# Lecture Notes in Computer Science

## 1275

T0223744

# Lecture Notes in Computer Science 1275

Edited by G. Goos, J. Hartmanis and J. van Leeuwen

Advisory Board: W. Brauer  D. Gries  J. Stoer

**Springer**
*Berlin*
*Heidelberg*
*New York*
*Barcelona*
*Budapest*
*Hong Kong*
*London*
*Milan*
*Paris*
*Santa Clara*
*Singapore*
*Tokyo*

Elsa L. Gunter  Amy Felty  (Eds.)

# Theorem Proving in Higher Order Logics

10th International Conference, TPHOLs '97
Murray Hill, NJ, USA, August 19-22, 1997
Proceedings

Springer

Series Editors

Gerhard Goos, Karlsruhe University, Germany

Juris Hartmanis, Cornell University, NY, USA

Jan van Leeuwen, Utrecht University, The Netherlands


Volume Editors

Elsa L. Gunter
Amy Felty
Lucent Technologies, Bell Labs Innovations
600 Mountain Avenue, Murray Hill, NJ 07974-0636, USA
E-mail: (elsa/felty)@research.bell-labs.com


Cataloging-in-Publication data applied for


Die Deutsche Bibliothek - CIP-Einheitsaufnahme

**Theorem proving in higher order logics** : 10th international
conference ; proceedings / TPHOLs '97, Murray Hill. NJ, USA,
August 19 - 22, 1997 / Elsa L. Gunter ; Amy Felty (ed.). - Berlin ;
Heidelberg ; New York ; Barcelona ; Budapest ; Hong Kong ;
London ; Milan ; Paris ; Santa Clara ; Singapore ; Tokyo : Springer,
1997
    ISBN 3-540-63379-0


CR Subject Classification (1991): B.6.3, D.2.4,F.3.1, F.4.1, I.2.3

ISSN 0302-9743
ISBN 3-540-63379-0 Springer-Verlag Berlin Heidelberg New York

This work is subject to copyright. All rights are reserved, whether the whole or part of the material is
concerned, specifically the rights of translation, reprinting, re-use of illustrations, recitation, broadcasting,
reproduction on microfilms or in any other way, and storage in data banks. Duplication of this publication
or parts thereof is permitted only under the provisions of the German Copyright Law of September 9, 1965,
in its current version, and permission for use must always be obtained from Springer -Verlag. Violations are
liable for prosecution under the German Copyright Law.

© Springer-Verlag Berlin Heidelberg 1997
Printed in Germany

Typesetting: Camera-ready by author
SPIN 10547850    06/3142 – 5 4 3 2 1 0    Printed on acid-free paper

# Preface

This volume contains the proceedings of the tenth international conference on *Theorem Proving in Higher Order Logics* (TPHOLs97), held at Bell Laboratories, Lucent Technologies, in Murray Hill, New Jersey, USA, during August 19-22, 1997. The previous meetings in this series were known initially as HOL Users Meetings, and later as Workshops on Higher Order Logic Theorem Proving and its Applications. The name Theorem Proving in Higher Order Logics was adopted for the first time last year to reflect a broadening in scope of the conference, which now encompasses work related to all aspects of theorem proving in higher order logics, particularly when based on a secure mechanization of those logics. These proceedings include papers describing work in Coq, HOL, Isabelle, LEGO, and PVS theorem provers.

The thirty-two papers submitted this year were generally of high quality. All submissions were fully refereed, each paper being reviewed by at least three reviewers appointed by the program committee (generally members of the committee themselves). Nineteen papers were selected for presentation as full research contributions. These are the papers appearing in this volume. The conference also continued its tradition of providing an open venue for the discussion and sharing of preliminary results and work in progress. Thus, the program included two informal poster sessions where twelve researchers were invited to present their work.

The organizers were pleased that Professor Robert L. Constable, Professor Deepak Kapur, and Dr. Doron Peled accepted invitations to be guest speakers at the conference. All three invited speakers also very kindly produced a written abstract or extended abstract of their talk for inclusion in these proceedings.

The conference was sponsored by Bell Laboratories, Lucent Technologies, and by the Department of Computer and Information Science of the University of Pennsylvania. We also want to thank Jennifer MacDougall who assisted in matters of local organization.

June 1997

Elsa L. Gunter
Amy Felty

# Conference Organization

**Conference Chair:**

Elsa L. Gunter (Bell Labs, Lucent)

**Organizing Committee:**

Amy Felty (Bell Labs, Lucent)
Elsa L. Gunter (Bell Labs, Lucent)

**Program Committee:**

Flemming Andersen (Tele Danmark)    Sara Kalvala (U. Warwick)
Yves Bertot (INRIA, Sophia)    Tom Melham (U. Glasgow)
Albert Camilleri (Hewlett-Packard)    Malcolm Newey (ANU)
Bill Farmer (MITRE)    Tobias Nipkow (TU München)
Amy Felty (Bell Labs, Lucent)    Christine Paulin-Mohring (ENS Lyon)
Elsa Gunter (Bell Labs, Lucent)    Larry Paulson (U. Cambridge)
Joshua Guttman (MITRE)    Tom Schubert (Portland State U.)
John Harrison (U. Cambridge)    Phil Windley (BYU)
John Herbert (SRI)    Jockum von Wright (Åbo Akademi)
Doug Howe (Bell Labs, Lucent)

**Invited Speakers:**

Robert L. Constable (Cornell U.)
Deepak Kapur (SUNY - Albany)
Doron Peled (Bell Labs, Lucent)

**Additional Referees:**

Robert Beers          J. Kelly Flanagan    Michael Norrish
Paul E. Black         Ranan Fraer          Maris A. Ozols
Annette Bunker        A. D. Gordon         Mark Steedman
P. Chartier           Jim Grundy           Javier Thayer
Graham Collins        Michael Jones        Myra VanInwegen
Katherine Eastaughffe Trent Larson         John Van Tassel

# Contents

# An Isabelle-Based Theorem Prover for VDM-SL

Sten Agerholm[1] and Jacob Frost[2]

[1] IFAD, Forskerparken 10, DK-5230 Odense M, Denmark
[2] Department of Information Technology, Technical University of Denmark,
DK-2800 Lyngby, Denmark

**Abstract.** This paper describes the theorem proving component of a
larger software development environment for the ISO standardized specification language VDM-SL. This component is constructed as an instantiation of the generic theorem prover Isabelle with a VDM-SL variant of
the Logic of Partial Functions (LPF). We describe the development of
this instantiation, focusing on both the embedding of syntax and the automation of proof support, which is a challenge due to the three-valued
nature of LPF.

## 1 Introduction

This paper is about mechanizing proof support for VDM-SL, which is a formal
notation for writing model-oriented specifications of software systems [13]. The
history of VDM-SL dates back to the late 70's, and it is now one of the most
widely used specification languages in industry and academia [15, 8]. Moreover,
it has an ISO standard [16] and is supported by a tool, the IFAD VDM-SL
Toolbox [9, 12], which is essential for the industrial adoption of a formal method.

Currently the VDM-SL Toolbox focuses on formal analysis of specifications
through test rather than proof [17, 3, 11]. However, there is an increasing de-
mand for proving facilities, in addition to testing facilities, due to emerging standards and higher quality requirements in general. For example, such enhanced
functionality of the Toolbox can be used to address the undecidability of type
checking in VDM-SL, by linking type checking and theorem proving to extend
the set of specifications that can be checked automatically [4]. But the enhanced
functionality can also be used to prove more general correctness requirements.

The long-term goal of our work is to develop an industrial proof support
tool for VDM-SL which can be integrated with the IFAD VDM-SL Toolbox.
However, at present we are merely making experiments to investigate the design
of such a proof tool. One of these experiments concerns a "proof engine", by
which we understand the basic theorem proving component of a more generally
usable proof environment (see [2]). This paper describes this basic component.

The proof engine, called Isabelle/VDM-LPF, or just VDM-LPF, has been
developed as an instantiation of the generic theorem prover Isabelle [18]. This
extends Isabelle (i.e. its Pure logic) with the Logic of Partial Functions (LPF) [5,
7] and rules for VDM-SL datatypes. LPF is a non-classical, three-valued logic
designed for reasoning about languages such as VDM-SL with partial functions.
Our instantiation exploits previous work done in the Mural project on proof

support for VDM-SL [14, 6], but extends this work by developing more powerful proof tools as well as a more flexible syntax.

The main contribution of our work is the instantiation of Isabelle with a VDM-SL variant of LPF, including automatic proof search. In particular, our research shows how the VDM-SL context-free grammar can be translated in a systematic way to Isabelle's priority grammar and syntax handling mechanisms, an observation which is generally useful. Furthermore, we solve some of the difficulties in building automatic proof support for the three-valued LPF in Isabelle, combining natural deduction and sequent calculus style reasoning (inspired by Cheng [7]). The syntax embedding supports a direct subset of the ISO standard VDM-SL ASCII notation. This has two important advantages: we have a standard format for exchanging information between tools, and VDM-LPF can be used conveniently as a stand-alone tool.

The paper gives an overview of the syntax embedding, the proof system and the proof tactics of our Isabelle instantiation. The paper also presents an example inspired by an industrial case study on formal methods [10]. We suggest future work in a number of directions before the conclusions.

## 2 VDM-SL Syntax in Isabelle

Isabelle is a generic theorem prover [18] which provides good features for embedding new logics (syntax and proof rules) and reasoning in these logics. Isabelle has a meta-logic, an intuitionistic higher order logic based on typed $\lambda$-calculus, in which constructs of new logics become constants, primitive proof rules become (meta-) axioms, and derived rules become (meta-) theorems. Moreover, it provides a few, but powerful tactics for applying these rules.

When embedding a language such as VDM-SL in Isabelle, two sometimes conflicting criteria must be met. Firstly, the language should allow smooth reasoning using features of Isabelle. Secondly, it should provide a user-friendly and familiar notation. These two goals are achieved by implementing an abstract and a concrete syntax, and by relating these using automatic translations. The purpose of this section, which is not important to understand the rest of the paper, is to give a light introduction to these concepts and the syntax embedding itself.

### 2.1 Abstract Syntax

This section provides a flavor of the core abstract syntax which is used internally in Isabelle for reasoning. It is a higher-order abstract syntax [19] in order to ensure smooth and elegant handling of bound variables. This means that object-level variables are identified with meta-level variables of a particular type. Meta-abstraction is used to represent variable binding, and substitution for bound variables is expressed using meta-application. Isabelle's $\beta$-conversion handles the variable capturing problem. Moreover, typical side-conditions involving free variables are handled using universal meta-quantification and meta-application.

The abstract syntax has two central categories, one of expressions and one of types. Consequently Isabelle's typed λ-calculus is extended with two new types **ex** and **ty** respectively. These types are logical in the sense that they are meant to be reasoned about, and new constants of these types are equipped with a standard prefix syntax.

Expressions and types of VDM-SL are represented in Isabelle using constants with result type **ex** and **ty**. Some examples of such constants are

```
not'    :: ex => ex
forall' :: [ty,ex => ex] => ex
eq'     :: [ex,ex] => ex
natty'  :: ty
succ'   :: ex => ex
```

These constants correspond to negation, universal quantification, equality, the type of natural numbers and the successor function. The constant for universal quantification is an example of a higher-order constant because it takes a function as its second argument. Using such constants as above it is possible to write expressions in a simple prefix form in the abstract syntax. The constants are primed in order to distinguish them from constants of the concrete syntax. The following example is a boolean expression which states that adding one is not the identity function for any natural number:

```
forall'(natty',%x.not'(eq'(x,succ'(x))))
```

This example illustrates how meta-abstraction % is used to express variable binding at the object-level.

## 2.2  Concrete Syntax

The purpose of the concrete syntax is to provide a user-friendly and familiar notation for presentation, while the role of the abstract syntax presented above was to support reasoning internally in Isabelle. The concrete syntax is based on the ISO standard of the VDM-SL ASCII notation [16]. This makes Isabelle/VDM-LPF relatively easy to use as a stand-alone tool for people who have experience with VDM-SL (and proof). Furthermore, it provides a standardized text-based format for exchanging data with other software components.

The VDM-SL syntax standard is expressed as a context free grammar with additional operator precedence rules to remove ambiguities. The concrete syntax of VDM-LPF is expressed as a priority grammar, i.e as a grammar where the nonterminal symbols are decorated with integer priorities [18]. This priority grammar is constructed by a systematic and fairly straightforward translation of productions and operator precedence rules into priority grammar productions. In most cases the base form of the priority grammar productions comes directly from the corresponding production in the VDM-SL grammar, while the priorities of the production are constructed from the corresponding operator precedences. Some simple examples of such priority grammar productions are:

$$ex^{(250)} \leftarrow \textbf{not } ex^{(250)}$$
$$ex^{(310)} \leftarrow ex^{(310)} = ex^{(311)}$$

The structure of the above productions matches the corresponding declarations of the abstract syntax. Consequently, in such cases the concrete syntax is implemented in Isabelle simply by adding a syntax annotation to the relevant constant declaration of the abstract syntax. The constant declarations corresponding to the two productions above are

```
not' :: ex => ex   ("(2not _/)" [250] 250)
eq'  :: [ex,ex] => ex   ("(_ = /_)" [310,311] 310)
```

where the types correspond to nonterminals of the productions. The syntax annotation in brackets consists of two parts: a quoted mixfix template followed by an optional priority part. The mixfix template describes the terminals and contains other printing and parsing directives (see [18]).

However, not all of the concrete syntax can be handled by adding syntax annotations to the constant declarations for the abstract syntax. In cases such as multiple binding quantifiers, set comprehensions, if-then-elseif expressions, enumerated sequences, etc., the structure of the concrete syntax differs from that of the abstract syntax. Such situations are handled using separate syntax declarations which declare a special kind of constants. These constants only serve a syntactic purpose and are never used internally for reasoning. The syntax declarations below are those needed for multiple binder universal quantifications:

```
""        :: tbind => tbinds   ("_")
tbinds_ :: [tbind,tbinds] => tbinds   ("(_,/ _)")
tbind_  :: [idt,ty] => tbind   ("(_ :/ _)")
forall_ :: [tbinds,ex] => ex   ("(2forall/ _ &/ _)" [100,100] 100)
```

Unlike when using syntax annotations, the relationship to the abstract syntax is not established automatically in such separate syntax declarations. Instead translations are defined to relate the abstract and the concrete syntax, as discussed in the following section.

## 2.3 Translations

A simple example of a translation is the expansion of the special notation for not equal <> in the concrete syntax to negated equality in the abstract syntax. This is implemented using Isabelle's macro mechanism. A macro is essentially a rewrite rule which works on Isabelle's abstract syntax trees. In this case the macro is

```
"x <> y" == "not x = y"
```

This transformation means that not equal will behave just as a negated equality in proofs. Another deliberate consequence is that any negated equality will be presented using the more readable not equal notation. In other words the original formatting is not always retained, but instead the implementation tries to improve it whenever possible.

Another more complicated example is that of universal quantification with multiple type bindings. In VDM-LPF such a quantifier is viewed simply as a syntactic shorthand for a number of nested single binding quantifiers. The translation between the concrete external first-order representation and the internal higher-order abstract representation is implemented using a mixture of macros and print translations. However, these are too complex to be included here. During parsing, the effect of these macros and translations is that concrete syntax such as

```
forall x:nat, y:nat & x = y
```

is automatically translated to the following abstract syntax:

```
forall'(nat,%x.forall'(nat,%y.eq'(x,y)))
```

Similarly, during printing, the abstract form is translated to the concrete form. Constants such as tbind_ and forall_ of the previous section do not occur explicitly here, since they are only used in the standard first-order syntax trees corresponding to the concrete syntax. However, they are used in the relevant macros and translations. Other variable binding constructs are handled in a similar fashion to universal quantification.

## 2.4 Examples

Through the use of the techniques described above, VDM-LPF is able to print and parse VDM-SL concrete syntax such as the following:

```
[3,1,2]
{x + 1 | x in set {1,2,3} & x >= 2}
forall x:nat, y:nat & x + y = y + x
let x = 5, y = x + 6, z = 7 in y + z
if n = 0 then 1 elseif n = 1 then 2 elseif n < 10 then 9 else n
mk_(x,5,z).#2 + mk_(1,2,3,4).#3 = 8
```

As illustrated in the last line, Isabelle's syntax handling features can be used to support something as exotic as arbitrary-length tuples and generalized projections.

# 3  Proof System of VDM-LPF

The proof system for VDM-SL axiomatized in Isabelle has been copied with minor modifications from the book [6]. In addition to primitive and derived rules for propositional and predicate LPF, this book contains a large number of rules for datatypes such as natural numbers, sets, sequences, maps, etc. As in many other formulations of LPF, these rules are formulated as natural deduction rules. This fits well with the choice of Isabelle which supports natural deduction style proof particularly well.

The following two subsections describe part of the VDM-SL proof system and its implementation in Isabelle. In particular we discuss the implementation of proof rules and judgments for sequent calculus style reasoning. The axiomatization of, for example, datatypes is not discussed since we do not contribute to the presentation in [6].

## 3.1 Proof Rules

The proof system of LPF contains most of the standard rules of propositional and predicate logic. However, it is a three-valued logic so it does not provide the law of excluded middle, and some rules have additional typing assumptions, for example, in order to ensure that equality is defined (see below).

Most of the rules of the Isabelle instantiation are taken from [6]. The adaptation consists mostly of changing the syntax. For example, consider the rules:

$$\frac{}{\text{true}} \qquad \frac{P;\ Q}{P \wedge Q} \qquad \frac{P \vee Q;\ P \vdash R;\ Q \vdash R}{R}$$

$$\frac{x : A \vdash_x \neg P(x)}{\neg(\exists x : A \cdot P(x))} \qquad \frac{b : A;\ a = b;\ P(b)}{P(a)}$$

These rules are translated into the following Isabelle axioms:

```
true_intr          "true"
and_intr           "[| P; Q |] ==> P and Q"
or_elim            "[| P or Q; P ==> R; Q ==> R |] ==> R"
not_exists_intr    "(!!x.x:A ==> not P(x)) ==> not (exists x:A & P(x))"
eq_subs_left       "[| a=b; P(b); b:A |] ==> P(a)"
```

In these axioms, ==> represents meta-implication, !! universal meta-quantification, while [| and |] enclose a list of assumptions separated by ;. Note that variable subscripts for locally bound variables in sequents are handled using meta-quantification. Apart from using the concrete ASCII syntax of VDM-LPF (see Section 2.2), these examples illustrate how the horizontal line and turnstile in the original rules are represented as meta-implication. In some cases, the order of assumptions is changed to make the rules work better with Isabelle's resolution tactics, which often use unification on the first assumption to instantiate variables. In particular, type assumptions are often moved from the front of the assumption list to the back, since these do not typically contain any important information for restricting the application of rules. An example of this is the last substitution rule above.

## 3.2 Combining Natural Deduction and Sequent Style Proof

In order to formalize proof rules as meta-level axioms in Isabelle it is necessary to define a judgment relating object-level formulas to meta-level formulas in Isabelle's higher-order logic. In the LPF variant used here, there is no distinction between expressions and formulas. Hence, expressions (and formulas) are represented as $\lambda$-calculus terms of type ex. In Isabelle meta-level formulas are terms of type prop. Consequently, the standard judgment relating object-level expressions to meta-level formulas is the following lifting constant:

```
TRUE' :: ex => prop    ("(_)" 5)
```

The concrete syntax associated with this constant in brackets specifies that TRUE' will not occur explicitly in (meta-) axioms representing proof rules. Hence, it was invisible above.

The standard judgment TRUE' is sufficient for implementing a natural deduction system for LPF. However, in order to automate proving in VDM-LPF, it is advantageous to be able to conduct (or simulate) sequent calculus style backward proof. In classical logic this can be done by representing multiple conclusions as negated assumptions. This issue is a consequence of the law of excluded middle. However, LPF is a three-valued logic and does not satisfy this law. Instead, we have therefore declared an additional judgment for this purpose:

```
FALSE' :: ex => prop    ("FALSE _" 5)
```

In this case the concrete syntax requires an object-level formula to be preceded by FALSE (specified in brackets). The idea is that this judgment acts as a kind of non-strict negation with respect to the third value of LPF. This form of negation, which can only occur at the outermost level, allows multiple conclusions to be represented as a kind of negated assumptions. This is discussed further in Section 4.

There are two new rules for the FALSE judgment:

```
FALSE_dup    "(FALSE P ==> P) ==> P"
FALSE_contr  "[| FALSE P; P |] ==> Q"
```

The first rule allows a conclusion to be duplicated as a kind of negated assumption using FALSE, while the second rule is a contradiction-like rule. Together these rules imply that FALSE behaves as desired.

The inclusion of the additional judgment FALSE to represent multiple conclusions has interesting consequences for the proof system. For example, the primitive rule

```
(!! y.y:A ==> def P(y)) ==> def exists x:A & P(x)
```

becomes derivable, and it is no longer necessary or useful to have in practice. This is fortunate since the rule appears to be hard to apply properly, especially in automatic backwards proof. An automatic proof of the rule is given in Section 4.2.

## 3.3   Soundness

We are confident, but have not formally proved, that the modifications of the proof system discussed above are sound. We base this confidence on Cheng's thesis [7], who have proved essentially this result for VDM-SL without datatypes. Cheng formulates both a sequent calculus and a natural deduction proof system for predicate LPF with equality and non-strict connectives[3]. Among other things, he proves that these proof systems are equivalent in terms of what can be derived.

---

[3] The connectives, in particular definedness (for "true or false"), in our variant of LPF are all strict.

However, he does not consider datatypes like those of VDM-LPF. Hence, we should eventually extend Cheng's work to ensure that the VDM-SL datatype extensions of LPF do not violate soundness. We have done some preliminary work on this.

# 4 Proof Tactics

Isabelle's built-in tactics can be used immediately with VDM-LPF for fine-grained proof. However, it is advantageous to build special-purpose tactics exploiting the FALSE judgment as well as tactics for doing automatic proof search. This section describes such basic tactics as well as proof search tactics.

## 4.1 Basic Tactics

In many cases Isabelle's standard resolution tactics are suitable for applying the rules of VDM-LPF directly. For example, consider a proof state with the following subgoal:

```
1.   Q and P ==> P or Q
```

The conclusion of this goal can be broken down using the standard resolution tactic resolve_tac with the or-introduction rule or_intr_left, which will apply this rule to the conclusion in a backward fashion. This can be written using Isabelle's useful shorthand br, where b stands for by:

```
- br or_intr_left 1;   (* same as: by(resolve_tac [or_intr_left] 1) *)
1.   Q and P ==> P
```

In a similar fashion the assumption of the subgoal can be broken down, this time using eresolve_tac to apply the and-elimination rule and_elim in a forward fashion on the assumption of the subgoal:

```
- be and_elim 1;   (* same as: by (eresolve_tac [and_elim] 1) *)
1.   [| Q; P |] ==> P
```

Finally, the remaining subgoal can be solved using assume_tac which simulates proof by assumption in natural deduction:

```
- ba 1;   (* same as: by (assume_tac 1) *)
No subgoals!
```

In addition to the above tactics, Isabelle has a few other basic resolution tactics for applying natural deduction rules (see [18]).

There are a few situations where the above tactics are not suitable for applying the rules of VDM-LPF. For example, consider the following subgoal where a multiple conclusion is represented as an assumption using the FALSE judgment:

```
1.   [| P and Q; FALSE P|] ==> Q
```

In this case `resolve_tac` cannot be used directly to apply `or_intr` to the conclusion P or Q, since it is represented as an assumption. Instead we have developed variants of the standard resolution tactics, which can be used in such situations. The names of these are obtained by just adding an additional prime on standard names, as in `resolve_tac'`. These tactics use the proof rules for the FALSE judgment to allow a rule to be applied to conclusions represented in assumptions using FALSE. In addition to these, a VDM-LPF variant of `assume_tac`, called `assume_tac'`, allows one step proofs of subgoals like:

```
[| P; Q |] ==> P
[| P; FALSE P; Q |] ==> R
[| P; not P; Q |] ==> R
```

The first case is just ordinary proof by assumption, the next covers the situation where a conclusion appears in the assumptions due to FALSE, while the last case deals with the situation where a proof branch is ended by an application of the primitive LPF contradiction rule [| P; not P |] ==> Q.

## 4.2 Proof Search Tactics

Isabelle provides a generic classical reasoning package for automating larger parts of proofs when instantiated to a particular object-logic than supported by the tactics above. However, VDM-LPF is not classical and therefore it seems hard to use this package. Classical laws are used for simulating sequents using natural deduction. Instead we have implemented a new package designed specifically for VDM-LPF. This package combines ideas from Cheng's thesis on LPF [7] with ideas and code from the classical reasoning package. As in Isabelle, the aim of this is to provide a practical tool and less emphasis is put on completeness issues.

The proof search tactics in the packages are based on the same basic idea: do sequent calculus style backward proofs using suitable rules to break assumptions and conclusions of subgoals gradually down, until the conclusion is provable from an assumption. In other words, natural deduction introduction rules are applied as right sequent style rules, while elimination rules are applied as left rules. Our package handles multiple conclusions using FALSE and by working as if using the primed versions of the tactics. Rules for both FALSE and strict negation not are required by the package. In contrast, the Isabelle classical reasoning package does not make such a distinction since it uses just classical negation to represent multiple conclusions (this is not possible in non-classical logics).

Rules applied by the tactics are organized in rule sets and are supplied directly as arguments of the tactics. As in Isabelle's classical reasoner, a rule set is constructed by dividing rules into groups of introduction rules, elimination rules, etc. For each of these groups, the rules are further divided into safe and hazardous rules. Roughly speaking, the idea is that a safe rule can always be attempted blindly, while an hazardous rule might, for example, sidetrack the search (thus requiring backtracking) or cause the search to loop. The search tactics generally try safe rules before the hazardous ones.

In most cases, the grouping is fairly straightforward, for example, consider the following rules for disjunction:

```
or_intr_left    "P ==> P or Q"
or_intr_right   "Q ==> P or Q"
or_intr         "[| FALSE P ==> Q |] ==> P or Q";
or_elim         "[| P or Q; P==>R; Q==>R |] ==> R"
not_or_intr     "[| not P; not Q |] ==> not (P or Q)"
not_or_elim     "[| not (P or Q); [| not P; not Q |] ==> R |] ==> R"
```

The first two rules are hazardous introduction rules, since they force a choice
between the two disjuncts. In contrast the third is a safe introduction rule using
FALSE to represent the two possible conclusions. The fourth rule is just the
standard elimination rule for disjunction. In addition to these, rules explaining
how negation behaves when combined with disjunction are needed. This is the
purpose of the last two rules. The reason why these are needed is that it is not
possible to give general rules for negation. These conjunction-like introduction
and elimination rules are both safe. The rule set prop_lpfs for propositional
VDM-LPF contains all the above rules, except the hazardous introduction rules
which are replaced by the single safe one.

In order to illustrate how the search strategy described above can be used to
find proofs, a sketch of a small proof following this strategy is shown below:

```
1.  not (Q and P) ==> not P or not Q

- br or_intr 1;
1. [| not (Q and P); FALSE  not P |] ==>  not Q

- be not_and_elim 1;
1. [| FALSE  not P;  not Q |] ==>  not Q
2. [| FALSE  not P;  not P |] ==>  not Q

- ba' 1; ba' 1;  (* same as: by (assume_tac' 1) *)
No subgoals!
```

The tactic lpf_fast_tac combines the strategy above and depth first search
with backtracking at suitable points (e.g. if more than one unsafe rule is applicable). This is probably the most used tactic in the package. For example,
when invoked as lpf_fast_tac prop_lpfs 1, this tactic proves the above theorem in one step. Other similar tactics support safe steps only to be carried out
(lpf_safe_tac), support the restriction of the depth of proofs (lpf_depth_tac),
etc. So far these tactics have been used to prove (in one step) essentially all of
the 120 derived propositional and predicate logic rules mentioned in [6].

We end this section by considering a last example where the assumption of
the rule is itself a generalized rule:

```
val [asm] =
goal Pred.thy "(!!y.y:A ==> def P(y)) ==> def exists x:A & P(x)";
by (lpf_fast_tac (exists_lpfs addDs [asm]) 1);
qed "def_exists_inh";
```

This situation is handled by adding the assumption to one of the intermediate
rule sets exists_lpfs used to build the theory of predicate VDM-LPF. Hence,

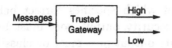

Messages | Trusted Gateway | High
Low

**Fig. 1.** A Trusted Gateway

the proof search tactics provide a universal strategy which also works for most proofs about quantifiers as long as a sufficient quantifier rule set is supplied as an argument. Moreover, this example shows that `lpf_fast_tac` can be used to prove a quantifier rule which is primitive in LPF (see Section 3.3).

# 5 Case Study

This section illustrates how the VDM-LPF instantiation works on an example VDM-SL specification of a trusted gateway (provided by John Fitzgerald). Though the example is small, it is inspired by an industrial case study on formal methods [10, 15]. Strictly speaking, we do not support reasoning about the specification itself, but about an axiomatization of the specification which is automatically generated by the more general proof support tool described in [2]. We will try to avoid the details of the axiomatization here.

In the following we first present excerpts from a specification of the trusted gateway and then illustrate the use of our proof tactics to prove invariant and safety properties.

## 5.1 A Trusted Gateway

A trusted gateway connects an input port to two output ports, which are a high- and a low-security port (see Fig. 1). The purpose of the gateway is to prevent accidental disclosure of classified or sensitive information on the low-security port. The trusted gateway reads messages from the input port into an internal block where it analyzes them according to two categories of high- and low-classification strings. It must send messages containing only low-classification strings to the low-security port and all other messages to the high-security port.

In VDM-SL we can model a trusted gateway as the following record type:

```
Gateway:: input: Port
          highOutput: Port
          lowOutput: Port
          high: Category
          low: Category
          block: Message
   inv g == (forall msg in set elems g.highOutput &
               classification(msg,g.high,g.low) = <HIGH>) and
            (forall msg in set elems g.lowOutput &
               classification(msg,g.high,g.low) = <LOW>) and
            g.high inter g.low = {}
```

This type has an invariant which specifies correct behavior of gateways, i.e. all messages on the high-security output port must be classified as high, all messages on the low-security output port must be classified as low, and the two categories of high- and low-classification should not have any strings in common. A message is modeled as a sequence of strings, a port as a sequence of messages, and a category as a set of strings.

The different operations on the gateway are modeled as functions acting on elements of type Gateway. These include a function for loading an element into the internal block, a function for analyzing the contents of the block and a function for emptying the block. For illustration, the specification of the analyze function is shown:

```
Analyze: Gateway -> Gateway
Analyze(g) ==
  if classification(g.block,g.high,g.low) = <HIGH>
  then mk_Gateway(g.input,
                  g.highOutput ^ [g.block],
                  g.lowOutput,
                  g.high,g.low,g.block)
  else mk_Gateway(g.input,
                  g.highOutput,
                  g.lowOutput ^ [g.block],
                  g.high,g.low,g.block);
```

This function copies messages from the internal block to the appropriate output port, depending on the result returned by the classification function. The definition of the classification function is fairly central:

```
classification: String * Category * Category -> (<HIGH> | <LOW>)
classification(s,high,low) ==
  if contains_category(s,high)
  then <HIGH>
  elseif contains_category(s,low)
  then <LOW>
  else <HIGH>
```

Note that the order of the if-conditions is important, and messages that contain neither high nor low classified strings are classified as high for security reasons.

## 5.2 Invariant Properties

In order to be well-formed, functions such as Analyze must respect the invariant of their result type. For Analyze, this means that assuming its argument is a gateway its body must yield a gateway as well:

```
"g : Gateway ==>
  if classification@(g.block, g.high, g.low) = <HIGH> then
    mk_Gateway(g.input, g.highOutput ^ [g.block], g.lowOutput,
      g.high, g.low, g.block)
  else
```

```
    mk_Gateway(g.input, g.highOutput, g.lowOutput ^ [g.block],
       g.high, g.low, g.block) :
  Gateway"
```

Note that object-level application is written using @ and postfix field selection is supported by declarations such as

```
  block' :: ex => ex  ("_.block" [500] 500)
  high'  :: ex => ex  ("_.high" [500] 500)
```

produced by the axiomatization (see [2]). The above statement, which is generated automatically using the proof obligation generator described in [4], has been proved in VDM-LPF. However, due to lack of space it is not possible to show the entire interactive proof here. Instead some central steps in the proof are discussed below.

The first obvious step is to use case analysis on the conditional expression. Due to the third value in VDM-LPF, we get three subgoals, the two obvious and one which says that the test condition must be true or false (it could potentially be undefined in some cases). Here we concentrate on the subgoal corresponding to the first branch of the conditional:

```
  [| g : Gateway; classification@(g.block,g.high,g.low) = <HIGH> |] ==>
  mk_Gateway
   (g.input, g.highOutput^[g.block], g.lowOutput, g.high,
    g.low, g.block) :
  Gateway
```

To prove this, we first unfold the type definition of Gateway in the assumptions and the conclusion, then we prove some trivial type judgment subgoals automatically, and what we obtain is the subgoal:

```
  [| classification@(g.block,g.high,g.low) = <HIGH>; g.input : Port;
     g.highOutput : Port; g.lowOutput : Port; g.high : Category;
     g.low : Category; g.block : Message;
     (forall m in set elems g.highOutput &
        classification@(m,g.high,g.low) = <HIGH>) and
     (forall m in set elems g.lowOutput &
        classification@(m,g.high,g.low) = <LOW>) and
     g.high inter g.low = {} |] ==>
  (forall m in set elems (g.highOutput^[g.block]) &
     classification@(m,g.high,g.low) = <HIGH>) and
  (forall m in set elems g.lowOutput &
     classification@(m,g.high,g.low) = <LOW>) and
  g.high inter g.low = {}
```

The hardest part is clearly to prove the first conjunct of the conclusion, the other two follow trivially from the assumptions. One tactic lpf_fast_tac proves the above subgoal:

```
  by (lpf_fast_tac
       (prop_lpfs addIs [foralls_lemma] addEs [Port_elim]) 1);
```

The rule set argument contains proof rules for propositional reasoning, a suitable lemma for the difficult conjunct and a single rule for type checking ports. The lemma states how to break the quantification according to the sequence concatenation, and it is proved from various properties about sets, sequences and of course the set-bounded universal quantifier.

## 5.3 Safety Property

The safety property for a trusted gateway states that all messages on the low security output port are given a low security classification:

```
"g : Gateway ==>
  forall m in set elems g.lowOutput &
    classification@(m, g.high, g.low) = <LOW>"
```

This has a single tactic proof:

```
by (lpf_fast_tac
    (prop_lpfs addEs [Gateway_elim] addDs [inv_Gateway_dest]) 1);
```

The rule set argument supports propositional reasoning, unfolding of the gateway type assumption and unfolding of the resulting gateway invariant. Inspecting the property more closely, it is not surprising that the proof turned out to be that simple, since the safety property is essentially a part of the invariant. Thus the real challenge is to prove that the invariant on Gateway is preserved.

## 6  Future Work

Although the current system can be used to reason about VDM-SL specifications, it can clearly be improved in many ways. Some of the most important improvements are discussed briefly below.

**Proof Rules** The proof system still needs work to be truly practical. Many of the rules for the different VDM-SL datatypes seem quite ad hoc and more work is needed here. Although often ignored, it is a major task to develop well-organized and powerful proof rules for datatypes like those of VDM-SL. Moreover, such proof rules should be organized in rule sets for the proof search tactics (if possible). This is also a major and important task.

**Tactics** The current version of VDM-LPF does not provide a simplifier. Unfortunately it does not seem easy to instantiate Isabelle's generic simplifier to support reasoning about equality in VDM-LPF, since in order to do this we must justify that we can identify the VDM-LPF object-level equality with Isabelle's meta-level equality. If we cannot use Isabelle's simplifier, a special-purpose VDM-LPF simplifier should be constructed.

In addition, it might be useful to construct a number of special purpose tactics, for example, for reasoning about arithmetic and for proving trivial type conditions, which tend to clutter up proofs.

**Compatibility** VDM-LPF is meant to be used to reason about VDM-SL and to be integrated with existing tools. A natural question is whether or not all these are compatible, and if not, what should then be changed. For example, is the proof system used sound with respect to the ISO standard (static and dynamic) semantics of VDM-SL? Although no inconsistencies have been found in the proof system itself, preliminary investigations suggest that there might be a problem with compatibility. For example, it is currently possible to derive **true** or 1 as a theorem in the proof system, but according to the semantics of VDM-SL this is undefined. Since the semantics of VDM-SL is defined by an ISO standard it is perhaps most tempting to try to modify the proof system to exclude theorems as the one above. However, the result might be a proof system which is not suited for practical reasoning. This compatibility issue requires further attention.

**Natural Deduction versus Sequent Calculus** The current instantiation is based on a natural deduction formulation of LPF. However, there are indications suggesting that a sequent calculus formulation of LPF might be a better foundation, in particular for automating proofs.

## 7 Conclusion

In this paper we have described the implementation of some central features of a VDM-LPF instantiation of Isabelle. In particular we have illustrated how Isabelle's syntax annotation and translation mechanisms can be used in a systematic way to implement a substantial part of the ISO standard of the VDM-SL ASCII syntax. We have also illustrated how existing LPF proof rules can be implemented in Isabelle. Finally, the new facilities for automatic proof search in VDM-LPF have been discussed, which automatically proved most of the 120 propositional and predicate logic derived rules listed in [6]. We feel that our experiments have shown Isabelle to be a very useful tool for quickly building specialized proof support for new and even non-standard logics such as VDM-LPF. Moreover, Isabelle is relatively easy to adapt to VDM-SL and to integrate with the IFAD VDM-SL Toolbox (see [2]), unlike a closed system such as PVS [1].

A generic framework like Isabelle allows quick implementation of powerful theorem provers through reuse. However, we have seen some limitations to reuse when dealing with a three-valued logic like VDM-LPF. In particular, the generic simplifier and classical reasoning package appear not to be easy to use with VDM-LPF. However, in our implementation of a special purpose reasoning package we were able to reuse many idea's and even code from the existing package.

## References

1. S. Agerholm. Translating specifications in VDM-SL to PVS. In J. von Wright, J. Grundy, and J. Harrison, editors, *Proceedings of the 9th International Conference on Theorem Proving in Higher Order Logics (TPHOLs'96)*, volume 1125 of *Lecture Notes in Computer Science*. Springer-Verlag, 1996.

2. S. Agerholm and J. Frost. Towards an integrated CASE and theorem proving tool for VDM-SL. In *FME'97*, LNCS. Springer-Verlag, September 1997.

3. S. Agerholm and P. G. Larsen. Modeling and validating SAFER in VDM-SL. In M. Holloway, editor, *Proceedings of the Fourth NASA Formal Methods Workshop*, September 1997.

4. B. Aichernig and P. G. Larsen. A proof obligation generator for VDM-SL. In *FME'97*, LNCS. Springer-Verlag, September 1997.

5. H. Barringer, J. H. Cheng, and C. B. Jones. A logic covering undefinedness in program proofs. *Acta Informatica*, 21:251–269, 1984.

6. J. C. Bicarregui, J. S. Fitzgerald, P. A. Lindsay, R. Moore, and B. Ritchie. *Proof in VDM: A Practitioner's Guide*. FACIT. Springer-Verlag, 1994.

7. J. H. Cheng. A logic for partial functions. Ph.D. Thesis UMCS-86-7-1, Department of Computer Science, University of Manchester, Manchester M13 9PL, England, 1986.

8. L. Devauchelle, P. G. Larsen, and H. Voss. PICGAL: Practical use of Formal Specification to Develop a Complex Critical System. In *FME'97*, LNCS. Springer-Verlag, September 1997.

9. R. Elmstrøm, P. G. Larsen, and P. B. Lassen. The IFAD VDM-SL Toolbox: A practical approach to formal specifications. *ACM Sigplan Notices*, 29(9):77–80, September 1994.

10. J. Fitzgerald, P. G. Larsen, T. Brookes, and M. Green. *Applications of Formal Methods, edited by M.G. Hinchey and J.P. Bowen*, chapter 14. Developing a Security-critical System using Formal and Convential Methods, pages 333–356. Prentice-Hall International Series in Computer Science, 1995.

11. B. Fröhlich and P. G. Larsen. Combining VDM-SL Specifications with C++ Code. In M.-C. Gaudel and J. Woodcock, editors, *FME'96: Industrial Benefit and Advances in Formal Methods*, pages 179–194. Springer-Verlag, March 1996.

12. IFAD World Wide Web page. http://www.ifad.dk.

13. C. B. Jones. *Systematic Software Development using VDM*. Prentice Hall International, 1990.

14. C. B. Jones, K. D. Jones, P. A. Lindsay, and R. Moore. *mural: A Formal Development Support System*. Springer-Verlag, 1991.

15. P. G. Larsen, J. Fitzgerald, and T. Brookes. Applying Formal Specification in Industry. *IEEE Software*, 13(3):48–56, May 1996.

16. P. G. Larsen, B. S. Hansen, et al. Information technology — Programming languages, their environments and system software interfaces — Vienna Development Method — Specification Language — Part 1: Base language, December 1996.

17. P. Mukherjee. Computer-aided validation of formal specifications. *Software Engineering Journal*, pages 133–140, July 1995.

18. L. C. Paulson. *Isabelle: A Generic Theorem Prover*, volume 828 of *Lecture Notes in Computer Science*. Springer-Verlag, 1994.

19. F. Pfenning and C. Elliott. Higher-order abstract syntax. In *Proceedings of the SIGPLAN'88 Conference on Programming Language Design and Implementation*, pages 199 – 208, Atlanta, Georgia, June 1998.

# Executing Formal Specifications by Translation to Higher Order Logic Programming

James H. Andrews

Dept. of Computer Science
University of British Columbia
Vancouver, BC, Canada V6T 1Z4

**Abstract.** We describe the construction and use of a system for translating higher order logic-based specifications into programs in the higher order logic programming language Lambda Prolog. The translation improves on previous work in the field of executing specifications by allowing formulas with quantifiers to be executed, and by permitting users to pose Prolog-style queries with free variables to be instantiated by the system. We also discuss various alternative target languages and design decisions in implementing the translator.

## 1  Introduction

One of the early goals of formal specification in software engineering was to provide a formal model against which an implementation of the software, or a more detailed model, could be checked. This goal has not been fully realized in practice. But even where no tools exist to check an implementation against a specification, the process of writing a formal specification (FS) from an informal specification (IS) can still be very useful. For instance, since formal specification languages are less ambiguous than natural language, writing the FS forces the writer to deal with ambiguous passages in the IS by asking the writers of the IS to clarify them. The FS also casts the IS in the form of more detailed requirements which can be tracked during the course of system development.

Regardless of how the FS is used, however, a problem remains: how do we know when it is correct? Any contradictory statements in the IS which are not directly ambiguous may be translated directly into the FS. Subtleties of the specification language or unstated assumptions made in the translation from IS to FS may introduce other problems. Thus, just as we check the soundness of a software project by writing a FS, we must somehow check the soundness of the FS before using it as the basis of a project.

To check the FS, we can of course prove properties and consequences of it using a general-purpose theorem prover such as HOL. But this may be needlessly time-consuming, and we may find errors in the FS only when we have already done a great deal of manually intensive verification based on the faulty version. To make an initial check of our FS, it is sometimes good enough simply to perform steps like unfolding definitions and checking for the existence of terms which satisfy given formulas; in other words, to execute the specification. Thus, ironically, we can test the feasibility of a program by writing a formal model, and test the feasibility of the formal model by treating it as a program.

How should a specification be executed? Building a custom environment in which to execute it is an obvious choice, but needlessly duplicates much of the effort that goes into building programming languages. A more expeditious approach is to implement a program which translates from the specification language to an existing programming language. This approach has the further advantage of giving the user access to the run-time environment and whatever static analysis tools have been developed for the programming language.

This paper discusses the implementation of a translator from the specification language S to the programming language Lambda Prolog. S is a higher order logic-based specification language developed at the University of British Columbia by Jeffrey Joyce, Nancy Day and Michael Donat [JDD94]. It is a central focus of the FormalWare project, an industry-funded technology transfer project concerning formal methods in software engineering. Lambda Prolog, developed initially by Dale Miller and Gopalan Nadathur at the University of Pennsylvania [MN86, MNPS91], is an elegant higher order logic extension of the Prolog programming language.

This work extends earlier work by Camilleri [Cam88], Murthy [Mur91] and Rajan [Raj92], who translated HOL to ML. Translating to Lambda Prolog allows us to use the backtracking and higher order unification capabilities of the target language to execute such constructs as the Hilbert epsilon operator and disjunctions inside quantifiers. The translation of quantified variables is more straightforward, since the target language also has a notion of quantification. It also allows the user to ask Prolog-style queries with free variables, to be instantiated by the system. The results are cast in terms of S, but are applicable to any higher order specification language.

This work can also been seen as extending work by Kahn [Kah87] and Hannan and Miller [HM90] on operational semantics and logic programming systems. These authors studied specifically translating operational semantics into Prolog or expressing them in Lambda Prolog; in contrast, this paper deals with the translation of general specifications, possibly involving higher order features, into Lambda Prolog.

The structure of this paper is as follows. Section 2 briefly describes the S specification language. Section 3 discusses Lambda Prolog as a target language for the translation, comparing it to S and to some alternate target languages. Section 4 describes the translation scheme and the translated program in greater detail. Section 5 discusses some of the design decisions taken for the implementation, mainly to deal with the problems inherent in trying to execute formulas without crossing into full theorem-proving. Section 6 presents an extended example and experiences with the translation system. Finally, Section 7 gives conclusions and describes future work.

## 2 The S Specification Language

S is a specification language developed at the University of British Columbia. It was designed to be more readable than other formal specification languages such as Z or the script language used as input to HOL, while still retaining the abstracting power of uninterpreted constants and higher order logic. There is a typechecker for S input files, called Fuss [JDD96]; getting an S input file to be accepted by Fuss is comparable to getting an ML program to typecheck. Various other tools associated with S are under development.

| S construct | Meaning | Equivalent Lambda Prolog construct |
|---|---|---|
| `: process;` | Type declaration | `kind process type.` |
| `: (A, B) array;` | Parameterized type declaration | `kind array`<br>`    type -> type -> type.` |
| `version_number: num;` | Constant declaration | `type version_number num.` |
| `: (A) tree :=`<br>`    leaf :A  |`<br>`    branch :(A) tree`<br>`        :(A) tree;` | Type definition | `kind tree type -> type.`<br>`type leaf A -> (tree A).`<br>`type branch (tree A) ->`<br>`    (tree A) -> (tree A).` |
| `: style == colour # size;` | Type abbreviation | No equivalent |
| `mother X :=`<br>`    (parent X) & (female X);` | Boolean function definition | `type mother person -> o.`<br>`mother X :-`<br>`    parent X, female X.` |
| `reverse X := rev_aux X [];` | Non-boolean function definition | No direct equivalent |
| `~(separation a1 a2 < 300);` | Boolean constraint | No general equivalent; Horn clause constraints declared with Prolog-style clauses |
| `function X . (g X X)` | Lambda abstraction | `X\ (g X X)` |

**Fig. 1.** Syntactic constructs of S and Lambda Prolog.

The syntactic constructs of S are summarized in Figure 1, along with a comparison to Lambda Prolog features which will be discussed later. In S, one can declare the names of new types (possibly parameterized), and declare new constants to be of those types. Types and "term constructor" constants can be declared together in ML-style "type definitions", and one can abbreviate one type by a new name. A type expression in S is a declared or built-in type name, or the type of functions from one type to another (written T1 -> T2), or the cross product of two types (written T1 # T2). The built-in types of S are num (the type of numbers) and bool (the Boolean values "true" and "false").

A constant can also be defined as a function with a given meaning, by constructs such as "reverse X := rev_aux X []". ML-style multi-clause function definitions are also available. For such function definitions, the Fuss typechecker will infer the type of the arguments and the range of the function.

Expressions are largely as they are in ML. The lambda-expression which would be written $\lambda X.(f\ X)$ in lambda notation is written as function X . (f X) in S; the formulas $\exists X(p\ X)$ and $\forall X(p\ X)$ are written "exists X . (p X)" and "forall X . (p X)" respectively. The expression $\epsilon X.(p\ X)$, where $\epsilon$ is Hilbert's epsilon operator, is written "select X . (p X)". (The meaning is "some individual $X$ such that $(p\ X)$ is true.") Constraints – that is, the actual formulas constituting the formal specification – are written as expressions of type bool terminated by semicolons, on the same level as definitions in an S source file.

An example of a full S specification is contained in Figure 2. It is a specification of a simplified version of CCS, Milner's Calculus of Concurrent Systems [Mil80]. In the example, we define a process as being of one of four forms:

- The "null process" nullprocess, which can do nothing;
- An (andthen L P) process, which can perform the action indicated by its label L and then become process P;
- A (plus P1 P2) process, which can choose between becoming P1 or P2; or
- A (par P1 P2) process, which represents processes P1 and P2 running in parallel and communicating via synchronized labels.

The relation can_do Process Label Newprocess holds if Process can do the action indicated by Label, becoming Newprocess. The function trace is intended to return a possible trace (sequence of actions) of its argument. The last few lines define some example processes.

Of course, this is only an example for the present purposes; it is possible to specify CCS in other formalisms as well. Readers may wish to compare this treatment with Nesi's specification of full value-passing CCS in HOL [Nes93].

# 3 Lambda Prolog as a Target Language

Lambda Prolog was chosen as the target language for the translation because of the relatively large number of features it shares with S, and its ability to reason both about logical connectives and quantifiers and about higher-order constructs.

## 3.1 A Comparison of S and Lambda Prolog

S and Lambda Prolog are both based on typed higher order logic. Both languages allow type declarations; parameterized type declarations; declarations of new uninterpreted constants of arbitrary types; and definitions of the meanings of functions with boolean range. Figure 1 shows the correspondences between the syntax of these constructions in the two languages.

The most important notational difference between the languages is that Lambda Prolog has an explicit notion of "kind". Kinds form a third level of objects above individuals and types; just as each individual belongs to some type, each type belongs to some kind. Thus, for example, list is of kind type -> type

```
%include startup.s

: label;
: process := andthen :label :process
          | plus :process :process
          | par :process :process
          | nullprocess;
tau: label;
prime: label -> label;

can_do (andthen Label Process) Donelabel Newprocess :=
  (Donelabel = Label) /\ (Newprocess = Process) |
can_do (plus Process1 Process2) Label Newprocess :=
  can_do Process1 Label Newprocess \/
  can_do Process2 Label Newprocess |
can_do (par Process1 Process2) Label Newprocess :=
  ( exists Newprocess1 .
    (  can_do Process1 Label Newprocess1
    /\ (Newprocess = (par Newprocess1 Process2)))) \/
  ( exists Newprocess2 .
    (  can_do Process2 Label Newprocess2
    /\ (Newprocess = (par Process1 Newprocess2)))) \/
  ( exists Newprocess1 Newprocess2 Handshakelabel .
    ( ( can_do Process1 Handshakelabel Newprocess1 /\
        can_do Process2 (prime Handshakelabel) Newprocess2 ) \/
      ( can_do Process2 Handshakelabel Newprocess2 /\
        can_do Process1 (prime Handshakelabel) Newprocess1 ) )
    /\ (Newprocess = (par Newprocess1 Newprocess2))
    /\ (Label = tau));

trace Process :=
  if (Process == nullprocess) then []
  else ( select Trace .
          ( exists Label Newprocess .
            (  (can_do Process Label Newprocess)
            /\ (Trace = (CONS Label (trace Newprocess))))));

% Example

a, b, c: label;
process1 := (andthen a (andthen b nullprocess));
process2 := (andthen a (plus (andthen b nullprocess)
                            (andthen c nullprocess)));
process3 := (plus (andthen (prime a) (andthen (prime b) nullprocess))
                  (andthen (prime a) (andthen (prime c) nullprocess)));
```

**Fig. 2.** A sample specification in S: The CCS formalism.

in Lambda Prolog, because it takes a type (the type of its elements) and returns another type (the type of lists of that element type). In S, the notion of kind is implicit in type expressions.

Some of the most important features which S (or its typechecker Fuss) has but which Lambda Prolog[1] does not have are: type inference on constant definitions; type abbreviations; the ability to define functions with arbitrary range; the "select" (Hilbert epsilon) operator; and constraint paragraphs.

As we shall see, the only one of these that causes a significant problem in the translation is the absence of function definitions. We must translate functions into predicate clauses in order to achieve the same effect. However, these features help make S a more useful specification language. Because of their absence, Lambda Prolog itself cannot be used effectively as a specification language.

The main features which Lambda Prolog has but S/Fuss does not have are, obviously, its explicit evaluation semantics, runtime environment and so on. Lambda Prolog also has a slightly richer type structure, theoretically allowing objects to be of kind (type -> type) -> type whereas in S we are implicitly restricted to "linear" kinds such as type -> (type -> (type -> type)); however, this added richness is not usually important in practice.

## 3.2 Alternative Target Languages

What other languages could be used as the target language for the translation from S? It can be assumed that we do not want to consider languages that involve explicit memory allocation and pointer manipulation for building dynamic data structures, since the task of building a translator to such a language would be of similar complexity to that of building an interpreter for S. There are several other programming languages with features which could make them useful as the translation target.

- ML was the target language for both Murthy's [Mur91] and Rajan's [Raj92] translations from HOL. It also has parameterized types, polymorphic functions, and lambda-expressions. Its main advantages over Lambda Prolog are that it is more widely known, used and supported, and that one can make explicit function declarations in it. However, it does not have built-in support for logical variables or explicit backtracking over disjunctions, as Lambda Prolog does. Thus the translation would have to use, or build, ML code to simulate these features, somewhat defeating the purpose of translating rather than custom-building an interpreter.
- Standard Prolog has logical variables and explicit backtracking, and is even more widely used and supported than ML. However, it does not handle lambda-expressions and has no built-in capabilities for checking the well-typedness of queries. Again, these things would have to be built.

---

[1] Unless described otherwise, all references to Lambda Prolog in this paper are to the Terzo implementation available from the University of Pennsylvania [Mil96].

– Aït-Kaci's language LIFE [AKP93] would be another interesting choice, insofar as it allows both function and predicate definitions, and can handle function calls containing uninstantiated variables. (This issue is an important one, as we will later see.) However, LIFE also lacks lambda-abstraction capabilities, and its type system has an entirely different foundation from that of the higher order logic type system.

Various other logic programming systems exist (see Section 5) which could provide other useful features in a target language. However, the crucial combination of lambda notation, unification and backtracking, which makes the execution of higher order logical constructs possible, is available only in Lambda Prolog.

# 4  The Translation Scheme

There are two main components to the translation scheme: a program called s2lp and a Lambda Prolog source file called s2lp_common.lp. s2lp acts as a Unix filter, translating an S file on its standard input into a Lambda Prolog file on its standard output. It is an adaptation of the S typechecking program Fuss [JDD96], and typechecks its input before translation. s2lp_common.lp contains declarations supporting the translated specifications, and is included in every translated file. Here we will look at the most important features of s2lp and s2lp_common.lp.

## 4.1  Translation of Type Declarations and Function Definitions

s2lp translates S type declarations into Lambda Prolog in the straightforward way; for instance, the declaration of the parameterized type array in Figure 1 is translated into the equivalent Lambda Prolog construct in Figure 1.

The main duty of s2lp is to generate Lambda Prolog clauses of the predicate eval for every constant declaration and definition in the S input file. eval is a predicate which takes two arguments of the same type, and (in its usual mode of use) instantiates its second argument to the "value" (according to the S input) of its first argument. The queries we will pose to the Lambda Prolog program will usually be of the form eval *expr* Result, where *expr* is some expression to be evaluated and Result is a variable which will be bound to its value.

Thus the S polymorphic function declaration

```
(:Element_type)
reverse (X: (Element_type) list) := rev_aux X [];
```

will (assuming rev_aux has been declared) produce the expected Lambda Prolog type declaration[2]

---

[2] Note that in Lambda Prolog, variable names start with an upper case letter and constant names start with a lower case letter, whereas case is not significant in S. This paper largely glosses over the difference by choosing names consistent with Lambda Prolog, but s2lp does do the required translation.

```
type    reverse ((list Element_type) -> (list Element_type)).
```

but also the **eval** clause

```
eval (reverse X) Result$ :-
    eval ((rev_aux X) 'NIL') Result$.
```

Because of this clause, when **eval** evaluates a call to **reverse**, it does so by immediately evaluating the corresponding call to **rev_aux**.

## 4.2  Translation of Constant Declarations and Type Definitions

The recursion of the **eval** predicate in the translated program "bottoms out" on declared constants, in keeping with the view of these constants as "uninterpreted". Thus the S constant declaration **version: num** will produce the Lambda Prolog declarations

```
    type    version num.
    eval (version) (version).
```

This indicates that the value of the expression **version** is the term **version** itself. Similarly, the type definition

```
    : (A) tree := leaf :A | branch :(A)tree :(A)tree;
```

which creates constructors **leaf** and **branch**, will produce the declarations

```
    kind    tree    type -> type.
    type    leaf    (A -> (tree A)).
    type    branch  ((tree A) -> ((tree A) -> (tree A))).
```

but also the clauses

```
    eval (leaf X$1) (leaf Y$1) :-
        eval X$1 Y$1.
    eval (branch X$1 X$2) (branch Y$1 Y$2) :-
        eval X$1 Y$1,
        eval X$2 Y$2.
```

These clauses ensure that, for instance, if an expression like (**branch Tree1 Tree2**) is evaluated, the arguments will be evaluated and the results will be assembled into a new **branch** structure as the value.

## 4.3  The Common Declarations

Every translated file contains a directive to include the Lambda Prolog source file **s21p_common.lp**. This file contains supporting declarations of the built-in types and constants of S (such as **'NIL'**), as well as the **eval** clauses for evaluating logical expressions.

These clauses are crucial to the success and ease of the translation. For example, in S one can write Hilbert-epsilon expressions of the form `select x . A`, where $A$ is any formula. In accordance with higher order logic conventions, these are parsed as `SELECT` ($\lambda$x. $A$). The `eval` clause in `s2lp_common.lp` which evaluates such expressions is simply

```
eval ('SELECT' Abstraction) Result :-
  eval (Abstraction Result) 'T'.
```

In other words, if the lambda-abstraction applied to the result is a formula which evaluates to the truth value 'T', then the value of the 'SELECT' expression is the result.

With the declarations in `s2lp_common.lp`, one can even compute goals involving implication and the universal quantifier, to the extent to which this is possible in Lambda Prolog; for instance, one can write boolean functions with bodies of the form `forall Pred . (Defn ==> Goal)`, where `Defn` is a Horn clause defining `Pred` and `Goal` is a boolean expression.

# 5 Design Decisions

A specification is a collection of logical formulas associated with some notion of what constitutes a proof; since even first order logic is undecidable, a proof cannot always be found by following a predefined strategy. A program, however, is an object associated with a predefined execution strategy. Thus an attempt to "execute a specification" must inevitably come up against the contrast between these two notions. These issues have long been explored in the functional and logic programming communities, and the design decisions made in the `s2lp` translation scheme reflect some of the knowledge that has been gained.

## 5.1 Negation

In the logic programming community there seems to be a consensus that trying to handle full negation in a sound and complete manner takes one into the realm of theorem proving. Some schemes, such as Loveland's "near-Horn" programming [LR91], provide for a graceful degradation of performance from regular Prolog when the user attempts to work with programs containing a small number of negations; but they are not available with Lambda Prolog.

`s2lp` deals with this issue by providing `eval` clauses for negation which perform the usual Lambda Prolog negation as failure, which is in some circumstances incomplete or unsound. Users should understand that if they wish to evaluate negation completely, they should move to a semi-automated theorem proving system such as HOL.

## 5.2 Uninstantiated Variables in Function Calls

When working with a combination of function and predicate definitions, the issue arises of what to do with a function call which contains an uninstantiated logical variable. This arises frequently in s21p translations when the source specifications involve both quantification and functional syntax.

For example, consider the expression `trace process1`, with respect to the specification of CCS (Fig. 2); we can evaluate this expression in the translated program by the query `eval (trace process1) Result`. The evaluation will eventually involve the solving of a subgoal of the form

   `eval (can_do process1 Label Newprocess) Result1`

which in turn will eventually involve the solving of a subgoal of the form

   `eval ('=$' Donelabel a) Result2`

where `'=$'` is the prefix binary operator corresponding to the S operator =. But now, if the Lambda Prolog program treats the arguments of `'=$'` exactly as it would any other expressions, it will try to "evaluate" the uninstantiated variable `Donelabel`. This results in an infinite recursion as the program matches variables against the existing `eval` clauses. Clearly this is not acceptable.

Aït-Kaci's language LIFE [AKP93] takes the approach of delaying function calls containing uninstantiated variables until such time as all their arguments are instantiated, a scheme called *residuation*. Again, this scheme is not available in combination with Lambda Prolog.

The scheme adopted in s21p is to assign a special meaning to the standard "=" operator. Normally, arguments to any function symbol appearing in a definition body are evaluated in that function's `eval` clause. In contrast, the clauses in `s21p_common.1p` handling = evaluate only the right-hand argument, and unify the value with the left-hand argument. Thus $s = t$ will succeed only if $s$ is syntactically identical to the `eval` value of $t$, or is some partially-instantiated generalization of that value (including an uninstantiated variable). With care, as in the CCS example, it can be used to instantiate uninstantiated variables in the correct pattern. The operator == is defined with the more expected semantics of evaluating both arguments and comparing the results.

## 5.3 Caller and Callee Evaluation

s21p adopts a "callee evaluation" scheme (sometimes referred to as "call-by-name"), where the called function is passed unevaluated arguments and evaluates them itself during the course of its computation. A potential alternative is a "caller evaluation" scheme: each `eval` clause assumes that all its function arguments contain no calls to defined functions (though they may contain uninstantiated variables), and pre-evaluates all the arguments of the functions it calls. For instance, the S declaration

   `stalled Y := ((trace Y) = []);`

would under s2lp's "callee evaluation" be translated into the form

```
eval (stalled Y) Result :-
    eval ('=$' (trace Y) []) Result.
```

but under a "caller evaluation" scheme be translated into the form

```
eval (stalled Y) Result :-
    eval (trace Y) Trace,
    eval ('=$' Trace []) Result.
```

Caller evaluation allows an uninstantiated variable to be passed through until it reaches an = expression and is unified straightforwardly. It therefore solves the problem of uninstantiated variables. However, it has the unfortunate effect of requiring that users similarly evaluate each function call in each query given to the Lambda Prolog interpreter, making queries clumsier.

Moreover, under caller evaluation it is not clear how to translate function definitions of the form apply X Y := (X Y) in such a way as to allow the first argument to be either a constant, a defined function, or a lambda expression. On the whole, the callee evaluation scheme seems less problematic for the user.

## 5.4  Uninterpreted Constants and Interpreted Operators

In specifications, we may occasionally want to declare uninterpreted boolean constants – for instance, heater_on: bool – to stand for conditions on the environment of the system under specification. When such constants are declared in S specifications, the s2lp translation essentially treats them as false rather than taking them as "new truth values", as we might prefer.

An alternative is for the translated program to take the expression to be evaluated, whether boolean or otherwise, and rewrite it to the most reduced form possible. Donat [Don97] has developed a rewriting package as an extension of Fuss for use in generating test cases from S specifications. This rewriting package is preferable to s2lp for this purpose because the truth of quantified formulas does not have to be determined.

Unfortunately, rewriting does not help when it comes to quantified formulas. For example, if (p 3) rewrites to heater_on and (p 4) rewrites to ac_on, it is not at all clear what the returned value of exists X . (p X) should be. Logic programming with boolean constraints, as is possible in SICStus Prolog [oCS94], essentially allows for such behaviour by allowing variables to be unified with "true" and "false" in whatever way will cause a goal to succeed.

The problem extends to constants of types other than bool. For instance, if temperature: num, we would like the expression temperature+2 = temperature+3 to evaluate to 'F', but temperature*2 = temperature*3 to evaluate to 'T' while unifying temperature with 0. In general, the problem of uninterpreted constants and interpreted operators leads us into the realm of constraint logic programming systems [JMSY92], which can process such queries correctly. Again, however, constraint processing is not available in Lambda Prolog.

In conclusion, then, it seems that the ideal target language for translation from a higher order specification language would be a higher order constraint logic programming language with near-Horn processing and residuation. In the absence of such a language, Lambda Prolog seems to be a reasonable choice given the design decisions made in the implementation of s2lp.

# 6 Working with the Translated Program

The following is an extended example to illustrate how the s2lp translation of an S specification works. After the command "s2lp <ccs.s >ccs.lp", which translates the CCS specification given in Fig. 2 into Lambda Prolog, we invoke the Lambda Prolog interpreter, terzo. Commands given to the Terzo loader start with #.

```
re[1]: /usr/bin/time terzo
loading /isd/local/generic/src/terzo/bin/sun4/.lpsml ....................
..... done
Terzo lambda-Prolog, Version 1.0b, Built Wed Jul 17 22:14:23 EDT 1996
[reading file /isd/local/generic/src/terzo/lib/terzo.rc]
[closed file /isd/local/generic/src/terzo/lib/terzo.rc]
Terzo> #load "ccs.lp".
[reading file ./ccs.lp]
[reading file ./s21p_common.lp]
GC #0.0.0.0.1.1:    (0 ms.)
module s21p_common
[closed file ./s21p_common.lp]
GC #0.0.0.1.2.14:    (80 ms.)
module s21p
[closed file ./ccs.lp]
Terzo> #query s21p.
?-
```

("GC" lines give Terzo garbage collection statistics.) We are now in an interpretive loop for the program, and can give queries. First we ask it to evaluate the simple function call process1 and return the result in the variable Result.

```
?- eval process1 Result.

Result = andthen a (andthen b nullprocess) ;

no more solutions
```

Next we ask it for the possible traces of this process (the sequences of actions which it can perform).

```
?- eval (trace process1) Result.
GC #0.0.0.2.3.81:    (130 ms.)

Result = CONS a (CONS b NIL) ;

no more solutions
```

We do the same for a more complex process.

```
?- eval (trace process2) Result.

Result = CONS a (CONS b NIL) ;

Result = CONS a (CONS c NIL) ;

no more solutions
```

We have obtained two results from the function call, and the **select** expression inside it, because there were two traces which met the given criteria. Next we look at the process made up by placing **process2** and **process3** in parallel; we evaluate the boolean function **can_do** with two uninstantiated variables, to see what possible ways the process can evolve. We should get five solutions.

```
?- eval (can_do (par process2 process3) Label Newp) Boolresult.
GC #0.0.0.3.4.287:   (140 ms.)

Label = a
Newp =
 par (plus (andthen b nullprocess) (andthen c nullprocess))
   (plus (andthen (prime a) (andthen (prime b) nullprocess))
     (andthen (prime a) (andthen (prime c) nullprocess)))
Boolresult = T ;

Label = prime a
Newp =
 par (andthen a (plus (andthen b nullprocess) (andthen c nullprocess)))
   (andthen (prime b) nullprocess)
Boolresult = T ;

Label = prime a
Newp =
 par (andthen a (plus (andthen b nullprocess) (andthen c nullprocess)))
   (andthen (prime c) nullprocess)
Boolresult = T ;

Label = tau
Newp =
 par (plus (andthen b nullprocess) (andthen c nullprocess))
   (andthen (prime b) nullprocess)
Boolresult = T ;
GC #0.0.0.3.5.519:   (50 ms.)

Label = tau
Newp =
 par (plus (andthen b nullprocess) (andthen c nullprocess))
   (andthen (prime c) nullprocess)
Boolresult = T ;
```

```
Label = Label
Newp = Newp
Boolresult = F ;
```

no more solutions

In fact we get a sixth solution, in which the variables have not been instantiated and the system returns a result of "false". This is to be expected as the final alternative, since we are backtracking on the value of a boolean expression and the only other possibility is falsehood. Note that the syntax of the output of Lambda Prolog is very close to that of simple S terms, and can in most cases be input back into Fuss if necessary.

```
?-         241.0 real        59.7 user        1.7 sys
re[2]:
```

After breaking out of the interpreter, we find that all this evaluation has taken about a minute of CPU time. We have been running the Terzo interpreter; on compiled Lambda Prolog systems like Prolog/MALI [BR93] this may be significantly reduced due to such techniques as first argument indexing.

Finally, we re-enter Terzo and try to see the possible traces of the (par process2 process3) process.

```
re[229]: terzo
...
Terzo> #query s2lp.
?- eval (trace (par process2 process3)) Result.
GC #0.0.0.2.3.83:    (150 ms.)
GC #0.0.0.3.4.260:   (270 ms.)
GC #0.0.1.4.5.380:   (380 ms.)
GC #0.1.2.5.6.494:   (400 ms.)
GC #0.1.2.5.7.620:   (30 ms.)
^C
interrupt
Terzo>
```

We have found a hole in the specification: there is a specification for the trace of the null process, but no specification for the trace of the process (par nullprocess nullprocess), one of the possible descendents of the process in the query. The system has responded by going into an infinite loop on one of the uninstantiated variables. Now we can return to the specification and patch the hole before basing any further work on it. Future edit-translate-execute cycles will allow our confidence in the correctness of our specification to increase.

s2lp has been run on a number of different specifications, including portions of an S specification of a telecommunications network being developed within the FormalWare project. The translated Lambda Prolog code returns results of function calls as expected and finds solutions within its capabilities.

# 7   Conclusions and Future Work

s2lp represents an advance over some previous schemes for evaluating higher order specifications, in that it allows a wider range of quantified formulas to be executed using the Prolog backtracking and unification features. With s21p, users can build formal specifications of their systems of interest in S, and translate them into Lambda Prolog in order to verify that desired properties hold before doing more extensive theorem-proving or implementation.

The results of this paper are not specific to S, but generalize to other specification languages. For instance, we should be able to translate HOL into Lambda Prolog via ML functions which traverse the ML internal representation of HOL terms. Future extensions of the scheme could include extensions for partially evaluating arithmetic expressions, or providing the option of "caller evaluation" (see Section 5.3) for situations which require it.

Ideally, one can envision an integrated logic and functional programming and specification language, in which computable functions and predicates can be defined in a natural style, but uninterpreted constants and assertions can be included where required to produce a readable and sufficiently abstract specification. Such a scheme might be built as a generalization of an existing programming language, such as ML or Lambda Prolog, or an existing specification language, such as Z or S.

# 8   Acknowledgments

Thanks to Jeff Joyce for suggesting the topic of this paper and, together with Nancy Day and Michael Donat, for the development of the Fuss typechecker on which s21p was based, for giving valuable comments on an earlier version of this paper, and for providing a stimulating working environment in which to explore ideas of logic, computation, and software engineering.

The FormalWare project is financially supported by the BC Advanced Systems Institute (BCASI), Hughes Aircraft of Canada Limited Systems Division (HCSD), and MacDonald Dettwiler Limited (MDA). The author derives half his funding from this project and half from the generous support of Dr. Paul Gilmore of UBC Computer Science, via his grant from the Natural Sciences and Engineering Research Council of Canada (NSERC).

# References

[AKP93]   Hassan Ait-Kaci and Andreas Podelski. Towards a meaning of Life. *Journal of Logic Programming*, 16(3/4):195, July 1993.

[BR93]   Pascal Brisset and Olivier Ridoux. The compilation of Lambda Prolog and its execution with MALI. Technical Report 1831, INRIA, 1993.

[Cam88]   Albert Camilleri. Simulation as an aid to verification using the HOL theorem prover. Technical Report 150, University of Cambridge Computer Laboratory, October 1988.

[Don97]   Michael R. Donat. Automating formal specification-based testing. In *TAP-SOFT: 7th International Joint Conference on Theory and Practice of Software Engineering*, April 1997.

[HM90]     John Hannan and Dale Miller. From operational semantics to abstract machines: Preliminary results. In *Proceedings of the ACM Conference on Lisp and Functional Programming*, pages 323–332, Nice, France, June 1990. ACM Press.

[JDD94]    Jeffrey J. Joyce, Nancy A. Day, and Michael R. Donat. S: A machine readable specification notation based on higher order logic. In *Higher Order Logic Theorem Proving and Its Applications, 7th International Workshop*, volume 859 of *LNCS*. Springer-Verlag, 1994.

[JDD96]    Jeffrey J. Joyce, Nancy A. Day, and Michael R. Donat. S – a general-purpose specification notation. Draft report, 1996.

[JMSY92]  Joxan Jaffar, Spiro Michaylov, Peter J. Stuckey, and Roland H. C. Yap. The CLP($\mathcal{R}$) language and system. *ACM Transactions on Programming Languages and Systems*, 14(3):339–395, July 1992.

[Kah87]    G. Kahn. Natural semantics. In *Proceedings of the Symposium on Theoretical Aspects of Computer Science*, volume 247 of *LNCS*, pages 22–39, Passau, Federal Republic of Germany, Feb 1987. Springer.

[LR91]     Donald W. Loveland and David W. Reed. A near-Horn Prolog for compliation. In *Computational Logic: Essays in Honor of Alan Robinson*, Cambridge, Mass., 1991. MIT Press.

[Mil80]    Robin Milner. *A Calculus of Communicating Systems*, volume 92 of *Lecture Notes in Computer Science*. Springer-Verlag, Berlin, 1980.

[Mil96]    Dale A. Miller. Lambda Prolog home page. http://www.cis.upenn.edu/ dale/lProlog/index.html/, 1996.

[MN86]     Dale A. Miller and Gopalan Nadathur. Higher-order logic programming. In *Proceedings of the Third International Logic Programming Conference*, Imperial College, London, July 1986.

[MNPS91]  Dale Miller, Gopalan Nadathur, Frank Pfenning, and Andre Scedrov. Uniform proofs as a foundation for logic programming. *Annals of Pure and Applied Logic*, 51:125–157, 1991.

[Mur91]    Chetan R. Murthy. An evaluation semantics for classical proofs. In *Proceedings of the Fifth Annual Symposium on Logic in Computer Science*. IEEE, 1991.

[Nes93]    Monica Nesi. Value-passing CCS in HOL. In *HOL Users' Group Workshop*, Vancouver, August 1993.

[oCS94]    SICS (Swedish Institute of Computer Science). SICStus Prolog user's manual. Technical report, Swedish Institute of Computer Science, Kista, Sweden, April 1994.

[Raj92]    P. Sreeranga Rajan. Executing HOL specifications: Towards an evaluation semantics for classical higher order logic. In L. J. M. Claesen and M. J. C. Gordon, editors, *Higher Order Logic Theorem Proving and its Applications*, Leuven, Belgium, September 1992. Elsevier.

# Human-Style Theorem Proving Using PVS*

Myla Archer and Constance Heitmeyer

Code 5546, Naval Research Laboratory, Washington, DC 20375
{archer,heitmeyer}@itd.nrl.navy.mil

**Abstract.** A major barrier to more common use of mechanical theorem provers in verifying software designs is the significant distance between proof styles natural to humans and proof styles supported by mechanical provers. To make mechanical provers useful to software designers with some mathematical sophistication but without expertise in mechanical provers, the distance between hand proofs and their mechanized versions must be reduced. To achieve this, we are developing a mechanical prover called TAME on top of PVS. TAME is designed to process proof steps that resemble in style and size the typical steps in hand proofs. TAME's support of more natural proof steps should not only facilitate mechanized checking of hand proofs, but in addition should provide assurance that theorems proved mechanically are true for the reasons expected and also provide a basis for conceptual level feedback when a mechanized proof fails. While infeasible for all applications, designing a prover that can process a set of high-level, natural proof steps for restricted domains should be achievable. In developing TAME, we have had moderate success in defining specialized proof strategies to validate hand proofs of properties of Lynch-Vaandrager timed automata. This paper reports on our successes, the services provided by PVS that support these successes, and some desired enhancements to PVS that would permit us to improve and extend TAME.

## 1 Introduction

Although the application of mechanical theorem provers to the verification of hardware designs has been somewhat successful, the use of such provers for verifying software is quite rare. A major barrier to more common use of mechanical theorem provers in both software and hardware verification, or verification of mathematical results in general, is the distance between the proof style natural to human beings and the proof style supported in various mechanical theorem provers.

Our goal is to make mechanical proof tools more useful to those who are not experts in one or more mechanical theorem provers. This group includes most mathematicians, algorithm designers, and industrial software and hardware developers. Our approach is to develop a tool on top of an existing theorem prover which reduces the distance between specifications and proofs natural to people and the specifications and proofs supported by existing theorem provers. In an ongoing case study, we have been developing the tool TAME [1, 2, 3] on top of the PVS environment [24, 20]. TAME can be used to specify and reason about Lynch-Vaandrager timed automata.

### 1.1 Some challenging questions

Reducing the distance between hand proofs and proofs generated mechanically is very difficult if not impossible to achieve in full generality, because different applications have their own specialized languages and conventions. This observation raises a number of questions:

* This work is funded by the Office of Naval Research. URLs for the authors are http://www.itd.nrl.navy.mil/ITD/5540/personnel/{archer,heitmeyer}.html

1. Can restricting the problem to specific application domains make the problem more manageable, and, if so, how large can the domain be?

2. Can a theorem prover specialized for an application domain be used directly by engineers?

3. Can a specialized theorem prover help with proof *search* as well as proof checking?

4. What is required of the underlying theorem prover to support natural proof steps tailored for a particular application domain?

We use our experience with TAME to address these questions.

## 1.2 Our approach

Our assumption in developing TAME is that the answer to the first question is positive. TAME, which supports the specification and mechanical verification of Lynch-Vaandrager timed automata, has been used to check a number of specifications and proofs developed by Lynch and her collaborators [10, 15, 14, 26]. The proofs checked with TAME apply human-style reasoning in the context of concepts specific to timed automata models. We believe that analogous combinations of human-style reasoning with model-specific concepts will make mechanization of verification natural for other mathematical models as well.

Our approach is not to build a new mechanical theorem prover from scratch but to build upon an existing prover that provides the basic features needed in a prover. Our goal is to support "human-style" reasoning in a particular mathematical model through an appropriate top layer to PVS. By human-style reasoning, we mean reasoning of the sort found in typical hand proofs. Such proofs usually include large proof steps, each of which corresponds to many small, detailed steps in a mechanized proof. Although mechanical provers can use powerful general tactics or strategies to take large steps, these steps rarely correspond to the steps that a human takes in reasoning. Our goal is to design the top layer so that large steps taken by the prover correspond closely to large steps taken by humans.

Supporting human-style proofs provides many benefits. First, a mechanical proof that corresponds closely to a hand proof provides documentation that allows a person who is expert in a given mathematical model, but not necessarily an expert in the use of a mechanical prover, to understand the proof and thus decide whether the property proved holds for the reasons expected. Second, the hand proof of a property can be used in a direct way to search for a mechanized proof and provides an opportunity for a person who is a domain expert but not an expert in the full mechanized proof system to do some proof checking. Finally, when a mechanized proof that is more natural fails, the prover can provide feedback at a high conceptual level explaining why the proof (or the associated specification) is in error.

Natural mechanized proof steps must not only be human-style; they must be *human-sized* as well. Humans can, of course, reason in tiny steps, but reasoning at too low a level can obscure the "big picture". For readability, human-sized steps are important. They are also important for the efficient creation of mechanized proofs.

Our current goal in TAME is to develop PVS strategies for proof steps that closely resemble the steps in hand proofs. Thus, we have concentrated so far on how to design the underlying theorem proving support for TAME, rather than a high-level interface. In the process, we have identified a set of services that a programmable prover should provide to facilitate the mechanization of natural proof steps. In particular, we have found that higher-order features are critical for efficient implementation of human-style steps. PVS has some of these higher-order features. However, we have identified both additional higher-order features and other features currently lacking in PVS, that would increase the range of human-style steps that we could mechanize using PVS. Such features should prove useful not only to support TAME in PVS; they should be generally useful for supporting human-style proofs in any programmable prover.

## 1.3 Related efforts

Some approaches to mechanical verification are designed to be totally automatic. Such approaches include model checking [19, 12, 13] and the protocol analyzer described in [6]. Tools based on these approaches can indeed be useful, but requiring the assertion checking to be completely automatic limits their range of application.

Significant progress towards supporting human-style proofs in a mechanical prover has been made in the Mizar project [21]. As noted in [22], Mizar proofs tend to be very detailed, and unless care is taken in their construction, not easily read. The Mizar system has been used primarily to check proofs in pure mathematics; whether Mizar can be applied efficiently to verify software is not clear. In [9], Harrison shows how Mizar can be emulated in HOL. As a result, HOL-based proofs can use human-style reasoning that follows the Mizar formalities and required level of detail and thus can be easily understood. Using either Mizar or the HOL Mizar mode requires that one learn the details and conventions of a general theorem proving system before one uses the system in conjunction with a specialized mathematical model. This is the problem that TAME is intended to remedy.

Although different in their approaches from TAME, both the Mizar system [9] and Brackin's protocol analyzer [6] demonstrate how specialized theorem proving support can be built using a programmable theorem prover. The proof assistant for the Duration Calculus (DC) [25] also illustrates this approach. Proofs in the DC proof assistant are not human-style but use a Gentzen-style sequent proof system developed especially for the tool.

## 1.4 Preview of the paper

Section 2 provides technical background needed in the rest of the paper, while Section 3 describes the degree of success TAME has had in mimicking human-style reasoning. Section 4 illustrates the PVS features that have been useful in supporting human-style reasoning and discusses additional features desirable in the underlying prover. Section 5 discusses the features desirable in the underlying system to support the development of specialized theorem-proving, and Section 6 responds to the questions posed above. Finally, Section 7 discusses our plans for the further development of TAME.

## 2 Background

This section describes the mathematical model upon which TAME is based, and gives a brief introduction to both PVS and TAME.

### 2.1 The Lynch-Vaandrager Timed Automata Model

A Lynch-Vaandrager (LV) timed automaton is a very general automaton, i.e., a labeled transition system that incorporates the notions of current time and timed transitions. In the model, a system is described as a set of timed automata, interacting by means of common actions. For verification purposes, these interacting automata can be composed into a single timed automaton. An automaton need not be finite-state: for example, the state can contain real-valued information, such as the current time, water level or steam rate in a boiler, velocity and acceleration of a train, and so on. This makes timed automata suitable for modeling not only computer systems but also real-world quantities, such as water levels and acceleration. LV timed automata can have nondeterministic transitions; this is particularly useful for describing how real-world quantities change as time passes.

The definition of timed automaton below, based on the definitions in [11, 10], was used in our case study involving a deterministic timed automaton [2].

A *timed automaton A* consists of five components:

– *states*($A$), a (finite or infinite) set of states.
– *start*($A$) $\subseteq$ *states*($A$), a nonempty (finite or infinite) set of start states.
– A mapping *now* from *states*($A$) to $R^{\geq 0}$, the non-negative real numbers.
– *acts*($A$), a set of actions (or events), which include special *time-passage* actions $\nu(\Delta t)$, where $\Delta t$ is a positive real number, and *non-time-passage* actions, classified as *input* and *output* actions, which are *visible*, and *internal* actions;
– *steps*($A$) : *states*($A$) $\times$ *acts*($A$) $\rightarrow$ *states*($A$), a partial function that defines the possible steps (i.e., transitions).

This definition describes a special case of Lynch-Vaandrager timed automata that requires the next-state relation, *steps*($A$), to be a function. By using the Hilbert choice operator $\epsilon$, we are able to use essentially the same definition in the nondeterministic case as well [3]. A challenge is how to make reasoning about nondeterminism in TAME resemble human-style reasoning as closely as possible.

The properties of timed automata that one wants to prove fall into three classes: (1) state invariants, typically proved by induction; (2) simulation relations; and (3) ad hoc properties of certain execution sequences of a timed automaton. Proofs in both (1) and (2) have a standard structure with a base case involving start states and a case for each possible action. They are thus especially good targets for mechanization. Below, we define timed executions, reachability and invariants, and simulation relations.

**Timed Executions.** A *trajectory* is either a single state or a continuous series (i.e., an interval) of states connected by time passage events. A *timed execution fragment* is a finite or infinite alternating sequence $\alpha = w_0 \pi_1 w_1 \pi_2 w_2 \cdots$, where each $w_j$ is a trajectory and each $\pi_j$ is a non-time-passage action that "connects" the final state $s$ of the preceding trajectory $w_{j-1}$ with the initial state $s'$ of the following trajectory $w_j$. A *timed execution* is a timed execution fragment in which the initial state of the first trajectory is a start state.

A timed execution is *admissible* if the total time-passage is infinity. The notion of admissible timed executions is important in expressing properties defined over time intervals (e.g., the gate at a railroad crossing is not down after a train has left unless a new train is about to arrive), rather than time points, and in defining simulation relations between timed automata.

**Reachability and Invariants.** A state of a timed automaton is *reachable* if it is the final state of the final trajectory in some finite timed execution of the automaton. An *invariant* of a timed automaton is any property true of all reachable states, or equivalently, any set of states containing the reachable states.

**Simulation Relations.** A *simulation relation* [18, 17, 16] relates the states of one timed automaton $A$ to the states of another timed automaton $B$ in such a way that the (visible) actions and their timings in admissible timed executions correspond. The existence of a simulation relation from $A$ to $B$ implies that each visible behavior (i.e., timed sequence of visible actions) of automaton $A$ is a member of the set of visible behaviors of automaton $B$.

## 2.2 PVS

PVS (Prototype Verification System) [24] is a specification and verification environment developed by SRI. The system provides a specification language, a parser, a type checker, and an interactive proof checker. The PVS specification language is based on a richly typed higher-order logic. Proof steps in PVS are either *primitive* steps or *strategies* defined using primitive proof steps, applicative Lisp code, and other strategies. Strategies may be built-in or user-defined. Proof goals in PVS are represented as Gentzen-style *sequents*. To satisfy a proof goal, one must establish that the antecedent formulae imply one of the (zero or more) consequent formulae.

The primitive proof steps of PVS incorporate arithmetic and equality decision procedures, automatic rewriting, and BDD-based boolean simplification. Thus, PVS provides *both* a highly expressive specification language and automation of most low-level proof steps, in contrast to to other widely used proof systems, such as HOL [8] (which is lacking in decision procedures) and the Boyer-Moore theorem prover [5] (whose specification language is first-order). The programmability of PVS makes it a candidate to be the basis for specialized tools.

## 2.3 TAME

TAME (for Timed Automata Modeling Environment) is based upon a standard template specification for the timed automata described in Section 2.1, a set of standard theories, and a set of standard PVS strategies. The TAME template for specifying Lynch-Vaandrager timed automata provides a standard organization for an automaton definition. To define a timed automaton, the user supplies the following six components:

- declarations of the non-time actions,
- a type for the "basic state" (usually a record type) representing the state variables,
- any arbitrary state predicate that restricts the set of states (the default is **true**),
- the preconditions for all transitions,
- the effects of all transitions, and
- the set of start states.

In addition, the user may optionally supply

- declarations of important constants,
- an axiom listing any relations assumed among the constants, and
- any additional declarations or axioms desired.

To support mechanical reasoning about timed automata using proof steps that mimic human proof steps, TAME provides a set of standard strategies we have constructed using PVS. These strategies are based on a set of standard theories and certain template conventions. For example, the induction strategy, which is used to prove state invariants, is based on a standard automaton theory called **machine**. To reason about the arithmetic of time, we have developed a special theory called **time_thy** and an associated simplification strategy called **TIME_ETC_SIMP** for time values that can be either non-negative real values or $\infty$.

# 3   Successes with Human-Style Proving in TAME

We have successfully created PVS strategies for many of the human-style proof steps needed to verify properties of timed automata. We discovered these strategies by constructing PVS proofs that resembled the corresponding hand proofs as much as possible. In constructing the proofs, we used the standard PVS rules and strategies and then generalized the results. In several cases, additional PVS features would have allowed us to more closely follow human-style steps. Section 4 describes these additional features.

We have applied TAME to several problems: the Generalized Railroad Crossing (GRC) problem [10, 11], a timed version of Fischer's mutual exclusion algorithm [15], the Boiler Controller problem [14], and a Vehicle Control System example [26]. Most recently, we have used TAME to check some properties of a Group Communication Service [7].

As noted in Section 2.1, the interesting properties of timed automata fall into three classes. Each class has its own associated proof styles. State invariants are proved either by induction or directly using other state invariants. Proofs of simulation either have a case structure similar to induction proofs or are direct proofs combining other simulation results. Proofs of properties of timed executions are more ad hoc in their structure but employ certain specialized types of inference in their domain-relevant steps. We have had moderate success in developing human-style proof steps for properties in the first and third classes and have used these steps to obtain proofs. Our major strategy for state invariant proofs, discussed in more detail below, sets up induction proofs. Due to limitations in the PVS specification language, we have not yet developed an analogous strategy for simulation proofs. Currently, PVS does not allow us to define the simulation property at a useful level of abstraction. Future improvements to PVS are expected to remove this barrier.

Below, we provide more detail about our PVS strategies, the extent to which they support the translation of hand proofs into PVS proofs, and the benefits we have gained from their use.

## 3.1   Some PVS strategies that support human-style proof steps

**Some existing strategies.** Below, we describe some of the PVS strategies we have built into TAME. These support steps that are frequently found in hand proofs of properties of timed automata.

*The induction strategy* performs the (usually implicit) step in human reasoning about state invariants that converts induction over the number of transitions from a start state to a reachable state into a base case (for start states) and a case for each possible action that could lead to a transition. Besides making this conversion, the induction strategy completes the trivial proof branches and presents the user with the nontrivial base or action cases. The knowledge that the prestate and poststate are reachable is carried along in the action cases; this facilitates the application of previously proved state invariant lemmas in a proof. For each TAME application, the appropriate induction strategy must be compiled from the declaration of the non-time actions entered into the template specification.

*The invariant-lemma strategy* supports the application of state invariants to arbitrary states during a proof, the default state in an induction proof being the prestate. When applied to a state whose reachability status has not been established, the reachability of that state is retained as a condition on the invariant for that state.

*The precondition strategy* simply invokes the specific precondition in an action case of an induction proof. (The full precondition may have other nontrivial components such as bounds on the time when the action can occur.)

*The constant-facts strategy.* This strategy introduces known facts about the constant "parameters" in a timed automaton description.

*The strategy* TIME_ETC_SIMP combines simple case-based reasoning and reasoning about time arithmetic, where time values can be nonnegative real numbers or $\infty$. The combination is particularly useful, since the definitions of the operations in time arithmetic are themselves case-based. This strategy is currently our best approximation to the human-style step "it is now obvious".

*The strategy* USE_EPSILON supports reasoning about nondeterministic components in the poststate. It introduces the constraints on a nondeterministic component on the main proof branch and forks a side branch for the existence proof entailed by the use of Hilbert's $\epsilon$-axiom. It (inconveniently) requires as one of its arguments the domain type of the predicate to which $\epsilon$ is applied. Thus, there is room for improvement in this strategy. Nevertheless, we have found it very helpful in our applications involving nondeterminism (even though $\epsilon$ does not fit our needs for reasoning about nondeterminism precisely [3]).

*The last-event and first-event strategies* have proved helpful in ad hoc proofs about timed executions. The last-event strategy adduces, on the main proof branch, the last event before a point in the execution that possesses a certain property. The property, the point in the execution, and the name to be assigned to the last event must be supplied as arguments. A side proof branch is created in which one is obliged to prove the existence of some event that occurs prior to the given point in the execution and has the property. The first-event strategy is symmetrically analogous. The strategies are supported by the lemmas last_event and first_event shown in Figure 2 in Section 4.

*The discretization strategy.* The discretization strategy is also mainly useful in proofs about timed executions. It permits the leap (when justified) from reasoning about all states during an execution to reasoning about all states at the beginning of some trajectory of an execution. Again, an appropriate side proof branch is created, in which one must show that the property to be proved itself satisfies the property trajectory_constant: i.e., it is constant in any trajectory. Improvements and variations on this strategy are under consideration.

**Some future strategies.** Once those PVS enhancements described in Section 4 that are currently under way are complete, we plan to implement additional strategies. We describe a few examples of these strategies below.

*The reachability strategy* will determine and make known in the course of a TAME proof the fact that a particular state is reachable. This strategy will make the invariant-lemma strategy more powerful in the context of proofs concerning timed executions. While obvious to a human that any state in an admissible timed execution is reachable, some effort is required to introduce this fact into a mechanized proof, due partly to the variety of ways one can represent a state. The strategy will invoke several lemmas, apply the relevant one, and remove

---

**Lemma 6.3.**  *In all reachable states of SystImpl, if Trains.r.status = I for any r, then Gate.status = down.*

**Proof:**  Use induction. The interesting cases are *enterI* and *raise*. Fix $r$.

1. *enterI* $(r)$

   By the precondition, $s.Trains.r.status = P$.

   If $s.Gate.status \in \{up, going-up\}$, then Lemma 6.1 implies that $s.Trains.first(enterI(r)) > now + \gamma_{down}$, so $s.Trains.first(enterI(r)) > now$. But, the precondition for *enterI* $(r)$ is $s.Trains.first(enterI(r)) \leq now$. This means that it is impossible for this action to occur, a contradiction.

   If $s.Gate.status = going-down$, then Lemma 6.2 implies that $s.Trains.first(enterI(r)) > s.Gate.last(down)$. By Lemma B.1, $s.Gate.status = going-down$ implies $s.Gate.last(down) \geq now$. This implies that $s.Trains.first(enterI(r)) > now$, which again means that it is impossible for this action to occur.

   The only remaining case is $s.Gate.status = down$. This implies $s'.Gate.status = down$, which suffices.

2. *raise*

   We need to show that the gate doesn't get raised when a train is in $I$. So suppose that $s.Trains.r.status = I$. The precondition of *raise* states that $\exists r : s.CompImpl.r.sched-time \leq now + \gamma_{up} + \delta + \gamma_{down}$, which implies that, for all $r$, $s.CompImpl.r.sched-time > now$. But Parts 1 and 3 of Lemma 5.1 imply that in this case, $s.Trains.r.status = P$, a contradiction.

---

**Fig. 1.** A typical hand proof we have mechanized in TAME is the proof of the Safety Property from [11].

the irrelevant information. Its implementation will combine formula naming and recognition by content.

*Naming strategies* will keep the expanded versions of complex expressions—most notably, the representation of the poststate in an induction proof—out of sight, but retrieve, use, and hide their definitions when simplification strategies are applied to the sequent. The implementation of these strategies will combine formula naming and improved access to hidden formulae.

*A skolemization-instantiation strategy* will coordinate skolemization and instantiation of pairs of quantified formulae. This strategy can improve the induction strategy for state invariants that are quantified formulae. Its implementation will require the ability to probe for information about the number and type of the quantified variables in a formula. Its argument formulae will usually be identified by name.

*The inductive-hypothesis strategy* will retrieve the uninstantiated inductive hypothesis from among the hidden formulae, in induction proofs of quantified state invariants. It is needed in those rare cases where the default instantiation provided by the improved induction strategy is not the one desired. Its implementation will use formula naming and improved access to hidden formulae.

### 3.2  Translation support from our strategies

In the GRC, Fischer's Algorithm, the Boiler System, and the Vehicle Control Systems examples, we used TAME successfully to check both induction proofs and direct proofs of state invariants. We succeeded in mechanizing all of the state invariant proofs in these examples with the exception of a few induction proof branches involving complex arithmetic reasoning that could be checked by hand, but for which discovering the extra hints needed to supplement the decision procedures in PVS would be very time-consuming. In the majority of the induction proofs we mechanized, TAME's specialized strategies alone were enough to obtain the proofs. Figure 1 shows a typical hand proof from the GRC example. The steps in this hand proof are induction, appeal to invariant lemmas, appeal to a precondition, and simple reasoning. Its mechanization uses only the induction strategy, the invariant-lemma strategy, the precondition strategy, and **TIME_ETC_SIMP**.

Other induction proofs sometimes required extra steps from the following four categories: (1) explicit substitutions to give the PVS decision procedures a boost, (2) manipulation to lift embedded quantified expressions to the top level, (3) expansion of a definition, and (4) application of lemmas about real arithmetic, sometimes accompanied by the use of the PVS CASE strategy to provide hints. They also occasionally involved what we consider a more legitimate application of the CASE strategy, namely, when reasoning by cases is a natural human proof step.

The degree of isomorphism between our TAME proofs and the hand proofs from which they were derived is very high for the GRC and Boiler System examples. For Fischer's Algorithm and the Vehicle Control Systems examples, the degree is less, but for different reasons. The hand proofs for Fischer's Algorithm used a different case breakdown than that supported by our induction strategy. In the Vehicle Control Systems example, the specification was in a form slightly different from the form TAME supports, and as a result the specification had to be translated into the required form. However, the TAME proofs did resemble the hand proofs in two important respects: the action cases considered significant by TAME and in the hand proofs were identical, and the facts required in the TAME proofs could be inferred from the hand proofs. Imposing some restrictions on the form of the human specification and proof would increase the degree of isomorphism.

## 3.3 Benefits of the TAME approach

We can construct induction proofs with TAME rather quickly. The initial capabilities of TAME were developed during our specification and verification of the GRC example. The next examples (with the exception of the Group Communication Service) took about two or three work weeks at most. Translating the specifications of each example into the TAME template required approximately two to three days. The proofs of individual invariants usually required approximately half an hour to half a day. Proofs of some of the more complicated invariants (whose hand proofs run from one to two and a half pages) often required two or three days to construct. The speed with which we can construct TAME proofs increases when we have a hand proof of similar structure as a guide. However, even in the absence of such a hand proof, or any hand proof at all, we have found TAME to be very helpful in proof exploration, because it simplifies the mechanization of many large steps natural in a hand proof.

In applying TAME to additional examples, we find that the previously developed strategies are highly reusable. This has contributed greatly to the speed with which we have been able to check new examples.

On occasion, a dead end was reached during an attempt to mechanize an induction proof using TAME. In the case of the original Boiler Controller specification, these dead ends revealed some errors in the specification and two of the proofs. Due to the form of the proofs, the contents of the sequents at these dead ends were easily traced to the specification and the point reached in the reasoning. Thus, the type of feedback we were able to provide in the Boiler Controller example was very specific in pinpointing both typographical and reasoning errors. In the case of the Group Communication Service, we are using TAME for proof exploration as well as proof checking. Thus, we cannot always anticipate the line of reasoning that will succeed nor the meaning of dead ends in a proof. In some cases, a dead end suggested the reformulation of complex invariants. In others, dead ends have uncovered additional invariants needed in the full correctness proof.

## 4  Desirable Capabilities in the Underlying Prover

In developing PVS strategies for human-style proofs, we have found certain PVS features to be particularly helpful and have discovered other features, currently missing in PVS, that would be helpful if provided. The features that we have identified should be useful for supporting human-style proof steps in other programmable theorem provers—not just PVS.

**Useful higher order features of PVS.** To define several of the generic steps, we found various higher-order features of PVS useful. The most useful higher-order feature is the ability to quantify over predicates in definitions and lemmas. This feature permits us (see Figure 2) to state the induction principle **machine_induct**, the existence lemmas **last_event** and **first_event**, and the definitions of the function **discretize** and related concepts involved in the discretization strategy. This feature would also permit support for reasoning that uses such higher-order concepts from real analysis as "convex function", which

---

**Example 1:** The theorem **machine_induct** and supporting definitions.

base(Inv) : bool = (FORALL s: start(s) => Inv(s));
inductstep(Inv) : bool = (FORALL s, a: reachable(s) & Inv(s) & enabled(a,s) => Inv(trans(a,s)));
inductthm(Inv): bool = base(Inv) & inductstep(Inv) => (FORALL s : reachable(s) => Inv(s));
machine_induct: THEOREM (FORALL Inv: inductthm(Inv));

**Example 2:** The lemmas **last_event** and **first_event** with supporting definitions.

state_event_prop: TYPE = [atexecs,states,posnat -> bool];
Q: state_event_prop;
last_event: LEMMA (FORALL (alpha:atexecs, s:states, P:state_event_prop):
  (LET Q = (LAMBDA(alpha:atexecs, s:states, n:pos_nat): (precedes_state(alpha)(n,s) & P(alpha,s,n))) IN
  (FORALL (n:posnat): (Q(alpha,s,n) => (EXISTS (m: posnat): m >= n & Q(alpha,s,m)
                          & (FORALL (k: posnat): k >= m & Q(alpha,s,k) => k = m)))));
first_event: LEMMA (FORALL (alpha:atexecs, s:states, P:state_event_prop):
  (LET Q = (LAMBDA(alpha:atexecs, s:states, n:pos_nat): (precedes_event(alpha)(s,n) & P(alpha,s,n))) IN
  (FORALL (n:posnat): (Q(alpha,s,n) => (EXISTS (m: posnat): m <= n & Q(alpha,s,m)
                          & (FORALL (k: posnat): k <= m & Q(alpha,s,k) => k = m)))));

**Example 3:** The theorem **discrete_equiv** and some supporting definitions.

state_pred: TYPE = [atexecs -> [states -> bool]];
index_pred: TYPE = [atexecs -> [nat -> bool]];
discretize (T: state_pred): index_pred =
  LAMBDA (alpha:atexecs): LAMBDA (n:nat): T(alpha)(fstate(w(alpha)(n)));
trajectory_constant(SP:state_pred): bool = FORALL (alpha:atexecs, s:states):
  (in_atexec(alpha)(s) => (SP(alpha)(s) = SP(alpha)(fstate(w(alpha)(traj_index(alpha)(s))))));
discrete_equiv_pred(T:state_pred):bool = (trajectory_constant(T) =>
  (FORALL (alpha:atexecs, s:states):
    (in_atexec(alpha)(s) => (T(alpha)(s) = (discretize(T))(alpha)(traj_index(alpha)(s))))));
discrete_equiv: THEOREM FORALL (T:state_pred): discrete_equiv_pred(T);

---

**Fig. 2.** Some higher-order definitions useful in supporting human-style proof steps.

turned up in the Boiler Controller example. Whether adding such support to TAME will prove worthwhile is at this point unknown.

The ability to define the state of an automaton as a record, some of whose components are functions, supports our strategies in a more indirect way, by simplifying the template conventions followed in specifying a particular automaton and relied upon by our strategies.

**Other useful PVS features.** Another feature of PVS useful for supporting human-style proof steps is the presence of built-in decision procedures. These decision procedures provide much of the support needed (for example, in our strategy **TIME_ETC_SIMP**) for taking the analogous mechanical steps in the many cases where a hand proof contains steps such as "it is obvious", "this is a contradiction", etc. The existing decision procedures handle propositional logic, equational reasoning, automatic rewriting, and linear arithmetic and can be invoked concurrently using built-in PVS strategies.

**Desirable higher-order features lacking in PVS.** PVS lacks some useful higher-order features. One such feature is parametric polymorphism, which permits the types of the parameters in definitions or lemmas to be type variables or to include type variables in their representation. Another higher-order capability missing in PVS is one that would permit us to express the definition of a simulation relation between automata. This capability is discussed in more detail below.

Parametric polymorphism requires on-the-fly type inference, but can simplify both specification and proof. Currently, the following cannot be done in PVS without explicit type information from the user:

  definition of a predicate stating that the value of a state component is unchanged by time passage events;

  - application of generic lemmas on parameterized types, such as queues and ordered lists;

  - definition of generic lemmas that support strategies for converting ∀ expressions to ¬∃¬ expressions and, similarly, ∃ to ¬∀¬; and

  - invocation of the Hilbert ε-axiom on a predicate.

Given parametric polymorphism, we could eliminate many instances where application-specific detail is required, and extend the set of generic human-style proof steps supported by TAME. PVS does support generic definitions, axioms, and lemmas by way of parameterized *theories*. However, using these in a specification currently requires either providing explicit type information in places or explicitly importing all relevant theory instantiations. In either case, explicit type information is needed when the axioms or lemmas are invoked in the course of a proof. The need for such type information is a barrier to creating generic strategies that are simple to apply. For example, our strategy **USE_EPSILON** (see Section 3.1) currently needs as an argument not only the predicate to which the ε-axiom is being applied, but the domain type of that predicate.

When we try to define a simulation mapping generically in PVS (see Figure 3), we encounter dead ends. For example, to refer to an automaton by name in a definition, we need an automaton type. The obvious representation of an element of this type is a record whose components are the states, actions, start state predicate, transition function, and so on. However, states and actions are most naturally represented as types, and record components (unlike parameters

---

Let $A$ and $B$ be timed automata, and $I_A$ and $I_B$ be, respectively, state invariants of $A$ and $B$. Let $f$ be a binary relation between *states* $(A)$ and *states* $(B)$. Then $f$ is a *simulation mapping* from $A$ to $B$ if it satisfies the following three conditions:

1. If $u \in f[s]$ then $now(u) = now(s)$.

2. If $s \in start(A)$ then $f[s] \cap start(B) \neq \emptyset$.

3. If $s \xrightarrow{\pi}_A s'$ is a step of $A$, $s, s' \in I_A$, and $u \in f[s] \cap I_B$, then there exists $u' \in f[s']$ such that there is a timed execution fragment from $u$ to $u'$ having the same timed visible actions as the step $\pi$.

---

**Fig. 3.** Definition of simulation between automata. The notation $f[s]$ stands for $\{u : (s, u) \in f\}$.

of theories) cannot have type "type" in PVS. All the alternative, less natural solutions we have considered also seem to require some feature currently missing in PVS.[1]

**Other desirable features lacking in PVS.** Several PVS features are being added. These will permit us to implement several human-style strategies for which we have designs. These features include the ability to name formulae and subformulae, to retrieve a hidden formula by name, and to identify formulae by content. They will permit the writing of strategies that can use specific formulae in a sequent without referring to their exact "address". The usefulness of such a feature in HOL has been noted by others [4]. Section 3.1 outlined some of our intended applications of these features.

We have also identified other features, some available in other mechanical provers, that would be extremely useful in supporting human-style reasoning steps. Examples include the ability to skolemize or instantiate embedded quantifiers, the expansion of the scope of the existing decision procedures to handle some obvious facts about nonlinear real arithmetic, better automated support for reasoning about expressions involving the constructors or destructors of an abstract data type, and the ability to do resolution-style reasoning with respect to all or part of a sequent. Below, we describe how these features would prove useful.

*Embedded quantifiers.* We have encountered many cases where a human reasoning step is sidetracked in a PVS proof because embedded quantifiers cannot be "reached" for skolemization or instantiation. Figure 4 illustrates two such cases. The first case in Figure 4 is a generic illustration of a situation in which instantiation of the quantified variables *in situ* would lead to a proof without splitting the current goal. The second case is an actual invariant lemma from the proof of the implementation of Fischer's Algorithm from [15], in particular, the Strong Mutual Exclusion invariant that guarantees that no two processes can simultaneously be in the critical section. In this case, the skolem constant of the embedded "FORALL" in the inductive conclusion must be used as the instantiation of the corresponding "FORALL" in the inductive hypothesis in nearly every proof branch. The structure of the mechanical proof is obscured by the need to extract the embedded quantified subexpressions. For both examples in Figure 4, the embedded quantifier problem could be dealt with by recasting the formulae as formulae quantified at the top level. For complex state invariants, however,

---

[1] In a future version of PVS, SRI plans to support both theory parameters for theories and theory interpretations [23]. For our purposes, either may be sufficient.

**Example 1:**

P(a)

(EXISTS (x): P(x)) => (FORALL (y): Q(y))

-----------------------------------------------------------------

Q(b)

**Example 2:**

Inv_5_4(s: states): bool = (FORALL (i: Index):
    (pc(i,s) = leave_trying OR pc(i,s) = critical OR pc(i,s) = reset) =>
      (user?(x(s)) & (name(x(s)) = i)
    & (FORALL (j: Index): ((NOT (j = i)) =>
      (NOT (pc(j,s) = set OR pc(j,s) = leave_trying OR pc(j,s) = critical OR pc(j,s) = reset))))));

lemma_5_4: LEMMA ( FORALL (s: states): reachable(s) => Inv_5_4(s) );

**Fig. 4.** A sequent and invariant with embedded quantifiers. The invariant *Inv_5_4* of *Lemma_5_4* embodies the Strong Mutual Exclusion property that implies that processors with different indices cannot simultaneously have their program counters in their critical region.

this cannot always be done; see, e.g., [7]. Even when recasting is possible, the resulting formulae are often less natural, and this violates the philosophy behind TAME.

*Extended arithmetic decision procedures.* In applying TAME to hybrid automata, we have encountered reasoning about nonlinear real arithmetic where PVS requires an interactive boost in the form of appropriate application of several lemmas about real arithmetic. Figure 5 shows the lemmas we have needed in practice. This list suggests useful extensions to the decision procedures.

*Abstract data type reasoning.* When an abstract data type is involved in a proof, many relevant inferences are obvious to a human but not to the prover. For example, in reasoning about the abstract data type **time** (see Figure 6), a human seeing $A = dur(B)$ immediately interprets this equality as equivalent to $fintime(A) = B$, but the prover requires detailed human guidance to make the same inference. Of course, if a data type constructor requires more than one argument, information about all the destructor-values are needed in drawing a conclusion about the constructor-value. A resolution-style step could be useful in handling this.

real_thy: THEORY
  BEGIN
    nonnegreal:TYPE = {r:real | 0 <= r};
    sq(x:real):real = x*x;
    % posreal_mult_closed: LEMMA (FORALL (x,y:real): (x > 0 & y > 0) => x*y > 0);
    nonnegreal_mult_closed: LEMMA (FORALL (x,y:real): (x >= 0 & y >= 0) => x*y >= 0);
    greater_eq_nonnegmult_closed: LEMMA (FORALL (x,y,z:real): (x >= 0 & y >= z) => x*y >= x*z);
    square_nonneg: LEMMA (FORALL (x:real): (sq(x) >= 0));
    nonpos_neg_quotient:LEMMA (FORALL (x:real,y:real): (x <= 0 & y < 0) => x/y >= 0);
    nonneg_pos_quotient:LEMMA (FORALL (x:real,y:real): (x >= 0 & y > 0) => x/y >= 0);
  END real_thy

**Fig. 5.** Some lemmas about real arithmetic

---

```
time: DATATYPE
  BEGIN
    fintime(dur:{r:real|r>=0}): fintime?
    infinity: inftime?
  END time
```

---

**Fig. 6.** The type time is a simple example of an abstract data type in PVS. It is the union type of nonnegative real numbers and ∞. The destructor *dur* extracts the argument of the constructor *fintime*. *fintime?* and *inftime?* are recognizer predicates.

*Resolution-style steps.* Another application we have encountered for a resolution-style step is in automatically proving that the value of a predicate is constant over a trajectory from its propositional structure and the properties of its atomic parts. This would be helpful in automating the proof obligation that would accompany the use of our discretization strategy.

## 5 Desirable Features in the Prover Environment

In developing specialized strategies in a programmable theorem prover, additional support beyond the services provided by the prover itself is highly desirable. Since strategy development involves much interactive experimentation with proofs, features that would allow the developer to experiment more efficiently are especially important. These features include efficient ways to save and test alternate proofs, efficient ways to continue incomplete branches of partial proofs without executing the remaining branches, and the ability to obtain timing information to help locate inefficient steps in a strategy under development (e.g., why does carrying along the reachability of the poststate in our induction strategy double its execution time?). The features mentioned are among the planned PVS enhancements.

## 6 Lessons Learned

Based on our experience with TAME, we have found at least partial answers to the four questions listed in Section 1.1. Section 4 addresses the fourth question. Below, we address the first three.

*Question 1:* Restricting the domain does make a significant difference in the extent to which human-style theorem proving can be supported. In a restricted domain in which a limited repertoire of proof steps is sufficient for most human proofs, we have been able to provide substantial support for human-style mechanical proofs. Many of the human-style steps we support, such as the induction strategy, the precondition strategy, and the invariant-lemma strategy, are highly specific to the mathematical model supported by TAME, and are effective only when applied to specifications of a highly restricted form. The induction strategy is quite complex and very finely tuned for its purpose. Thus, we do not expect our techniques to be useful in supporting human-style proofs across the board. With respect to how large the restricted domain can be, we note that TAME's domain is significantly larger than that of other proof tools aimed at verifying automata—particularly model checkers, which require finite-state automata.

*Question 2.* So far, TAME has not been used by any engineers, so we still have no answer to this question. However, we have demonstrated that it is possible for a theorem proving expert to provide useful feedback to practitioners.

*Question 3.* Tackling the Group Communication Service problem has provided us with some experience in using TAME to search interactively for a proof. We have succeeded in constructing several induction proofs without the aid of a hand proof. Using TAME to keep track of the details and to identify the significant cases has helped in focusing the interactive contribution required in a search on determining which previously proved state invariants to apply. Making the current proof goals readable would be a significant help during proof search. In this, the naming strategies planned by SRI can play an important role.

# 7 Future Directions

The TAME proofs that we have produced have a structure which reflects the human-style proof steps that comprise them. However, what these human-style steps are is currently discernible only to a TAME expert. We plan to make TAME proofs more readable by non-experts in two ways, both of which require the enhancements to PVS in progress. First, we plan to name the TAME proof steps uniformly. Since some strategies, such as the induction strategy, are compiled for each particular automaton, doing this may require the ability to set and access a global variable through PVS whose value is the automaton name. Second, we plan to print, in the form of comments, the information introduced in certain proof steps, such as application of an invariant lemma or invocation of the precondition. To do this, we need the ability to retrieve the content of a named formula in the sequent.

Currently, we must compile the automaton-specific strategies by hand from the user's description of the nontime actions and a user-defined set of abbreviations. We plan to automate this procedure, either internally or externally to PVS.

The PVS enhancements we have discussed were inspired by our experience in developing TAME. We hope to use our continuing experience with the design of strategies for human-style reasoning and the development of specialized tools based upon PVS to motivate the further development of PVS, and perhaps other theorem proving systems, in what we consider to be an important direction.

## Acknowledgments

We wish to thank N. Lynch, G. Leeb, V. Luchangco, H. B. Weinberg, A. Fekete, A. Shvartsman, and R. Khazan for providing us with challenging examples for testing TAME. We also thank R. Jeffords and S. Garland for helpful discussions.

## References

1. M. Archer and C. Heitmeyer. Mechanical verification of timed automata: A case study. In *Work-In-Progress Proc. 1996 IEEE Real-Time Systems Symp. (RTSS'96)*, pages 3–6, 1996.
2. M. Archer and C. Heitmeyer. Mechanical verification of timed automata: A case study. In *Proc. 1996 IEEE Real-Time Technology and Applications Symp. (RTAS'96)*. IEEE Computer Society Press, 1996.
3. M. Archer and C. Heitmeyer. Verifying hybrid systems modeled as timed automata: A case study. In *Hybrid and Real-Time Systems (HART'97)*, volume 1201 of *Lecture Notes in Computer Science*, pages 171–185. Springer-Verlag, 1997.
4. P. Black and P. Windley. Automatically synthesized term denotation predicates: A proof aid. In *Higher Order Logic Theorem Proving and Its Applications (HOL'95)*, volume 971 of *Lect. Notes in Comp. Sci.*, pages 46–57. Springer-Verlag, 1995.

5. R. Boyer and J. Moore. *A Computational Logic*. Academic Press, 1979.
6. S. Brackin. Deciding cryptographic protocol adequacy with HOL. In *Higher Order Logic Theorem Proving and Its Applications (HOL'95)*, volume 971 of *Lecture Notes in Computer Science*, pages 90–105. Springer-Verlag, 1995.
7. A. Fekete, N. Lynch, and A. Shvartsman. Specifying and using a partitionable group communication service. in preparation.
8. M. J. C. Gordon and T. Melham, editors. *Introduction to HOL: A Theorem Proving Environment for Higher-Order Logic*. Cambridge University Press, 1993.
9. J. Harrison. A Mizar mode for HOL. In *Proc. 9th Intl. Conf. on Theorem Proving in Higher Order Logics (TPHOLs'96)*, volume 1125 of *Lecture Notes in Computer Science*, pages 203–220. Springer-Verlag, 1996.
10. C. Heitmeyer and N. Lynch. The Generalized Railroad Crossing: A case study in formal verification of real-time systems. In *Proc., Real-Time Systems Symp.*, San Juan, Puerto Rico, Dec. 1994.
11. C. Heitmeyer and N. Lynch. The Generalized Railroad Crossing: A case study in formal verification of real-time systems. Technical Report MIT/LCS/TM-51, Lab. for Comp. Sci., MIT, Cambridge, MA, 1994. Also Technical Report 7619, NRL, Wash., DC 1994.
12. T. Henzinger and P. Ho. Hytech: The Cornell Hybrid Technology Tool. Technical report, Cornell University, 1995.
13. R. P. Kurshan. *Computer-Aided Verification of Coordinating Processes: the Automata-Theoretic Approach*. Princeton University Press, 1994.
14. G. Leeb and N. Lynch. Proving safety properties of the Steam Boiler Controller: Formal methods for industrial applications: A case study. In J.-R. Abrial, et al., eds., *Formal Methods for Industrial Applications: Specifying and Programming the Steam Boiler Control*, vol. 1165 of *Lect. Notes in Comp. Sci.* Springer-Verlag, 1996.
15. V. Luchangco. Using simulation techniques to prove timing properties. Master's thesis, Massachusetts Institute of Technology, June 1995.
16. N. Lynch. Simulation techniques for proving properties of real-time systems. In *REX Workshop '93*, volume 803 of *Lecture Notes in Computer Science*, pages 375–424, Mook, the Netherlands, 1994. Springer-Verlag.
17. N. Lynch and F. Vaandrager. Forward and backward simulations – Part II: Timing-based systems. To appear in *Information and Computation*.
18. N. Lynch and F. Vaandrager. Forward and backward simulations for timing-based systems. In *Proc. of REX Workshop "Real-Time: Theory in Practice"*, volume 600 of *Lecture Notes in Computer Science*, pages 397–446. Springer-Verlag, 1991.
19. K. L. McMillan. *Symbolic Model Checking*. Kluwer Academic Publishers, 1993.
20. S. Owre, N. Shankar, and J. Rushby. User guide for the PVS specification and verification system (Draft). Technical report, Computer Science Lab., SRI Intl., Menlo Park, CA, 1993.
21. P. Rudnicki. An overview of the MIZAR project. In *Proc. 1992 Workshop on Types and Proofs for Programs*, pages 311–332, June 1992. Also available through anonymous ftp as pub/cs-reports/Bastad92/proc.ps.Z on ftp.cs.chalmers.se.
22. P. Rudnicki and A. Trybulec. A note on "How to Write a Proof". In *Proc. 1992 Workshop on Types and Proofs for Programs*, June 1996. Available through P. Rudnicki's web page at http://www.cs.ualberta.ca/~piotr/Mizar/.
23. J. Rushby. Private communication. NRL, Jan. 1997.
24. N. Shankar, S. Owre, and J. Rushby. The PVS proof checker: A reference manual. Technical report, Computer Science Lab., SRI Intl., Menlo Park, CA, 1993.
25. J. Skakkebaek and N. Shankar. Towards a duration calculus proof assistant in PVS. In *Third Intern. School and Symp. on Formal Techniques in Real Time and Fault Tolerant Systems, Lect. Notes in Comp. Sci. 863*. Springer-Verlag, 1994.
26. H. B. Weinberg. Correctness of vehicle control systems: A case study. Master's thesis, Massachusetts Institute of Technology, February 1996.

# A Hybrid Approach to Verifying Liveness in a Symmetric Multi-Processor

Albert J Camilleri

Hewlett-Packard Company, 8000 Foothills Boulevard, Roseville CA 95747

**Abstract.** The verification of increasingly complex multiprocessor systems has become a formidable challenge. Given the complexity of each of the multi-processor components and the complex interactions between them, simulation may no longer provide the desired level of coverage to detect possible starvation and deadlocks. The Formal Verification Group at Hewlett-Packard has used a combination of model checking and theorem proving techniques with great effect to analyse the correctness of the RUNWAY bus arbitration protocols in models representing several members of the HP 9000 K-CLASS servers and J-CLASS workstations. This paper presents some basic ideas behind this verification methodology, highlights its strengths and shortcomings, and discusses how it can be used to enhance the existing system-verification methodology.

## 1  Introduction

Hewlett-Packard's latest line of computer servers and workstations, such as the K-CLASS servers which won the *1997 Datamation Product of the Year Award* [5] and the J-CLASS workstations which won the US Government TAC-4 contract, are all based on a multiprocessor bus called RUNWAY [1], designed to interconnect multiple CPUs (such as the HP PA 7200 and HP PA 8000 processors), multiple IO adapters, and a memory controller.

RUNWAY is a high-speed, highly-pipelined, multiple-issue, and variable latency bus which allows out-of-order returns. In a RUNWAY based multi processing configuration, several CPUs and IO adapters compete for bus resources, and interactions between modules can become very complex. So much so that it was recognised early in the design cycle that there was significant potential for some of these interactions to result in deadlock or starvation.

Traditional simulation techniques do not adequately screen for deadlock and starvation problems because the interactions leading up to them are too complex to anticipate, and the exact combination of operations is too unlikely to occur by chance during the simulations. A hardware prototype system may run at full speed for hours or days before encountering a failure of this type, while all the simulation vectors we can run in a year add up to only a few milliseconds of actual run time. Even a high-speed emulator cannot run enough vectors in a year to give good confidence that these bugs are completely eliminated. Previous experience has shown us that deadlock and starvation problems are often not discovered until late in the design cycle, sometimes only after hardware prototypes are running the operating system and manufacturing is ramping up for production.

Given the complexities involved with liveness on RUNWAY, we elected to use formal verification to determine that no deadlocks would occur under correct use of the bus. Our approach to the use of formal verification is very pragmatic, and is largely driven by *time-to-market* constraints. The product range we were working on is not classed as safety-critical, so iron-clad guarantees of freedom from defects were not our goal. Our goals were to reach a level of confidence higher than that possible by using simulation alone, to identify defects as early as possible, and to *shorten* the overall design time by reducing the likelihood of requiring design recycles.

To this effect, the work proved extremely successful. Several functional defects were identified at various stages of the designs, demonstrating the productivity of these techniques. Formal verification is now recognised in Hewlett-Packard as a significant contribution to the development of the RUNWAY family of computers.[1]

This paper describes the methodology adopted to realise this success, and presents details of the verification of liveness of the RUNWAY protocols. We advocate a *hybrid* approach based on both model checking and theorem proving and discuss the reasoning behind the decisions on when to favour one technique over the other. This approach for verifying liveness is only one of several investigated in Hewlett-Packard—alternatives are described in [4, 7].

## 2   The Runway Bus

The RUNWAY bus is a synchronous, 64-bit, processor-IO-memory interconnect ideally suited for high-performance, symmetric multiprocessing. In the K-CLASS servers, for example, four CPUs (HP PA 7200 or 8000), two IO adaptors (IOAs) and one master memory controller (with 4 GB of memory) can be connected by means of RUNWAY (see Figure 1) to operate at a bus frequency of 160–180 MHz.

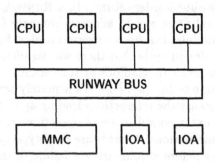

**Fig. 1.** Typical Configuration of a RUNWAY-Based Multi Processor

[1] The work described in this paper was carried out in various stages over the period 1992–1994 [3] but could not be published until recently for product-confidentiality reasons.

RUNWAY uses a *snoopy* algorithm to ensure *cache coherency* and supports both coherent and non-coherent transactions.[2] Coherent transactions include data requests, such as READ_PRIV and READ_SHAR, cache line flush requests, called FLUSH_BACK, and memory barrier transactions, called SYNC. Non-coherent transactions include READs and WRITEs to IO space as well as error transactions. Table 1 summarizes a sample of RUNWAY transactions, focusing mainly on those discussed later in this paper.

| Transactions | Meaning |
|---|---|
| READ_PRIV | Request *private* copy of a cache line. |
| READ_SHAR | Request *shared* copy of a cache line. |
| FLUSH | Broadcast request to flush cache line. |
| SYNC | Broadcast request to synchronise caches, i.e. request completion of all outstanding FLUSHes. |
| TLB_PURGE | Broadcast request to purge data TLB entries for a specified page. |
| FLUSH_BACK | Coherent write-back in response to a FLUSH. |
| WRITE_BACK | Coherent write-back except from FLUSH. |
| CACHE_2_CACHE | Coherent cache-to-cache copy of data. |
| SYNC_DONE | SYNC completion response. |
| TLB_PURGE_DONE | TLB_PURGE completion response. |
| READ | Non-coherent data request, typically from IO space. |
| WRITE | Non-coherent data write, typically to IO space. |

**Table 1.** Sample RUNWAY Transactions

To control access to the bus, RUNWAY uses a sophisticated arbitration scheme designed to minimise arbitration latency without reducing bus frequency. RUNWAY supports split transactions and time multiplexes addresses and data. This means that both addresses and data use the same bus, and that a request for data does not lock the bus until a response is made. Since in this way several transactions can be outstanding at any one time, there needs to be some control over the number (and type) of transactions that can be in flight at any one time to avoid queue overflow within the multi-processor components. To do this, the memory controller drives a multi-value control signal called CLIENT_OP which acts as a throttle to control which types of transactions, if any, can access the bus at any one time. Table 2 summarises the different flow-control features used by CLIENT_OP.

So for example, if the CLIENT_OP indicated RET_ONLY then new, read transactions such as READ_PRIV cannot be issued, but data can be copied back to

---

[2] For a comprehensive description of computer architecture terminology used in this paper, especially this section, the reader is refered to [8].

| CLIENT_OP values | Meaning |
|---|---|
| ANY_TRANS | Any transaction allowed. |
| NO_IO | Any transaction allowed except transactions to IO. |
| RET_ONLY | Only return or response transactions allowed. |
| ONE_CYCLE | Only one-cycle transactions allowed. |
| NONE_ALLOWED | No transactions allowed. |
| MMC_CONTROL | Master Memory Controller controls bus. |
| ATOMIC | Atomic owner (IOA) can issue any transaction; all others issue only returns or responses. |

**Table 2.** Flow Control Features Allowed on RUNWAY

memory from a CPU by means of a WRITE_BACK transaction. Conversely, under a ONE_CYCLE CLIENT_OP, a multi-cycle transaction such as a WRITE_BACK cannot be issued, but a one-cycle transaction like a READ_PRIV could.

Arbitration for RUNWAY is pipelined in three phases during which each module on the bus is responsible for determining the arbitration result, i.e. there is no single arbitration controller. Each module drives a unique arbitration request signal and receives arbitration signals from other modules. So on the first pipeline cycle all arbitrating parties assert their arbitration signals and the memory controller drives the CLIENT_OP flow-control signal. On the second cycle all modules evaluate the information received and decide on which module won ownership of the bus. On the third cycle, the winning module may begin to drive an allowed transaction.

A winning client can drive RUNWAY for a default of two cycles (unless CLIENT_OP indicates ONE_CYCLE). To drive a transaction for longer than two cycles the module needs to drive a special signal called *long* to prevent other transactions from being issued simultaneously. The *long* signal is a form of bus-lock and takes precedence over other arbitration requests.

For performance and liveness reasons RUNWAY arbitration operates at three levels of priority. The master memory controller (MMC) has highest priority. When it arbitrates (by driving MMC_CONTROL on CLIENT_OP) it becomes the next bus winner.[3] IOAs are the next priority modules and the CPUs have least priority. Obviously, various *back-off* mechanisms are necessary, and are implemented, to ensure fairness.

## 3 Verification Approach

At the time of undertaking this work, and still to this day, no single formal tool or technique existed that was singly and universally applicable to a problem

---

[3] If *long* is asserted the MMC will still win the bus but it will wait until *long* is deasserted before using it.

of the complexity and scale of RUNWAY within the enforced time constraints. From the start it was clear that to stand any chance of success, different aspects of the design would have to be handled using different methods and different abstraction levels. The approach we adopted, therefore, was to use a *hybrid* technique consisting of model checking and theorem proving.

The property we set out to prove was liveness of the RUNWAY bus protocol.[4] To facilitate the proof, the verification goal was split into two parts. The first stage was to prove that if a client on RUNWAY (whether CPU, IOA or memory) issues a transaction on the bus, then the transaction always reaches its destination (liveness), provided arbitration is fair. The second stage was to prove that arbitration is indeed fair, i.e. that if a client requests use of the bus, it always eventually wins arbitration (fairness).

The analysis of the first stage involved detailed modelling of the clients' queues, and of the conditions under which the clients could be forced to stall (i.e. temporarily suspend processing). The proof therefore involved showing that all stalls always eventually become unstalled. This demanded a fairly detailed representation of the state of the queues of all clients, and the use of a proof technique called *course-of-values induction*.[5] Interactive theorem provers are ideally suited to tackle this kind of problem so HOL [6] was used to carry out the proof.

Among the advantages of interactive theorem provers is that they are powerful enough to facilitate the construction of fairly complex proofs at very high levels of abstraction. For example structures like queues can be handled abstractly without state-space explosion (see Section 5). Their disadvantage is that they are often time consuming, so our task was to identify the areas which could really benefit from theorem proving, and to use HOL only there.

The second stage of the RUNWAY proof involved constructing a finite state machine representation of the arbitration protocol, and checking that this satisfied the properties required for fairness, i.e. that if a client enters an arbitration state, it is always eventually able to enter the *arbitration winner* state. For this we used the SMV model checker [9]. Although this tool seemed perfectly suited for this type of problem, careful modelling was still required to avoid state explosion.

In fact, the overall feasibility of conducting the proofs within the time allocated, both in HOL and SMV, depended almost entirely on being able to construct models at the right level of abstraction. The levels of abstraction used in the two stages of the proof were different, but both were very abstract indeed, capturing exactly the amount of detail necessary to model and verify the problems in question, but no more. In the case of model checking this was necessary to avoid state explosion, whereas in the case of theorem proving it was necessary to limit the amount of work required. Indeed, a large part of our formal methods research has involved finding suitable abstraction levels for handling proofs. The RUNWAY verification could not have been completed without it.

---

[4] Liveness ensures that if something needs to be done, it eventually happens. It entails that there are no deadlocks.

[5] Course-of-values induction allows induction over intervals by means of the theorem
$$\vdash \forall P. (\forall x. (\forall y. y < x \supset P\,y) \supset P\,x) \supset (\forall x. P\,x)$$

# 4 Verifying Fairness

The ability to model check Verilog finite-state machines directly is often discussed as an advantage. It minimises the effort spent on writing models and reduces the potential risk for human error. There are, however, advantages in working at a higher level of abstraction, manually constructing finite state machines from their specification. Not only can larger models be verified this way, but more importantly, verification can start long before HDL models become available.

Even at this more abstract level than HDLs, overcoming the state explosion problems for a design of this scale was still a challenge and required careful crafting of the models. In this section we describe some of the techniques used to verify the RUNWAY arbitration protocol.

## 4.1 Abstraction Techniques

The main technique that enabled the verification of this large a model was to partition the proof into different parts. This was largely possible due to the symmetry inherent in this type of problem which enabled independent checking of separate components. Care has to be taken, of course, that this is done in a way that does not eliminate important correctness criteria. For example, two components of a system which communicate together cannot simply be separated and verified independently if one is trying to verify properties which are influenced by that very communication. The communication protocol itself may need to be broken down, or partitioned, into simple phases until a starting point for the verification is identified. If a problem is cyclic it may not be possible to partition it, but many problems are not cyclic and a useful partitioning can be found. The partitions used to verify RUNWAY arbitration are described in Section 4.2.

Splitting the problem into components by itself was not enough to overcome the state-explosion problem. It had to be coupled with other abstraction techniques. The challenge here was to simplify the model by eliminating unnecessary detail without modifying the behaviour that had to be verified.

### 4.1.1 Data Abstraction

Several data structures in the model could be simplified in a way which significantly reduced the number of states required to represent them. For example, a counter implemented with nine bits for performance reasons could be represented using just one bit for model checking purposes if one were confident that the size of the counter did not affect correctness.

Queues are a predominant data structure in many designs and they are notoriously bad to model accurately using finite-state machines due to the large number of states that must be represented. From a communication viewpoint, however, queue-size is often unimportant, as is the exact nature of the queue entries. For example, if one were interested in whether a queue that only accepted WRITE_BACKs could accept another WRITE_BACK one wouldn't necessarily need to model the exact nature of the WRITE_BACKs in the queue, the size of the queue, or even the FIFO nature of the queue. One would just care about whether the queue had space or not, and if not, whether it would clear. The abstract behaviour of the queue (without FIFO) would be summarised as follows:

- if a queue never receives any input, it cannot fill up.
- once a queue is full, it stays so until it sends at least one output.

The above properties are valid irrespective of queue size, as long as the size is at least one. So queues of arbitrary size can be modeled effectively by means of the above properties, and by means of a non-deterministic decision on when a queue becomes full as shown by the simple SMV statements below.

```
VAR      QueueFull : boolean;
ASSIGN   init (QueueFull) := 0;
         next (QueueFull) :=
             case popTrans    : 0;
                  pushTrans   : {QueueFull, 1};
                  1           : QueueFull;
             esac;
```

The statements describe a state machine for a boolean state variable QueueFull, set to 0 when the queue is not full, 1 when full. Initially the queue is not full. Whenever an entry is *popped* from the queue, the state is reset to *not* full. Whenever an entry is *pushed* into the queue there is a non-deterministic choice which allows the queue to fill, and stay so until an entry is popped. If nothing happens, QueueFull retains its value. Note that pushTrans and popTrans can themselves have complex definitions.

### 4.1.2 Timing Abstractions

Timing characteristics play a crucial part in the functionality of a protocol or design and it is often crucial to model these accurately when proving correctness. For example, timing in the three stage pipeline algorithm for RUNWAY arbitration is crucial and needed to be modeled with utmost care.

There are times, however, when the full-blown details are unnecessary and careful abstractions can once again save on valuable state space. For example, the precise length of transactions was not relevant for proving arbitration fairness. Indeed the length of transactions is often arbitrarily chosen, so in fact it is even desirable to model transactions of arbitrary length because then correctness results would apply to any length of transactions.

In SMV this was again possible by means of non-determinism and *fairness* constraints. For example, upon driving the bus, the owner can make a non-deterministic choice to assert the *long* signal, and then to make a non-deterministic choice on when to deassert *long*. A fairness constraint is necessary to ensure that *long* is never asserted forever.

In fact, this was quite an accurate abstraction of RUNWAY because one of the features in the protocol is that clients are allowed to insert idle cycles in the middle of transactions for timing purposes. So even though a WRITE_BACK transaction typically takes 5 cycles (1 address and 4 data, say), theoretically it can take more. The non-deterministic handling of *long* was a good representation of this feature.

## 4.2 Verification of Runway Arbitration

The verification of fair arbitration was based on four straightforward assumptions which were left for the designers to ensure their correctness. These were:

- CPUs and IOAs do not drive transactions that are infinitely long.
- IOAs do not drive an infinite sequence of atomically-linked transactions.
- Memory, having highest priority, will not arbitrate indefinitely.
- Memory will not postpone responding to requests indefinitely.

The proof was then constructed in four parts using different models, or in other words, the problem was partitioned into four parts, for efficiency reasons, as described in Section 4.1. As already mentioned in Section 2 the memory controller is the master of arbitration. From an arbitration viewpoint, the memory controller does not recognise any difference between transactions received from a CPU or an IOA, and neither does it recognise that there may be several CPUs or IOAs that could be arbitrating. Being the module of highest priority, the memory controller merely observes that a client of lesser priority may be competing with it for resources. So the first part of the proof was to model the interaction between memory and *one* client (Figure 2), which can behave as either a CPU or an IOA.

**Fig. 2.** Proof I: Fairness between Memory Controller and Client

The proof of this first model involves showing that memory always allows *sufficient* idle, winnable cycles under all possible communication sequences between clients and memory so that if a client ever arbitrated it would eventually have the opportunity to win the bus.[6] This was done by proving a statement which states that whenever the value of CLIENT_OP is other than ANY_TRANS, it will eventually return to ANY_TRANS.[7]

```
SPEC AG !(client_op = ANY_TRANS) -> (AF (client_op = ANY_TRANS))
```

The expression AG P means that on all paths of the state machine, P holds in all states, and AF Q means that on all paths, there is a future state where Q holds [9].

Once such a result is established, i.e. that a client may eventually always access the bus, the next stage is to show that CPUs and IOAs share RUNWAY fairly, i.e. an idle cycle can be won by either an IOA or a CPU infinitely often. For this, it is enough to model the interaction between *only one* CPU and *only one* IOA, as shown in Figure 3.

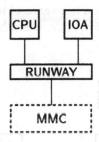

**Fig. 3.** Proof II: Fairness across Subnets

Whether the system is composed of only one CPU or one hundred, only one CPU can win arbitration at any one time. So the important criterion to model to demonstrate fairness between the different priority levels is not the arbitration between clients, but the arbitration between *subnets* of the different priority levels. Moreover, since memory has already been shown to be fair, in that it will always allow idle, winnable cycles, we no longer need to model memory in full detail. The use of *non-determinism* and *fairness* possible in model checking now allows us to model memory as a simple finite-state machine that non-deterministically always allows idle cycles.

```
FAIRNESS (client_op = ANY_TRANS)
```

---

[6] In RUNWAY, once a client begins to arbitrate, it must keep doing so until it wins arbitration. It cannot back-off capriciously; IOAs can, and must, back-off only when in explicit back-off mode.

[7] Of course we could have simply proved AG (AF (client_op = ANY_TRANS)), but this is less efficient to model check as it involves more state exploration.

This makes a tremendous saving in state-space. In fact the approach consisted of the verification result of one stage becoming the fairness constraint in the next. This stage was verified by checking the CTL statements:

```
SPEC  AG (io.arb  -> (AF (io.winner  & ppAnyTrans)))
SPEC  AG (cpu.arb -> (AF (cpu.winner & ppAnyTrans)))
SPEC  AG !(cpu.runwayOwner & io.runwayOwner)
```

The first two SPECs say that if either client arbitrated (i.e. the value of io.arb or cpu.arb was high) it would eventually win arbitration (the value of io.winner or cpu.winner would be true accordingly) two cycles after ANY_TRANS occurred (indicated by ppAnyTrans—a macro used to retain the value of (CLIENT_OP = ANY_TRANS) from two cycles earlier[8]). The third SPEC is a safety condition and says that a CPU and an IOA never own RUNWAY simultaneously.

Having established that the CPU and IOA subnets share idle cycles fairly, the final parts of the proof involve modeling the interaction within the subnets. It now suffices to model each of these subnets independently, and to show that all the clients within each subnet get a fair share of idle cycles. Two further models were therefore constructed: one for CPUs, the other for IOAs (see Figure 4). In

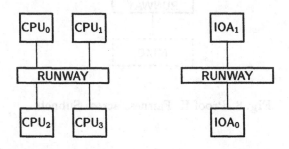

**Fig. 4.** Proof III: Fairness between CPUs and IOAs

each of these models it was assumed that idle, winnable cycles were available infinitely often to each subnet and it was proved that all possible configurations of processors and IOAs allowed by the RUNWAY specification permitted fair access to the bus. Again the results from the previous proof were used as fairness constraints, and the following kind of property was checked for CPUs 0–3 and IOAs 0–1.

```
SPEC  AG ((cpu0.needAnyTrans & cpu0.arb) ->
            (AF (cpu0.runwayOwner & newTrans & ppAnyTrans)))
```

---

[8] Remember that arbitration is done in three stages, as described in Section 2, so a client wins on cycle $n$ based on the value of CLIENT_OP from cycle $n-2$.

The specification roughly says that if a CPU needs to send a transaction which requires the CLIENT_OP to be ANY_TRANS (cpu.needAnyTrans), and it arbitrates (cpu.arb), then it will eventually become the bus owner (cpu.runwayOwner) for a *new* transaction (newTrans), two cycles after the CLIENT_OP was ANY_TRANS (ppAnyTrans).

# 5  Verifying Liveness

Proving liveness in RUNWAY-based multi-processors required details of both the nature of the outstanding transactions and their location as they executed within the system. It was not possible to prove liveness with respect to a single transaction or cache line[9] because forward progress depended on the interaction between different kinds of transactions. For example, a coherence response to a SYNC transaction (which has reached the top of a *Cache Coherency Check* (CCC) queue—see Section 5.2) cannot be given (it is stalled) until all FLUSH_BACK responses required for transactions that entered the CCC queue before the SYNC have been sent on RUNWAY. In general, the internal state of *several* queues can be crucial.

From a liveness perspective, the key features necessary to model the components of a multi-processor are the queues and devices through which transactions flow as they are processed. We adopted the approach developed in [2] which was intended for reasoning at this level, and we were able to prove liveness in terms of the queue-like behaviour of all relevant components of the system within the time constraints available. Reuse of much of the queuing theory developed for [2] played a significant part in keeping the verification work on schedule.

## 5.1  The Abstraction Level

The approach advocates the treatment of interfaces between components as *partial signals*. That is, signals which occur at these interfaces are only *valid* at certain specified points of time. We use the predicate Ps $s$ $m$ $t$ to mean that the partial signal $s$ has value $m$ at time $t$. As is conventional in hardware modelling, device ports are modelled as signals. So Ps $s$ $m$ $t$ can alternatively be read as: value $m$ is communicated on port $s$ at time $t$. It is not required that something should occur at every point in time. A time $t$ at which there is no $m$ being signaled on the interface $s$ (i.e. $\neg \exists m.$ Ps $s$ $m$ $t$) is a time when the signal is not *valid*. In implementation terms, there must usually be an extra control signal indicating when the value is valid. Such control signals do not appear explicitly in our models—an abstraction which intentionally omits them is chosen to make the proof-load lighter.

To deal with the asynchronous behaviour exhibited by many devices, we build into the partial signal datatype the property of when they are ready for data. We

---

[9] A useful abstraction often possible when verifying cache coherence properties [10].

introduce the predicate Rfd $s\,m\,t$ to mean that value $m$ may be communicated on signal $s$ at time $t$, with the property:

$$\vdash \forall s\; m\; t.\, \mathsf{Ps}\, s\, m\, t \supset \mathsf{Rfd}\, s\, m\, t$$

Various definitions can be made in terms of Ps and Rfd to capture commonly used properties. For example, the predicate Done $s\,m\,t$ is used to refer to an event $m$ which happens on $s$ at, or before, $t$, SDone $s\,m\,t$ to refer to an event which happens on $s$ strictly before $t$, and Defined to simply refer to events that happen (at some time) on a signal. The abbreviation RfdAll is used to signify that a port is ready for all types of transactions, and Earlier $s\,m\,m'$ to indicate that $m$ happens before $m'$ on $s$.

$$\vdash \mathsf{Done}\, s\, m\, t = \exists t'.\, t' \leq t \wedge \mathsf{Ps}\, s\, m\, t'$$
$$\vdash \mathsf{SDone}\, s\, m\, t = \exists t'.\, t' < t \wedge \mathsf{Ps}\, s\, m\, t'$$
$$\vdash \mathsf{Defined}\, s\, m = \exists t.\, \mathsf{Ps}\, s\, m\, t$$
$$\vdash \mathsf{RfdAll}\, s\, t = \forall m.\, \mathsf{Rfd}\, s\, m\, t$$
$$\vdash \mathsf{Earlier}\, s\, m\, m' = \exists t\, t'.\, \mathsf{Ps}\, s\, m\, t \wedge \mathsf{Ps}\, s\, m'\, t' \wedge t < t'$$

With such definitions we can now define some liveness concepts used to show that a device can always make progress. We introduce the predicate PortLive $s$ to capture the notion that a port $s$ is always eventually ready for data and the predicate TransLive $in\;out$ to capture the notion that anything input will eventually be output. A safety property, TransSafe, to indicate that all outputs must have been input, can be similarly defined.

$$\vdash \mathsf{PortLive}\, s = \forall t.\, \exists t'.\, t \leq t' \wedge \mathsf{RfdAll}\, s\, t'$$
$$\vdash \mathsf{TransLive}\, in\, out = \forall m\, t.\, \mathsf{Ps}\, in\, m\, t \supset \exists t'.\, t \leq t' \wedge \mathsf{Ps}\, out\, m\, t'$$
$$\vdash \mathsf{TransSafe}\, in\, out = \forall m\, t.\, \mathsf{Ps}\, out\, m\, t \supset \exists t'.\, t' \leq t \wedge \mathsf{Ps}\, in\, m\, t'$$

Queues are structures which input and output transactions in an order-preserving fashion. We do not, however, generally wish to say that anything that is input is later output. This would risk contradiction if the device which receives the output of the queue could deadlock, and refuse to receive data. We start, therefore, by defining the rather weaker property that the outputs are an initial segment of the inputs:

$$\vdash \mathsf{InitSeg}\, in\, out =$$
$$\mathsf{TransSafe}\, in\, out \wedge$$
$$\forall m\, m'\, t\, t'\, t''.\, \mathsf{Ps}\, in\, m\, t \wedge \mathsf{Ps}\, in\, m'\, t' \wedge t < t' \wedge \mathsf{Ps}\, out\, m'\, t'' \supset$$
$$\exists t'''.\, t''' < t'' \wedge \mathsf{Ps}\, out\, m\, t'''$$

We then loosely specify a queue by stating that if the output port is live, inputs eventually work their way through as outputs in an order preserving fashion. Our queue can now be defined as

$$\vdash \mathsf{Queue}\, in\, out =$$
$$(\mathsf{PortLive}\, out \supset (\mathsf{TransLive}\, in\, out \wedge \mathsf{PortLive}\, in)) \wedge$$
$$\mathsf{InitSeg}\, in\, out$$

The definitions of TransLive, TransSafe, InitSeg and Queue above are all transitive; a property extremely useful for accelerating proofs.

Finally, we define a notion of *filtering* on partial signals. We define a partial signal filter to be a function which restricts a partial signal to transactions satisfying a given predicate, i.e. we define a partial signal Filter $P$ $s$ which filters a partial signal $s$ with a predicate $P$ to be such that

$$\vdash\; \mathsf{Ps}\,(\mathsf{Filter}\,P\,s)\,m\,t = \mathsf{Ps}\;s\;m\;t \wedge P\;m$$

So if a device only exhibits queue-like behaviour on certain ports and for certain transactions, say, we can selectively refer to those queue-like properties as follows.

$$\mathsf{Queue}\,(\mathsf{Filter}\,P\,in)\,(\mathsf{Filter}\,P\,out)$$

As these filtered relations are commonplace, we introduce the abbreviation

$$\vdash\; \mathsf{Fltr}\,R\,P\,in\,out = R\,(\mathsf{Filter}\,P\,in)(\mathsf{Filter}\,P\,out)$$

A more detailed description of this modelling style can be found in [2].

## 5.2 The Multi-Processor Model

Figure 5 shows a simplified version of our abstract representation of RUNWAY based multiprocessors, used to verify liveness of the flow control protocols. The diagram distinguishes only the queues and features required to reason about liveness and shows a representation of CPUs, an IOA and the MMC in terms of such queues. The diagram depicts the CPUs and the IOA very similarly because, from a liveness viewpoint, it was actually possible to model the flow control behaviour of the CPUs and the IOAs almost identically: the same components were used in both models, but with slightly different specifications due to the different handling of certain transactions. Due to the similarity in the models a description of the IOA models is not presented here.

A CPU is depicted as able to issue new transactions (e.g. READ_PRIV) onto RUNWAY via a queue named the OutQ, and to issue data returns or responses (e.g. FLUSH_BACKs, WRITE_BACKs and CACHE_2_CACHE copies) via a separate queue, the RtnQ. Separate queues are necessary here for liveness reasons—if the CLIENT_OP was RET_ONLY, say, a CPU must be able to issue returns, which would not be possible if these were queued up behind non-returns in the OutQ. All coherent transactions coming in from RUNWAY enter the CPU's CccQ via the port ccc. When a transaction gets to the top of the CccQ, the CPU checks the TLB and issues an appropriate coherency response via the *coh* line before proceeding to the next entry in the CccQ. If the coherency response causes data to be cast out from cache, a FLUSH_BACK response must first be put in the RtnQ (via port *fb*) before a coherency response can be completed. Some coherency responses are more complex. Data returns from RUNWAY do not enter the CccQ; they go straight to cache, or registers, via *data_rtn*[10]. The ports *tdne* and *trtn* are interfaces for TLB_PURGE and acknowledgement transactions.

---

[10] In actuality, there are not different ports to the bus as shown—this is an abstract model.

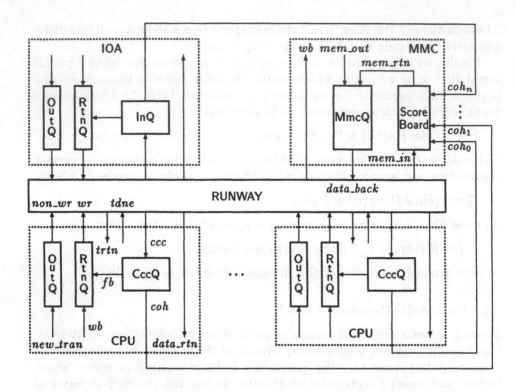

**Fig. 5.** Queue-Based Model of a RUNWAY Multi-Processor

The MMC receives data transactions via port *wb*. Such transactions include FLUSH_BACKs, WRITE_BACKs and CACHE_2_CACHE copies because the MMC implements a *write-back* memory. All other transactions enter the MMC via *mem_in* where coherent transactions get *scoreboarded* by means of the coherency responses sent by the CPU and IOA devices via the *coh* lines. Those transactions requiring a response (such as data) from memory get one via *mem_rtn*. For example, if a READ_PRIV enters *mem_in* and a coherency response indicates that data is *private dirty* and will be copied *cache-to-cache*, no response will be required from the MMC. If all coherency responses indicated *shared* or *idle* cache lines, however, then a data response would be needed, and would be queued via *mem_rtn*. The formal relation between *mem_in* and *mem_rtn*, in fact, is a good example of the use of filtered queues, described in Section 5.1. Memory responses queued via *mem_rtn* are interleaved with transactions generated by the MMC via *mem_out*, such as error transactions, and sent to RUNWAY via *data_back*.

## 5.3 The Formal Model

It would be impractical to present the formal specification for the entire system here, so we describe only a couple of components of the CPU to illustrate the specification style. The specifications for the MMC and the IOAs are constructed in similar fashion.

We construct the specification of the CPU mainly as a conjunction of the specifications of each of the component queues present, along with the additional property that CPUs must always be live for returns, such as data returns from memory or other CPUs. This property is captured in the overall CPU specification below by the conjunct PortLive ($data\_rtn\ i$).

> ⊢ Cpu $n\ i\ wr\ non\_wr\ ccc\ coh\ data\_rtn\ new\_tran\ wb\ tdne\ trtn$ =
>    ∃ $fb$. PortLive ($data\_rtn\ i$) ∧
>        RtnQ $i\ wb\ fb\ wr$ ∧
>        OutQ $n\ i\ new\_tran\ data\_rtn\ non\_wr\ trtn\ wr$ ∧
>        CccQ $i\ ccc\ coh\ fb\ wr$ ∧
>        TlbQ $i\ data\_rtn\ fb\ tdne\ trtn$

The specification is parameterised by all the external ports, by an index $i$ to identify the CPU, and by the total number of CPUs in the system, $n$. Note that most of the ports shown in Figure 5, except those belonging to the MMC, are actually indexed to identify the client they belong to. Thus, $data\_rtn\ i$ denotes the $data\_rtn$ port interfacing RUNWAY to client $i$. Below we examine the specifications of RtnQ and CccQ in further detail.

The return queue, RtnQ, is the simplest queue in the CPU[11]. It is an interleave of two inputs:

- one for WRITE_BACKs or error transactions originating from the CPU ($wb$) and
- one for replies to dirty coherent read transactions or FLUSHes ($fb$), in other words FLUSH_BACKs or CACHE_2_CACHE writes.

each of which needs to be output in the same order they were input. In [2] we showed that such *multiplexers* can be modelled as an overlay of filtered queues as follows:

> ⊢ RtnQ $i\ wb\ fb\ wr$ =
> Fltr Queue IsRetOnly ($wb\ i$) ($wr\ i$) ∧
> Fltr Queue (IsCpuReply $i$) ($fb\ i$) ($wr\ i$)

where the definitions of Fltr and Queue are given in Section 5.1, and the definitions of IsRetOnly and IsCpuReply select the appropriate kinds of transactions as follows:

> ⊢ IsRetOnly $m$ = IsWrBack $m$ ∨ IsError $m$
> ⊢ IsCpuReply $i\ m$ = IsDirtyFlush $i\ m$ ∨ IsDirtyRead $i\ m$

---

[11] Despite appearances the OutQ is actually a little more sophisticated than the RtnQ because the ability to issue a new transaction via $non\_wr$ does not solely depend on access to the bus, but also on whether the CPU must process outstanding transactions before new ones are allowed.

where IsWrBack and IsError are identifiers for WRITE_BACK and error transactions respectively, and IsDirtyFlush $i$ and IsDirtyRead $i$ denote FLUSH and coherent read transactions which *hit* dirty (modified) data in the cache of client $i$. Note that the definition of Queue used in the RtnQ definition does not imply liveness. It does not say the RtnQ *will* output transactions on RUNWAY (we need to prove this); it only says that if returns are output, certain ordering constraints are observed.

The coherency queue is again an overlay of queues. The transactions entering the queue via $ccc$ have responses sent out via $coh$ in the same order, i.e. $ccc$ is an *initial segment* of $coh$.

InitSeg $(ccc\ i)\ (coh\ i)$

The queue input line $ccc$ is also an initial segment of the data return line $fb$, but only for transactions requiring a data response, i.e. for coherent read and FLUSH transactions which hit dirty in cache (identified by the predicate IsCpuReply defined earlier).

Fltr InitSeg (IsCpuReply $i$) $(ccc\ i)\ (fb\ i)$

For cache hits requiring a data return, the CPU must ensure that the data *will* be returned (by casting it out of cache and enqueuing it in the RtnQ) after sending the appropriate coherency response. This liveness dependency is specified by means of the predicate CpuReturnLive below which states that provided the data response port $fb$ is live, then if a coherency response is given on $coh\ i$ for a dirty cache hit, data will be returned via $fb\ i$. Note that the coherency response must be given before data is sent.

⊢ CpuReturnLive $coh\ fb\ i =$
PortLive $(fb\ i) \supset$ Fltr TransLive (IsCpuReply $i$) $(coh\ i)\ (fb\ i)$

The remaining issue to specify in the behaviour of the CccQ is when coherency responses can happen. This is done by means of a *ready-to-send* predicate (CohRts) because of the possibility of a stall on the CccQ.

⊢ CohRts $wr\ ccc\ coh\ fb\ i\ m\ t =$
Done $(ccc\ i)\ m\ t\ \wedge$
AllPrevCohDone $ccc\ coh\ fb\ i\ m\ t\ \wedge$
(IsSync $m \supset$ AllPrevFBacksDone $ccc\ wr\ i\ m\ t$)

The above definition says that the CccQ becomes ready to send a transaction $m$ at time $t$ on port $coh$ if $m$ has entered the $ccc$ port by time $t$, all previous coherency checks have been completed by time $t$, and if $m$ is a SYNC transaction, all previous FLUSH_BACKs have also been done. The predicate for denoting that all previous FLUSH_BACKs have been done is specified as follows:

⊢ AllPrevFBacksDone $ccc\ wr\ i\ m\ t =$
$\forall m'.$ Earlier $(ccc\ i)\ m'\ m\ \wedge$ IsDirtyFlush $i\ m' \supset$ SDone $(wr\ i)\ m'\ t$

and the one to denote that all previous coherency checks have been done is:

$\vdash$ AllPrevCohDone $ccc\ coh\ fb\ i\ m\ t =$
$\forall m'.$ Earlier $(ccc\ i)\ m'\ m \supset$
Done $(coh\ i)\ m'\ t \wedge$
(IsCpuReply $i\ m' \supset$ Done $(fb\ i)\ m'\ t)$

The liveness property that describes the constraints of when coherency responses can happen is now defined in terms of the ready-to-send predicate CohRts. From our (simplified) discussion above, the only thing that can hold up a coherency response from ever getting sent is the inability to issue outstanding FLUSH_BACKs on RUNWAY (in the case of a SYNC transaction). The liveness of coherency responses, therefore, is dependent on the port $wr$ being live. We wish to say that if port $wr$ is live then if the CccQ ever becomes ready to send a coherency response (i.e. CohRts becomes true) it will eventually send it. Formally we define a predicate CohLive as follows:

$\vdash$ CohLive $wr\ ccc\ coh\ fb\ i =$
PortLive $(wr\ i) \supset$ RtsLive (CohRts $wr\ ccc\ coh\ fb\ i$ ) $(coh\ i)$

where RtsLive is defined as:

$\vdash$ RtsLive $Rts\ s = \forall m\ t.\ Rts\ m\ t \supset \neg$SDone $s\ m\ t \supset \exists t'.\ t \leq t' \wedge$ Ps $s\ m\ t'$

The overall specification of the CccQ is given in terms of all the properties described above.

$\vdash$ CccQ $i\ ccc\ coh\ fb\ wr =$
InitSeg $(ccc\ i)\ (coh\ i) \wedge$
Fltr InitSeg (IsCpuReply $i$) $(ccc\ i)\ (fb\ i) \wedge$
CpuReturnLive $coh\ fb\ i \wedge$
CohLive $wr\ ccc\ coh\ fb\ i$

## 5.4 Proving Liveness

The overall specification for a multi-processor system is given in terms of the specifications of all the components: $n$ CPUs, $m$ IOAs and an MMC. Several liveness-related lemmas and theorems were proved about this system, with the most important and global result being that if a CPU (or IOA) $i$ say, issued a transaction on port $new\_tran\ i$ which required a reply (such as data), then that reply would eventually happen on port $data\_rtn\ i$. Formally, if RunwaySpec were the predicate for the entire RUNWAY system specification, and IsMmcReply an identifier for the above mentioned transactions, we prove for any number of CPUs (or IOAs):

$\vdash$ RunwaySpec $n\ new\_tran\ data\_rtn \ldots \supset$
$\forall m.$ IsMmcReply $m \supset$
$\forall i.\ i \leq n \supset$
$\forall t.$ Ps $(new\_tran\ i)\ m\ t \supset \exists t'.\ t \leq t' \wedge$ Ps $(data\_rtn\ i)\ m\ t'$

Several assumptions on fairness had to be made to prove such liveness theorems. These assumptions, though not shown explicitly here, were proven using model checking, so the model checking and theorem proving activities turned out to be very closely coupled due to the interdependencies inherent between liveness and fairness.

At first glance, the circularity in the argument that liveness depends on fairness and fairness depends on liveness, makes a proof of liveness seem impossible. In other words, the system is live if arbitration is fair, but the system cannot be fair if deadlocks are possible. Upon closer examination of the behaviour of the system, however, the proofs of liveness and fairness are found to be intricately woven together, but not circular. The apparent circularity of the argument is broken by identifying the *root* argument that unfolds the rest of the proof.

This root argument, or first step, in our proof turned out to depend on showing that the MMC is always live for RET_ONLY transactions[12]; an argument which follows from the assumption on the memory controller in Section 4.2. From this, we then proved using model checking that arbitration for RET_ONLY transactions is fair (Section 4.2) — a result which followed from the assumption that the MMC will not arbitrate indefinitely.

Having shown that clients could always win arbitration to send RET_ONLY transactions we proved (using the theorem prover) that coherency responses can always be given, that the CCC queue is live, and hence, that the system is live to complete outstanding transactions. The next stage was then to show (in model checking) that the CLIENT_OP will return to ANY_TRANS infinitely often (Section 4.2) and that indeed arbitration is fair. This only left it to be shown, using theorem proving, that if arbitration were fair then the system is live for new transactions, as indicated in the above theorem.

# 6 Results

One somewhat alarming result that emerged from this work concerns the number of bugs that were discovered in designs which had already been subjected to several months of simulation. We expected such designs to yield no bugs whatsoever. Even more surprising, though, were the number of these bugs that concerned the specification, e.g. arbitration algorithms that were found to be unfair. Such defective specifications are extremely dangerous because they cannot lead to correct implementations, and fixes to implementations to circumvent faulty specifications are typically messy and often lead to further problems. In one of these cases several engineer months were spent in trying to work out the best way to fix a specification bug with minimum impact.

The desire to attain correct specifications suggests that these techniques should be used early in the design cycle, as a design-aid, rather than as a post-hoc verification tool. The deliverable to the design and simulation engineers is then not just the result of a formal proof, but correctness conditions (which we

---

[12] Transactions allowed under a CLIENT_OP of RET_ONLY i.e. WRITE_BACK, FLUSH_BACK and CACHE_2_CACHE transactions.

call *meta-protocol*) which must be implemented correctly for the design to work. Simulation can then be directed to ensure that such conditions are met.

From the results of this work it is clear that formal verification was being applied to areas where simulation was not achieving sufficient coverage. We believe that by further developing formal verification tools, maybe to better incorporate model checking, theorem proving and simulation in ways which exploit all their strengths, a more effective design process can be achieved overall, and time-to-market can be reduced.

## Acknowledgements

I wish to thank several colleagues for numerous discussions and technical reviews. In particular, this work would not have succeeded without the help and support of Roger Fleming, Bob Odineal and David Prekeges. Thanks are also due to Cheryl Harkness and Mark Heap for enhancing SMV, and to Dave Burns, Francisco Corella, Debendra Das Dharma, Rob Shaw and Liz Wolf for commenting on drafts of this paper.

## References

1. Bryg W., Chan K., Fiduccia N., 'A High-Performance, Low-Cost Multiprocessor Bus for Workstations and Midrange Servers', *Hewlett-Packard Journal*, 47 (1), February 1996.
2. Bainbridge S., Camilleri A., Fleming R., 'Theorem Proving as an Industrial Tool for System Level Design', in *Theorem Provers in Circuit Design*, Stavridou V., Melham T., Boute R. (eds.), North-Holland, 1992, pp. 253–274, Proceedings of the IFIP TC 10/WG 10.2 International Conference, Nijmegen, 22–24 June, 1992.
3. Camilleri A., Fleming R., Odineal R., Prekeges D., 'Formal Verification of Liveness of a Multi-Processor Bus Protocol', pp. 409–412, Proceedings of the 1993 HP Design Technology Conference, Portland, 25–28 May, 1993. HP Confidential.
4. Corella F., Shaw R., Zhang C., 'A formal proof of absence of deadlock for any acyclic network of PCI buses', Proceedings of 13$^{th}$ International Conference on Computer Hardware Description Languages and their Applications, Chapman & Hall, 1997.
5. *Datamation* Magazine, February 1997.
6. Gordon M. J. C., Melham T. F., *Introduction to HOL — A theorem proving environment for higher order logic*, Cambridge University Press, 1993.
7. Harkness C., Wolf, E., 'Verifying the Summit Bus Converter Protocols with Symbolic Model Checking', Formal Methods in System Design, 4 (2), pp. 83–97, February 1994.
8. Hennessy J., Patterson D., *Computer Architecture: A Quantitative Approach*, Morgan Kaufmann Publishers, Inc., 1990.
9. McMillan K. L., *Symbolic Model Checking*, Kluwer Academic Publishers, 1993.
10. McMillan K. L., Schwalbe J., 'Formal Verification of the Encore Gigamax Cache Consistency Protocol', in *International Symposium on Shared Memory Multiprocessors*, 1991.

# Formal Verification of Concurrent Programs in LP and in COQ: A Comparative Analysis

Boutheina Chetali & Barbara Heyd

CRIN-CNRS and INRIA-Lorraine
University of Henri Poincaré,Nancy I,
Campus Scientifique —B.P. 101,
54602 Villers-les-Nancy — FRANCE
e-mail: chetali@loria.fr,heyd@loria.fr

**Abstract.** This paper describes the formal verification of parallel programs using a rewrite and induction based theorem prover like LP and a higher order theorem prover based on the Calculus of Inductive Construction, namely COQ. The chosen specification environment is UNITY, a subset of temporal logic for specifying and verifying concurrent programs. By means of an example, a *lift-control* program, we describe the embedding of UNITY and we show how to verify mechanically program properties using the two provers. Then we summarize a comparison between the theorem proving environments, based on our practical experience with both systems for the verification of UNITY programs.

**Keywords:** Formal Verification, UNITY, theorem prover methodology, LARCH Prover, COQ, Computer Checked Proof.

## 1 Introduction

The verification of parallel programs have inspired several methodologies. One of these, UNITY introduced by Chandy & Misra [5], has been used and developed in several provers [4, 18, 6, 16, 1]. UNITY is a theory to specify and verify concurrent programs. It provides us with a formalism to express the relevant properties of a program, an appropriate language to construct well-formed formulas and a proof system to construct proofs.

The aim of the paper is not to identify the best tool to mechanically prove UNITY specifications, if such a tool exists, but to evaluate the compromises of the different approaches associated with the power of the prover by comparing the implementations of UNITY made in LP [6] and in COQ [18]. Moreover, the comparison takes UNITY as a means and not as a goal in the sense that we will discuss the implementation of the objects one could find in any embedding of a programming theory, such as *state*, *variables* and *assignments*.

This comparison is based on our practical experience for the verification of a *lift-control* program taken from [2] and already completed with the HOL-UNITY system [1]. This example is interesting because it is a good archetypical problem that allows us to show how we deal with a program manipulating naturals, booleans, and abstract data types such as arrays. As the correctness proof has been verified independently with the CoQ proof assistant and with the LARCH prover, it allows us fruitful comparisons on the use of a theorem prover with regards to the mechanization of UNITY proofs.

The design and development of the LARCH proof assistant LP were motivated primarily as a means to debug LSL specifications [17] but they have also been used to establish the correctness of hardware designs [23, 7] and to reason about algorithms involving concurrency [13, 21]. It is a general-purpose theorem prover for multi-sorted first-order logic, it is based on equational term rewriting [14] and it supports proofs about axiomatic specifications. All proofs are carried out by applying rewrite rules, proofs by case splitting, induction, contradiction and application of inference rules. LP does not contain any predefined theory, but automatically declares the sort *bool* with the corresponding logical operators.

CoQ [9] is a theorem prover based on *the Calculus of Inductive Construction* (CiC) which is a higher order typed calculus with inductive definitions [29]. It has been used to prove the correctness of hardware designs [10, 26] and to reason about different theories on protocols [15, 3]. The system CoQ is divided into three parts. The first part is the logical language in which we write our axiomatizations and specifications. The second part is the proof assistant which allows the development of mathematical proofs. It provides several tactics to built the proof. It is important to note that the tactics implement the backward reasoning, that is the construction of the proof is made in the top-down manner. The proofs, when they are achieved, are considered as terms of $\lambda$-calculus due to the Curry-Howard isomorphism. The third part is a program extractor which allows the synthesis of a functional program from the constructive part of its proof of correctness. This last feature of CoQ is not taken into account in the comparison.

The paper is organized as follows. We start by a brief description of the fundamental concepts of UNITY. Next we describe the mechanization of UNITY logic in both theorem provers and we point out the differences between the embeddings of the *lift-control* program using LP and CoQ. Following that, we discuss the automation in the two provers and the facilities given by the logic.

## 2 Unity and the Lift-Control Program

A UNITY program consists of four sections: a **Declare** section that declares the variables used in the program, an **Initially** section that describes the initial values of the variables, an **Always** section that is a set of shorthands, and an **Assign** section that consists of a non-empty set of assignment statements.

The following example is taken from [2]. It describes a lift that moves between a number of floors to serve requests on these. The bottom and top floors are specified with two constant parameters *min* and *max*.

**Program** {Lift(min,max)}
**Declare**
    *floor* : *integer* [] *up, move, stop, open* : *bool* [] *req* : *array*[*min..max*] *of bool*
**Initially**
    *floor* = *min* [] *up, move, stop, open* = *false, true, true, false* [] $\forall i.min \leq i \leq max \wedge req[i]$ = *false*
**Always**
    *above* = $\exists i : floor < i \leq max \wedge req[i]$

$below = \exists i : min \leq i < floor \land req[i]$
$queueing = above \lor below$
$goingup = above \land (up \lor \neg below)$
$goingdown = below \land (\neg up \lor \neg above)$
$ready = stop \land \neg open \land move$

**Assign**

| | | | |
|---|---|---|---|
| $\{request\_act\}$ | $stop, move$ | $:= true, false$ | $if \neg stop \land req[floor]$ |
| $[]\{open\_act\}$ | $open, req[floor], move$ | $:= true, false, true$ | $if\ stop \land \neg open \land req[floor]$ |
| | | | $\land\neg(move \land queueing)$ |
| $[]\{close\_act\}$ | $open$ | $:= false$ | $if\ open$ |
| $[]\{req\_up\}$ | $stop, floor, up$ | $:= false, floor + 1, true$ | $if\ ready \land goingup$ |
| $[]\{req\_down\}$ | $stop, floor, up$ | $:= false, floor - 1, false$ | $if\ ready \land goingdown$ |
| $[]\{move\_up\}$ | $floor$ | $:= floor + 1$ | $if \neg stop \land up \land \neg req[floor]$ |
| $[]\{move\_down\}$ | $floor$ | $:= floor - 1$ | $if \neg stop \land \neg up \land \neg req[floor]$ |

**end**$\{$Lift$\}$

The symbol $[]$ acts as a separator between actions. The bracketed expressions ($\{\}$) are "names" that we add to identify the program actions, which are very helpful when describing the program and its proofs.

The state space of the lift is represented by six variables : *floor* denotes the current position of the lift, *open* whether the doors are opened at *floor*, *stop* whether the lift is stopped at *floor*, *req[i]* whether the lift is requested at the floor *i*, *up* denotes the current direction of the movement, and *move* whether moving the lift takes precedence over opening of the doors.

Execution of every UNITY actions terminates for every program and a program execution consists of an infinite number of steps in which each statement is executed infinitely often (weak fairness). There are five relations on predicates in UNITY theory[1]: *unless, stable, invariant, ensures* and *leads_ to*. The first three are used for stating *safety* properties whereas the last two are used to express *progress* properties, a subset of *liveness* properties [19].

For example, the main *progress* property to prove about the *lift-control* program is the following (where $\leadsto$ stands for *leadsto*):

$$\forall n : min \leq n \leq max \Rightarrow req[n] \leadsto open \land floor = n$$

which states that any request for service will eventually be served.

## 3 Embedding UNITY into LP and into COQ

### 3.1 Types

In COQ definitions, type information has to be supplied by the user, but the type checking is automatic. Types can be polymorphic or type dependent. In the CIC, type and terms have the same syntactic structure. There is three distinct hierarchies of sorts: **Prop**, **Set** and **Type**. The sort **Prop** is intended to be the type of logical propositions. An object of type **Prop** is often called a predicate. The sort **Set** is intended to be the type of usual sets (or *collections*). Objects of type **Set** are said to be concrete sets. The sort **Type** is intended to be the type of abstract sets. The set of *natural* or the type of *lists* are considered as concrete

---

[1] A revised version has been proposed by Misra [24], where new operators are introduced to simplify formal manipulations, but it is not relevant to our study.

sets. The *less than equal* relation is a predicate taking two natural arguments. The type of this relation is : nat → nat → Prop. The sort of these concrete sets is Type. The judgment $t : T$ represents the fact that the term $t$ is of type $T$. Due to the Curry-Howard isomorphism, a term inhabiting one type witnesses a proof of the proposition. For the purpose of the paper and in order to make the notations more readable, we have slightly modified the syntax of CoQ: we will use ∀x:T.B and λx:T.B for (x:T) B and [x:T] B respectively and f a ≡ b for Definition f = [a:?] b.

LP is the theorem prover of LARCH, a (multi-sorted) frame (a larch shared language, a set of interface languages, a checker and a theorem prover). It is based on a multi-sorted first-order logic. There is no notion of *type* in LP but there are *sort*. The user has to define a collection of sorts to represent the objects to use. A sort represents a non-empty set of objects. In LP, distinct sorts represent disjoint sets of objects. LP automatically declares the sort Bool and treats it as representing a set containing two objects, true and false. LP automatically declares the usual logical operators for this sort. All sorts other than Bool must be declared in a declare sort command.

Since distinct sorts represent disjoint sets of objects, users who want to consider one "sort" (e.g., Nat) as a subset of another (e.g., Int) must resort to one of two devices. They can define the larger as a sort and the smaller by means of a unary predicate (e.g., isNat:Int → Bool). Alternatively, they can define both as sorts and introduce a mapping from one into the other (e.g., isInt:Nat → Int). We take the second solution in our formalization.

## 3.2   Variables, Programs and Actions

**Variables:** UNITY variables are of two kinds. The *identifiers* appear in the program text and the *proof variables* appear in the UNITY proofs. It is important to distinguish between UNITY program variables (*state* variables), and proof variables that are logical variables whose value do not change over time.

In LP, the *identifiers* appearing in the program are encoded as *constants* of sort Id and the *proof variables* as LP *variables* of sort Id_of_var. To ensure that the name *identifiers* are distinct, we define the sort Id inductively using two constructors :

```
declare operators
   firstId:    -> Id
   nextId : Id -> Id
assert sort Id generated freely by firstId,nextId
```

The last line, which is an induction rule, asserts that all elements of sort Id can be obtained by finitely many applications of nextid to firstId. Besides the induction principle, this axiom introduces (by the freely option) two formulas stating that elements of sort Id must be distinct. For example in this framework, the *lift* variables *floor*, and *move* are declared as follow:

```
declare operators floor, move:-> Id
   assert
```

```
floor = FirstId;
move = nextid(floor);
```

The identifiers take their value from different sorts. The specifications of the abstract data types, such as naturals (Nat), sequences (seq), and records (rec) are part of the Larch Shared Language [17], which we have modified in order to axiomatize customized data types [6]. To say that an identifier is of type T, we apply a conversion function id_to_T (a mapping), of signature Id → T. To say that the identifier *floor* is equal to 0, we write id_to_nat(floor)=0, using a function that "transforms" an identifier into a natural. Moreover, we define a conversion function for each used sort.

In COQ, we define the set of *identifiers* as an object of type Set and the domain of these variables as the type of functions from variable to Set.

```
Variable variable : Set.
Variable domain   : variable -> Set.
```

Here variable is just the name of a new data type in COQ. When we load the COQ-Unity[2] theory, all the definitions written using variable and domain are represented as closed terms (in λ-calculus) with the abstraction of variable and domain. For an actual program, we must give the specification of the type variable. This one is an inductive definition which specifies the *identifiers* as a collection of variables. The constructors of this Set are the *identifiers* of the program. As the inductive definitions are primitive, all program variables are distinct by construction. In this framework, for the *lift-control* program, the variable data type is defined as follows:

```
Inductive variable : Set :=
  req  : variable | open : variable | stop : variable
| move : variable | up   : variable | floor: variable.
```

A *state* is a mapping from a set of *identifiers* to *values* constrained by types. However, to be able to define such a notion, we must decide for each *identifier* the type of its values. As the *identifiers* are defined using an inductive definition, a specific elimination rule for variable is now available, which allows case analysis on variable constructors. The function domain gives for each constructor (or *identifier*) the corresponding type. The type of *req*, representing a boolean array, is a function from *naturals* to *booleans*. The other variables are either of type bool or of type nat. A state, which is the set of all the valuations of the variables, is defined as a function from *identifiers* to their *value domain*, written as a dependent product. Note that, in COQ, the dependent product and the universal quantification have the same syntax.

```
domain v ≡ Cases v of
  req => (nat -> bool) | open  => bool | stop => bool
| move => bool | up => bool | floor  => nat
end.
state ≡ ∀ v:variable. (domain v).
```

---

[2] The COQ data base formalizing UNITY

In LP, we could use a similar concept to define the variable identifiers, i.e. to replace the induction rule for the sort Id given below (p.4) by the following one:

**assert sort** Id **generated freely by** req,open,stop,move, up, floor

where the constructors of the sort Id are now the program variables. So doing, we will change the constructors of the sort Id, for each new UNITY program to prove. Therefore, the global database could not be loaded automatically for each new program to prove and will depend on the program to its validity.
We note that in the two formalizations, we use the inductive definitions to ensures that the program identifiers are distinct. The main difference is the ability in CoQ to handle any kind of data type manipulated by the programs using the predefined types.

One way to illustrate the facilities given by the higher order of CoQ is the formalization of the arrays. The *lift_ control* program uses an array of booleans to store the requests. The expression $req[i] := e$ is an assignment, where the modified variable is *req* and not an hypothetical variable $req[i]$ for a some value $i$. Hence, the assignment $req[i] := e$ is actually:

$$req := (\forall j \in Dom(index) : if \ i = j \ then \ e \ else \ req(j))$$

Therefore the array *req* is a function from the range of the index to the type of the array elements. If we formalize the assignment using a substitution function, the assignment of an array variable will use a function applied to a function. This require a higher order facility.

In the LP formalization, we define a new sort **array** with three operators, and a conversion function id_to_array. Two of those operators allow us to distinguish the term req[i], which represents the $i^{th}$ element of the array *req* that can be modified by the program (and then it is an *identifier* of the program), from the term val(req,i) which represents the value of this $i^{th}$ element (the value of the *identifier*).

In CoQ, the array is not a new type but mainly a function from *naturals* (range of the index) to the type of the array elements (bool, the range of the values). So in LP we needed a function val to return explicitly the value of $req[i]$ (of type Bexp) whereas in CoQ, the value of $req[i]$ is (req i) (as req is a function from natural to booleans).

**Programs and Actions:** There are two possibilities for encoding the program actions: either as a set or as a list. In LP as in CoQ, the two solutions are possible. From an operational point of view, the LP encoding of a program as a set or as a list is equivalent, because the sorts sets and lists are both inductively defined (see [17] for details). So lists have been chosen. In CoQ, they have not the same encoding. As the use of sets is more intuitive, we took that solution. Let's see now how a program is actually encoded.

In LP, to represent the actions and the programs, we define two sorts, Act and Actlist. A UNITY program is then represented as a list of actions, i.e. a constant of sort Actlist. We define the usual list operators for the sort Actlist as follows:

**declare operators**
```
nil :                  -> Actlist
cons: Act,Actlist -> Actlist
```

**assert sort** Actlist **generated** by nil, cons

The last line defines an induction rule for the sort Actlist. It provides the basis for definitions and proofs by induction.

The actions are encoded using four operators, one per each kind of assignment. For example, a simple assignment and a conditional multiple assignment are encoded as follow:

- assg:pair → Act is the operator for single assignment with pair of type (Id, Exp) or (Id, Bexp). According to whether Id is an integer identifier or a boolean identifier, this operator assigns the expression Exp or the boolean structure Bexp (*predicate*), the corresponding definition of Bexp will be given in the sequel).
- c_mult_assg:Set,Bexp → Act is the operator for multiple[3] conditional assignment, where Set is a list of pairs and Bexp the condition.

In COQ, our implementation is based on the state-transition model. An action is a transition, i.e. a function from states to states.

```
transition ≡ state -> state.
```

We use a single formalization for both simple and multiple assignments. Moreover, using the definition by case analysis, we say explicitly that the variables that do not occur in the assignment keep their previous value. For example, the action x:= x+1 if b, where x and b are the program identifiers is formalized as follows:

```
example_transition s v ≡ <domain> Cases v of
   x => (Ifb nat (s b) ((s x) + 1) (s x)) | b => (s b)
end.
```

A COQ-UNITY program is encoded as a triple made of initial conditions, transitions and context[4]. So program is an inductive type with one constructor:

**Inductive** program : **Type** :=
```
Triple: (a_set state)->(a_set transition)->(a_set transition)->program.
```

where a_set is the characteristic function of sets:

```
a_set (X:Set) ≡ X -> Prop.
```

---

[3] Details about how we safely encode the parallel assignment can be found in [6]
[4] The context of a program is the set of transitions that can be used by any programs it is composed with. This is the dual of the classical notion of interface or environment and it imposes restrictions from the context on the programs it calls. We refer to [18] from details.

## 3.3  Functions and Predicates

For a given UNITY program, the main properties to be proved are based on the *unless*, *ensures* and *leads_to* operators. These are higher-order functions applied to predicates, which are non-modal formulas. We discuss in the following section the different strategies taken to formalize these functions in both theorem provers. Those formalizations take into account the power of the used logic.

LP specifications consist of two kinds of symbols, *sorts* and *operators*, similar to the programming language concepts of *type* and *procedures* or *functions*. To prove the UNITY assertion $p\,R\,q$ for a given program *prg* in the framework of LP, where $R$ is one of the UNITY temporal operators, the signature of $R$ should be of the form *Pred, Pred, Prog → bool*. As LP is a first-order language, we encode the UNITY temporal predicates by first-order functions yielding the question of how the *first order predicates* (on which the temporal predicates are applied) are encoded ?

A *predicate* in the object language (i.e. UNITY, the language to be encoded in the theorem prover) is defined as a *boolean structure* [12]. A *boolean structure* is constructed from two structures and a boolean operator. A *structure* is an abstraction of "expressions in program variables". These *expressions* are either of types *boolean* or *integer*. To represent these boolean structures (predicates), we define a new sort called Bexp. The sort Bexp is not (and cannot be) an extension of bool, the basic sort provided by LP. Therefore we need to redefine the usual boolean connectives, namely *true, false, imply, or, and*.

declare operators
```
T,F   :  -> Bexp
|=>,\or,\and : Bexp,Bexp -> Bexp
```

The *integer* structures, for which we define a new sort Exp, are the arithmetic expressions built with the operators +, -, and * of signature Exp,Exp → Exp. To manipulate these *boolean* and *integer* structures, we define a database of axioms for which we prove a set of theorems. These axioms and theorems are oriented into rewriting rules using the predefined ordering[5] provided by LP.

In Coq, the predicates are usual functions of type Prop, the basic sort of propositions. As we choose the state-transition model, a UNITY first order predicate is considered as a *state abstracted predicate*, encoded as a function from state to Prop. Let pred be the name of this function. Then we define the state abstracted logical connectives using the prefix u_ to distinguish these operators from the built-in notation of the logical Coq operators. The definitions of a state abstracted predicate and operators are the following:

```
pred ≡ state -> Prop.
u_or p q ≡ λ (p s) \/ (q s).
```

Although the two formalizations are similar, i.e the re-definition of the *state abstracted predicates* and the connectives, in Coq these definitions are only shorthands used to simplify the manipulation of the formulas and the proofs.

---

[5] noeq-dsmpos, a *Recursive Path ordering*

In fact, pred is not a new type, but mainly the name of a function from state to Prop, while Bexp is a new sort in LP. As a sort is useless without a set of operators to manipulate its objects, we had to formalize all the theory of first order predicates. In COQ, the *new* connectives are defined using the predefined logical connectives. This is due to the higher order of the logic supported by the prover.

**Temporal Operators:** Proofs in UNITY are based on two temporal predicates, namely *unless* and *leads_ to*. For a given program, *p unless q* means that once the predicate *p* is true, it remains true as long as *q* is not true. Formally,

$$p \textbf{ unless } q \stackrel{def}{=} \langle \forall s : s \textit{ in pgm } :: \{p \wedge \neg q\}s\{p \vee q\} \rangle$$

In LP we choose the Dijkstra's weakest pre-condition as the formal tool to reason about UNITY programs. We define a *textual substitution* to encode the semantics of the UNITY actions using *wp*.

```
declare operators
  wp      : Act,Bexp -> Bexp
  sub_exp : Set,Exp  -> Exp
  sub_Bexp: Set,Bexp -> Bexp
```

The wp operator takes an action and a predicate and returns a predicate. We formalize the wp-calculus for assignment statements as follows:

```
assert
  wp(mult_assg(l),q)  = sub_Bexp(l,q);
  wp(c_mult_assg(l,b),q) = (b |=> wp(mult_assg(l),q)) \and (nnot(b) |=> q)
```

The function sub_Bexp(l,q), where l is a list of pairs (Id,Exp), substitutes each occurrence[6] of the identifier Id by Exp in the boolean structure q. We define the substitutions on atomic expressions and homomorphically extend them to the whole structure. For the atomic substitutions, we need to consider the different possibilities of atomic expressions [6].

Using the *wp* operator, we specify the *unless* operator as follow[7].

```
assert
  unless(p,q,nil)  = true;
  unless(p,q,a) = (((p \and nnot(q)) |=> wp(a,p \or q))=T);
  unless(p,q,cons(a,act_l)) = unless(p,q,a) /\ unless(p,q, act_l)
```

This definition could be written using only two axioms, one for the empty program and one for the general case, but we use an additional axiom for readability.

In COQ, the state-transition model is used because the translation of the definitions in terms of HOARE triples is straightforward. It is due to the fact that the "substitution" is related to the β-reduction of the lambda-calculus. Indeed, if *t* is a transition and *s* is a state, the new state resulting from the substitution of

---

[6] There is no quantifier in our language of *boolean structures*

[7] It is a binary relation on state predicates, but we add a third argument to represent the program.

the transition $t$ in the state $s$ is equal to *(t s)*. Moreover, our Coq formalization of the UNITY logic is not the same as the one given by Chandy and Misra, as we take into account the problematic *substitution axiom*, required for the UNITY logic to be complete. In order to achieve the substitution axiom as a theorem, the properties need to be defined on reachable states [28]. As proposed by B. Sanders, we restrict the state space to the reachable states, which we characterize inductively : an initial state is a reachable state, a state resulting from the application of a transition (of the program or of the context) to a reachable state is also a reachable state.

```
Inductive reachable [P:program]: state -> Prop :=
   reach_init : ∀ s. (initial_of P s) -> (reachable P s)
 | reach_trans: ∀ s, t.
      (transition_of P t) -> (reachable P s) -> (reachable P (t s))
 | reach_ctxt: ∀ s, t.
      (context_of P t) -> (reachable P s) -> (reachable P (t s)).
```

Here (initial_of P s) checks if s belongs to the set of initial states of the given program P and (transition_of P t) checks if the transition t belongs to the set of program transitions.

The *unless* formalization is then a translation of its HOARE triples definition :

```
unless p q P ≡ ∀ s. (reachable P s) -> ∀ t. (transition_of P t) ->
                 ((u_and p (u_not q)) s) -> ((u_or p q) (t s)).
```

**Progress** The basis of the definition of progress in UNITY is the *ensures* operator, whose meaning is that once $p$ is true it remains true at least as long as $q$ is not true (the UNITY definition of the *ensures* operators uses the *unless* one). But the most important operator is the *leads_to* relation, which is defined as the transitive and disjunctive closure of the *ensures* relation. A program has the property $p$ *leads_to* $q$ iff once $p$ is true, $q$ will eventually be true ($\rightsquigarrow$ stands for *leads_to*). Formally,

$$\frac{p \text{ ensures } q}{p \rightsquigarrow q} \qquad \frac{p \rightsquigarrow r, r \rightsquigarrow q}{p \rightsquigarrow q} \qquad For \text{ any set } W, \quad \frac{\langle \forall m \in W :: p_m \rightsquigarrow q \rangle}{\langle \exists m \in W :: p_m \rangle \rightsquigarrow q}$$

In LP, we define the *leads_to* operator using three axioms formalized as implications as follows:

```
assert
when ensures(p,q,pgm) yield leads_to(p,q,pgm)
(leads_to(p,r,pgm) /\ leads_to(r,q,pgm)) => leads_to(p,q,pgm)
(leads_to(p,r,pgm) /\ leads_to(q,r,pgm)) => leads_to(p \or q,r,pgm)
```

The first axiom is a **deduction** rule, which allows to infer $p$ *leads_to* $q$ once we have proved $p$ *ensures* $q$. The *when* clause contains the hypotheses of the rule and the *yield* clause the fact inferred when the hypotheses are true. The reason for formalizing the first inference rule as a deduction rule and the other two as implications is for convenience, to keep control on the use of these rules. To use an implication, we must instantiate explicitly the variables with the corresponding terms in order to infer the conclusion of the implication. For a deduction rule, the conclusion is automatically inferred by LP as soon as the hypothesis becomes true in the system. But if a deduction rule contains two (or more) hypotheses (as for the transitivity), as soon as one of the hypotheses holds, a new instance of the deduction rule is added to the system. This can introduce many unnecessary facts to the system.

Using CoQ, we formalize the *leads_ to* operator using the inductive definition. The inductive predicate is described by three constructors : *ens_ leads*, *leads_ trans* and *leads_ disj* that give respectively the clauses for the basis case, the transitivity rule and the infinite disjunction rules.

```
lub E s ≡ ∃ p. (E p) /\ (p s).

Inductive leads_to [P:program] : pred -> pred -> Prop :=
    ens_leads   : ∀ p,q. (ensures p q P) -> (leads_to P p q)
  | leads_trans : ∀ p,r. (leads_to P p r) ->
                      ∀ q. (leads_to P r q) -> (leads_to P p q)
  | leads_disj  : ∀ p,q. ∀ E. (∀ r. (E r) -> (leads_to P r q)) ->
                      (u_eqv p (lub E)) -> (leads_to P p q).
```

lub defines the least upper bound of a family of predicates as the infinite disjunction. u_eqv checks the equivalence between the predicate *p* and the least upper bound of $E$ ((lub E)).

To summarise, we can say that due to the higher order logic of CoQ, the encoding of UNITY is more easier and elegant than in LP. Some choices that we made about the state-transition model, the encoding of the variables, the *leads_ to* operator, the reachable states and the program actions depend on the powerful logic. For example, if you consider a *state* as a function from *variables* to *values* then a transition, which is a function from state to state, is a higher order function. In LP, we choose a concrete syntactical representation of both the state dependent predicates and the programming notation in first order logic. All objects are defined using a new sort and a set of axioms and theorems about these objects. This leads to a cumbersome formalization but the proof are easier that those in CoQ.

In the next section, the discussion is based on the mechanization of the correctness proof of the *lift-control* program. We will discuss the facilities given by the logic of the two provers for the the encodding and the proofs.

# 4 Discussion

## 4.1 Strategy

CoQ and LP are proof assistants in the sense that they require help from the user to achieve proofs. The proofs are built step by step. The steps of a proof are implemented by applying tactics in CoQ and proof methods in LP.

In CoQ, at each step of a proof development, we apply a tactic to the goal. A tactic is a mechanism or a small program which allows backward proofs. The user can design his own tactics oriented to a specific class of proofs, as for example, with the tactic BreakUnl that we develop for the *unless* properties. This tactic BreakUnl does not prove automatically an *unless* property, it simply unfolds the definition of a program into several actions. Moreover, we develop two other tactics, LetIntro and Un Elim that automatize sequences of basis tactics that are tedious to write. LetIntro simplifies the *introduction* of complex conjunctions and Un Elim *destructs* a disjunction and creates as many subgoals as there are elements in the disjunction. By building complex tactics the user can customize his own proof strategy. Therefore the user has to give the sequence of tactics to use in order to solve each subgoal. This is the main difference with LP, where the concept of tactic does not exist.

Using LP, the user decides in advance the proof methods he will use. For example, we could define a general proof strategy using the command: set proof-methods normalization, /\, =>. Those commands tell LP to attempt to prove conjectures by the first applicable proof method specified in the given list. To prove an *unless* property, LP uses the /\-method to split the conjecture after rewriting it to its normal form, and uses the =>-method for each generated subgoal. As the proofs of a property *p unless q* are the same for all *p* and *q*, that is, a single /\-command followed by a number of resume by =>-m command (one per action), the mechanized proof could be fully automated with a single command: prove unless(p,q,pgm). Although this strategy leads to less interaction with LP, it has not been used in our comparative case study in order to keep control of the lower steps of the proof. Indeed, if the above general strategy is used and if the proof stops because LP needs help from the user, finding the problematic action may be hard.

## 4.2 Automation

Automation is an important issue when comparing two theorems provers with respect to complex proofs. Although both theorem provers are semi-automatic, LP provides the user with more automation as it is based on rewriting systems. For instance, the simplification of the equations and subgoals is transparent to the user. In particular, the normalization of terms with respect to the asserted definitions is natural, whilst in CoQ the process must be explicitly conducted by the user. This is important when several lemmas have to be proved and used later. In a CoQ proof, these lemmas must be explicitly invoked, but in an LP proof they are used as rewrite rules. However, the Auto tactic of CoQ is a partial attempt towards automatization as it allows one to prove simple propositional or arithmetic goals. Since arithmetic proofs can be trivial but tedious for CoQ, P. Crégut [11] has developed a tactic, called Omega, which solves goals in Pressburger arithmetic. Thus, as each user of CoQ can develop their own tactics, the resulting library is useful for the interaction and the mechanization of proofs.

Unlike fully automatic theorem provers, LP provides several means to debug a proof that fails, allowing the user to find the origin of the failure and to backtrack to try another strategy. This is an important feature when we deal with large and complex proofs where the root of a failure is buried in a large number of proof obligations and details. As automation is desirable when the proof succeeds and when it fails, it is important to have backtracking mechanisms that help us to find the precise rewriting rules used by LP to deduce the problematic equation [8].

Moreover a user should not expect too much from automatization. Contrary to fully automatic theorem provers, our experiments confirmed that the user must have the architecture of his proof clear in mind. If several attempts and failures are possible in the proof of short lemmas, this failures can not be accepted for large proofs such as the *lift-control* program. For each subgoal to solve, the CoQ user has several possibilities: he can either solve it by applying an hypothesis or a lemma with the tactic Apply, or by finding a contradiction (tactic Contradiction) or an absurdity (tactic Absurd) among the hypotheses of the context. Sometimes, a lemma is missing and then the user has to state it and to prove it. However, we must be careful before applying a lemma or an hypothesis since it can generate a unprovable or inconsistent subgoal. Creating general tactics or tacticals can automatize some parts of proofs.

## 4.3 Induction

Induction schemes can be easily defined and used as a proof techniques in both systems. Although LP is a first order theorem prover, it provides the user with some second order features, such as the possibility to prove induction rules (structural or well-founded induction rule). For example, we define two induction principles for the naturals, namely Nat:

```
assert sort  Nat generated by 0,s              %nat.1
assert sort  Nat generated by  0,1,+           %nat.2
```

Having the first induction rule on the natural nat.1, we prove the second one (nat.2) using nat.1. Those higher order features are important when we use large specifications. When we define a new inductive data type, sometimes we want to use another induction aspect. For example, in our proof of a communication protocol [8], we define the *sequences* as being generated by *empty* and *push* constructors. But we need another induction rule, namely that a sequence is also generated by an *empty*, a *singleton* or a *union* constructor. Thus we prove the new induction rule using the axioms and theorems previously defined and checked for the sequence data type.

The induction rules of LP allows us to define the abstract data types such as *naturals, stacks, queues, lists* but the main use of the induction was to prove properties about these objects. This allows us to construct a database of objects and properties that someone else can reuse for his own framework and which is useful in many contexts beyond those involving UNITY and which need not be redone for each application [6]. Another important use of the LP induction was to prove the general properties satisfied by the UNITY temporal predicates. This is the main reason that leads us to define the identifier sort as an inductive sort, the program as list of actions,, etc. When the properties are proved, we use them as theorems in the proofs of the correctness of an actual program. We prove most of the properties (formalized as implications) about *unless* and *ensures* [5] by induction on the list of the actions of the program [6], because these temporal predicates are defined inductively on the actions of the program, but not those about *leads_ to*. Those ones require a structural induction on the length of proof that is not possible in LP.

In CoQ, induction is an important feature that allows the definition of inductive sets, enumerated sets and predicates families. For example, the $\leq$ relation are defined as follows:

<u>Inductive</u> le [n:nat] : nat -> Prop :=
  le_n : (le n n) | le_s : (m:nat)(le n m) -> (le n (S m)).

le defines a predicates family parameterized by n, it corresponds to introducing the binary relation $n \leq m$ as a family of predicates ($n \leq$ to be greater or equal than a given $n$). le is the minimal predicate verifying clauses le_n and le_s. When a property is proved about the le predicates, the Elim tactic is used to generate the corresponding induction subgoals. In CoQ, we can also use a well-founded induction with a relation $R$ and a set $A$, using the following theorem:

Theorem well_founded_induction  : $\forall$ A, R. (well_founded A R) ->
  $\forall$ P. ($\forall$ x. ($\forall$ y. (R y x) ->(P y)) ->(P x)) -> $\forall$ a. (P a).

In the framework on UNITY, the inductive definitions of CoQ allows us to define the program as a triple of three sets (initial states, program transitions and context transitions), the set of the reachable states and the set of variable identifiers. Moreover, the importance of the induction definition appeared in the formalization of the *leads_ to* operator that permit an intuitive and correct definition [18] with respect to its semantic meaning as the smallest relation verifying the three inference rules of the UNITY definitions. The theorems about the *leads_ to* operator that require a structural induction on the length of proof are proved using the induction principle automatically generated by the inductive definition of *leads_ to*.

## 4.4   Soundness

Although our aim was not to investigate the soundness and completeness of the UNITY theory, our CoQ implementation of UNITY handles the problem of the substitution axiom. B. Sanders [28] proposed restricting the state space to the reachable states. But this solution has some drawbacks related to the compositions of programs mentioned by I.S.W.B. Prasetya [27]. This problem was solved by considering the transitions of the context in order to increase the number of reachable states. Our formalization of UNITY has been proved correct and complete with respect to the operational semantics, and the proof has been done in CoQ [18]

In LP, we do not encode the substitution axiom[8], necessary for the UNITY logic to be complete. Therefore our UNITY formalization is incomplete but sound.

---

[8] In order to achieve the substitution axiom as a theorem in our model, we need the state properties to be defined on reachable states, but we do not use a notion of *state*.

The non-completeness is a theoretical limitation without practical incidence, since our aim in LP is a mechanized verification and not a proof search.

In LP, to ensure the soundness of the encoding, we use an incremental method for the specifications and standard techniques for the verification. The whole system (abstract data types) has been verified. When proving a UNITY program, its formalization in LP does not introduce any new facts that could made the system inconsistent. As mentioned before, the formalization of the UNITY theory developed in LP is defined to satisfy properties for any program states and the properties are defined as special cases of pre- and post-conditions between state transitions. We choose a concrete syntactical representation of state dependent predicates and the programming notation in first order logic.

LP does not use heuristics to formulate additional conjectures that might be useful in a proof. Instead, LP makes easy for us to employ standard techniques such as proofs by cases, induction, and contradiction, either to construct proofs or to understand why they have failed using backtracking mechanism. In fact, even if LP "does not suggest solutions", it provides a lot of information about the state of the proof, the current hypotheses, the subgoal and the technical reason for the failure.

## 5 Conclusion

In this paper, we described the implementation of UNITY using a higher order theorem prover such as CoQ, and a first order theorem prover like LP. Our goal was to compare the verification of concurrent programs done by two different theorem provers. We choose UNITY as a tool but having in mind to compare the implementations of the basic features encountered in the framework of parallel programming theory, namely *states*, *variables* and *assignments*. Our aim was not to identify the best tool but mainly to provide the user with some guidelines about the features of the two provers and to help him in the choice of an adequate tool with respect to his specifications and proofs.

The mechanized verification using CoQ is semi-automatic and can be tedious without the possibility of developing ones own tactics oriented to a very specific class of proofs. Unlike LP, there is no automatic rewriting techniques inside CoQ, so the user help the prover for the use of given rules. Research towards more automation in CoQ, such as the attempt in [11], will certainly improve considerably its efficiency and the user interaction.

On another hand, the higher order of the logic supported by CoQ allows us to write more intuitive specifications of *state* and *transition*. Moreover, the choice of the state-transition model has been motivated by the fact that the $\beta$-reduction allows to implement the substitution needed for assignment. In LP, as the substitution has not been implemented, the model chosen is the weakest-predicate and the substitution is textual.

This paper presented a somewhat toy example, namely the *lift-control* protocol. CoQ and the CoQ-UNITY theory is currently used in an industrial projet, namely the mechanized verification of a telecommunication protocol based on the ATM technology.

Proof engineering is a new emerging field that requires the design of new methodologies. As for other engineering fields, the advance in knowledge comes from exchange of experiment information. Making these works public enables other people to re-use skilled methodology and results. Obviously, what we have done can be helpful for people using UNITY, LP and COQ, we claim that it should be also interesting in experiments with other provers such as PVS [25], etc., and other formalisms. such as TLA [20] or more generally temporal logic [22].

# References

1. F. Andersen. *A theorem Prover for UNITY in Higher Order Logic*. PhD thesis, Technical University of Denmark, 1992.
2. F. Andersen, K.D. Petersen, and J.S. Pettersson. Program verification using HOL-Unity. In J.J. Joyce and C.H. Seger, editors, *Proceedings sixth International Workshop on Higher Order Logic theorem proving and its applications*, volume 780 of *Lecture Notes in Computer Science*, pages 1–15, Vancouver, Canada, August 1993. Springer-Verlag.
3. D Bolignano. Towards a Mechanization of Cryptographic Protocol Verification. In *Conference On Computer-Aided Verification*, Haifa, Israël, Jun 1997. Springer-Verlag.
4. N. Brown and D. Mery. A proof environment for concurrent programs. In *In Proceedings FME'93 Symposium*, volume 670 of *Lecture Notes in Computer Science*. Springer-Verlag, 1993.
5. K. M. Chandy and J. Misra. *Parallel Program Design: A Foundation*. Addison-Wesley, 1988. ISBN 0-201-05866-9.
6. B. Chetali. *Vérification Formelle des Systèmes Parallèles décrits en UNITY à l'aide d'un outil de Démonstration Automatique*. PhD thesis, Université Henri Poincaré, Nancy I, May 1996.
7. B. Chetali and P. Lescanne. An exercise in LP: The proof of the non restoring division circuit. In U. Martin and J.M. Wing, editors, *Proceedings First International Workshop on Larch*, volume 780 of *Workshops in Computing*, pages 55–68, Dedham, Boston, August 1992. Springer-Verlag.
8. B. Chetali and P. Lescanne. Formal verification of a protocol for communications over faulty channels. In *Proc. of the 8th International Conference on Formal Description Techniques for Distributed Systems and Communications Protocols (FORTE'95)*, Montréal, Quebec, Canada, October 1995. IFIP.
9. Projet Coq. The coq proof assistant (version 6.1). Reference Manual, 1996.
10. S Coupet-Grimal and L Jakubiec. Coq and Hardward Verification : A Case Study. In J von Wright, J Grundy, and J Harrison, editors, *Theorem Proving In Higher Order Logics*, volume 1125 of *Lecture Notes in Computer Science*, pages 125–139, Turku, Finland, August 1996. Springer-Verlag.
11. P Crégut. Omega: A solver of quantifier-free problems in presburger arithmetic. Supplied in the contrib directory of Coq V6.1, 1996.
12. E. W. Dijkstra and C. S. Scholten. *Predicate Calculus and Program Semantics*. Springer-Verlag, 1989.
13. D. Doligez and G. Gonthier. Portable, unobtrusive garbage collection for multiprocessor systems. In *POPL'94*. ACM, 1994.

14. S. V. Garland and J. V. Guttag. A guide to LP, the Larch prover. Technical Report 82, Digital Systems Research Center, 130 Lytton Ave., Palo Alto, CA 94301, USA., 1991.

15. E. Giménez. *A Calculus of Infinite Constructions and its application to the verification of communicating systems*. PhD thesis, Ecole Normale Supérieure de Lyon, 1996.

16. D. M. Goldschlag. Mechanically verifying concurrent programs with the Boyer-Moore Prover. *IEEE Transactions on Software Engineering*, 16(9):1005-1022, September 1990.

17. J. V. Guttag, J.J. Horning, S.J Garland, K.D. Jones, A. Modet, and J. M. Wing. *Larch: Languages and Tools for Formal Specification*. Springer-Verlag, 1993.

18. B Heyd and P. Crégut. A modular coding of Unity in Coq. In J von Wright, J Grundy, and J Harrison, editors, *Theorem Proving in Higher Order Logic*, volume 1125 of *Lecture Notes in Computer Science*, pages 251-266, Turku, Finland, August 1996. Springer-Verlag.

19. L. Lamport. Proving the correctness of multiprocess programs. *IEEE Transactions on Software Engineering*, 3(2):125-143, 1977.

20. L. Lamport and S. Owicki. The temporal logic of actions. *ACM Transactions on Programming Languages and Systems*, 16(3):872-923, may 1994.

21. Victor Luchangco, Ekrem Söylemez, Stephen Garland, and Nancy Lynch. Verifying timing properties of concurrent algorithms. In *FORTE'94: Seventh International Conference on Formal Description Techniques*, Berne, Switzerland, October 4-7 1994. Chapman and Hall.

22. Z. Manna and A. Pnueli. *The Temporal Logic of Reactive and Concurrent Systems,Specification*. Springer-Verlag, 1991.

23. N. Mellergaard and J. Staunstrup. Generating proof obligations for circuits. In Ursula Martin and Jeannette M. Wing, editors, *First International Workshop on Larch*, pages 185-199. Springer-Verlag, July 1992.

24. J. Misra. A logic for concurrent programming. unpublished manuscripts, 1994.

25. S. Owre, J. Rushby, N. Shankar, and F. von Henke. Formal verification for fault-tolerant architectures: Prolegomena to the design of PVS. *IEEE Transactions on Software Engineering*, 21(2), February 1995.

26. C Paulin-Mohring. Circuits as Streams in Coq : Verification of a Sequential Multiplier. *Basic Research Actions "Types"*, 1995.

27. I.S.W.B. Prasetya. Error in the UNITY Substitution Rule for Subscripted Operators(Short Communication). 6(4):466-470, 1994.

28. B. A. Sanders. Eliminating the substitution axiom from UNITY logic. *Formal Aspects of Computing*, 3:189-205, 1991.

29. B Werner. *Une théorie des constructions inductives*. PhD thesis, Université Paris 7, 1994.

# ML Programming in Constructive Type Theory

Robert L. Constable

Department of Computer Science
Cornell University
Ithaca, N.Y., USA
email: rc@cs.cornell.edu

## Abstract

ML programs can be considered as the terms of a constructive type theory such as Nuprl, and the rules of the theory become a programming logic for ML. We are using such an embedding of ML to support the Ensemble fault-tolerant group communication system with the Nuprl prover. The Ensemble system is a successor to the widely used Isis system built by Ken Birman's group at Cornell and now sold by Stratus Corporation. It was first written in C, under the name Horus, and re-coded in ML as part of an effort to make it more modular and reliable by building a "reference" implementation. The ML version consists of many small protocols that can be configured into stacks for processing messages. The reference version performed so well that it has become the production system.

This talk will discuss the ML embedding into Nuprl and the type theoretic semantics this provides. It will also discuss tactic support for programming in this logical environment and how tactics are being used to support the Ensemble work. Plans to use Nuprl-Light, a light weight version of the system as a partner to Ensemble will be mentioned as well.

# Possibly Infinite Sequences in Theorem Provers: A Comparative Study

Marco Devillers[1], David Griffioen[*1,2] and Olaf Müller[†3]

[1] Computing Science Institute, University of Nijmegen, The Netherlands.
{marcod|davidg}@cs.kun.nl
[2] CWI, Amsterdam, The Netherlands, griffioe@cwi.nl
[3] Computer Science Department, Technical University Munich, Germany.
mueller@informatik.tu-muenchen.de

**Abstract.** We compare four different formalizations of possibly infinite sequences in theorem provers based on higher-order logic. The formalizations have been carried out in different proof tools, namely in Gordon's HOL, in Isabelle and in PVS. The comparison considers different logics and proof infrastructures, but emphasizes on the proof principles that are available for each approach. The different formalizations discussed have been used not only to mechanize proofs of different properties of possibly infinite sequences, but also for the verification of some non-trivial theorems of concurrency theory.

## 1 Introduction

Sequences occur frequently in all areas of computer science and mathematics. In particular, formal models of distributed systems often employ (possibly infinite) sequences to describe system behavior over time, *e.g.* TLA [Lam94] or I/O automata [LT89]. Recently, there is a growing interest in using theorem provers not only to verify properties of systems described in such a model, but also to formalize (parts of) the model itself in a theorem prover. For this reason, formalizations of possibly infinite sequences in proof tools are needed.

In this paper, we compare a number of such formalizations, which were carried out in theorem provers based on higher-order logic. We compare to what extent the formalizations have been worked out, and draw conclusions on general applicability. In the comparison we consider the following representative requirements on the datatype of possibly infinite sequences: A predicate *finite* characterizes finite sequences, operations on sequences include *hd, tl, map, length, concat* (also known as *append*), *filter* (removal of elements) and *flatten* (concatenation of possibly infinitely many finite sequences).

In particular, *filter* and *flatten* are chosen, because defining them and reasoning about them turned out to be rather complicated in various formalizations,

[*] Research supported by the Netherlands Organization for Scientific Research (NWO) under contract SION 612-316-125
[†] Research supported by BMBF, *KorSys*

especially because of their result depend on infinite calculations. These functions are especially motivated by concurrency theory: for abstraction and modularity purposes, internal messages are often hidden in behaviors using the *filter* function. The *flatten* function is required for proofs about system refinement, where infinitely many steps of a system may be simulated by finite behaviors.

The following four approaches are evaluated and compared:

- HOL-FUN: Sequences are defined as functions by $(\alpha)\mathsf{seq} = \mathsf{N} \rightarrow (\alpha)\mathsf{option}$, where the datatype $(\alpha)\mathsf{option} \equiv \mathsf{None} \mid \mathsf{Some}(\alpha)$ is used to incorporate finite sequences into the model: None denotes a "non-existing" element. This approach has been taken by Nipkow, Slind and Müller [NS95, MN97], where it has been used to formalize parts of I/O automata meta-theory. It has been carried out in Isabelle/HOL [Pau94].

- HOL-SUM: Sequences are defined as the disjoint sum of finite and infinite sequences: $(\alpha)\mathsf{seq} \equiv \mathsf{FinSeq}((\alpha)\mathsf{list}) \mid \mathsf{InfSeq}(\mathsf{N} \rightarrow \alpha)$. Here $(\alpha)\mathsf{list}$ stands for ordinary finite lists. This approach has been taken by Chou and Peled [CP96] in the verification of a partial-order reduction technique for model checking and by Agerholm [Age94] as an example of his formalization of domain theory. Both versions have been carried out independently from each other in Gordon's HOL [GM93].

- PVS-FUN: Sequences are defined as functions from a downward closed subset of N, where the cardinality of the subset corresponds to the length of the sequence. This is achieved by the dependent product $(S \in \mathbb{I} \times (S \rightarrow \alpha))$, where $\mathbb{I} \subseteq \wp(\mathsf{N})$ denotes the set of all downward closed subsets of N. This approach has been taken by Devillers and Griffioen [DG97], who also formalized I/O automata meta-theory. It has been carried out in PVS [ORSH95].

- HOL-LCF: In domain theory, sequences can be defined by the simple recursive domain equation $(\alpha)\mathsf{seq} \equiv \mathsf{nil} \mid (\alpha) : (\alpha)\mathsf{seq}$, where the "cons"-operator : is strict in the first and lazy in its second argument. This approach has been taken by Müller and Nipkow [MN97] as a continuation of the first approach, as that one caused some difficulties that will be sketched later on. It has been carried out in Isabelle/HOLCF [Reg95].

The aim of every formalization is a rich enough collection of theorems, such that independence on the specific model is reached. As this, up to our experience, will not completely be possible, we focus our comparison on the proof principles that are offered by the respective approaches. Their usability, applicability and degree of automation are especially essential for the user of the sequence package and influence proof length considerably. In addition, specific features of the tools and of the respective logics are taken into account.

## 2  Theorem Provers and Logics

In this section we summarize the distinguishing aspects of the different tools used, as far as they are relevant to the sequence formalizations.

## 2.1 The different Logics

**Isabelle/HOL and Gordon's HOL.** Gordon's HOL [GM93] is a theorem prover for higher-order logic developed according to the LCF approach [Pau87]. Isabelle [Pau94] is a *generic* theorem prover that supports a number of logics, among them first-order logic (FOL), Zermelo-Fränkel set theory (ZF), constructive type theory (CTT), higher-order logic (HOL), and others. As Isabelle/HOL and Gordon's HOL are similar, we will in general not distinguish between them and refer to both of them as HOL. Both logics are based on Church's formulation of simple type theory [Chu40], which has been augmented by a ML-style polymorphism and extension mechanisms for defining new constants and types. The following section gives a quick overview, mainly of the notation we use.

*Types.* The syntax of types is given by $\sigma ::= v \mid (\sigma_1, ..., \sigma_n)op$ where $\sigma, \sigma_1, ..., \sigma_n$ range over types, $v$ ranges over type *variables*, and $op$ ranges over $n$-ary type *operators* $(n \geq 0)$. Greek letters (e.g. $\alpha, \beta$) are generally used for type variables, and sans serif identifiers (e.g. list, option) are used for type operators. In this paper, we use the type constants $N$ and $\mathbb{B}$, denoting natural numbers and booleans, and the type operators $\rightarrow$ for the function space and $\times$ for the cartesian product.

*Terms.* The syntax of terms is given by $M ::= c \mid v \mid (MN) \mid \lambda v.M$ where $c$ ranges over constants, $v$ ranges over variables, and $M$ and $N$ range over terms. Sans serif identifiers (e.g. a,b,c) and non-alphabetical symbols (e.g. $\Rightarrow$, $=$, $\forall$) are generally used for constants, and italic identifiers (e.g. $x,y,z$) are used for variables. Every term in HOL denotes a *total* function and has to be *well-typed*. HOL incorporates Hilbert's choice operator $\varepsilon$ as a primitive constant.

**HOLCF.** HOLCF [Reg95] conservatively extends Isabelle/HOL with concepts of domain theory such as complete partial orders, continuous functions and a fixed point operator. As a consequence, the logic of the original LCF tool [Pau87] constitutes a proper sublanguage of HOLCF.

HOLCF uses Isabelle's *type classes*, similar to Haskell, to distinguish between HOL and LCF types. A type class is a constraint on a polymorphic variable restricting it to the class of types fulfilling certain requirements.

For example, there is a type class $\alpha :: $ po (partial order) that restricts the class of all types $\alpha$ of the universal type class term of HOL to those for which the constant $\sqsubseteq: \alpha \times \alpha \rightarrow \mathbb{B}$ is reflexive, transitive and antisymmetric. Showing that a particular type is an *instance* of this type class, requires to prove the properties above for this particular definition of the symbol $\sqsubseteq$. Once this proof has been done, Isabelle can use this semantic information during static type checking.

The default type class of HOLCF is pcpo (pointed complete partial order), which is a subclass of po, equipped with a least element $\perp$ and demanding completeness for $\sqsubseteq$. There is a special type for continuous functions between pcpos. Elements of this type are called *operations*, the type constructor is denoted by $\rightarrow_c$, in contrast to the standard HOL constructor $\rightarrow$. Abstraction and application of continuous functions is denoted by $\Lambda$ (instead of $\lambda$) and $f`t$ (instead of

$f\ t$). The fixed point operator $\mathit{fix} : (\alpha :: \mathsf{pcpo} \to_c \alpha) \to_c \alpha$ enjoys the fixed point property $\mathit{fix}\,f = f(\mathit{fix}\,f)$. Note that the requirement of continuity is incorporated in the type of $\mathit{fix}$ ($\to_c$ instead of $\to$). This illuminates the fact, that checking continuity in HOLCF is only a matter of automatic type checking, as far as terms belong to the proper LCF sublanguage ($\Lambda$ abstractions and ' applications). HOLCF includes a datatype package that allows the definition of domains by recursive equations.

**PVS Logic.** Similar to HOL, the PVS logic [ORSH95] is based on higher order logic, but type expressions are more expressive, featuring set theoretic semantics. Whereas HOL only allows simple types, PVS offers mechanisms for *subtyping* and *dependent types*. Again, we only give a quick overview, mainly clarifying syntax.

Subtyping is expressed with the usual set notation, e.g., $\{n \in \mathbb{N}\,.\,even(n)\}$ is the set of all even natural numbers. The dependent sum $(x : A \times B_x)$ – in which the second component $B_x$ depends on a member $x$ of the first set $A$ – denotes the set of all pairs $(a, b)$ where $a \in A$ and $b \in B_a$. For example, if $S^i$ denotes a sequence of length $i$ then members of $(i : \mathbb{N} \times \{a, b, c\}^i)$ would be $(2, ab)$ and $(3, bac)$. A dependent product $(x : A \to B_x)$ denotes all functions $f$ where if $a \in A$ then $f(a) \in B_a$. For example, if $f$ is a member of the dependent product $(i : \mathbb{N} \to \{a, b, c\}^i)$, then $f(2) = ab$ and $f(3) = acb$ would be type-correct. Furthermore, we use $\pi_0$ and $\pi_1$ for the left- and right-hand projection in a tuple, e.g., $\pi_0((a, b)) = a$.

Whereas the general type checking problem in HOL is decidable, in PVS it is not. The PVS system solves this problem by generating type correctness conditions (TCCs) for those checks it cannot resolve automatically.

Similar to HOL, the specification language of PVS is organized into theories and datatypes, which, in contrast to HOL, can be parameterized by types and constants. This enables an easy handling of generic theories. HOL's type variables and Isabelle's type classes offer a similar mechanism.

## 2.2 Design Philosophies and Tool Specifics

Both Gordon's HOL and Isabelle/HOL, were developed according to the LCF-system approach [Pau87], which ensures soundness of extensions to the logic. The main idea of the LCF approach is to use abstract data types to derive proofs. Predefined values of a data type corresponded to instances of axioms, and the operations correspond to inference rules. By using a strictly typed language, wherefore ML was developed, theorem security is assured.

PVS, however, is a closed tool. There is no document that describes the exact syntax and semantics of the PVS logic, which is hardwired in the tool. On the other hand, PVS features a tight integration of rewriting and various decision procedures (*e.g.* for arithmetic and propositional logic based on BDDs), which results in a high degree of automation. This is in particular an advantage in comparison to Isabelle/HOL, which in the present version does not offer effective support for arithmetic.

# 3 HOL-Fun: Functions in Isabelle/HOL

**Definition 1 (Type of Sequences).** Sequences are defined by the type

$$(\alpha)\mathsf{seq} = \mathbb{N} \to (\alpha)\mathsf{option}$$

using the option datatype defined as: $(\alpha)\mathsf{option} = \mathsf{None} \mid \mathsf{Some}(\alpha)$. None denotes "nonexisting" elements and is used to model finite sequences. To avoid the case in which None appears within a sequence – otherwise the representation would not be unique – the predicate

$$is\_sequence(s) = (\forall i.s(i) = \mathsf{None} \Rightarrow s(i+1) = \mathsf{None})$$

is introduced, which has to hold for every sequence. Sequences therefore can be regarded as a quotient structure, where *is_sequence* characterizes the normal form of each equivalence class. Of course, every operation has to yield a term in normal form. This is the main disadvantage of this approach, as it is not straightforward to construct the normal form for *e.g.* the *filter* function, which will be discussed below.

**Definition 2 (Basic Operations).** Functions on sequences are defined pointwise. This is especially simple if the output length is equal to the input length (as for *map*) or if it can easily be computed from it (as for $\oplus$ ).

$$
\begin{aligned}
&\mathsf{nil} &&= \lambda i.\mathsf{None} &&hd(s) &&= s(0)\\
&tl(s) &&= \lambda i.s(i+1) &&len(s) &&= \sharp\{i\,.\,s(i) \neq \mathsf{None}\}\\
&map\,f\,s &&= f \circ s &&s \oplus t &&= \lambda i.\,\text{if } i < len(s) \text{ then } s(i) \text{ else } t(i - len(s))
\end{aligned}
$$

where the codomain for *len* and $\sharp$ (cardinality) are the natural numbers, extended by an infinity element: $\mathbb{N}^\infty = \mathsf{Fin}(\mathbb{N})|\mathsf{Inf}$. Arithmetic operations and relations (as *e.g.* $-, <$ have been extended accordingly.

**Definition 3 (Filter).** Filtering is divided into two steps: first, $proj : (\alpha)\mathsf{seq} \to (\alpha)\mathsf{seq}$ replaces every element not satisfying $P$ by None, then the resulting sequence is brought into normal form. Normalization is achieved by an index transformation $it : \mathbb{N} \to \mathbb{N}$, that has to meet three requirements: first, normalization has to maintain the ordering of the elements, second, every Some$(a)$ has to appear in the normal form, and third, if there is a None in the normal form, then there will be no Some afterwards. These requirements can directly serve as the definition for $it$ using Hilbert's description operator $\varepsilon$.

$$
\begin{aligned}
proj\,P\,s &= \lambda i.\,\mathsf{case}\ s(i)\ \mathsf{of}\ \mathsf{None} \Rightarrow \mathsf{None}\\
&\qquad\qquad\quad\mid \mathsf{Some}(a) \Rightarrow \text{if } P(a) \text{ then } \mathsf{Some}(a) \text{ else } \mathsf{None}\\
it(s) &= \varepsilon\, it.\ monotone(it) \wedge\\
&\qquad \forall i\,.\,s(i) \neq \mathsf{None} \Rightarrow i \in range(it) \wedge\\
&\qquad is\_sequence(s \circ it)\\
NF(s) &= s \circ it(s)\\
filter\,P\,s &= NF \circ (proj\,P\,s)
\end{aligned}
$$

The definition for *it* is a nice requirement specification, but it is not simple to work with it, as for every $\varepsilon x.P(x)$ the existence of an $x$ satisfying $P$ has to be shown. Theoretically, this can be done using proof by contradiction, as we are in a classical logic, but it was not obvious how to do this in this case. In practice, an explicit construction seemed to be unavoidable.

One reason why Müller and Nipkow stopped this sequence formalization at this point [MN97] and changed to a formalization in HOLCF was the complexity of this construction. A second reason was the unsufficient support for arithmetic, provided by Isabelle/HOL up to now, as reasoning about normal forms heavily involves index calculations. However, a version without normal forms has been successfully used to model parts of the meta-theory of I/O-automata [NS95].

Anyway, it will turn out, that the PVS approach is very close to the one presented here, so that an impression of the practicability can be gained from the experiences that have been made there. In particular, *it* reappears in the PVS approach in a very similar fashion, and an explicit construction of it will be presented in that context.

## 4 HOL-SUM: Lists and Functions in Gordon's HOL

Chou and Peled [CP96] use a disjoint union type of a list for finite sequences, and a function from the natural numbers for infinite sequences.

**Definition 4 (Type of Sequences).**

$$(\alpha)\mathsf{seq} = \mathsf{FinSeq}((\alpha)\mathsf{list}) \mid \mathsf{InfSeq}(\mathbb{N} \to \alpha)$$

An advantage of this approach is that no normalization of elements in this type is needed. A disadvantage is that a number of the operators on sequences are implemented twice, once in case the argument is a finite sequence, and once in the infinite case.

**Definition 5 (Basic Operations).** For instance, consider the length *len* and *tl* functions shown below.

$$len(\mathsf{FinSeq}\ l) = \mathsf{Fin}(len\ l)$$
$$len(\mathsf{InfSeq}\ f) = \mathsf{Inf}$$

$$tl(\mathsf{FinSeq}\ l) = TL\ l$$
$$tl(\mathsf{InfSeq}\ f) = \mathsf{InfSeq}(\lambda i\ .\ f(i+1))$$

In the above definitions, the length function returns an element in $\mathbb{N}^\infty$. The *tl* function is defined twice, for finite sequences the usual *TL* operator on lists is used, and for infinite sequences it uses a transposition function.

Whenever it is not easy to define a sequence in such a way, Chou and Peled make use of under-specified functions from the natural number to the data set. Such functions are not specified for all arguments greater than the length of a sequence. A conversion function *seq*, which takes a number $n : \mathbb{N}^\infty$ and such a function $f$ as arguments, constructs the corresponding sequence to $f$ of length $n$. In the definition below, *genlist f n* is the finite list of the first $n$ values $f(1), \ldots, f(n)$.

$$seq(\text{Fin } n)(f) = \text{FinSeq}(genlist\ f\ n)$$
$$seq(\text{Inf})(f) \quad = \text{InfSeq}(f)$$

For instance, the concatenation function, which takes two sequence arguments, is defined by means of this function. If this function were defined using normal case distinctions on the arguments, one would need four cases.

$$s \oplus t = seq\ (len(s) + len(t))\ (\lambda i\ .\ \text{if } i < len(s) \text{ then } nth\ s\ i \text{ else } nth\ t\ (i - len(s)))$$

**Definition 6 (Filter).** Chou and Peled define the *filter* function as the limit of an ascending chain of finite sequences according to the prefix ordering $\sqsubseteq$ on sequences. Below the definitions of chains and limits are given. The argument of both functions is a variable $c$ of type $\mathbb{N} \to (\alpha)\text{list}$.

$$chain(c) = (\forall j\ .\ (c\ j) \sqsubseteq (c\ (j + 1)))$$

$$limit(c) \ = seq\ (lub\ (\lambda n\ .\ \exists j\ .\ n = len(c\ j)))\ (\lambda i\ .\ nth\ (c\ (least(\lambda j\ .\ i < len(c\ j))))\ i)$$

The chain function is a predicate which states that $c$ is a chain iff all the elements satisfy the prefix ordering. The limit function returns the sequence *seq* where the length is the least upper bound *lub* of all lengths in the chain, and the $i$-th element in a sequence (if any) is the $i$-element of the first sequence in the chain which holds at least $i$ elements.

The filter function then is defined as the limit of all projections on initial segments of a given argument.

$$FilterChain(p)(s)(j) = \text{FinSeq}(FILTER(p)(list(take\ s\ j)))$$

$$filter(p)(s) \qquad = limit(FilterChain(p)(s))$$

The function *FilterChain* produces a chain of lists where the $j$-th element in such a list is the projection of $p$ on the first $j$ elements of $s$. For instance, when filtering all even numbers out of the sequence $(1, 4, 9, 16, 25, \ldots)$ the resulting chain will be nil $\sqsubseteq$ (4) $\sqsubseteq$ (4) $\sqsubseteq$ (4, 16) $\sqsubseteq \ldots$. The limit of this chain is, of course, the infinite sequence of squares of even numbers.

Properties proven about these limits include that every sequence is the limit of the chain of all of its finite prefixes, and that concatenation is continuous in its right argument, in the sense of Scott's topology. Theorems proven about the *filter* function include that *filter* distributes over concatenation when the first argument is a finite sequence. The *flatten* function has not been defined in this setting; however, a construction similar to *filter* would be necessary.

**Definition 7 (Proof Principles).** The basic proof principles are structural induction on finite lists and extensionality for infinite sequences. Using *seq*, proofs have to be split up as follows:

$$\frac{(\forall n, f\ .\ P(seq\ (\text{Fin } n)\ f)) \qquad (\forall g\ .\ P(seq\ \text{Inf}\ g))}{\forall y\ .\ P(y)}$$

The following more general extensionality proof principle is also available:

$$\frac{len(x) = len(y) \wedge (\forall i < len(x) . nth \, x \, i = nth \, y \, i)}{x = y}$$

For particular functions as *filter* and $\oplus$, the notions of chains, limits and sometimes continuity are used to prove equality of sequences only by proving their equality for all finite sequences.

After writing the paper we became aware of [Age94], where Agerholm takes the same approach as Chou and Peled, but in a more domain theoretic style and to a much greater extent.

## 5 PVS-FUN: Functions in PVS

The specification of possibly infinite sequences in PVS by Devillers and Griffioen made use of dependent types. In this manner, sequences are defined as functions from downward closed subsets of the natural numbers to a data set. Below, the definition of the set of all downward closed sets, called index sets, $\mathbb{I}$ is given.

$$\mathbb{I} = \{S \in \wp(\mathbb{N}) . (\forall i \in S, j \in \mathbb{N} . j < i \Rightarrow j \in S)\}$$

In the case of finite sequences, the domain of such a function will be an initial segment of the natural numbers which can be constructed with the *below* function (for any $n \in \mathbb{N}$, $below(n)$ is the set of the first $n$ natural numbers $\{0, \dots, n-1\}$). In case of infinite sequences, the domain of the sequence is the set of natural numbers $\mathbb{N}$. Note, that $\mathbb{I}$ is isomorphic to $\mathbb{N}^\infty$. In the following, $\lfloor S \rfloor$ denotes the smallest element of the set $S$.

The definition of possibly infinite sequences is given as a dependent product of an index set, and a mapping from that index set to the data set. The sets of finite and infinite sequences are defined with the use of predicate subtyping.

**Definition 8 (Type of Sequences).**

$$A^\infty = (S \in \mathbb{I} \times (S \to A))$$
$$A^\star = \{x \in A^\infty . finite(\pi_0(x))\}$$
$$A^\omega = \{x \in A^\infty . \neg finite(\pi_0(x))\}$$

Note that a tuple of a set and a function is used in this implementation because there does not exists a domain operator in PVS (an operator returning the domain of a given function). In the rest of the paper, we will write $dom(x)$ for the domain of a sequence $x$, and $x(i)$ for the $i$-th element in such a sequence.

Simple operators are defined in a straightforward fashion. What is practical about these definitions is that no distinction is made between finite or infinite sequences in the mappings used. As a result, during some proofs no explicit split in reasoning is needed between finite and strictly infinite sequences.

However, sometimes it is needed to make that distinction to derive the appropriate domain for a function. Please consider, for instance, the concatenation operator $\oplus$ defined in the list below.

**Definition 9 (Basic Operations).**

$$
\begin{array}{ll}
nil & : A^* \\
nil & = (\emptyset, f) \text{ where } f \in \emptyset \to A \\[1ex]
len & : A^* \to \mathbb{N} \\
len(x) & = \sharp dom(x) \\[1ex]
map & : (A \to B) \to A^\infty \to B^\infty \\
map(f)(x) & = (dom(x), (\lambda i : dom(x).f(x(i)))) \\[1ex]
\oplus & : A^* \times A^\infty \to A^\infty \\
x \oplus y & = (S, (\lambda i : S. \text{ if } i < l \text{ then } x(i) \text{ else } y(i - l) \text{ fi })) \\
\text{where} & l = len(x), S = \text{ if } finite(y) \text{ then } below(l + len(y)) \text{ else } \mathbb{N} \text{ fi}
\end{array}
$$

The filter function is basically defined with the use of an enumeration function on ordered sets. Let $W(S, x)$ be the witness set of all indexes $i$ which satisfy $x(i) \in S$, and let $it_{S'}$ be the enumerated sequence of elements of the ordered countable set $S'$. Then $x \circ it_{W(S,x)}$ is a filtered sequence. For example, suppose one wants to filter all symbols $a$ in the sequence $x = (b, a, a, b, a, \ldots)$. Then $W(\{a\}, x) = \{1, 2, 4, \ldots\}$, and $it_{W(\{a\},x)}$ is the sequence $(1, 2, 4, \ldots)$. Therefore, $x \circ it_{W(\{a\},x)} = (b, a, a, b, a, \ldots) \circ (1, 2, 4, \ldots) = (a, a, a, \ldots)$.

**Definition 10 (Filter).**

$$
\begin{array}{ll}
W(S, x) & = \{i \in dom(x) \mid x(i) \in S\} \\[1ex]
\tilde{S} & = \text{ if } finite(S) \text{ then } below(\sharp(S)) \text{ else } \mathbb{N} \text{ fi} \\[1ex]
S^{-0} & = S \\[1ex]
S^{-(n+1)} & = \begin{cases} \emptyset & , S^{-n} = \emptyset \\ S^{-n} \backslash \lfloor S^{-n} \rfloor & , \text{ otherwise} \end{cases} \\[1ex]
it_S(i) & = \lfloor S^{-i} \rfloor \\[1ex]
filter(S, x) & = (\tilde{W}(S, x), x \circ it_{W(S,x)})
\end{array}
$$

Although most proofs concerning sequence operators are simple in this setting, a proof of even a simple property about *filter* is complicated (which in a similar fashion is expected for *flatten* that has not been formalized yet). Proofs performed about *filter* include proofs that the *it* function is a monotonic bijective function, and of the primitive recursive characterization of *filter*:

$filter_S(a \hat{\ } x) = \text{ if } a \in S \text{ then } a \hat{\ } filter_S x \text{ else } filter_S x \text{ fi}$

**Definition 11 (Proof Principles).** The most used proof principle in this setting is called extensionality, point-to-point wise equality

$$
\frac{dom(x) = dom(y) \land (\forall i \in dom(x) . x(i) = y(i))}{x = y}
$$

As a corollary, we would like to mention that properties over down-ward closed subsets of the natural numbers can easily be proven with a generalized induction scheme on these subsets. Let $S$ be a down-ward closed subset of the natural numbers then

$$\frac{((0 \in S \Rightarrow p(0)) \wedge (\forall (n+1) \in S . p(n) \Rightarrow p(n+1)))}{(\forall n \in S . p(n))}$$

For finite sequences, also structural inductions rules and induction to the length of sequences are given.

# 6 HOL-LCF: Domain Theory in Isabelle/HOL

**Definition 12 (Type of Sequences).** Using the HOLCF datatype package sequences are defined by the simple recursive domain equation

$$\mathbf{domain} \, (\alpha)\mathsf{Seq} = \mathsf{nil} \mid (\alpha) \star (\mathbf{lazy} \, (\alpha)\mathsf{Seq})$$

where nil and the "cons"-operator $\star$ are the constructors of the datatype. By default domain constructors are strict, therefore $\star$ is strict in its first argument and lazy in the second. This means, that elements of the type $(\alpha)\mathsf{Seq}$ come in three flavors:

- Finite total sequences: $a_1 \star \ldots \star a_n \star \mathsf{nil}$
- Finite partial sequences: $a_1 \star \ldots \star a_n \star \bot$
- Infinite sequences: $a_1 \star a_2 \star a_3 \ldots$

The domain package automatically proves a number of user-relevant theorems, *e.g.* concerning the constructors, discriminators, and selectors of the datatype.

**Sequence Elements in HOL.** Domain definitions, like $(\alpha)\mathsf{Seq}$, require the argument type $\alpha$ to be in type class pcpo. However, in Müller's case, domains are appropriate for recursively defining sequences, but *elements* in sequences are often easier to handle in a total fashion, as types of class **term**. Therefore types of class **term** are lifted to *flat domains* using the type constructor lift:

$$(\alpha)\mathsf{lift} = \mathsf{Undef} \mid \mathsf{Def}(\alpha)$$

Here, both $\alpha$ and $(\alpha)\mathsf{lift}$ are elements of **term**, but by adding the two definitions

$$\bot = \mathsf{Undef}$$
$$x \sqsubseteq y = (x = y) \mid x = \mathsf{Undef}$$

and proving the properties of a complete partial order with a least element, $(\alpha)\mathsf{lift}$ becomes an instance of pcpo. Note that $\bot$ and $\sqsubseteq$ are overloaded and this definition only fixes their meaning at type $(\alpha)\mathsf{lift}$. In the sequel, $\bot$ is written instead of Undef.

Sequences are now defined as $(\alpha)\mathsf{seq} = ((\alpha)\mathsf{lift})\mathsf{Seq}$ and a new "cons"-operator for elements of type class **term** is introduced: $x \hat{\ } xs = (\mathsf{Def} \, x) \star xs$. Using the lift constructor has several advantages:

- If sequence elements do not need support for infinity or undefinedness, we are not forced to press the overhead of domain theory into them, but lift them as late as possible to a domain, just when it is really needed.
- Many datatypes are well supported in HOL, *e.g.* lists or natural numbers. We can make reuse of these theories, theorem libraries, and tailored proof procedures.
- Within the new "cons"-operator $x\hat{}xs$ the Def constructor serves as an implicit tag showing definedness of an element. As we will show later with an example, this simplifies or even eliminates reasoning about the $\bot$ case.

Besides lifting basic types it is necessary to lift also domains and codomains of functions, built by the type constructor $\to$. Furthermore the automatic proof support for continuity has to be extended. Details can be found in [MN97, MS96].

**Definition 13 (Basic Operations).** Operations are defined as fixed points, from which recursive equations are derived automatically. For example, *map* has type

$$map \;:\; (\alpha \to \beta) \to (\alpha)\mathsf{seq} \to_c (\beta)\mathsf{seq}$$

and the following rewrite rules

$$map \; f'\bot = \bot$$
$$map \; f'\mathsf{nil} = \mathsf{nil}$$
$$map \; f'(x\hat{}xs) = f(x)\hat{}map \; f'xs$$

are automatically derived from the definition

$$map \; f = fix'(\Lambda h.\Lambda s \,.\, \mathsf{case} \; s \; \mathsf{of} \; \mathsf{nil} \Rightarrow \mathsf{nil}$$
$$\mid (x\hat{}xs) \Rightarrow f(x)\hat{}(h'xs))$$

According to domain theory, the argument of *fix* in this definition has to be a continuous function in order to guarantee the existence of the least fixed point. This continuity requirement is handled automatically by type checking, as every occuring function is constructed using the continuous function type $\to_c$.

Note, that the derived recursive equations are just the algebraic definitions of the corresponding functions for finite lists, extended for the $\bot$ case. Therefore, informally speaking, defining operations on finite lists smoothly carries over to infinite lists.

**Definition 14 (Filter and Flatten).** All other operations are defined likewise easily. This is especially remarkable for the *filter* and *flatten* operations that would cause some trouble especially in the functional formalizations:

$$filter \;:\; (\alpha \to \mathbb{B}) \to (\alpha)\mathsf{seq} \to_c (\alpha)\mathsf{seq}$$
$$filter \; P'\bot = \bot$$
$$filter \; P'\mathsf{nil} = \mathsf{nil}$$
$$filter \; P'(x\hat{}xs) = \mathsf{if} \; P(x) \; \mathsf{then} \; x\hat{}filter \; P'xs \; \mathsf{else} \; filter \; P'xs$$

Flatten is defined in a similar simple fashion. Note, that these fixed point definitions incorporate the intuition of computability. Therefore, lemmas like *filter* $P(x \oplus y) =$ *filter* $P x \oplus$ *filter* $P y$ do not only hold for finite $x$. Consider the example $P = (\lambda x.x = a)$, $x = (a, b, b, b, ......)$ and $y = (a, a, a, a....)$. Whereas in HOL-LCF the mentioned lemma would hold (because $(a, \bot) = (a, \bot)$), in other formalizations this lemma would not $((a, \text{nil}) = (a, a, a...))$.

**Definition 15 (Proof Principles).** The proof principles that are discussed in the following are all automatically proved by the HOLCF datatype package.

A very strong proof principle is **structural induction**, as it allows one to reason about infinite sequences, as if they were finite, modulo an admissibility requirement:

$$\frac{adm(P) \quad P(\bot) \quad P(\text{nil}) \quad (\forall x, xs . P(xs) \Rightarrow P(x \hat{\ } xs))}{\forall y.P(y)} \quad (1)$$

Note, how Def serves here as an implicit tag for definedness: In the equivalent rule for $(\alpha)$Seq the last assumption of this rule would be $(\forall x, xs . x \neq \bot \wedge P(xs) \Rightarrow P(x \star xs))$. The nasty case distinction $x \neq \bot$ can be omitted, as $(\text{Def } x) \neq \bot$ and $x \hat{\ } xs = (\text{Def } x) \star xs$.

A predicate $P$ is defined to be admissible, denoted by $adm(P)$, if it holds for the least upper bound of every chain satisfying $P$. However, in practice, one rather uses a syntactic criterion (see *e.g.* [Pau87]): Roughly, it states that if $P$, reduced to conjunctive normal form, contains no existential quantifier or negation, admissibility of $P$ boils down to continuity of all functions occuring in $P$. Therefore, if one stays within the LCF sublanguage, admissibility in theses cases can be proven automatically, *i.e.* we get the proof of the infinite case for free. The following exceptions and extensions of the rough guideline above are especially useful when trying to satisfy the syntactic criterion: Firstly, $t(x) \not\sqsubseteq c$ and $t(x) \neq \bot$ are admissible in $x$, if $t$ is continuous. Secondly, predicates over chain-finite domains are admissible, and finally, substitution maintains admissibility.

Besides (1) and conventional fixed point induction, there are also weaker structural induction rules, that do not need admissibility, namely for the finite case

$$\frac{P(\text{nil}) \quad (\forall x, xs . P(xs) \wedge finite(xs) \Rightarrow P(x \hat{\ } xs))}{\forall y . finite(y) \Rightarrow P(y)}$$

and an analogous rule for the partial case. Furthermore, the **take lemma**

$$\frac{\forall n.take\, n^{\,\iota}x = take\, n^{\,\iota}y}{x = y}$$

and the **bisimulation** rule, that follows easily from the take lemma, are available:

$$\frac{bisim R \quad R(x, y)}{x = y}$$

where $bisim\, R = \forall x, y.R(x, y) \Rightarrow$
$\quad (x = \bot \Rightarrow y = \bot) \wedge$
$\quad (x = \text{nil} \Rightarrow y = \text{nil}) \wedge$
$\quad (\exists a, x'.x = a \hat{\ } x' \Rightarrow \exists b, y'.y = b \hat{\ } y' \wedge R(x', y') \wedge a = b)$

# 7 Comparison

**Comparing the functional Approaches.** As mentioned earlier, HOL-FUN and PVS-FUN are similar to the extent that they both use functions to define sequences. To achieve this common goal, two complementary ways are chosen: Whereas HOL-FUN *extends* the *codomain* of the function by the element None modeling partiality, PVS-FUN *restricts* the *domain* of the function. Therefore, the main proof principle within such a setting is extensionality. Since the approaches are very similar and HOL-FUN (at least the version including normal forms) has not been extensively studied, we will concentrate on the experiences made with PVS-FUN.

**Experiences with PVS-FUN.** It turned out that the extensionality principle works very well for the standard operators, since these operators often only perform but simple index transformations on their arguments. As an example, consider the concatenation operator $\oplus$ in the PVS-FUN section. Because these index transformations often involve simple linear expressions, and the PVS prover has considerable support for linear arithmetic, most proofs are done with a minimum of human guidance, typically by just expanding the definitions involved. However, the definition of *filter* was tedious, and proofs of basic properties about it were very hard, since this involved more than just reasoning over basic index transformations. In conclusion, the definition given seems to be too ad-hoc. An approach where in a more general fashion definitions can be given, together with matching proof principles, should be the focus of future research for such a formalization.

**Experiences with HOL-SUM.** The HOL-SUM approach is a pragmatic mixture of algebraic lists for finite sequences and functions for infinite sequences. Equality of sequences therefore can be proven with structural induction for the finite case, and function equality in the infinite case. Therefore proofs show a twofold character. The *filter* function, however, still is a problem, as there the two representations have to be related, since *filter* may produce either finite or infinite sequences from an infinite one. For this reason, notions of chains, limits and continuity were introduced, which in [CP96], however, are only used for proofs about specific functions, whereas general proof principles involving continuity are not developed. Agerholm [Age94] takes this step and carries over the whole world of domain theory to this setting. Agerholm concludes that his development of sequences was long and tedious (50 pages of 70 lines each) and in his opinion rather an "ad-hoc approach". The main difficulties arise from a threefold definition of $\sqsubseteq$ — both sequences finite, both infinite, and finite/infinite — which results in several versions of every single fact throughout the whole development.

**Experiences with HOL-LCF.** HOL-LCF employs domain theory to extend algebraic lists to infinity, so that a uniform approach is obtained. Of the formalizations discussed, it is the most powerful formalization incorporating a number of proof principles, and the largest body of proven lemmata. However, at first sight it seems that domain theory has two drawbacks: all types must denote domains; all functions must be continuous. But the first requirement can effectively be relaxed by the ($\alpha$)lift type constructor. And the latter rather offers advantages than disadvantages. Firstly, arbitrary recursion can be defined by fixed points. Unfortunately, this means also that definitions of non-continuous functions are delicate, *e.g.* the fair merge function cannot be defined without leaving the LCF sublanguage. Secondly, continuity extends the familiar structural induction rule to infinite objects for free, at least for equations about lazy lists. For general formulae a rather liberal syntactic criterion exists. Here, Müller's experience in formalizing I/O automata was quite encouraging: in almost all cases it was possible (sometimes by reformulating the goal) to satisfy this criterion or to get by with the finite induction rule. In the remaining cases, it seems not to be advisable to prove admissibility via its definition, as this then often becomes the hardest part of the entire proof. Instead, one should switch to other proof principles, that do not require admissibility. These are the take-lemma (which is similar to extensionality), or bisimulation. For these principles a corecursive characterization of the operators would be useful in order to automate coinductive proofs, that usually – compare the experiences by Paulson [Pau97] – involve more case distinctions than the inductive proofs.

**Overall Evaluation.** In conclusion, we may distinguish three basic proof schemata for sequences: extensionality (point-wise equality), rules using admissibility or at least continuity, and bisimulation. The first of the three principles turned out to be inconvenient in practice to prove equalities of arbitrary functions. The second principle is strong, but builds on top of an extensive theory: In HOLCF this theory is provided, for HOL-SUM it would be a lot of work to incorporate these notions in a more general fashion. Experience with the application of the bisimulation principle to sequences seems to be rather preliminary (see also next section). Of course, it should be possible to derive all three proof principles in every setting. However, proof principles can only easily be applied when corresponding definitions or characterizations of the occuring functions exist. It is not known, for instance, whether it is easy to derive coalgebraic lemmata from definitions given in a functional manner.

**Related Work.** Concerning coalgebraic approaches, there is, up to our knowledge, no published work on a coalgebraic formalization with an equally large body of lemmata as the formalizations discussed. Paulson [Pau97] provided a mechanization of coinduction and corecursion in Isabelle/HOL – independent of domain theory –, which he applied also to the formalization of lazy lists. Unfortunately, the *filter* function – which indeed turned out to be very crucial – has not been mechanized there. Leclerc and Paulin-Mohring use Coq to formalize possibly infinite sequences coalgebraically as well [LPM93]. A problem is that they cannot express the *filter* function, as it does not fit into their *constructive* framework. Hensel and Jacobs [HJ97] showed how to obtain inductive and coinductive proof principles for datatypes with iterated recursion from a categorical analysis. They formalized a number of these datatypes in PVS and have also some promising recent results in formalizing coalgebraic possibly-infinite sequences. Recently, Feferman [Fef96] developed a recursion theory and applied it to the formalization of sequences. Similar to HOL-LCF, his solution incorporates finite, partial and infinite sequences. However, it does not require continuity. His approach has not been mechanized in a proof tool yet.

## 8 Conclusion and Future Research

We compared four formalizations of possibly infinite sequences in different higher-order logics and proof tools. Two of them – the Isabelle/HOLCF and the PVS solution – have been extensively used by the authors to model the meta-theory of I/O automata. The sequence theories include more than 100 theorems and required between 3 and 6 man months.

In general we have the following view on the formalizations; with respect to automation and usability the HOL-LCF package is developed the furthest. It offers a strong definitional scheme, and multiple proof principles for proofs by induction, extensionality or bisimulation.

Although domain theory gets simpler to use and to automate by integrating as much as possible from HOL, some users might be reluctant to take the significant step to switch to domain theory. These users probably will have to develop further one of the other approaches. The HOL-FUN and PVS-FUN approaches were not worked out completely. Within the PVS-FUN approach it became clear that ad-hoc definitions like the *filter* function result in too large proof obligations. The extensionality principle also seems to be not adequate for reasoning about infinite sequences.

The approaches taken by Chou and Peled HOL-SUM and Agerholm [Age94] are pragmatic and more "ad-hoc" ways to deal with sequences. For specific purposes such a theory is built up quickly and may be satisfactory, but in general the twofold or even threefold character of proofs is inconvenient. Basically, the approach suffers from the fact, that domain theory is (partly) used to define recursive functions, but not to define recursive domains, which, however, is the crucial point of domain theory.

Coinductive types are being implemented in different proof tools in the moment. As the packages also offer definitional principles, and coinduction (or bisimulation) seems much stronger than the extensionality principle, they are an interesting candidate for possibly infinite sequences as well. However, to our knowledge, at the moment there is not much experience with coinductive types used in sophisticated verifications.

**Acknowledgement.** We thank Ching-Tsun Chou for intensive and fruitful discussions on his formalization of sequences.

## References

[Age94]   Sten Agerholm. *A HOL Basis for Reasoning about Functional Programs.* PhD thesis, University of Aarhus, Denmark, 1994.

[Chu40]   Alonzo Church. A formulation of the simple theory of types. *J. Symbolic Logic*, 5:56–68, 1940.

[CP96]     Ching-Tsun Chou and Doron Peled. Formal verification of a partial-order reduction technique for model checking. In T. Margaria and B. Steffen, editors, *Proc. 2nd Workshop Tools and Algorithms for the Construction and Analysis of Systems (TACAS'96)*, volume 1055 of *Lecture Notes in Computer Science*. Springer-Verlag, 1996.

[DG97]     Marco Devillers and David Griffioen. A formalization of finite and infinite sequences in PVS. Technical Report CSI-R9702, Computing Science Institute, University of Nijmegen, 1997.

[Fef96]    Solomom Feferman. Computation on abstract data types. the extensional approach, with an application to streams. *Annals of Pure and Applied Logic*, 81:75–113, 1996.

[GM93]     M.C.J. Gordon and T.F. Melham. *Introduction to HOL: a theorem-proving environment for higher-order logic*. Cambridge University Press, 1993.

[HJ97]     U. Hensel and B. Jacobs. Proof principles for datatypes with iterated recursion. Technical Report CSI-R9703, Computing Science Institute, University of Nijmegen, 1997.

[Lam94]    Leslie Lamport. The Temporal Logic of Actions. *ACM Transactions on Programming Languages and Systems*, 16(3):872–923, May 1994.

[LPM93]    Francois Leclerc and Christine Paulin-Mohring. Programming with streams in Coq, a case study: the sieve of eratosthenes. In H. Barendregt and T. Nipkow, editors, *Proc. Types for Proofs and Programs (TYPES'93)*, volume 806 of *Lecture Notes in Computer Science*, 1993.

[LT89]     Nancy Lynch and Mark Tuttle. An introduction to Input/Output automata. *CWI Quarterly*, 2(3):219–246, 1989.

[MN97]     Olaf Müller and Tobias Nipkow. Traces of I/O-Automata in Isabelle/HOLCF. In *Proc. 7th Int. Joint Conf. on Theory and Practice of Software Development (TAPSOFT'97)*, Lecture Notes in Computer Science. Springer-Verlag, 1997.

[MS96]     Olaf Müller and Konrad Slind. Isabelle/HOL as a platform for partiality. In *CADE-13 Workshop: Mechanization of Partial Functions, New Brunswick*, pages 85–96, 1996.

[NS95]     Tobias Nipkow and Konrad Slind. I/O automata in Isabelle/HOL. In P. Dybjer, B. Nordström, and J. Smith, editors, *Types for Proofs and Programs*, volume 996 of *Lecture Notes in Computer Science*, pages 101–119. Springer-Verlag, 1995.

[ORSH95]   S. Owre, J. Rushby, N. Shankar, and F. von Henke. Formal verification for fault-tolerant architectures: Prolegomena to the design of PVS. *IEEE Transactions on Software Engineering*, 21(2):107–125, February 1995.

[Pau87]    Lawrence C. Paulson. *Logic and Computation*. Cambridge University Press, 1987.

[Pau94]    Lawrence C. Paulson. *Isabelle: A Generic Theorem Prover*, volume 828 of *Lecture Notes in Computer Science*. Springer-Verlag, 1994.

[Pau97]    Lawrence C. Paulson. Mechanizing coinduction and corecursion in higher-order logic. *J. Automated Reasoning*, 7, 1997.

[Reg95]    Franz Regensburger. HOLCF: Higher Order Logic of Computable Functions. In E.T. Schubert, P.J. Windley, and J. Alves-Foss, editors, *Higher Order Logic Theorem Proving and its Applications*, volume 971 of *Lecture Notes in Computer Science*, pages 293–307. Springer-Verlag, 1995.

# Proof Normalization for a First-Order Formulation of Higher-Order Logic

Gilles Dowek

INRIA-Rocquencourt, B.P. 105, 78153 Le Chesnay Cedex, France,
Gilles.Dowek@inria.fr

**Abstract.** We define a notion of cut and a proof normalization process for a class of theories, including all equational theories and a first-order formulation of higher-order logic. Proof normalization terminates for all equational theories. We show that the proof of termination of normalization for the usual formulation of higher-order logic can be adapted to a proof of termination of normalization for its first-order formulation. The "hard part" of the proof, that cannot be carried out in higher-order logic itself, i.e. the normalization of the system $F_\omega$, is left unchanged. Thus, from the point of view of proof normalization, defining higher-order logic as a different logic or as a first-order theory does not matter. This result also explains a relation between the normalization of propositions and the normalization of proofs in equational theories and in higher-order logic: normalizing of propositions does not eliminate cuts, but it transforms them.

It is well-known that higher-order logic can be formulated as a (many-sorted) first-order theory. Such a formulation permits to separate in a clear way the logic that describes the general rules of reasoning and a theory that describes the rules specific to the objects of the discourse (in this case, the sets and the functions).

From a more technical point of view, such a reduction permits to deduce Henkin's higher-order completeness theorem from Gödel's first-order completeness theorem (see for instance [4]). It permits also to use well-known first-order proof search methods for higher-order logic. In particular, as this theory is some kind of extended equational theory, the powerful methods designed for equational theories can be used for higher-order logic. However most efficient first-order proof search methods rely on the proof normalization theorem and the fact that searching for normal proofs (or proofs containing a very restricted form of cuts) is complete. In this paper, we are concerned with proofs normalization in the sense of Prawitz [9], i.e. in natural deduction.

The proof normalization theorem for higher-order logic cannot be deduced from the first-order one. Indeed, unlike completeness that is proved once for all the first-order theories, the proof normalization theorem needs a specific proof for each theory. The so called proof normalization theorem for first-order logic is only a proof normalization theorem for the the empty theory in first-order logic. Other theories, such as equality or arithmetic, have their own notion of cut and their own proof normalization theorem.

We define, in this paper a notion of cut for the first-order formulation of higher-order logic and we show that the proof of proof normalization for higher-order logic can be adapted to prove proof normalization for this theory. The "hard part" of the proof, that cannot be carried out in higher-order logic itself, i.e. the normalization of the system $F_\omega$ [6], is left unchanged.

# 1   A first-order formulation of higher-order logic

Higher-order logic is an extension of first-order logic with function variables, predicate variables, function terms to be substituted to function variables and predicate terms to be substituted to predicate variables.

In its first-order formulation, if $t$ is a function term of arity $n$ and $u_1$, ..., $u_n$ are terms we cannot write the application of $t$ to $u_1$, ..., $u_n$ as $t(u_1, ..., u_n)$, but we need to introduce a $(n+1)$-ary function symbol $\alpha_n$ (for *apply*) and write this term $\alpha_n(t, u_1, ..., u_n)$. In the same way if $t$ is a predicate term of arity $n$ and $u_1$, ..., $u_n$ are terms we cannot write the application of $t$ to $u_1$, ..., $u_n$ as $t(u_1, ..., u_n)$, but we need to introduce a predicate symbol $\in_n$ and write this proposition $\in_n (t, u_1, ..., u_n)$. When $n = 1$ we usually write $a \in A$ instead of $\in_1 (A, a)$. When $n = 0$, $t$ is a zero-ary predicate term (i.e. a proposition term) and $\in_0 (t)$ is the corresponding proposition.

If we curry the functions and define the predicates as functions mapping objects to proposition terms, we only need a binary function symbols $\alpha_1$, from now on written $\alpha$, and a unary predicate $\in_0$, from now on written $\varepsilon$. The term $\alpha_n(t, u_1, ..., u_n)$ is now written $\alpha(..., \alpha(t, u_1)..., u_n)$ and the proposition $\in_n (t, u_1, ..., u_n)$ $\varepsilon(\alpha(..., \alpha(t, u_1)..., u_n))$. As usual, we write $(t\ u)$ for $\alpha(t, u)$ and $(t\ u_1 ... u_n)$ for $(...(t\ u_1)...u_n)$.

Then, as in higher-order logic, we have functionals having functions as arguments, arity must be generalized to simple types defined as follows.

**Definition 1.** *Simple types* are inductively defined by

- $\iota$ and $o$ are simple types,
- if $T$ and $U$ are simple types then $T \rightarrow U$ is a simple type.

As usual we write $T_1 \rightarrow ... \rightarrow T_n \rightarrow U$ for $T_1 \rightarrow (... \rightarrow (T_n \rightarrow U)...)$. The symbol $\alpha$ is generalized to $\alpha_{T,U}$.

To construct functional terms and predicate terms we have the comprehension schemes.

$$\exists f\ \forall x_1\ ...\ \forall x_n\ ((f\ x_1\ ...\ x_n) = t)$$

and

$$\exists E\ \forall x_1\ ...\ \forall x_n\ (\varepsilon(E\ x_1\ ...\ x_n) \Leftrightarrow P)$$

As equality may be defined in higher-order logic (the proposition $a = b$ is an abbreviation for $\forall p\ (\varepsilon(p\ a) \Leftrightarrow \varepsilon(p\ b))$) the first scheme can be rephrased

$$\exists f\ \forall x_1\ ...\ \forall x_n\ \forall p\ (\varepsilon(p\ (f\ x_1\ ...\ x_n)) \Leftrightarrow \varepsilon(p\ t))$$

In fact, it is well-known that the first scheme is equivalent to the instances

$$\exists s \, \forall x \, \forall y \, \forall z \, \forall p \, (\varepsilon(p \, (s \, x \, y \, z)) \Leftrightarrow \varepsilon(p \, ((x \, z) \, (y \, z))))$$
$$\exists k \, \forall x \, \forall y \, \forall p \, ((\varepsilon(p \, (k \, x \, y)) \Leftrightarrow \varepsilon(p \, x))$$

and the second is equivalent to the instances

$$\exists I \, \forall x \, \forall y \, (\varepsilon(I \, x \, y) \Leftrightarrow (\varepsilon(x) \Rightarrow \varepsilon(y)))$$
$$\exists A \, \forall x \, (\varepsilon(A \, x) \Leftrightarrow \forall y \, \varepsilon(x \, y))$$

To have a genuine notation for objects we would rather skolemize these axioms, and introduce symbols $S$, $K$, $\Rightarrow$ and $\dot{\forall}$. Together with the symbols $\alpha_{T,U}$ and $\varepsilon$, these symbol form the language $\mathcal{L}$.

**Definition 2.** The language $\mathcal{L}$ is the many-sorted first-order language sorted by simple types containing the individual symbols

- $S_{T,U,V}$ of sort $(T \to U \to V) \to (T \to U) \to T \to V$,
- $K_{T,U}$ of sort $T \to U \to T$,
- $\Rightarrow$ of sort $o \to o \to o$
- $\dot{\forall}_T$ of sort $(T \to o) \to o$,

the function symbols

- $\alpha_{T,U}$ of rank $(T \to U, T, U)$,

the predicate symbol

- $\varepsilon$ of rank $(o)$.

At last, we take the following instances of the skolemized comprehension scheme.

**Definition 3.** The theory $\mathcal{H}$ is a many-sorted first-order theory in the language $\mathcal{L}$ with axioms

$$\forall x \, \forall y \, \forall z \, \forall p \, \varepsilon(p \, (S_{T,U,V} \, x \, y \, z)) \Leftrightarrow \varepsilon(p \, ((x \, z) \, (y \, z)))$$
$$\forall x \, \forall y \, \forall p \, \varepsilon(p \, (K_{T,U} \, x \, y)) \Leftrightarrow \varepsilon(p \, x)$$
$$\forall x \, \forall y \, \varepsilon(\Rightarrow x \, y) \Leftrightarrow (\varepsilon(x) \Rightarrow \varepsilon(y))$$
$$\forall x \, \varepsilon(\dot{\forall}_T \, x) \Leftrightarrow (\forall y \, \varepsilon(x \, y))$$

*Remark.* Notice that all the types, including the functional ones, are sorts in this theory. As usual, in a many sorted theory, the rank of a function symbol is a sequence of sorts: those of its arguments and of its result and the rank of a predicate symbol a is a sequence of sorts: those of its arguments.

There are two notions of function that must not be confused. The individual symbol $S$ is a term and thus it has a sort. This term denotes an object of the theory that happens to be a function, thus its sort is a functional type. In contrast, the function symbol $\alpha_{T,U}$ is not a term and does not denote an object of the theory, but a function mapping objects of the theory to objects of the theory. The sorts of the mapped objects is indicated in the rank of this symbol.

This distinction can be compared to that of set theory we are used to distinguish relations as objects of the theory and relations on the objects of the theory such as the denotation of the symbol $\in$.

Now we want to define a notion of cut and a proof normalization process associated to the theory $\mathcal{H}$.

# 2 Proof normalization for equational theories

## 2.1 First-order logic with equality

**Definition 4.** *First-order logic with equality* in a language containing a predicate symbol $=$ is the theory formed with the axioms

$$\forall x \ (x = x) \qquad \qquad \text{(Identity)}$$

$$\overline{\forall} \ (x = y \Rightarrow (P[z \leftarrow x] \Rightarrow P[z \leftarrow y])) \qquad \qquad \text{(Leibniz' scheme)}$$

where $\overline{\forall} \ P$ is the universal closure of the proposition $P$.

In this section, $\mathcal{T} \vdash P$ means that $P$ is provable from the axioms of $\mathcal{T}$ and the axioms of equality.

**Definition 5.** An *equality cut* is a proof of the form

$$\cfrac{\cfrac{\overline{\forall} \ (x = y \Rightarrow (P[z \leftarrow x] \Rightarrow P[z \leftarrow y]))}{t = t \Rightarrow (P'[z \leftarrow t] \Rightarrow P'[z \leftarrow t])} \text{\scriptsize $\forall$-elim} \quad \cfrac{\cfrac{\forall x \ (x = x)}{t = t} \text{\scriptsize $\forall$-elim}}{} }{\cfrac{P'[z \leftarrow t] \Rightarrow P'[z \leftarrow t]}{P'[z \leftarrow t]} \text{\scriptsize $\Rightarrow$-elim} \quad \cfrac{\pi}{P'[z \leftarrow t]}} \text{\scriptsize $\Rightarrow$-elim}$$

where $P'$ is an instance of $P$.

It reduces to the proof

$$\cfrac{\pi}{P'[z \leftarrow t]}$$

**Proposition 6.** *Proof normalization (including the elimination of equality cuts) terminates in the theory of equality.*

## 2.2 Proof normalization in equational theories

**Definition 7.** An *equational theory* is a theory whose axioms are universal closures of propositions of the form $t = u$.

**Definition 8.** Let $\mathcal{T}$ be an equational theory. An *elementary conversion step* in $\mathcal{T}$ relating a proposition $P'[z \leftarrow t]$ and $P'[z \leftarrow u]$ is a part of a proof of the form

$$\cfrac{\cfrac{\overline{\forall} \ (x = y \Rightarrow (P[z \leftarrow x] \Rightarrow P[z \leftarrow y]))}{t = u \Rightarrow (P'[z \leftarrow t] \Rightarrow P'[z \leftarrow u])} \text{\scriptsize $\forall$-elim} \quad \cfrac{\cfrac{\overline{\forall}(t_0 = u_0)}{t = u} \text{\scriptsize $\forall$-elim}}{} }{\cfrac{P'[z \leftarrow t] \Rightarrow P'[z \leftarrow u]}{P'[z \leftarrow u]} \text{\scriptsize $\Rightarrow$-elim} \quad \cfrac{}{P'[z \leftarrow t]}} \text{\scriptsize $\Rightarrow$-elim}$$

A *conversion step* is a sequence of elementary conversion steps. We write such a conversion step relating two propositions $P$ and $Q$

$$P$$

$$\boxed{\phantom{xx}}$$

$$Q$$

**Proposition 9.** *From a proof in the theory $\mathcal{T}$, we can build a proof where axioms of $\mathcal{T}$ are used in conversion steps only.*

*Proof.* We replace the axioms

$$\overline{\forall\ (t = u)}$$

by

$$\frac{\forall x\ (x = x)}{t = t}\ \forall\text{-elim}$$

$$\boxed{\phantom{xx}}$$

$$\frac{t = u}{\overline{\forall\ (t = u)}}\ \forall\text{-intro}$$

**Proposition 10.**    — *From a conversion step from $P$ to $Q$, we can build a conversion step from $Q$ to $P$.*
- *From a conversion step from $P$ to $Q$, we can build a conversion step from $P[x \leftarrow t]$ to $Q[x \leftarrow t]$.*
- *If $P$ and $Q$ have the same toplevel connective or quantifier, then from a conversion step relating $P$ and $Q$ we can build a conversion step relating their toplevel subformulas.*
- *From a conversion step relating $t = u$ and $t' = u'$ we can build a conversion step relating $P[x \leftarrow t]$ and $P[x \leftarrow t']$ and another relating $P[x \leftarrow u]$ and $P[x \leftarrow u']$.*

*Proof.* By induction on the length of the conversion step.

**Definition 11.** A *cut*, in natural deduction, in the theory $\mathcal{T}$ is an introduction rule followed by a conversion step and an elimination rule.

**Definition 12.** (Proof normalization)

- The cut

$$\frac{\dfrac{\pi_1}{P} \quad \dfrac{\pi_2}{Q}}{P \wedge Q}\ \wedge\text{-intro}$$

$$\boxed{\phantom{xx}}$$

$$\frac{P' \wedge Q'}{P'}\ \wedge\text{-elim}$$

is transformed into the proof

$$\frac{\pi_1}{P}$$

$$\square$$

$$P'$$

The conversion step form $P$ to $P'$ is given by the third point of proposition 10. The case of the cuts using the right elimination rule is similar.

- The cut

$$\cfrac{\cfrac{\cfrac{\pi_1}{P}}{P \vee Q} \text{ V-intro}}{\cfrac{\square}{P' \vee Q'} \quad \cfrac{\cancel{P'}}{\cfrac{\pi_2}{R}} \quad \cfrac{\cancel{Q'}}{\cfrac{\pi_3}{R}}}{R} \text{ V-elim}$$

is transformed into the proof

$$\frac{\pi_1}{P}$$

$$\square$$

$$P'$$

$$\frac{\pi_2}{R}$$

The conversion step form $P$ to $P'$ is given by the third point of proposition 10. The case of the cuts using the right introduction rule is similar.

- The cut

$$\cfrac{\cfrac{\cfrac{\pi_1}{Q}}{P \Rightarrow Q} \Rightarrow\text{-intro}}{\cfrac{\square}{P' \Rightarrow Q' \quad \cfrac{\pi_2}{P'}}}{Q'} \Rightarrow\text{-elim}$$

is transformed into the proof

$$\frac{\pi_2}{P'}$$

$$\square$$

$$P$$

$$\frac{\pi_1}{Q}$$

$$\square$$

$$Q'$$

The conversion step form $P'$ to $P$ and from $Q$ to $Q'$ are given by the first and third point of proposition 10. The cases of the cuts on negation ($\neg$) and equivalence ($\Leftrightarrow$) are similar.

– The cut

$$\frac{\dfrac{\pi}{P}}{\forall x\, P}\ \forall\text{-intro}\ (x \text{ not free in the hypotheses})$$

$$\frac{\boxed{\phantom{xx}}}{\dfrac{\forall x\, P'}{P'[x \leftarrow t]}}\ \forall\text{-elim}$$

is transformed into the proof

$$\frac{\pi[x \leftarrow t]}{P[x \leftarrow t]}$$

$$\frac{\boxed{\phantom{xx}}}{P'[x \leftarrow t]}$$

The conversion step form $P[x \leftarrow t]$ to $P'[x \leftarrow t]$ is given by the second point of proposition 10.

– The cut

$$\frac{\dfrac{\pi_1}{P[x \leftarrow t]}}{\exists x\, P}\ \exists\text{-intro}$$

$$\frac{\dfrac{\boxed{\phantom{xx}}}{\exists x\, P'} \qquad \dfrac{\dfrac{P'}{\pi_2}}{Q}}{Q}\ \exists\text{-elim}\ (x \text{ not free in } Q)$$

is transformed into the proof

$$\frac{\pi_1}{P[x \leftarrow t]}$$

$$\frac{\boxed{\phantom{xx}}}{\dfrac{P'[x \leftarrow t]}{\dfrac{\pi_2[x \leftarrow t]}{Q}}}$$

The conversion step form $P[x \leftarrow t]$ to $P'[x \leftarrow t]$ is given by the second point of proposition 10.

– The cut

$$\frac{\forall x\, (x = x)}{t = t}\ \forall\text{-elim}$$

$$\frac{\dfrac{u = u' \Rightarrow P[z \leftarrow u] \Rightarrow P[z \leftarrow u'] \qquad u = u'}{P[z \leftarrow u] \Rightarrow P[z \leftarrow u']}\ \Rightarrow\text{-elim} \qquad \dfrac{\pi}{P[z \leftarrow u]}}{P[z \leftarrow u']}\ \Rightarrow\text{-elim}$$

is transformed into the proof

$$\frac{\pi}{P[z \leftarrow u]}$$
$$\boxed{\phantom{xxxx}}$$
$$P[z \leftarrow u']$$

where the conversion step from $P[z \leftarrow u]$ to $P[z \leftarrow u']$ is built using the fourth and the first point of proposition 10.

**Proposition 13.** *If there is a conversion step from $P$ to $Q$ then $P$ and $Q$ have the same toplevel connective or quantifier (and if one is atomic, the other also).*

*Proof.* By induction on the length of the conversion step.

**Proposition 14.** *Proof normalization terminates in the theory $T$.*

*Proof.* Let $\pi_1, \pi_2, \ldots$ be a proof normalization sequence in the theory $T$. By proposition 10 and 13, the sequence $\pi'_1, \pi'_2, \ldots$ obtained by removing the conversion steps and replacing all the atomic propositions by a propositional constant is a proof normalization sequence in first-order logic with equality. Thus it is finite.

## 2.3 Equivalence axioms

We may also include, in the theory $T$, axioms of the form $\overline{\forall} (P \Leftrightarrow Q)$ where $P$ and $Q$ are atomic propositions. For instance Peano's fourth axiom

$$\forall x \, \forall y \, (S(x) = S(y) \Leftrightarrow x = y)$$

The notion of conversion step is a bit more difficult to define, because we do not have an equivalent of Leibniz' scheme for equivalence. Thus we inductively define a set $L$ of proofs containing the proofs of the form

$$\frac{\overline{\forall} (P \Leftrightarrow Q)}{P' \Leftrightarrow Q'} \; \forall\text{-elim}$$

and closed by the following constructions: if

$$\frac{\pi}{P \Leftrightarrow Q}$$

is an element of $L$ then

$$\frac{\dfrac{\pi}{P \Leftrightarrow Q} \quad \dfrac{\cancel{Q \wedge R}}{Q}}{\dfrac{P}{\dfrac{P \wedge R}{(P \wedge R) \Leftrightarrow (Q \wedge R)}}} \qquad \dfrac{\cancel{Q \wedge R}}{\dfrac{R}{}}$$

$$\frac{\dfrac{\pi}{P \Leftrightarrow Q} \quad \dfrac{\cancel{P \wedge R}}{P}}{\dfrac{Q}{\dfrac{Q \wedge R}{}}} \qquad \dfrac{\cancel{P \wedge R}}{R}$$

is an element of $L$, and similar rules for the other connectives and quantifiers.

We extend the definition of elementary conversion steps to consider also parts of proofs of the form

$$\cfrac{\cfrac{\pi}{P \Leftrightarrow Q} \qquad P}{Q} \; \Leftrightarrow\text{-elim}$$

and

$$\cfrac{\cfrac{\pi}{P \Leftrightarrow Q} \qquad Q}{P} \; \Leftrightarrow\text{-elim}$$

where $\pi$ is a proof of $L$.

Proposition 9 that every proof can be transformed into a proof where axioms are used in conversion steps only still holds, replacing the axioms

$$\overline{\forall \, (P \Leftrightarrow Q)}$$

by

$$\cfrac{\cfrac{\cfrac{\overline{P} \quad \overline{Q}}{\begin{array}{cc}\Box & \Box\end{array}}}{\cfrac{Q \qquad P}{P \Leftrightarrow Q}} \; \Leftrightarrow\text{-intro}}{\forall \, (P \Leftrightarrow Q)} \; \forall\text{-intro}$$

Proposition 10 still holds. Thus the cuts and the proof normalization process can be defined as in definition 11 and 12. Proposition 13 still holds, thus the termination of proof normalization can be proved as in proposition 14.

## 2.4 Normalizing propositions and normalizing proofs

In first-order logic with equality, consider a theory $T$ and a confluent and normalizing rewrite system $\triangleright$ on terms and propositions, such that if $t \triangleright u$ then $T \vdash t = u$. Call $R$ the decidable equivalence relation on propositions defined by: $P \, R \, Q$ if and only if $P$ and $Q$ have the same normal form.

**Proposition 15.** *If $P \, R \, Q$ and $T \vdash P$ then $T \vdash Q$.*

**Proposition 16.** $\quad$ – *If $P \, R \, Q$ then $Q \, R \, P$.*
- *If $P \, R \, Q$, then $P[x \leftarrow t] \, R \, Q[x \leftarrow t]$.*
- *If $P \, R \, Q$ then $P$ and $Q$ have the same toplevel connective or quantifier (and if one is atomic, the other also) and their toplevel subformulas are pairwise equivalent.*

Thus, we can define the same deduction rules on classes of $\mathcal{P}/\mathcal{R}$ as on propositions of $\mathcal{P}$ (Plotkin-Andrews quotient [1, 8]). Proof checking is still decidable, provided we indicate the substituted term in the elimination rule of the universal quantifier and the introduction rule of the existential quantifier. As representative of classes, we can chose normal forms.

We have the following equivalence lemma.

**Proposition 17.** $\mathcal{T} \vdash P$ *if and only if* $\overline{\mathcal{T}} \vdash \overline{P}$, *where* $\overline{P}$ *is the class of* $P$ *in the quotient and* $\overline{\mathcal{T}}$ *is the set of classes of the propositions of* $\mathcal{T}$.

**Corollary 18.** *If* $\mathcal{T}$ *is an equational theory such that all the classes of propositions of* $\mathcal{T}$ *are provable in first-order logic with equality, then* $\mathcal{T} \vdash P$ *if and only if* $\vdash \overline{P}$.

*Remark.* In the quotient, there are fewer axioms and proofs are simpler, thus proof search is more efficient. Unification must however be replaced by equational unification. Indeed, a unifier of two terms $t$ and $u$ is a substitution $\theta$ such that $\theta t$ and $\theta u$ are equal in the quotient i.e. have the same normal form.

*Remark.* If we also have axioms of the form $\overline{\forall} (P \Leftrightarrow Q)$, we must also have rewrite rules on atomic propositions, for instance

$$S(x) = S(y) \rhd x = y$$

*Example 1.* Consider [8] the associativity axiom $(A)$

$$\forall x \, \forall y \, \forall z \, ((x + y) + z = x + (y + z))$$

and the confluent and normalizing rewrite system defined by the single rule

$$(x + y) + z \rhd x + (y + z)$$

The normal form of the associativity axiom is

$$\forall x \, \forall y \, \forall z \, (x + (y + z) = x + (y + z))$$

and thus it is subsumed by the identity axiom

$$\forall x \, (x = x)$$

Thus $\mathcal{T} \vdash P$ if and only if $\vdash \overline{P}$.

Call $t = (a + b) + c$ and $u = a + (b + c)$. The proof

$$\dfrac{\dfrac{\overline{\forall} \, (x = y \Rightarrow (P[z \leftarrow x] \Rightarrow P[z \leftarrow y]))}{t = u \Rightarrow (P'[z \leftarrow t] \Rightarrow P'[z \leftarrow u])} \, \forall\text{-elim} \quad \dfrac{\overline{A}}{t = u} \, \forall\text{-elim}}{\dfrac{P'[z \leftarrow t] \Rightarrow P'[z \leftarrow u]}{P'[z \leftarrow u]} \Rightarrow\text{-elim} \quad \dfrac{\pi}{P'[z \leftarrow t]} \Rightarrow\text{-elim}}$$

can be simplified to

$$\dfrac{\pi}{P'[z \leftarrow u]}$$

*Remark.* If $\mathcal{T}$ is an equational theory such that all the classes of propositions of $\mathcal{T}$ are provable in first-order logic with equality, then, in the quotient, conversion steps relate identical propositions and they can be removed. Thus a cut in the quotient is just an introduction rule followed by an elimination rule. Normalizing propositions does not eliminate cuts, but it transforms them.

The notion of cut of definition 11 corresponds to the standard notion of cut (i.e. an introduction rule followed by an elimination rule) in the quotient. But the notion of cut of definition 11 does not require the existence of a confluent and nomalizing rewrite system, and can be formulated completely as a proof transformation system in first order logic (without quotient).

# 3 Proof normalization for the first-order formulation of higher-order logic

## 3.1 Plotkin-Andrews quotient for higher-order logic

We first define Plotkin-Andrews quotient for higher-order logic, that will be useful in the following.

**Definition 19.** Let $\triangleright$ be the following rewrite system on terms and propositions of the theory $\mathcal{H}$ (actually, since the language of propositions contains binders (quantifiers), it is rather a combinatory reduction system [7]).

$$(S_{T,U,V} \; x \; y \; z) \triangleright ((x \; z) \; (y \; z))$$

$$(K_{T,U} \; x \; y) \triangleright x$$

$$\varepsilon(\dot{\Rightarrow} \; x \; y) \triangleright \varepsilon(x) \Rightarrow \varepsilon(y)$$

$$\varepsilon(\dot{\forall}_T \; x) \triangleright \forall y \; \varepsilon(x \; y)$$

**Proposition 20.** *This rewrite system is confluent and strongly normalizing.*

*Proof.* As this system is orthogonal, it is confluent [7].

To prove that it is strongly normalizing we define a translation of the terms and the propositions of the theory $\mathcal{H}$ into the typed combinatory language $S$, $K$. In each type $T$, we chose a variable $z_T$.

- $\|x\| = z_T$,
- $\|S_{T,U,V}\| = S_{T,U,V}, \|K_{T,U}\| = K_{T,U}$,
- $\|\dot{\Rightarrow}\| = (I_{o \to o \to o} \; z_{o \to o \to o}), \|\dot{\forall}_T\| = (S_{T \to o,T,o} \; I_{T \to o} \; (K_{T,T \to o} \; z_T))$, where $I_T = (S_{T,T,T} \; K_{T,T \to T} \; K_{T,T})$,
- $\|(t \; u)\| = (\|t\| \; \|u\|)$,
- $\|P \wedge Q\| = \|P \vee Q\| = \|P \Rightarrow Q\| = \|P \Leftrightarrow Q\| = (z_{o \to o \to o} \; \|P\| \; \|Q\|)$,
- $\|\neg P\| = \|P\|$,
- $\|\forall x \; P\| = \|\exists x \; P\| = \|P\|$.

We check that if $P$ rewrites in one step to $Q$, then $\|P\|$ rewrites in at least one step to $\|Q\|$. Let $P_1, P_2, \ldots$ be a reduction sequence in the system above, the sequence $\|P_1\|, \|P_2\|, \ldots$ is a reduction sequence in the typed combinatory language $S$, $K$, thus it is finite [11].

Like for equational theories, we can take the quotient of the set of propositions by the equivalence relation defined by $P \, \mathcal{R} \, Q$ is $P$ and $Q$ have the same normal form for the rewrite system above (or chose the normal forms to represent their classes and define deduction rules on normal propositions, normalizing the conclusion after each rule).

As the normal forms of all axioms of $\mathcal{H}$ are provable in first-order logic, we have $\mathcal{H} \vdash P$ if and only if $\vdash \overline{P}$.

## 3.2 Proof normalization

The axioms of the theory $\mathcal{H}$ of definition 3 have the form $\overline{\forall} \, (P \Leftrightarrow Q)$, but $P$ and $Q$ are not always atomic propositions. Conversion steps can be defined as above. Proposition 9 that from a proof in the theory $\mathcal{H}$, we can build a proof where axioms of $\mathcal{H}$ are used in conversion steps only still holds and proposition 10 also, although the proof of the third point is different.

**Proposition 21.** *If $P$ and $Q$ have the same toplevel connective and quantifier, then from a conversion step relating $P$ and $Q$ we can build a conversion step relating their toplevel subformulas.*

*Proof.* From a conversion step relating the propositions $P$ and $Q$ we can build a conversion sequence from $P$ to $Q$ for the rewrite system of definition 19. Since this system is confluent, we can build reduction sequences from $P$ and $Q$ to a proposition $R$. This proposition $R$ has the same toplevel connective and quantifier as $P$ and $Q$ and we can build a reduction sequence from the toplevel subformulas of $P$ and $Q$ to the toplevel subformulas of $R$. From these reduction sequences, we can build a conversion step relating the toplevel subformulas of $P$ and $Q$.

Thus the cuts and the proof normalization process can be defined as in definition 11 and 12. But as we shall see the proposition 13 does not hold and thus, the termination proof of proposition 14 does not go through.

## 3.3 Termination

In the usual formulation of higher-order logic, the substitution of a predicate or a proposition variable may increase the complexity of the proposition. For instance, substituting $P \Rightarrow P$ for $X$ in

$$X \Rightarrow X$$

yields

$$(P \Rightarrow P) \Rightarrow (P \Rightarrow P)$$

Thus the termination of proof normalization cannot be proved like in the empty theory of first-order logic, by proving that the complexity of cut propositions decreases.

This is also the case in the quotient, if we chose normal forms as representative of their classes, as substituting $(\Rightarrow p\ p)$ for $x$ in the proposition

$$\varepsilon(x) \Rightarrow \varepsilon(x)$$

yields

$$(\varepsilon(p) \Rightarrow \varepsilon(p)) \Rightarrow (\varepsilon(p) \Rightarrow \varepsilon(p))$$

In the first-order formulation, predicate and proposition variables are just variables of sort $T_1 \to ... \to T_n \to o$ and substituting such a variable does not change the complexity of a proposition. For instance, substituting $(\Rightarrow p\ p)$ for $x$ in the proposition

$$\varepsilon(x) \Rightarrow \varepsilon(x)$$

yields

$$\varepsilon(\Rightarrow p\ p) \Rightarrow \varepsilon(\Rightarrow p\ p)$$

which has the same complexity as $\varepsilon(x) \Rightarrow \varepsilon(x)$.

But, this complexity may be increased by a conversion step, for instance the proposition above can be transformed into

$$(\varepsilon(p) \Rightarrow \varepsilon(p)) \Rightarrow (\varepsilon(p) \Rightarrow \varepsilon(p))$$

Thus because the third and fourth axiom permits to transform atomic propositions into non-atomic ones, the proposition 13 does not hold for the theory $\mathcal{H}$ and the termination proof of proposition 14 does not go through. However, we have the following termination proof which is an adaptation of the proof of [6].

**Proposition 22.** *Proof normalization terminates in the theory* $\mathcal{H}$.

*Proof.* We associate to each sort of the theory $\mathcal{H}$ a sort of the system $F_\omega$ [6] (see also [5]).

- $|o| = |\iota| = *$,
- $|T \to U| = |T| \to |U|$.

To each term of sort $T$ we associate a type constructor of sort $|T|$ in $F_\omega$

- $|S_{T,U,V}| = \lambda x : |T|\ \lambda y : |U|\ \lambda z : |V|\ ((x\ z)\ (y\ z))$,
- $|K_{T,U}| = \lambda x : |T|\ \lambda y : |U|\ x$,
- $|\Rightarrow| = \lambda x : *\ \lambda y : *\ (x \to y)$,
- $|\forall_T| = \lambda x : |T| \to *\ \forall y : |T|\ (x\ y)$,
- $|(t\ u)| = (|t|\ |u|)$.

To each proposition we associate a type in $F_\omega$. Atomic propositions are translated like their arguments.

- $|\varepsilon(t)| = |t|$,

and the translation follows that of [6] for the other propositions, e.g.

- $|P \Rightarrow Q| = |P| \rightarrow |Q|$,
- $|\forall x\ P| = \forall x : |T|\ |P|$,
- $|P \wedge Q| = \forall X : * ((|P| \rightarrow |Q| \rightarrow X) \rightarrow X)$.

To each proof of a proposition $P$, we associate a term in $F_\omega$ of type $|P|$. To a proof of the form

$$\frac{\pi}{P}$$

$$\boxed{\phantom{xxx}}$$

$$P'$$

we associate the term $|\pi|$, and the translation follows that of [6] for the other propositions, e.g. to a proof of the form

$$\frac{\overset{\pi_1}{P \Rightarrow Q}\ \overset{\pi_2}{P}}{Q}\ \Rightarrow\text{-elim}$$

we associate the term $(|\pi_1|\ |\pi_2|)$.

If a proof $\pi$ contains a cut then the term $|\pi|$ contains a redex and eliminating the cut in $\pi$ corresponds to reducing the redex in $|\pi|$.

Let $\pi_1, \pi_2, \dots$ be a proof normalization sequence in the theory $\mathcal{H}$. The sequence $|\pi_1|, |\pi_2|, \dots$ is a reduction sequence in $F_\omega$. Thus, by the strong normalization theorem of $F_\omega$ [6], it is finite.

*Remark.* Instead of mapping both $\iota$ and $o$ to $*$, we could follow the closer the proof of [6] and drop the first-order terms, i.e. take $|o| = *$ and $|\iota|$ to be undefined then $|T \rightarrow U| = |T| \rightarrow |U|$ when both $|T|$ and $|U|$ are defined, is equal to $|U|$ when $|U|$ is defined but $|T|$ is not and is undefined otherwise.

## Conclusion

We have defined a notion of cut (an introduction rule followed by a conversion step and an elimination rule) and a proof normalization process for a large class of theories, including all equational theories and a first-order formulation of higher-order logic $\mathcal{H}$. Although the proof normalization process is the same, the termination proof is different for equational theories and the theory $\mathcal{H}$. The termination of proof normalization for equational theories is proved by an elementary reduction to first-order logic with equality. By Gödel's second incompleteness theorem, there is no such reduction for the theory $\mathcal{H}$.

In some equational theories and in the theory $\mathcal{H}$, the Plotkin-Andrews quotient permits to remove the conversion steps.

The notion of cut introduced here correspond to standard notion of cut (i.e. an introduction rule followed by an elimination rule) in the quotient. This explains a relation between the normalization of propositions and the normalization of proofs: normalizing of propositions does not eliminate cuts, but it transforms them by removing the conversion steps.

From the point of view of proof normalization, defining higher-order logic as a different logic or as a first-order theory does not matter because the "hard part" (i.e. the normalization of $F_\omega$ that cannot be carried out in higher-order logic itself) is the same in both cases.

# References

1. P.B. Andrews, Resolution in type theory, *The Journal of Symbolic Logic*, 36, 3 (1971) pp. 414-432.
2. P.B. Andrews, An introduction to mathematical logic and type theory: to truth through proof, *Academic Press*, Orlando (1986).
3. A. Church, A formulation of the simple theory of types, *The Journal of Symbolic Logic*, 5 (1940) pp. 56-68.
4. M. Davis, Invited commentary to [10], *proceedings of the international federation for information processing congress*, North-Holland (1968).
5. J.H. Geuvers, M.J. Nederhof, A modular proof of strong normalization, *Journal of Functional Programming* 2, 1 (1991) pp. 155-189.
6. J.Y. Girard, Interprétation fonctionnelle et élimination des coupures dans l'arithmétique d'ordre supérieur, *Thèse d'État*, Université de Paris 7 (1972).
7. J.W. Klop, V. van Oostrom, F. van Raamsdonk, Combinatory reduction systems: introduction and survey, *Theoretical Computer Science* 121 (1993) pp. 279-308.
8. G. Plotkin, Building-in equational theories, *Machine Intelligence*, 7, (1972) pp. 73-90
9. D. Prawitz, Natural deduction. A proof-theoretical study. Almqvist & Wiksell (1965).
10. J.A. Robinson, New directions in mechanical theorem proving, *proceedings of the international federation for information processing congress*, North-Holland (1968).
11. W.W. Tait, Intensional Interpretation of Functionals of Finite Type I, *Journal of Symbolic Logic*, 32, 2 (1967) pp. 198-212.

# Using a PVS Embedding of CSP to Verify Authentication Protocols

Bruno Dutertre[1] and Steve Schneider[2]

[1] Department of Computer Science, Queen Mary and Westfield College,
University of London, London E14NS, UK
[2] Department of Computer Science, Royal Holloway,
University of London, Egham, Surrey TW20 0EX, UK

**Abstract.** This paper presents an application of PVS to the verification of security protocols. The objective is to provide mechanical support for a verification method described in [14]. The PVS formalization consists of a semantic embedding of CSP and of a collection of theorems and proof rules for reasoning about authentication properties. We present an application to the Needham-Schroeder public key protocol.

## 1 Introduction

Authentication protocols are used in insecure networks by principals who want to get assurance about their correspondent's identity. Designing such protocols is notoriously error-prone and attacks can often exploit weaknesses or subtle flaws. Validating authentication protocols requires a rigorous analysis and several formal approaches have been advocated for this purpose [3, 16, 12, 9].

In [14], Schneider presents such a method based on CSP [7]. The approach relies on a general network model which includes legitimate protocol participants, the users, and an intruder, the enemy. Both the users and the enemy are specified as CSP processes and authentication properties are expressed as constraints on the sequences of messages the whole network can produce.

The verification strategy uses rank functions, that is, functions which assign an integer value to messages. A key theorem shows that authentication properties can be verified by finding a rank function which satisfies appropriate conditions. These depend on the nature of the encryption mechanism used, on the definition of the users, and on the property to be verified. An important benefit of the technique is to decompose an authentication property – a global property of a network – into local properties of the protocol participants.

This paper shows how the PVS theorem prover [5] can provide effective mechanical support to the above method. Using a semantics embedding of CSP, we specify the general network model in PVS and derive the important theorems about authentication and rank functions. We then define specialised PVS rewrite rules and proof commands to facilitate the verifications. With these rules and commands, the proofs of authentication are very systematic and require only little manual guidance. This allows the user to concentrate on the most important aspects of the analysis: finding rank functions.

In the remainder of this paper, we give a brief introduction to CSP and an overview of the modelling and analysis approach. We then describe the formalization of the network model and of the verification method in PVS. We give a simple example of application to the Needham Schroeder public key protocol[10]. Finally, we discuss and compare our developments with other mechanisations of CSP and with other verification methods for security protocols.

# 2 Authentication Protocols in CSP

## 2.1 CSP Notation

CSP is an abstract language for describing concurrent systems which interact through message passing [7]. Systems are modelled in terms of the events they can perform, each event corresponding to a potential communication between a system and its environment. CSP is a process algebra: systems are constructed from a set of elementary processes which can be combined using operators such as prefixing, choice, or parallel composition. Different semantic models are available; in this paper only the simplest – the so-called trace semantics – is considered.

We assume that a fixed set $\Sigma$ of all possible events is given. A process is characterised by a set of *traces*, that is, finite sequences of elements of $\Sigma$. Each trace represents a possible sequence of communications one can observe on the process interface. The set of traces of a process $P$ is prefix-closed; if one observes a trace $tr$ then all the prefixes of $tr$ have been seen before.

The particular dialect we use includes four primitive notions. The syntax of process expressions is as follows:

$$P ::= Stop \mid a \to P \mid \Box_{i \in I} P_i \mid P_1 \Box P_2 \mid P_1 \,\|[A]\| \, P_2 \mid P_1 \,\|\|\, P_2,$$

where $a$ is an element of $\Sigma$, $I$ a non-empty set, and $A$ a subset of $\Sigma$. These expressions have the following informal interpretation.

- *Stop* is the process which cannot engage in any event (deadlock).
- $a \to P$ is able initially to perform only the event $a$ after which it behaves as $P$.
- $\Box_{i \in I} P_i$ is the choice among an indexed family of processes $P_i$. The resulting process can behave as any one of the $P_i$. When only two processes are involved, choice is denoted by $P_1 \Box P_2$.
- $P_1 \,\|[A]\| \, P_2$ is the parallel composition of $P_1$ and $P_2$ with synchronization on events in $A$. If one of the processes is willing to engage in an event of $A$ then it has to wait until the other is ready to perform the same event. On events which do not belong to $A$, $P_1$ and $P_2$ do not synchronise; they can perform any such event independently of each other. $P_1 \,\|\|\, P_2$ is an abbreviation for $P_1 \,\|[\emptyset]\| \, P_2$.

## 2.2 A Model for Authentication Protocols

In the analysis of authentication protocols, we consider the general network architecture shown in Fig. 1. The network consists of a set of user processes and of an enemy which has full control over the communication medium. The enemy can block, re-address, duplicate, corrupt, or fake messages but we assume that it cannot decrypt or encrypt messages without the appropriate keys.

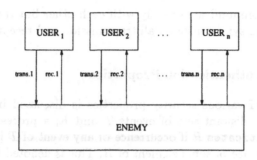

**Fig. 1.** The network

Each user has a unique identity. Its interface with the medium consists of two channels, one for transmission and one for reception. Accordingly, communications are modelled by two types of events. A transmission event is of the form $trans.i.j.m$ and is interpreted as "user $i$ sends a message $m$ destined for user $j$". A reception event is of the form $rec.i.j.m$ and means "$i$ receives a message $m$, apparently from user $j$". The communication channels are private; no user other than $i$ can produce events of the form $trans.i.j.m$ or $rec.i.j.m$.

In order to model the capabilities of the enemy, we use a relation $\vdash$ which specifies when new messages may be generated from existing ones: $S \vdash m$ means that knowledge of all the messages of the set $S$ is enough to produce the message $m$. The relation depends on the particular encryption mechanism used but we can assume that certain natural conditions are satisfied, such as,

$$\forall S, m \ \ m \in S \Rightarrow S \vdash m,$$
$$\forall S, S', m \ \ S \subseteq S' \wedge S \vdash m \Rightarrow S' \vdash m.$$

With the preceding notations, the enemy is specified as follows:

$$ENEMY(S) = (\Box_{i,j,m} \ trans.i.j.m \rightarrow ENEMY(S \cup \{m\}))$$
$$\Box \ (\Box_{i,j,(m|S \vdash m)} \ rec.i.j.m \rightarrow ENEMY(S)).$$

This describes the behaviour of an enemy which has knowledge of a set of messages $S$. Such a process can either allow a user to transmit a message $m$ after which it behaves as $ENEMY(S \cup \{m\})$ or generate a new message from the set

$S$ and send it to an arbitrary destinator. The enemy's behaviour at the start of a protocol is modelled by the process $ENEMY(INIT)$ where $INIT$ represents the information initially available to the enemy.

The user description depends entirely on the protocol being modelled and consists of a family of processes $USER(i)$. The whole network is the following composition of users and enemy:

$$NET = (\ |||_i \ USER(i)\ )\ |[trans, rec]|\ ENEMY(INIT).$$

The users do not communicate directly with each other but the enemy and the composition of users synchronize on all transmission and reception events.

## 2.3 Checking Authentication Properties

The specification of various security properties is discussed in [13]. Authentication involves two disjoint sets of events $T$ and $R$; a process $P$ satisfies the property $T$ **authenticates** $R$ if occurrence of any event of $T$ in a trace of $P$ is preceded by occurrence of some element of $R$. This is denoted by

$$P \ \text{sat} \ T \ \textbf{authenticates} \ R. \tag{1}$$

Examples in [14] illustrate how this relates concretely to authentication. Formally, $T$ **authenticates** $R$ is an abbreviation for the trace predicate

$$tr{\restriction}R = \langle\rangle \Rightarrow tr{\restriction}T = \langle\rangle, \tag{2}$$

where $\restriction$ denotes projection[3] and $\langle\rangle$ is the empty trace. The statement (1) is interpreted as "all the traces $tr$ of $P$ satisfy predicate (2)", that is, any trace of $P$ which does not contain events of $R$ does not contain events of $T$ either.

In order to verify authentication properties of a protocol, we have to prove statements of the form $NET$ **sat** $T$ **authenticates** $R$. It can be seen that this condition is equivalent to

$$NET\ |[R]|\ Stop \ \text{sat} \ tr{\restriction}T = \langle\rangle. \tag{3}$$

This equivalence is the basis of the proof strategy described in [14]. The idea is to assign to every message $m$ an integer value $\rho(m)$ called its rank in such a way that messages occurring in events of $T$ have non-positive rank while only messages of positive rank can be produced by $NET\ |[R]|\ Stop$.

Let $\mathcal{M}$ be the message space for a given protocol. A rank function is a function $\rho$ from $\mathcal{M}$ to the integers. Given such a function, we denote by $\rho^+$ the set of messages of positive rank and by $M(tr)$ the set of messages which occur in a trace $tr$. From the definition of $NET$ and $ENEMY$, one can derive the following key theorem [14].

---

[3] $tr{\restriction}R$ is the maximal subsequence of $tr$ all of whose elements belong to $R$.

**Theorem 1.** *If the four conditions below are satisfied,*

$$INIT \subseteq \rho^+,$$
$$\forall S, m. \ S \subseteq \rho^+ \wedge S \vdash m \Rightarrow \rho(m) > 0,$$
$$T \cap \rho^+ = \emptyset,$$
$$\forall i. \ USER(i) \,\|[R]\| \, Stop \ \text{ sat } \ M(tr \lceil rec) \subseteq \rho^+ \Rightarrow M(tr \lceil trans) \subseteq \rho^+,$$

*then*

$$NET \text{ sat } T \text{ authenticates } R.$$

With this result, one can verify authentication properties by finding an appropriate rank function. Showing that the four conditions are satisfied is simpler than a direct approach because user processes can be considered individually.

## 3  Embedding CSP in PVS

Our mechanization is based on a semantic embedding of CSP: Traces are represented by lists of events, processes are prefix-closed sets of traces, and the CSP operators are functions on processes which preserve the closure condition. Such a formalization is classic and similar to Camilleri's HOL embedding of CSP [4]. The main differences are the representation of events and processes, and the variant of CSP considered. In [4], events are considered as atomic symbols and are represented by strings. Our formalisation is more general and uses parametric types. Given any type T, trace[T] and process[T] represent traces and processes with events of type T. The CSP dialect considered by Camilleri is Hoare's original definition of deterministic processes [7]. In this model, a process has two components, a set of traces and an alphabet of events representing the interface. Due to this interface, there are restrictions on certain CSP operators. For our purpose, it is better to follow [14] and use the CSP variant presented previously.

Our definition of processes relies on PVS subtyping; process[T] is a subtype of set[trace[T]] defined as follows:

```
S: VAR set[trace[T]]
process: TYPE = { S | S(null) AND prefix_closed(S) }.
```

A process is any set of traces which contains the empty trace null and which is prefix-closed. All general results about sets or sets of traces apply then immediately to processes.

The CSP primitives are easily defined[6]. It is also convenient to generalise the two parallel composition operators to arbitrary (non-empty) families of processes. This non-standard extension of CSP does not pose any theoretical problem in the trace model and generalises the results presented in Sec. 2. We can consider networks with infinitely many users and all the theorems still hold. Moreover, the PVS statement and proof of these theorems are much simpler if infinite parallel composition is allowed.

Since PVS has a fixed syntax, we cannot use the standard CSP notations. Instead we use existing PVS symbols as indicated in Tab. 1. The operators `Choice` and `Interleave` are polymorphic functions which apply to indexed families of processes. For example, `Choice` is of parametric type `[[U -> process[T]] -> process[T]]`. PVS has a special syntax for denoting the applications of such functions to lambda terms; `Choice(lambda i: P(i))` can be written `Choice! i: P(i)`. More complex expressions are also valid:

```
Choice! i, j: Q(i) // P(i, j)

Choice! i, (j | i < j): i >> (j >> Stop[nat]).
```

In the two expressions above, PVS infers the correct parameter instantiation from the types of the variables and processes. In the first case, `U` is instantiated with a tuple type and in the second case, `U` is instantiated with the dependent type `[i:nat, {j:nat| i < j}]`.

**Table 1.** Syntax of process expressions.

| Operation | CSP | PVS |
|---|---|---|
| Stop | $Stop$ | Stop |
| Prefix | $a \rightarrow P$ | a >> P |
| Choice | $P_1 \Box P_2$ | P1 \/ P2 |
| | $\Box_{i \in I} P_i$ | Choice! i : P(i) |
| Parallel Composition | $P_1 \|[A]\| P_2$ | Par(A)(P1, P2) |
| | $P_1 \||| P_2$ | P1 // P2 |
| | $\||\|_{i \in I} P_i$ | Interleave! i : P(i) |

Recursive processes are defined as least fixed points of monotonic functions. Given such a function `F` of type `[[U -> process[T]] -> [U-> process[T]]]`, `mu(F)` denotes the least fixed point of `F`. This form of the `mu` operator is necessary for defining recursive processes with parameters. A simpler form is available for the non-parametric case.

The preceding elements allow us to define CSP processes in PVS. In order to reason about such processes, we provide various lemmas such as the associativity of choice and parallel composition [6]. For specifying properties of processes we imitiate the **sat** operator. Properties are predicates on traces, that is, sets of traces, and the satisfaction relation is

```
|>(P, E): bool = subset?(P, E).
```

For example, we can translate the statement $P$ **sat** $tr{\restriction}D = \langle\rangle$ to

```
P |> { tr | proj(tr, D) = null }.
```

Various rules about satisfaction and induction theorems for reasoning about fixed points are provided [6].

# 4 The Authentication Model in PVS

## 4.1 Network

It is routine to specify the network. Events are represented by an abstract data type parameterized by the types of user identities and messages.

```
event[I, M: TYPE]: DATATYPE
  BEGIN
    trans(t_snd, t_rcv: I, t_msg: M): trans?
    rec(r_rcv, r_snd: I, r_msg: M): rec?
  END event
```

From this specification, PVS generates an axiomatic definition of the data type. The functions **trans** and **rec** are constructors; events are either of the form **trans(i, j, m)** or **rec(i, j, m)**. Functions such as **t_snd** give access to the components of events. The two functions **trans?** and **rec?** are recognisers of type [**event -> bool**] and characterize transmission and reception events, respectively.

The enemy is defined using the least fixed point operator. The process depends on two type parameters as above and on a message generation relation.

```
enemy[Identity, Message: TYPE,
      |- : [set[Message], Message -> bool]]: THEORY
  BEGIN

  ...

  F(X)(S): process[event] =
      (Choice! i, j, m: trans(i, j, m) >> X(add(m, S)))
      \/ (Choice! i, j, (m | S |- m): rec(i, j, m) >> X(S))

  enemy: [set[Message] -> process[event]] = mu(F)

  END enemy.
```

For such a definition to be sound, PVS requires us to show that **F** is monotonic by generating a proof obligation (TCC) [11].

Users can be arbitrary processes provided they satisfy the interface constraints. The type **user_process** below captures this restriction:

```
LocalEvents(i): set[event] =
  {e | EXISTS m, j: e = trans(i,j,m) OR e = rec(i,j,m)}

user_process: TYPE =
  [i: Identity -> {P | subset?(sigma(P), LocalEvents(i))}].
```

The function **sigma** gives the set of events P can generate. Any **user** of the above type is a function of domain **Identity** and range **process[T]** such that the set of events generated by **user(i)** is included in **LocalEvents(i)**. For defining networks, we use the function

```
network(baddy, P): process[T] = Par(fullset)(baddy, Interleave(P)),
```

where **baddy** is any process and P is of type [**Identity -> process[T]**]. The constant **fullset** is the set of all transmission and reception events.

## 4.2 Key Theorems

The main results of Sec. 2 are proved in a theory **network** which has the same
parameters as **enemy** and makes the following assumption:

```
montonic_gen: ASSUMPTION
    FORALL A, B, m: subset?(A, B) AND (A |- m) IMPLIES (B |- m).
```

Within the theory, **monotonic_gen** can be used like an axiom, but PVS generates a TCC to check that the assumption holds when one imports a particular
instance of **network**.

A first lemma follows from the previous assumption and is proved using the
induction rule for least fixed points:

```
Gen(S): set[Message] = { m | S |- m }

Prop(S): set[trace[event]] =
    { tr | subset?(rec_msg(tr), Gen(union(S, trans_msg(tr)))) }

enemy_prop: THEOREM enemy(S) |> Prop(S).
```

Informally, this means that any message **enemy(S)** can produce is generated
from the set **S** and the messages the enemy has intercepted from users.

Now, given a function **rho** of type **[Message->int]**, we define two trace
predicates:

```
RankUser(rho): set[trace[event]] =
    {tr | pos_trans(rho, tr) IMPLIES pos_rec(rho, tr) }

RankEnemy(rho): set[trace[event]] =
    {tr | pos_rec(rho, tr) IMPLIES pos_trans(rho, tr) },
```

where **pos_rec(rho, tr)** and **pos_trans(rho, tr)** are true if all the reception
or transmission events of **tr**, respectively, have positive rank by **rho**. The first
half of the main theorem is a corollary of **enemy_prop**:

```
rank_property: COROLLARY  positive(rho, INIT)
        AND (FORALL S: positive(rho, S) implies positive(rho, Gen(S))
    IMPLIES enemy(INIT) |> RankEnemy(rho).
```

If the two premisses are satisfied then the enemy cannot generate messages of
non-positive ranks unless it receives such messages from the users.

For convenience, we use a specific restriction operator; the process $P\|[R]\|Stop$
is written **P # R** in PVS. We then get the following essential property:

```
main_result: LEMMA  baddy |> RankEnemy(rho)
        AND (FORALL i: user(i) # R |> RankUser(rho))
    IMPLIES network(baddy, user) # R |> {tr | positive(rho, tr)}.
```

In this lemma, the two premisses are symmetric: **baddy** does not generate messages of negative rank if the users send messages of positive ranks and **user(i)**
**# R** does not send messages of negative ranks if it only receives messages of positive ranks. By induction, the two conditions imply that no message of positive
rank can ever appear in a trace of **network(baddy,user) # R**. From this and
lemma **rank_property** we obtain the main theorem:

```
authentication_by_rank: THEOREM
     positive(rho, INIT)
  AND (FORALL S, m:
          positive(rho, S) AND (S |- m) IMPLIES rho(m) > 0)
  AND (FORALL i: user(i) # R |> RankUser(rho))
  AND non_positive(rho, T)
IMPLIES network(enemy(INIT), user) |> auth(T, R).
```

## 4.3 Automating the Verifications

The previous theorem is the main tool for verifying authentication properties. When using it, most of the effort concentrates on properties of the form `user(i) # R |> RankUser(rho)`. There are also hidden conditions which arise from the type of `user`: we have to prove that `user(i)` can only generate events which belong to `LocalEvents(i)`. All these proofs can be partially automated by using the PVS rewriting facilities and by defining specific proof strategies.

The interface constraints are of the form `subset?(sigma(P), E)` where P is a CSP expression and E is a set of events. We can systematically develop rules which rewrite the above inclusion in a simpler form according to the top-level operator of P. There is such a rule for every CSP primitive; a few examples are given below:

```
interface_pref: LEMMA subset?(sigma(a >> P), E) IFF
     E(a) AND subset?(sigma(P), E)

interface_choice3: LEMMA subset?(sigma(Choice(P)), E) IFF
     FORALL i: subset?(sigma(P(i)), E)

interface_stop: LEMMA subset?(sigma(Stop), E)

interface_par: LEMMA subset?(sigma(P1), E) AND subset?(sigma(P2), E)
     IMPLIES subset?(sigma(Par(A)(P1, P2)), E).
```

All such lemmas can be installed as automatic rewrite rules which PVS applies in conjunction with built-in simplification and decision procedures. The first two rules are inconditional rewritings which applies in the left to right direction; `interface_stop` is also inconditional but matching terms are rewritten to `true`. The last rule is conditional: terms matching the right hand side of the implication reduce to `true` provided the premisses are also reduced to `true` by the decision procedures or by further rewriting.

Lemma `interface_pref` introduces expressions of the form `E(a)`. For user processes, E is `LocalEvents(i)` for some fixed i and two more rewrite rules are necessary:

```
local_transmission: LEMMA LocalEvents(i)(trans(i, j, m))

local_reception: LEMMA LocalEvents(i)(rec(i, j, m)).
```

In practice, automatic rewriting with these two rules and the preceding lemmas prove almost all interface constraints. The few exceptions are usually due to fixed points. The presence of quantifiers in the rules for fixed points interrupts the chain of rewrites and little manual intervention is required before rewriting can proceed.

For properties of the form P # R |> RankUser(rho), rewrite rules can also largely reduce the proof effort. However, rewriting is not sufficient and the rules must be supplemented with specific proof strategies.

In a similar way as above, two sets of rewrite rules are constructed which apply to expressions of the form P # R or P |> RankUser(rho). For example, the rules for prefix and Stop are:

> restriction_pref: LEMMA
>     (a >> P) # B = IF B(a) THEN Stop ELSE a >> (P # B) ENDIF
>
> rank_user_output: LEMMA (trans(i,j,m) >> P) |> RankUser(rho)
>     IFF rho(m)>0 AND P |> RankUser(rho)
>
> rank_user_input: LEMMA (rec(i,j,m) >> P) |> RankUser(rho)
>     IFF (rho(m)>0 IMPLIES P |> RankUser(rho))
>
> restriction_stop: LEMMA Stop # B = Stop
>
> rank_user_stop: LEMMA Stop |> RankUser[rho].

Such lemmas are more complex than the interface rules and automatic rewriting does not work as well. The first three examples illustrate some of the difficulties. PVS considers restriction_pref as a conditional rule which applies only if B(a) reduces to true or false. This cannot be expected in general since B depends on the authentication property being checked. The other two lemmas introduce terms involving rank functions which cannot systematically reduce to true. As a result, the chains or reductions required to apply conditional rules often fail.

Despite these limitations, some form of automation is still possible. The proofs of P # R |> RankUser(rho) have a regular pattern and the same sequences of proof commands are applied repeatedly. For example, if P is of the form rec(i,j,m) >> Q then the corresponding PVS proof starts by the following sequent:

> |----
> {1} (rec(i,j,m) >> Q) # R |> RankUser(rho).

The natural first step is to apply (rewrite "restriction_pref"). This yields

> |----
> {1} IF R(rec(i,j,m)) THEN Stop
>     ELSE rec(i,j,m) >> (Q # R) ENDIF |> RankUser(rho).

The obvious case split generates two subgoals. The first one can be solved immediately using the rewrite rules for Stop and the second is:

> |----
> {1} rec(i,j,m)>> (Q # R) |> RankUser(rho)
> {2} R(rec(i,j,m)).

Lemma rank_user_input can be applied and further propositional simplification yields:

```
{-1} rho(m)>0
    |----
{1} Q # R |> RankUser(rho)
{2} R(rec(i,j,m)).
```

At this point, the same sequence of proof commands applies if Q is a prefix expression which starts by a reception event. More generally, successive goals in such proofs are of the form

```
    ...
    |----
{1} P # R |> RankUser(rho)
    ...
```

and the syntactic form of P determines a sequence of commands which can be used systematically.

We exploit this regularity by defining specific proof strategies. An initialisation strategy installs automatic rules for Stop together with rank_user_input and rank_user_output. The other strategies correspond to particular CSP operators. For example, the strategy (prefix) applies the following command:

```
(try (rewrite "restriction_pref")
     (then* (lift-if) (assert) (prop))
     (skip)).
```

This performs the four steps of the proof sketched previously. The strategy attempts to rewrite the current goal with restriction_pref. If this fails, (skip) leaves the goal unchanged, otherwise, an expression of the form IF R(a) THEN Stop ELSE a >> (P # R) ENDIF is introduced. Three commands are then applied successively. In the second step, (assert) activates automatic rewriting. As a result, the first branch of the conditional is reduced to true and the second branch is rewritten by one of rank_user_input or rank_user_output. The effect of (prefix) depends on whether a is a transmission or a reception event and is described in Fig. 2.

Reception Events: $a = rec.i.j.m$

$$\frac{\Gamma, \rho(m) > 0 \vdash P \# R \text{ sat } RankUser(\rho), R(a), \Delta}{\Gamma \vdash (a \to P) \# R \text{ sat } RankUser(\rho), \Delta}$$

Transmission Events: $a = trans.i.j.m$

$$\frac{\Gamma \vdash \rho(m) > 0, R(a), \Delta \qquad \Gamma \vdash P \# R \text{ sat } RankUser(\rho), R(a), \Delta}{\Gamma \vdash (a \to P) \# R \text{ sat } RankUser(\rho), \Delta}$$

**Fig. 2.** Effect of the prefix strategy.

With similar strategies for the other CSP primitives, the proofs can be conducted at a fairly abstract level. The details of the PVS mechanics are hidden from the user who simply selects the right strategy. When none applies, the remaining sequents do not contain any process expression and correspond to simple properties of the rank function which have to be proved by other means. The structure of the proofs is for a large part independent of the rank function under investigation. It is easy to experiment with various rank functions and most of the proofs remain unchanged.

# 5  Applications

We have experimented the PVS mechanization on two versions of the Needham Schroeder public key protocol [10]. All the properties examined in [14] have been mechanically verified [6]. In the sequel, we consider the following variant proposed by Lowe[9][4]:

$$A \rightarrow B : \{N_a, A\}_{K_b}$$
$$B \rightarrow A : \{N_a, N_b, B\}_{K_a}$$
$$A \rightarrow B : \{N_b\}_{K_b}.$$

## 5.1  Encryption

The first step in the analysis is to model public key encryption. We follow [14] and represent messages by an abstract data type:

```
message: DATATYPE WITH SUBTYPES key, nonkey
  BEGIN
  text    (x_text: Text)                       : text?   : nonkey
  nonce   (x_nonce: Nonce)                      : nonce?  : nonkey
  user    (x_user: Identity)                    : user?   : nonkey
  public  (x_public: Identity)                  : public? : key
  secret  (x_secret: Identity)                  : secret? : key
  conc    (x_conc, y_conc: message)             : conc?   : nonkey
  code    (x_code: key, y_code: message)        : code?   : nonkey
  END message.
```

In this data type, the subtypes **key** and **nonkey** are similar to extra recognisers. The first five constructors define elementary messages of different natures and the last two correspond to concatenation and encryption.

Asymmetric cryptosystems satisfy the identity $\{\{m\}_{K_a}\}_{K_a^{-1}} = m$ but the equivalent PVS assumption

```
code(secret(i), code(public(i), m)) = m
```

is not sound; it contradicts the data type axioms. Instead we use a function **crypto** which performs message normalisation. We can then define the message generation relation |- as follows:

---

[4] $K_x$ and $K_x^{-1}$ are $x$'s public and private key; $\{m\}_K$ is $m$ encrypted using $K$.

```
Gen(S)(m): INDUCTIVE bool =
    S(m)
 OR (EXISTS m1, m2: Gen(S)(m1) AND Gen(S)(m2) AND m=conc(m1, m2))
 OR (EXISTS m1: Gen(S)(conc(m1, m)) OR Gen(S)(conc(m, m1)))
 OR (EXISTS m1, k: Gen(S)(m1) AND Gen(S)(k) AND m=crypto(k, m1));

|-(S, m): bool = Gen(S)(m).
```

Gen(S) is the set of messages which can be generated from S and is defined inductively. PVS automatically generates two induction axioms for Gen from which we can show the required monotonicity assumption:

```
gen_monotonic2: COROLLARY
    subset?(S1, S2) AND (S1 |- m) IMPLIES (S2 |- m).
```

## 5.2   Users and Verifications

The modelling allows several variants of the protocol to be analysed, from the simple case of two participants executing a single run to multiple runs executed concurrently. In a simple example, the initiator is described by the process below

```
userA: process[event] =
  Choice! i, x:
    ( trans(a, i, pub(i, conc(Na, user(a)))) >>
      ( rec(a, i, pub(a, conc3(Na, x, user(i)))) >>
        ( trans(a, i, pub(i, x)) >> Stop[event]))).
```

User $A$ non-deterministically initiates a single run with some user $i$ by sending the message $\{N_a, a\}$ encrypted with $K_i$. Then $A$ is ready to receive a message of the form $\{N_a, x, i\}_{K_a}$ coming from $i$ where $x$ is any nonce. $A$ responds to this message by sending back $\{x\}_{K_i}$.

We assume that the responder $B$ behaves as if participating in a run with $A$:

```
userB: process[event] =
  Choice! y:
    ( rec(b, a, pub(b, conc(y, user(a)))) >>
      ( trans(b, a, pub(a, conc(y, Nb, user(b)))) >>
        ( rec(b, a, pub(b, Nb)) >> Stop[event]))),
```

and we want to prove that reception of $\{N_b\}_{K_b}$ by $B$ ensures that $B$ is effectively communicating with $A$. More precisely, we want to prove that the network satisfies $T$ authenticates $R$ where $T$ and $R$ are as follows:

```
T: set[event] = { e | e = rec(b, a, pub(b, Nb)) }
R: set[event] = { e | e = trans(a, b, pub(b, Nb)) }.
```

As shown in [9], this property does not hold for the original Needham-Schroeder protocol; reception of $\{N_b\}_{K_b}$ still ensures that $A$ sent the message but to a user which may be different from $B$. The property holds for Lowe's variant, provided the ENEMY does not know $N_b$ or the secret keys of $A$ and $B$.

The rank function we use for the property above is defined in [14]. It satisfies the essential property below:

```
rho(pub(i, m)) =
  IF i=a AND (EXISTS x: m=conc3(x, Nb, user(b))) THEN 1
  ELSE rho(m) ENDIF.
```

In order to apply the main theorem, the most important part of the verification is to show the four following lemmas:

```
interface_userA: LEMMA subset?(sigma(userA), LocalEvents(a))

interface_userB: LEMMA subset?(sigma(userB), LocalEvents(b))

rank_user_a: LEMMA userA # R |> RankUser(rho)

rank_user_b: LEMMA userB # R |> RankUser(rho).
```

The interface constraints are easily checked. The proof script for **interface_userA** is given below:

```
(AUTO-REWRITE "local_transmission" "local_reception"
  "interface_pref[event]" "interface_stop[event]")
(EXPAND "userA")
(REWRITE "interface_choice3").
```

The first command installs the automatic rewrite rules presented in Sec. 4.3 and the second expands the definition of **userA**. The third step is a manual application of the interface rule for unbounded choice. This triggers automatic rewriting and the goal is solved at once.

The proofs of the rank preservation properties apply the strategies for choice and prefix. On the remaining goals, we use the predefined strategy **(grind)** which expands the definitions of **rho** and **R** and applies the decision procedures. This is often enough to solve the goals but sometimes the extensionality axioms for the message data type are needed (see [6] for details). For example, the proof script of **rank_user_a** is

```
(INIT-CSP "Identity" "message")
(EXPAND "userA")
(CHOICE3)
(PREFIX)
(("1" (DELETE 2) (GRIND))
 ("2"
  (PREFIX)
  (PREFIX)
  (DELETE 3 4)
  (GRIND)
  (CASE "x_user(y_conc(conc(conc(....)))) = b")
  (("1" (APPLY (REPEAT (APPLY-EXTENSIONALITY))))
   ("2" (REPLACE -2) (ASSERT)))))).
```

The proofs of authentication properties we have performed with PVS are all similar to the previous example. The most general situations, where concurrent protocol runs are considered, require much more complex rank functions. But, even in such cases, the PVS proofs are not substantially harder. The same proof strategies are used together with **(grind)** and extensionality rules.

# 6  Discussion and Related Work

This paper shows that PVS can provide efficient support for a non-trivial application of CSP. The usefulness of the mechanisation is clear. In our experience, manual verification of the constraints on rank functions simply does not work. PVS has found many errors in our own manual proofs of authentication properties. The proofs we performed generalise the results presented in [9] to more complex variants of the Needham Schroeder protocol. In recent works, larger protocols have been verified [2].

The basis of our mechanisation is a semantics embedding of CSP and PVS is adequate for this purpose. Camilleri [4] and Thayer [17] present similar embeddings in HOL and IMPS. Our main contribution compared with these works is the application to the specific problem of authentication and the development of PVS theories for this purpose.

In the analysis of security protocols, tools exist which support various belief logics [3, 1]. Closer to our approach are methods based on modelling protocols as collections of rules for transforming and reducing messages. Tool support in this area [9, 8] is mostly based on analysis for reachability of an insecure state which corresponds to the existence of an attack. This usually requires finitary models and the inability to find an attack does not in itself guarantee correctness of the full-scale protocol. Our verification approach is then a useful complement to these state exploration techniques.

Paulson [12] investigates the application of Isabelle/HOL to proving security properties of protocols by induction. He specifies protocols in terms of traces and rules about how traces can be augmented. This is clearly very close to the CSP trace model but gives no control over when rules may apply. In contrast, the CSP approach maintains the order of protocol steps and the order in which proof rules are applied. Paulson has some useful results about proof reuse while at present we know little about the potential reusability of rank functions.

In future developments we envisage to increase the level of proof automation. Currently, we provide specialised proof commands but the user still has to manually select the right rule. This could be automatized; the rule to apply can be determined from the top-level operator in a CSP process. Another extension would be to allow a more flexible modelling of the space of messages. The use of a PVS data type implies that messages constructed in different ways are different. Algebraic properties (such as the associativity of concatenation or the fact that public-key and private-key encryption are inverse of each other) cannot be introduced as equations. The approach of [14] remains valid even in the presence of more complex equational properties. This can be implemented with PVS but requires extra developments, such as a quotient construction for data types.

Another important avenue to explore will be the extent to which construction of rank functions can be assisted by the attempt to provide a PVS proof. Particular constraints on the rank function arise when instantiating the CSP rules and could be generated by a "blank" run of the PVS proof: the rank constraints appear as unresolved leaves in the proof-tree. Collecting the information may then help us to identify a suitable rank function.

In conclusion, we have presented a viable mechanical support in PVS for the verification of security protocols with respect to authentication properties. There is still much to be done to support verification in the presence of algebraic properties of cryptographic mechanisms, to improve automation, and to gain experience by investigating further protocols.

## Acknowledgements

This work was partially funded by DRA/Malvern.

## References

1. S. H. Brackin. Deciding Cryptographic Protocol Adequacy with HOL: The Implementation. In *TPHOLs'96*. Springer-Verlag, LNCS 1125, 1996.
2. J. Bryans and S. Schneider. Mechanical Verification of the full Needham-Schroeder public key protocol. Technical report, Royal Holloway, University of London, 1997.
3. M. Burrows, M. Abadi, and R. Needham. A Logic of Authentication. Technical Report 39, Digital Equipment Corporation, System Research Center, 1989.
4. A. J. Camilleri. Mechanizing CSP trace theory in higher order logic. *IEEE Transactions on Software Engineering*, 16(9):993–1004, 1990.
5. J. Crow, S. Owre, J. Rushby, N. Shankar, and M. Srivas. A tutorial introduction to PVS. In *Workshop on Industrial-Strength Formal Specification Techniques*, 1995.
6. B. Dutertre and S. Schneider. Embedding CSP in PVS. An Application to Authentication Protocols. Technical report, Royal Holloway, CSD-TR-97-12.
7. C. A .R. Hoare. *Communicating Sequential Processes*. Prentice-Hall International, 1985.
8. R. Kemmerer, C. Meadows, and Millen J. Three systems for cryptographic analysis. *Journal of Cryptology*, 7(2), 1994.
9. G. Lowe. Breaking and Fixing the Needham-Schroeder Public-Key Protocol Using FDR. In *Proc. of TACAS'96*. Springer-Verlag, LNCS 1055, 1996.
10. R. M. Needham and M. D. Schroeder. Using Encryption for Authentication in Large Networks of Computers. *Comm. of the ACM*, 21(12):993–999, 1978.
11. S. Owre, N. Shankar, and J. M. Rushby. *The PVS Specification Language*. Computer Science Lab., SRI International, 1993.
12. L. Paulson. Proving Properties of Security Protocols by Induction. Technical Report TR409, Computer Laboratory, University of Cambridge, 1996.
13. S. Schneider. Security Properties and CSP. In *IEEE Symposium on Security and Privacy*, 1996.
14. S. Schneider. Using CSP for protocol analysis: the Needham-Schroeder Public Key Protocol. Technical Report CSD-TR-96-14, Royal Holloway, 1996.
15. J. U. Skakkebæk and N. Shankar. Towards a duration calculus proof assistant in PVS. In *Formal Techniques in Real-Time and Fault-Tolerant Systems*. Springer-Verlag, LNCS 863, September 1994.
16. P. Syverson and P. van Oorschot. On Unifying Some Cryptographic Protocol Logics. In *Proc. of the 1994 IEEE Symp. on Research in Security and Privacy*, 1994.
17. F. J. Thayer. An approach to process algebra using IMPS. Technical Report MP-94B193, The MITRE Corporation, 1994.

# Verifying the Accuracy of Polynomial Approximations in HOL

John Harrison*

University of Cambridge Computer Laboratory
New Museums Site, Pembroke Street
Cambridge CB2 3QG, England

**Abstract.** Many modern algorithms for the transcendental functions rely on a large table of precomputed values together with a low-order polynomial to interpolate between them. In verifying such an algorithm, one is faced with the problem of bounding the error in this polynomial approximation. The most straightforward methods are based on numerical approximations, and are not prima facie reducible to a formal HOL proof. We discuss a technique for proving such results formally in HOL, via the formalization of a number of results in polynomial theory, e.g. squarefree decomposition and Sturm's theorem, and the use of a computer algebra system to compute results that are then checked in HOL. We demonstrate our method by tackling an example from the literature.

## 1 Introduction

Many algorithms for the transcendental functions such as *exp*, *sin* and *ln* in floating point arithmetic are based on table lookup. Suppose that a transcendental function $f(x)$ is to be calculated. Values of $f(a_i)$ are prestored for some approximately equally-spaced family of values $a_i$. When $f(x)$ is required, there are enough $a_i$ that $x$ will lie very close to one of them. By the use of some sort of interpolation formula, whose exact nature depends on $f$, one can reduce the problem of calculating $f(x)$ to calculating some similar function $g(x')$ for a small argument $x' = x - a_k$. For example, when calculating $e^x$, we can evaluate $e^{x'}$ and then multiply it by the prestored constant $e^{a_k}$, since $e^x = e^{a_k + x'} = e^{a_k} e^{x'}$. Because $x'$ is so small, the appropriate interpolating function $g(x')$ can be approximated adequately by a fairly low-order polynomial. As part of a verification effort for such an algorithm that will be reported elsewhere (Harrison 1997), we need to prove some mathematical results about the accuracy of such polynomial approximations.

Suppose we are interested in approximating a function $f(x)$ over a closed interval $[a, b]$, i.e. $\{x \mid a \le x \le b\}$, by a polynomial of degree $n$. The natural choice is the polynomial $p(x)$ that, out of all polynomials of degree $n$, has the best *minimax* error behaviour, i.e. minimizes the maximum magnitude of the error:

* Work supported by the EPSRC grant 'Floating Point Verification'

$$\|f(x) - p(x)\|_\infty = sup_{a \leq x \leq b}|f(x) - p(x)|$$

A fundamental theorem of Chebyshev states that such a polynomial always exists and has an interesting 'equal ripple' property: the maximum value of $|f(x) - p(x)|$ is attained at some $n + 2$ points in the interval such that the sign of $f(x) - p(x)$ alternates between successive points. However the theorem does not yield an analytical expression for the coefficients, or the maximum error. Certainly the truncated Taylor expansion is normally not the best approximation in this sense. The truncated expansion in terms of *Chebyshev polynomials* is usually close. In fact there are special cases, typically for rational functions, where the coefficients in such a series are those for a best approximation, or can be converted into them analytically — see Rivlin (1962) for example. But these are no good for the functions we are interested in, and the only general methods known are iterative numerical ones that rely on numerically approximating extrema as part of the intermediate steps. The standard algorithm is usually attributed to Remes (1934), and also often referred to as the *exchange algorithm*.

## 2 Our approach

In summary, then, it seems difficult to calculate the maximum error in the best approximation by analytical methods. Besides, any value so found would need slight but messy modifications when the coefficients are stored as approximate floating point numbers; typically the required coefficients will not be exactly representable. Instead, we allow the approximation to be calculated outside the theorem prover by arbitrary means, with coefficients truncated to the form actually used. Then we prove a theorem characterizing the maximum error in this polynomial approximation. Our procedure has the added advantage that we can take from the literature the polynomial approximations actually considered by other workers, without worrying about whether they coincide with the best approximations as we would calculate them.

The function $f(x)$ that we are interested in approximating is typically fairly well-behaved, and therefore so is the error $e(x) = f(x) - p(x)$ for a polynomial $p(x)$. In particular, we can normally assume that $e(x)$ is differentiable at least once throughout the interval. Moreover, it is usually easy to arrive at a (pessimistic) bound $B$ for the absolute value of the derivative $e'(x)$. This isn't the case for pathological functions such as $x \, sin(1/x)$ near zero, but for the basic transcendentals, it is easy over the intervals typically considered. By the mean value theorem (proved in HOL), this ensures that $B$ is a fixed bound for uniform continuity, meaning that:

$$\forall x, x' \in [a, b]. \, |e(x) - e(x')| \leq B|x - x'|$$

Therefore it is easy in principle to approximate the extremal values of $e(x)$ to an accuracy $\epsilon$ simply by dividing up the interval into a set of values $a_i$ at most $\epsilon/B$ apart and finding the maximum of the $e(a_i)$. In fact, this method works for a weaker notion of uniform continuity, normally assumed in the definition of 'computable real function', and for functions of more than one variable (Pour-El and Richards 1980).

Nevertheless, the above is too expensive in practice, since it involves a large number of calculations. This is all the more true in HOL, where a single evaluation of a transcendental function to moderate accuracy can take many seconds (Harrison 1996). A much more refined approach is to use the fact that if a function is differentiable in an interval, then its maximum and minimum are each attained either at the endpoints of the interval or at one of the points of zero derivative. This is easy to prove in HOL using the existing real analysis theory. So if we can approximate the points of zero derivative to within $\epsilon/B$, we can get the maximum and minimum to accuracy $\epsilon$ by evaluating $e(x)$ only at these points.

However, we are now faced with the problem of locating the points of zero derivative. It's generally pretty easy in practice to approximate all the derivative's roots $x_i$ numerically, e.g. using a Newton iteration. Provided they are simple roots, we can then find (rational) numbers $\alpha_i$ and $\beta_i$ such that $\alpha_i < x_i < \beta_i$ and the signs of $e'(\alpha_i)$ and $e'(\beta_i)$ differ. Now the intermediate value theorem (already proved in HOL) assures us that there is a root between $\alpha_i$ and $\beta_i$. If we also ensure that $\beta_i - \alpha_i \leq \epsilon/B$ this approximation serves for the later calculations. However there are two difficulties. First, if $x_i$ is a double root, or in general a root of even order, we will no longer have different signs for $e'(\alpha_i)$ and $e'(\beta_i)$ and it will be more complicated to prove in HOL that there is a root between those points. A more serious problem is that we have no HOL proof that we have located *all* the roots of $e'(x)$, and without that we have no way of proving our final result.

We are not aware of any simple general theory that can prove exactly how many roots an equation involving transcendental functions has. Therefore the above approach seems very difficult. Instead we modify it as follows.[2] We approximate $f(x)$ by a truncated Taylor series $t(x)$, choosing the degree so large that truncation incurs an error well below the tightness of the bound we are trying to achieve, say $\epsilon/2$. (An alternative would be to truncate the Chebyshev expansion, but although that might lead to a lower-degree polynomial, the analytical details are messier.) Now instead of working with $f(x)$ above we work with $t(x)$, and we then need only locate all the zeros of a *polynomial* $e'(x)$. Moreover this polynomial has rational coefficients, since floating point numbers are rational and the coefficients in all the typical Taylor series are rational. This problem is tractable. It is not hard to prove (see later) that a polynomial of degree $n$ can have at most $n$ roots. If we find exactly $n$, our task is necessarily complete. This favourable situation can't be relied on, but in general we can calculate the exact number of roots using a classical result due to Sturm. The main difficulties are that we must prove this theorem in HOL and then apply it. In principle, it would be possible to use the general quantifier elimination procedure for the reals that has already been developed by Harrison (1996), but in practice it is far too slow.

---

[2] Thanks to David Wheeler for this suggestion.

# 3 Polynomials in HOL

The ring $\mathbb{R}[X]$ of univariate polynomials over the reals may be characterized abstractly via a universal property. The most natural concrete definition is that it is the space of functions $c : \mathbb{N} \to \mathbb{R}$ such that for all sufficiently large $n$ we have $c_n = 0$.[3] We define the degree of $c$, written $\partial(c)$ or $deg(c)$, to be the least $d$ such that $\forall i > d.c_i = 0$. The function $c$ is thought of as $\Sigma_{i=0}^{deg(c)} c_i x^i$, and this motivates the definition of addition and negation componentwise, e.g. $(b + c)_i = b_i + c_i$, and multiplication by:

$$(bc)_n = \Sigma_{i=0}^{n} b_i c_{n-i}$$

Rather than define a type of polynomials in this way, we deal directly with the *functions* $\mathbb{R} \to \mathbb{R}$ determined by polynomials. For a polynomial $c$, this is the function that takes $x$ to $\Sigma_{i=0}^{deg(c)} c_i x^i$. Actually, in the case of the reals, nothing is lost by this, since every polynomial function determines a unique polynomial, and vice versa.[4] We define a function poly that maps a list of coefficients $[c_0; \ldots; c_n]$ into the corresponding polynomial function $\lambda x. \, \Sigma_{i=0}^{n} c_i x^i$:[5]

```
|- (poly [] x = &0) /\ (poly (CONS h t) x = h + x * poly t x)
```

Note that `poly` is not injective, since lists with trailing zeros give the same function, and so the salient notion of equality for polynomial functions arising from two lists $l_1$ and $l_2$ is that poly $l_1$ = poly $l_2$, or equivalently $\forall x.$ poly $l_1 \, x =$ poly $l_2 \, x$, rather than simply $l_1 = l_2$. If desired, we could introduce an equivalence relation between lists corresponding to this notion. We can now define arithmetic operations on lists by primitive recursion, including addition (++):

```
|- ([] ++ 12 = 12) /\
   (CONS h t ++ 12 = if (12 = []) then CONS h t
                     else CONS (h + (HD 12) (t ++ (TL 12))))
```

multiplication by a constant (##):

```
|- (c ## [] = []) /\
   (c ## CONS h t = CONS (c * h) (c ## t))
```

and multiplication of two polynomials (**):

```
|- ([] ** 12 = []) /\
   (CONS h t ** 12 =
    if t = [] then h ## 12 else h ## 12 ++ CONS (&0) (t ** 12))
```

---

[3] We write $c_n$ rather than $c(n)$, since it is probably more natural.

[4] This depends on the fact that the underlying ring is infinite. For example in a 2-element ring the polynomials $x$ and $x^2$ are distinct even though they both determine the same function.

[5] The symbol & is the injection $\mathbb{N} \to \mathbb{R}$, and hence appears in real numeral constants.

From these, we can define negation and exponentiation in an obvious way:

```
|- neg p = --(&1) ## p

|- (p exp 0 = [&1]) ∧
   (p exp (SUC n) = p ** p exp n)
```

We also need to define differentiation of polynomials. This can be expressed purely as a formal manipulation of the list of coefficients, conveniently done via an auxiliary function:

```
|- (diff_aux n [] = []) ∧
   (diff_aux n (CONS h t) = CONS (&n * h) (diff_aux (SUC n) t))

|- diff l = if l = [] then [] else diff_aux 1 (TL l)
```

We then prove that all these operations do indeed work as expected on the corresponding polynomial functions. These are all straightforward single or double structural inductions on lists:

```
|- ∀p1 p2 x. poly (p1 ++ p2) x = poly p1 x + poly p2 x

|- ∀p c x. poly (c ## p) x = c * poly p x

|- ∀p x. poly (neg p) x = --(poly p x)

|- ∀x p1 p2. poly (p1 ** p2) x = poly p1 x * poly p2 x

|- ∀p n x. poly (p exp n) x = (poly p x) pow n

|- ∀l x. ((poly l) diffl (poly (diff l) x)) x
```

The last of these uses a notion from the HOL real analysis theory: it says that poly $l$ is locally differentiable at $x$ with derivative poly (diff $l$) $x$ there. From the above results, it is straightforward to verify all the basic properties that one would expect of polynomial functions, e.g. that addition and multiplication are commutative, and that all polynomial functions are infinitely continuously differentiable, and that the product rule holds for derivatives of polynomial products. Note a subtle point however: not all identities hold at the level of *lists*. For example we have:

```
|- ([] ** [&1; &2] = []) ∧
   ([&1; &2] ** [] = [&0])
```

We do however define a function that deletes trailing zeros, and prove that it does not affect the polynomial function. Proving the opposite, that if $l_1$ and $l_2$ give rise to the same polynomial function then their normalized forms are equal, is harder, and it's convenient to wait till we've proved the key property that a nontrivial polynomial only has finitely many roots.

```
|- (normalize [] = []) ∧
   (normalize (CONS h t) = if normalize t = [] then
                              if h = &0 then [] else [h]
                           else CONS h (normalize t))

|- ∀p. poly (normalize p) = poly p
```

If desired, we could redefine the addition operation to use this at the end, and then all operations would return normalized results for normalized inputs. However we do not do that, merely using it to define the notion of degree:

```
|- ∀p. degree p = PRE (LENGTH (normalize p))
```

Although we don't really want to rely on representation details, it's very convenient to get us started to prove one key result at the level of lists, rather than polynomial functions. This is that if a polynomial derived from a nonempty list is divided by a linear polynomial, there is a constant remainder:

```
|- ∀t h. ∃q r. CONS h t = [r] ++ [-- a; &1] ** q
```

(Note that [-- a; &1] is thought of as '$x - a$'.) From this, we find that if $a$ is a root of a nontrivial polynomial, then the polynomial is divisible by $(x - a)$ *at the level of lists*:

```
|- ∀a p. (poly p a = &0) = (p = []) ∨ (∃q. p = [-- a; &1] ** q)
```

Now since we also have:

```
|- ∀q. LENGTH ([-- a; &1] ** q) = SUC (LENGTH q)
```

it is a straightforward induction on the length of a generating list to show that a nonzero polynomial can only have finitely many roots, bounded, in fact, by the length of the list, and therefore by the degree of a normalized polynomial:

```
|- ∀p. ¬(poly p = poly [])
       ⟹ (∃i. ∀x. (poly p x = &0)
           ⟹ (∃n. n <= (LENGTH p) ∧ (x = i n)))
```

or more abstractly, using a notion from the HOL set theory:

```
|- ∀p. ¬(poly p = poly []) ⟹ FINITE {x | poly p x = &0}
```

Several key results flow immediately from this fact. The polynomial ring has no zerodivisors, i.e. if the product of two polynomials is trivial, so is one of the factors. Hence cancellation holds. We can also get a more constructive definition of what it means for a polynomial to be zero.

```
|- ∀p q. (poly (p ** q) = poly []) =
        (poly p = poly []) ∨ (poly q = poly [])

|- ∀p q r. (poly (p ** q) = poly (p ** r)) =
          (poly p = poly []) ∨ (poly q = poly r)

|- ∀p. (poly p = poly []) = FORALL (λc. c = &0) p
```

where here, and later, we use the logical operations on lists defined by:

```
|- (FORALL P [] = T) ∧
   (FORALL P (CONS h t) = P h ∧ FORALL P t)

|- (EX P [] = F) ∧
   (EX P (CONS h t) = P h ∨ EX P t)
```

After this, there are no real mathematical difficulties left in getting the results we want; it is merely necessary to accumulate a number of lemmas. Many of these are concerned with divisibility of polynomials, which we define, no longer at the list level, by:

```
|- p1 divides p2 = ∃q. poly p2 = poly (p1 ** q)
```

There are various obvious properties collected, e.g:

```
|- ∀p. p divides p

|- ∀p q r. p divides q ∧ q divides r ⟹ p divides r

|- ∀p q m n. p exp n divides q ∧ m <= n ⟹ p exp m divides q

|- ∀p q r. p divides q ∧ p divides r ⟹ p divides q ++ r

|- ∀p q r. p divides q ∧ p divides q ++ r ⟹ p divides r

|- ∀p q. (poly p = poly []) ⟹ q divides p
```

A slightly less trivial property is that the linear polynomials are prime elements in the polynomial ring:

```
|- ∀a p q. [a; &1] divides p ** q =
           [a; &1] divides p ∨ [a; &1] divides q
```

A major result in what follows is that for each nonzero polynomial $p$ and real number $a$, we have a welldefined 'order' $n$ for $a$ such that $p(x)$ is divisible by $(x - a)^n$ but not by $(x - a)^{n+1}$. Hence $a$ is a root of $p$ precisely if its order is nonzero. The definition as a choice term is trivial:

```
|- order a p =
        εn. [-- a; &1] exp n divides p ∧
            ¬([-- a; &1] exp SUC n divides p)
```

Some tedious but straightforward proofs are required to show that it has the required properties for any nontrivial polynomial:

```
|- ∀p a. ¬(poly p = poly [])
        ⟹ ([-- a; &1] exp (order a p)) divides p ∧
            ¬(([-- a; &1] exp (SUC(order a p))) divides p)

|- ∀p a. (poly p a = &0) = (poly p = poly []) ∨ ¬(order a p = 0)

|- ∀p a n. [-- a; &1] exp n divides p =
        (poly p = poly []) ∨ n <= order a p

|- ∀p a. ¬(poly p = poly [])
        ⟹ (∃q. (poly p = poly ([-- a; &1] exp (order a p) ** q)) ∧
            ¬([-- a; &1] divides q))
```

## 4   Squarefree decomposition

Given a polynomial $p(x)$, we are interested in locating its roots. As we have already mentioned, given an isolating interval $[\alpha, \beta]$ for a root such that $p(\alpha)$ and $p(\beta)$ have opposite signs, we can straightforwardly prove in HOL from the intermediate value theorem and the known continuity of polynomials that there must be at least one root in the interval. However, this doesn't work for roots of even order (in the precise sense of 'order' we have defined above), since in that case the function has the same sign at either side of the root. This is one reason why we would prefer the polynomial to have no multiple real roots. Another reason is that Sturm's theorem is easier to prove for polynomials without multiple real roots — this is actually the only form we have proved in HOL.

Therefore, it's convenient to start off by finding the so-called 'squarefree decomposition' of $p$. To get this, we divide $p$ by $gcd(p, p')$ where $p'$ is the derivative polynomial. It is easy to see that the resulting polynomial has the same roots but that they are all of order 1. If $a$ is a root of $p(x)$ of order $n + 1$, then we have $p(x) = (x - a)^{n+1}q(x)$ for $q(a) \neq 0$. Differentiating, we have $p'(x) = (n + 1)(x - a)^n q(x) + (x - a)^{n+1}q'(x)$. This is obviously divisible by $(x-a)^n$ but not by $(x-a)^{n+1}$, for that would, by the primality of linear factors, imply that $(x - a)$ divides $q(x)$, a contradiction since we assumed $q(a) \neq 0$. Hence $a$ has order $min(n, n + 1) = n$ in $gcd(p, p')$, and so order 1 in $p/gcd(p, p')$.

We start by defining what it means for a polynomial to be 'squarefree', i.e. to have no quadratic factors. Actually, since we only consider real factors, we prepend the letter 'r':

```
|- ∀p. rsquarefree p =
       ¬(poly p = poly []) ∧ (∀a. (order a p = 0) ∨ (order a p = 1))
```

We prove without much trouble that this is equivalent to the fact that $p$ and $p'$ have no common factors, and deduce a simple decomposition theorem for squarefree polynomials:

```
|- ∀p. rsquarefree p =
       (∀a. ¬((poly p a = &0) ∧ (poly (diff p) a = &0)))

|- ∀p a.
       rsquarefree p ∧ (poly p a = &0)
       ⟹ (∃q. (poly p = poly ([-- a; &1] ** q)) ∧ ¬(poly q a = &0))
```

Now we need to show that dividing by $gcd(p, p')$ always converts a polynomial $p$ into a squarefree one with the same roots. Rather than defining $gcd(p, p')$ explicitly in HOL, we will simply assume some $d$ such that the following hold for some polynomials $r$ and $s$, $q$ and $e$:

$$p = qd$$
$$p' = ed$$
$$d = rp + sp'$$

It is clear that this constrains $d$ to be a gcd of $p$ and $p'$, since any other common divisor of $p$ and $p'$ must divide $d$. We can calculate the gcd externally together with the coefficients $r$ and $s$, using the gcdex function of the Maple computer algebra system, and get $q$ and $e$ via its division function. These are then plugged into the following HOL theorem for checking.

```
|- ∀p q d e r s.
       ¬(poly (diff p) = poly []) ∧
       (poly p = poly (q ** d)) ∧
       (poly (diff p) = poly (e ** d)) ∧
       (poly d = poly (r ** p ++ s ** diff p))
       ⟹ rsquarefree q ∧
           (∀a. (poly q a = &0) = (poly p a = &0))
```

The proof of this is not too difficult, by deriving a couple of additional facts about how orders of roots interact with operations:

```
|- ∀a p q.
       ¬(poly (p ** q) = poly [])
       ⟹ (order a (p ** q) = order a p + order a q)

|- ∀p a.
       ¬(poly (diff p) = poly []) ∧ ¬(order a p = 0)
       ⟹ (order a p = SUC(order a (diff p)))
```

Now fix $a$ and consider the orders of $a$ in the various polynomials we consider above. We have, assuming $p$ and $p'$ are nontrivial (the latter obviously implies the former):

$$order_a(p) = order_a(q) + order_a(d)$$
$$order_a(p') = order_a(e) + order_a(d)$$
$$order_a(d) \geq min(order_a(p'), order_a(p))$$

These together imply (over the natural numbers) that $order_a(q) = 0$ if $order_a(p) = 0$ and $order_a(q) = 1$ otherwise. The proof is done automatically by HOL's linear natural number arithmetic package, after case-splitting over whether $order_a(p)$ is zero and throwing in the fact that $order_a(p) = order_a(p') + 1$ in the latter case.

# 5  Sturm's theorem

Sturm's theorem (Benedetti and Risler 1990) gives a precise figure for the number of (distinct) real roots a polynomial has in an interval. Assuming the polynomial has rational coefficients and the endpoints of the interval are rational, it requires only rational arithmetic. The key concept is a *Sturm sequence* for a polynomial $p$. This is a finite sequence of polynomials, with $p$ as the first element that has certain important properties. Rather than deal abstractly in terms of these properties, we use the 'standard' Sturm sequence directly. This starts with $p_0 = p$ and $p_1 = p'$ and thereafter proceeds by division, with a change of sign, so that $p_i = q_i p_{i+1} - p_{i+2}$ for some quotient $q_i$, and $deg(p_{i+2}) < deg(p_{i+1})$. Actually we can relax this slightly by rescaling the polynomials to keep the coefficients as simple as possible, provided we do not change their signs. We thus define the property of being a Sturm sequence in HOL as follows.

```
|- (STURM p p' [] = p' divides p) ∧
   (STURM p p' (CONS g gs) = (∃k. &0 < k ∧ p' divides (p ++ k ## g)) ∧
                             degree g < degree p' ∧
                             STURM p' g gs)
```

Note that we separate out the first two elements of the list, to give simpler manipulation, and do not yet assume that $p'$ is the derivative of $p$. We next define the number of variations in sign of a finite sequence of numbers (or a list in our formalization), not counting zeros:

```
|- (varrec prev [] = 0) ∧
   (varrec prev (CONS h t) =
      if prev * h < &0 then SUC (varrec h t)
      else if h = &0 then varrec prev t else varrec h t)

|- variation l = varrec (&0) l
```

Sturm's theorem involves calculating the number of variations in sign of the polynomials in a Sturm sequence, evaluated at a point. It asserts that the number of roots of $p$ between $a$ and $b$ is the difference in this variation when calculated at $a$ and $b$ respectively. The proof proceeds by analyzing how this variation changes across roots of polynomials in the Sturm sequence. We can break the problem down so that we only need to consider one root at a time. It is easy to prove by induction on the definition of finiteness that any finite set of reals can be laid out in an ordered linear sequence $i_0, \ldots, i_{N-1}$:

```
|- ∀s. FINITE s
      ⟹ (∃i N.
            (∀x. x IN s = (∃k. k < N ∧ (x = i k))) ∧
            (∀k. i k < i (SUC k)))
```

The set of zeros of a list of nontrivial polynomials is finite (optionally in any interval, since any subset of a finite set is finite), by list induction, so we can find such an enumeration of the points that are roots of any of the polynomials in a sequence. Now by considering the mid-points between adjacent $i_k$, we can split up an interval $[a, b]$ into intervals so that there is at most one root in each (though it may be a root of more than one of the polynomials at once). This is actually quite tedious to prove, since we need to take care at the endpoints.

Now we can confine ourselves to intervals containing at most one root, and such that if the root is one of the endpoints, it is not a root of the starting polynomial $p$. (This is ruled out for the two endpoints $a$ and $b$ by hypothesis; for internal endpoints this holds for the other polynomials too.) We just need to prove that if such an interval contains no root of $p$, the variation is the same at both ends, while if there is a root, it decreases by 1 in passing from left to right.

The first is pretty easy, under fairly weak hypotheses. Consider an interval $[a, b]$ and suppose that $p_i(c) \neq 0$ but $p_{i+1}(c) = 0$. Since we have $p_i = q_i p_{i+1} - k p_{i+2}$ for positive $k$, this means that $p_i(c)$ and $p_{i+2}(c)$ have opposite signs. Since $c$ is the only possible root, neither $p_i$ nor $p_{i+2}$ changes sign throughout the interval, so they have opposite signs at both ends. Now the signs of $p_{i+1}(a)$ and $p_{i+1}(b)$ make no difference to the overall variation between $p_i$ and $p_{i+2}$, which is one in each case. This argument is easily formalized in HOL using induction, though not pure structural induction. Depending on whether the head element of a list is zero, we either move to the consideration of a list one element or two elements shorter, so we need to perform wellfounded induction on the length of the list. The final result is:

```
|- ∀l f f' c.
      STURM f f' l ∧ a <= c ∧ c <= b ∧
      (∀x. a <= x ∧ x <= b ∧
            EX (λp. poly p x = &0) (CONS f (CONS f' l))
            ⟹ (x = c)) ∧
      ¬(poly f c = &0)
      ⟹ (varrec (poly f a) (MAP (λp. poly p a) (CONS f' l)) =
          varrec (poly f b) (MAP (λp. poly p b) (CONS f' l)))
```

We just need to prove that if the starting polynomial does have a root in the interval, then the variation changes by 1. Now we use an assumption that the starting polynomial is squarefree. Therefore the derivative has no zero in the interval, and so by the above lemma we get no change in variation from the tail of the sequence. We need only consider the change in sign from $p(x)$ to $p'(x)$. In fact there must be exactly one change of sign, because $p$ crosses the axis precisely once, the root being simple. This is easily formalized using the mean value theorem: the derivative does not change sign over the interval, so either the derivative is positive everywhere and the function goes from negative to positive, or vice versa. In either case the result follows. Plugging this together with the lemma for the rest of the sequence, we get the result for a single interval, and so by summing over the intervals, we get the final result:

```
|- ∀f a b l.
     a <= b ∧ ¬(poly f a = &0) ∧ ¬(poly f b = &0) ∧
     rsquarefree f ∧ STURM f (diff f) l
     ⟹ {x | a <= x ∧ x <= b ∧ (poly f x = &0)} HAS_SIZE
           (variation (MAP (λp. poly p a) (CONS f (CONS (diff f) l))) -
            variation (MAP (λp. poly p b) (CONS f (CONS (diff f) l))))
```

where, because the HOL cardinality function is total and hence does not encode finiteness, we use:

```
|- s HAS_SIZE n = FINITE s ∧ (CARD s = n)
```

The main result also holds without the restriction that the starting polynomial be squarefree, but it is more complicated to prove (using the above squarefree case as a lemma) and we do not need it. However, note that the Sturm sequence is up to rescaling a Euclidean division sequence for the polynomial and its derivative. Hence we expect the last term of the Sturm sequence to be a constant polynomial, and this itself implies that the original polynomial must have been squarefree without a separate check. Thus we can sharpen the above slightly, if we rule out a few degenerate cases. The form we actually use, as proved in HOL, is:

```
|- ∀f a b l d.
        a <= b ∧
        ¬(poly f a = &0) ∧
        ¬(poly f b = &0) ∧
        ¬(poly (diff f) = poly []) ∧
        STURM f (diff f) l ∧
        ¬(l = []) ∧
        (LAST l = [d]) ∧
        ¬(d = &0)
        ⟹ {x | a <= x ∧ x <= b ∧ (poly f x = &0)} HAS_SIZE
              variation (MAP (λp. poly p a) (CONS f (CONS (diff f) l))) -
              variation (MAP (λp. poly p b) (CONS f (CONS (diff f) l)))
```

# 6 Applications

We will consider an example taken from a paper by Tang (1989) giving algorithms for the exponential function in single and double IEEE standard arithmetic. They use polynomials to approximate $e^x - 1$ over the range $[-\frac{ln(2)}{64}, \frac{ln(2)}{64}]$ for the respective precisions. The paper gives the coefficients as IEEE numbers in hexadecimal form. Translated into rational numbers, the approximating polynomial for single precision is:

$$p_{single}(x) = x + \frac{8388676}{2^{24}}x^2 + \frac{11184876}{2^{26}}x^3$$

Tang asserts an error of approximately $2^{-33.2}$ for the approximation, obtained by 'locating numerically all the extreme points of $e^t - 1 - p(t)$ in the interval $[-0.010831, 0.010831]$'. It is this result that we will formalize in HOL. Consider the error in truncated Taylor expansions. There are several versions of Taylor's theorem proved in the HOL real analysis theory, and the most convenient one for our purposes is the one for infinitely everywhere differentiable functions:

```
|- ∀f diff.
       (diff 0 = f) ∧ (∀m x. (diff m diffl diff (SUC m) x) x)
    ⟹ (∀x n.
           ∃t. abs t <= abs x ∧
           (f x =
            Sum (0,n) (λm. diff m (&0) / &(FACT m) * x pow m) +
            diff n t / &(FACT n) * x pow n))
```

Note that `Sum (0,n) f` means $\sum_{i=0}^{n-1} f_i$, so the above says that for some $t$ with $|t| \le |x|$ we have

$$f(x) = (\Sigma_{i=0}^{n-1} \frac{f^{(i)}(0)}{i!}x^i) + \frac{f^{(n)}(t)}{n!}x^n$$

We can sharpen the above to $|t| < |x|$ when $x \neq 0$ and $n \neq 0$, but that is unnecessary here. Instantiating to the exponential function and using the known derivative, we get:

```
|- ∀x n. ∃t. abs t <= abs x ∧
            (exp x = Sum (0,n) (λm. x pow m / &(FACT m)) +
             exp t / &(FACT n) * x pow n)
```

that is, $e^x = (\Sigma_{i=0}^{n-1} x^i/i!) + e^t x^n/n!$. We need only consider $x$ with $|x| \le ln(2)/64$. In this case, $e^t$ for $|t| \le |x|$ is almost 1, so the maximum error from truncating the series before the $n^{th}$ term is approximately $\epsilon_n = (ln(2)/64)^n/n!$. We can see that an additional 3 terms gives an error of about $\epsilon_7 = 2^{-58}$, easily small enough for our purposes. [6]

---

[6] Note that the $n = 4$ value indicates that the minimax approximation we are concerned with is 5 times as accurate as the truncated Taylor series of the same order, a difference that suffices to make a significant change to the overall error in the algorithm.

$$t(x) = x + \frac{1}{2}x^2 + \frac{1}{6}x^3 + \frac{1}{24}x^4 + \frac{1}{120}x^5 + \frac{1}{720}x^6$$

Hence the error polynomial $e(x) = t(x) - p_{single}(x)$ is:

$$e(x) = -\frac{17}{4194304}x^2 - \frac{49}{50331648}x^3 + \frac{1}{24}x^4 + \frac{1}{120}x^5 + \frac{1}{720}x^6$$

Differentiating with respect to $x$ yields:

$$e'(x) = -\frac{17}{2097152}x - \frac{49}{16777216}x^2 + \frac{1}{6}x^3 + \frac{1}{24}x^4 + \frac{1}{120}x^5$$

This is already squarefree, so the squarefree decomposition is trivial. It has fewer real roots than its full complement of 5, just 3 of them, all in the interval of interest. Hence we need to use Sturm's theorem. The Sturm sequence given by Maple, after rescaling the original derivative and all the members of the sequence to make all the coefficients integers, can easily be checked in HOL by expanding the definitions and doing arithmetic. We can then deduce from Sturm's theorem that there are exactly 3 real roots in the interval concerned. First, we want to isolate them to a reasonable accuracy. For the accuracy of the polynomial bound to be well above the tightness of the error bound required, we choose $\epsilon = 2^{-48}$. It is straightforward to give a crude upper bound on the derivative using the following theorem:

```
|- ∀x k p. abs x <= k ⟹ abs (poly p x) <= poly (MAP abs p) k
```

and we duly find that $B = 2^{-21}$ suffices. Therefore we want to isolate the roots to within $\epsilon/B = 2^{-27}$. Maple offers the following isolating intervals when given the required accuracy: $[0, 0]$, $[\frac{936399}{2^{27}}, \frac{936400}{2^{27}}]$ and $[\frac{-935680}{2^{27}}, \frac{-935679}{2^{27}}]$.

We can now prove that an ordered list of these isolating intervals does indeed include all the roots, using the following general lemma:

```
|- ∀l a b.
     {x | a <= x ∧ x <= b ∧ (poly p x = &0)} HAS_SIZE (LENGTH l) ∧
     recordered a l b ∧
     FORALL (λ(u,v). poly p(u) * poly p(v) <= &0) l
     ⟹ ∀x. a <= x ∧ x <= b ∧ (poly p(x) = &0)
         ⟹ EX (λ(u,v). u <= x ∧ x <= v) l
```

where:

```
|- (recordered a [] b = a <= b) ∧
   (recordered a (CONS h t) b =
        a < FST h ∧ FST h <= SND h ∧ recordered (SND h) t b)
```

As we said, there is already a theorem in HOL asserting that we can maximize a differentiable function in an interval by considering values only at the endpoints and points of zero derivative:

```
|- ∀f f' a b K.
      (∀x. a <= x ∧ x <= b ⟹ (f diffl (f' x)) x) ∧
      abs(f a) <= K ∧ abs(f b) <= K ∧
      (∀x. a <= x ∧ x <= b ∧ (f'(x) = &0) ⟹ abs(f x) <= K)
      ⟹ (∀x. a <= x ∧ x <= b ⟹ abs(f x) <= K)
```

This can be modified to take account of our approximate knowledge of the points of zero derivative:

```
|- ∀f f' l a b.
      (∀x. a <= x ∧ x <= b ⟹ (f diffl f'(x)) x) ∧
      (∀x. a <= x ∧ x <= b ⟹ abs(f'(x)) <= B) ∧
      abs(f a) <= K + B * e ∧ abs(f b) <= K + B * e ∧
      (∀x. a <= x ∧ x <= b ∧ (f'(x) = &0)
           ⟹ EX (λ(u,v). u <= x ∧ x <= v) l) ∧
      FORALL (λ(u,v). a <= u ∧ v <= b ∧
                      abs(u - v) <= e ∧ abs(f(u)) <= K) l
      ⟹ ∀x. a <= x ∧ x <= b ⟹ abs(f(x)) <= K + B * e
```

We now have all the ingredients required by this theorem, so we get the final result for the error in approximating the higher degree Taylor series. We now include the error from the Taylor truncation, using the following theorem to give a crude bound on the error term:

```
|- ∀x. &0 <= x ∧ x <= inv(&2) ⟹ exp(x) <= &1 + &2 * x
```

Thus we get the final result:

```
|- ∀x. --(&10831) / &1000000 <= x ∧ x <= &10831 / &1000000
       ⟹ abs((exp(x) - &1) - (x + (&8388676 / &2 pow 24) * x pow 2 +
                              &11184876 / &2 pow 26 * x pow 3))
       <= (&23 / &27) * inv(&2 pow 33)
```

# 7 Conclusion and future work

This paper illustrates how we can incorporate an important form of numerical reasoning into a formal HOL proof. This is appealing since it allows us to conduct the whole verification in a single system, without relying on the correctness of external tools or stepping outside the usual logic. At the same time, the proof is nontrivial, with the development of the material described here taking several weeks' work. In addition, the eventual runtimes are large (over an hour on a fast machine) owing to the extensive need for numerical calculation, which is rather slow when done by pure inference. The difficulty in both these senses is all the more striking when one considers that an informal error analysis of this numerical approximation occupies about two lines of the source paper.

One of the motivations behind ACL2, the successor to NQTHM (Boyer and Moore 1979), is that calculation is an important part of proof in verifications, and deserves to be a key consideration in the design of theorem provers. In one sense, our work suggests that an ordinary theorem prover may be adequate for the task, but it would obviously be preferable to make the calculations here much faster. This could certainly be done in ACL2, which can perform rational arithmetic in proofs at almost the same speed as in the host machine. Nevertheless, ACL2 would not be particularly convenient for the whole proof, since it does not support real numbers. It would be impossible to use many of the proofs here in ACL2, or even to *state* our final theorem, without artificial paraphrases.

A key objective of future work is to automate this class of proofs. We have already automated most of the internal manipulations such as multiplying polynomials, and it would not be difficult to package up the polynomial-bounding as an automatic HOL derived rule. Then we could use it in the future for say *ln* or *sin* with minimal effort. The very final part, using the error in the Taylor series, could also be automated, but only with more work. There are optimizations that can be made on a case-by-case basis, which would also be tricky to automate. For example, since the example derivative above only has 3 real roots *in total*, we could evaluate the variation at $\pm 1$ and save some rational arithmetic.

The extension to rational functions would be fairly straightforward since the zeros of these can be located in much the same way. We may consider this if we ever need to deal with rational functions in our future verifications.

# References

Benedetti, R. and Risler, J.-J. (1990) *Real algebraic and semi-algebraic sets*. Hermann, Paris.

Boyer, R. S. and Moore, J S. (1979) *A Computational Logic*. ACM Monograph Series. Academic Press.

Harrison, J. (1997) Floating point verification in HOL Light: The exponential function. Unpublished draft, to appear.

Harrison, J. (1996) Theorem proving with the real numbers. Technical Report 408, University of Cambridge Computer Laboratory, New Museums Site, Pembroke Street, Cambridge, CB2 3QG, UK. Author's PhD thesis.

Pour-El, M. B. and Richards, J. I. (1980) *Computability in Analysis and Physics*. Perspectives in Mathematical Logic. Springer-Verlag.

Remes, M. E. (1934) Sur le calcul effectif des polynomes d'approximation de Tchebichef. *Comptes Rendus Hebdomadaires des Séances de l'Académie des Sciences*, **199**, 337–340.

Rivlin, T. J. (1962) Polynomials of best uniform approximation to certain rational functions. *Numerische Mathematik*, 4, 345–349.

Tang, P. T. P. (1989) Table-driven implementation of the exponential function in IEEE floating-point arithmetic. *ACM Transactions on Mathematical Software*, **15**, 144–157.

# A Full Formalisation of π-Calculus Theory in the Calculus of Constructions

Daniel Hirschkoff*

CERMICS - ENPC/INRIA and
Dipartimento di Scienze dell'Informazione - Università di Roma "La Sapienza"

**Abstract.** A formalisation of π-calculus in the Coq system is presented. Based on a de Bruijn notation for names, our implementation exploits the mechanisation of some proof techniques described by Sangiorgi in [San95b] to derive several results of classical π-calculus theory, including congruence, structural equivalence and the replication theorems. As the proofs are described, insight is given to the main implementational issues that arise in our study, without entering too much the technical details. Possible extensions of this work include the full verification for the "functions as processes" paradigm, as well as the design of a system to check bisimilarities for processes.

## 1  Introduction

This work is a continuation of [Hir97]; it presents a formalisation of some results of π-calculus theory in the Calculus of Inductive Constructions. π-calculus [MPW92, Mil91] has become a widely accepted theoretical model for concurrency, and aims at playing the rôle λ-calculus does play for (functional) sequential computation. Implementing the proofs for some classical laws of the algebraic theory of π-calculus in a logical framework like Coq raises many interesting questions, that help to understand both the results we prove and the techniques we use for these proofs. The main paradigm we focus on to compare π-calculus terms is *bisimulation*, which does not seem to be a handy notion to manage when it comes to proof mechanisation (see Section 3). To perform bisimulation proofs, we have implemented a theory described by Sangiorgi in [San95b], called in this paper *theory of progressions*, that turns out to be very tractable for our purposes, and allows us to prove many bisimilarity results of classical π-calculus theory in a simple and uniform way. Moreover, the generality of the results we derive within the theory of progressions gives a great expressiveness to our implementation, as the proof of the so-called *replication theorems* testifies.

In this paper, we will not describe precisely the whole Coq implementation we have built, but rather focus on the many implementational issues that arise as we formalise the theory of π-calculus. We believe that the present work at the same time shows the expressiveness of a logical framework like Coq and provides some insight on verification in the field of concurrency. The plan of the paper is the following: the remainder of this section is devoted to a very brief

---

* email: dh@cermics.enpc.fr

presentation of Coq. Section 2 presents our implementation of $\pi$-calculus syntax and semantics and describes the de Bruijn representation for names. The next Section presents Sangiorgi's theory of progressions, and the proof of the up to context bisimulation theorem, which is the main technique we use to establish bisimilarity relations. Section 4 presents some classical theorems of $\pi$-calculus theory that we prove this way, namely congruence and structural equivalence, and Section 5 is devoted to the proof of the replication theorems. We also discuss in Section 5 the encoding of $\lambda$-calculus into $\pi$-calculus, and the corresponding proof of operational correspondence, which has not been implemented yet. In the conclusion, we give some technical informations about our proofs, describe some related work and discuss future extensions of this implementation.

Coq [BBC+96a] is a proof-assistant based on the Calculus of Inductive Constructions [Wer94]. Let us briefly recall the syntax of Coq declarations (in the following, Coq text will be in typewriter style): product types can be written (_)_ (dependent product) or _->_ (non dependent product); abstraction is written [_]_, while application is as usually written (_ _). A new inductive type is introduced by defining its constructors with their respective types; this automatically generates elimination lemmas, that allow one to perform induction over elements of these types. Among the primitive objects, let us mention inductive type nat for natural numbers, whose constructors are 0 and S.

## 2  A $\pi$-Calculus Implementation

In this Section, we first briefly describe the syntax and semantics for the $\pi$-calculus we have implemented. We then turn to our implementation, stressing the consequences of our choice of a de Bruijn notation for names.

### 2.1  Syntax and Semantics of Processes

Terms of the $\pi$-calculus, called *processes*, are built upon an infinite set of names $N = x, y, z, a, b, \ldots$ (also called *channels*). In the following, we range over (possibly empty) name lists with $\mathbf{a}, \mathbf{x}, \ldots$, and over processes with $P, Q, R, \ldots$. The language we have implemented can be described by the following syntax:

$$P \equiv 0 \mid a(\mathbf{b}).P \mid \overline{a}[\mathbf{b}].P \mid (P|Q) \mid (\nu a)P \mid {!}P.$$

$0$ is the inactive process; together with the two kinds of prefixes ($\overline{a}[\mathbf{b}].$ for output and $a(\mathbf{b}).$ for input), we have operators $\mid$ (parallel composition), $\nu$ (restriction), and $!$ (replication). Several consecutive restrictions $(\nu a_1)(\nu a_2) \ldots (\nu a_n)$ may be written as $(\nu \mathbf{a})$, and we further generalize this notation by saying that if $\mathbf{a}$ is the empty list, then $(\nu \mathbf{a})P$ is $P$.

The operational semantics of processes is given through the definition of a transition relation, stating that a process $P$ can perform an *action* $a$ to become process $P'$; we write this $P \xrightarrow{a} P'$. Actions are described by

$$A \equiv a(\mathbf{b}) \mid (\nu \mathbf{c})\overline{a}[\mathbf{b}]_{(\mathbf{c} \subseteq \mathbf{b})} \mid \tau,$$

where $\tau$ is a special action, called the silent action, and denoting an internal communication in a process. The side condition for output actions ($\mathbf{c} \subseteq \mathbf{b}$) will be explained below. Bound and free names both for processes and actions are defined as usual. The rules for early operational semantics are stated in table 1; symmetrical version of rules $PAR_l$ and $CLOSE_1$ are omitted.

$$\text{INP} \quad x.(\mathbf{y})P \xrightarrow{x(\mathbf{z})} P\{\mathbf{y} := \mathbf{z}\}$$

$$\text{OUT} \quad \bar{x}.[\mathbf{y}]P \xrightarrow{\bar{x}[\mathbf{y}]} P$$

$$\text{OPEN} \quad \frac{P \xrightarrow{(\nu \mathbf{z})\bar{x}.[\mathbf{y}]} P'}{(\nu t)P \xrightarrow{(\nu\, t::\mathbf{z})\bar{x}.[\mathbf{y}]} P'} \quad t \in \mathbf{y}, t \neq x$$

$$\text{CLOSE}_1 \quad \frac{X \xrightarrow{a(\mathbf{l})} P \quad Y \xrightarrow{(\nu \mathbf{k})\bar{a}[\mathbf{l}]} Q}{X \,|\, Y \xrightarrow{\tau} (\nu \mathbf{k})(P \,|\, Q)} \quad \mathbf{k} \cap fn(X) = \emptyset$$

$$\text{RES} \quad \frac{P \xrightarrow{\mu} P'}{(\nu x)P \xrightarrow{\mu} (\nu x)P'} \quad x \notin n(\mu)$$

$$\text{PAR}_l \quad \frac{P \xrightarrow{\mu} P'}{Q \,|\, P \xrightarrow{\mu} Q \,|\, P'} \quad bn(\mu) \cap fn(Q) = \emptyset$$

$$\text{BANG} \quad \frac{!P \,|\, P \xrightarrow{\mu} P'}{!P \xrightarrow{\mu} P'}$$

**Table 1.** Early operational semantics for $\pi$-calculus terms

Let us make a few remarks about the version of $\pi$-calculus we have chosen. Our processes belong to a polyadic (in the sense that many names can be transmitted in a single communication), and sum free $\pi$-calculus; both polyadic communications and the sum operator (also called *choice operator*) can be encoded into a monadic, sum free $\pi$-calculus (see [Mil91, NP96]). While sum can be useful from a theoretical point of view to build axiomatisations, it turns out that it can be discarded without much loss of convenience for implementation tasks. Polyadicity, on the other hand, is a very useful feature when taken as primitive, because it makes the treatment of many examples (like the study of $\lambda$-calculus encoding discussed in Section 5) much easier. The PICT programming language [Pie95] is another example of a $\pi$-calculus implementation where polyadicity is in some way "more primitive" than the choice construct (which is available, though, through the notion of *event channel*).

Terms possibly having an infinite behaviour are encoded using replication (!) instead of recursive definitions, mainly for the task of simplicity and clarity in our implementation (a single constructor is easier to introduce in Coq than a construction to represent recursive definitions). This is not a limitation, as

[Mil91] shows how to encode recursive definitions into replicated terms; as will be discussed below, this choice influences the shape of our proofs.

Finally, let us remark that our choice of an *early* transition semantics (as opposed to *late* or *open*, for example) was taken to stay as close as possible to the proofs given in [San95b], that are described in Section 3.

## 2.2   The de Bruijn Notation for Names

**Processes**  For the task of our Coq implementation, we represent the basic notion of $\pi$-calculus syntax, that is names, with a de Bruijn notation (following the ideas of [Hue93]). In the de Bruijn representation (which is defined in [dB72]; a description of a de Bruijn notation for monadic $\pi$-calculus can be found in [Amb91]), a name is defined by a natural number indicating its *binding depth* inside the term where it occurs, i.e. the number of binding operators that have to be crossed to reach the operator it refers to. Let us give an example: in $\lambda$-calculus, there is one binding operator, abstraction, and the (closed) $\lambda$-term $\lambda x \lambda y.(y\ x)$ is represented with de Bruijn indexes as $\lambda\lambda.(0\ 1)$. If free variables occur, they are considered to be bound "above" the term, or alternatively one supposes that a binding list (the environment) is provided with the term. Such a way of writing the syntax of a term has an immediate advantage, in that it provides a canonical representation for bound names, and hence gives $\alpha$-conversion for free. It turns out, however, that free names have to be handled with care in such a setting, and in some way one could say that *what is gained on bound names gets lost for free names*, as will be discussed in the next Section.

In the $\pi$-calculus, there are two binders for names, namely input prefix $a(\mathbf{b})$, that binds names of $\mathbf{b}$ in its continuation (i.e. the process being prefixed), and restriction $(\nu x)$. This means that a de Bruijn index can either represent a name that is not yet known (bound by input prefix), or private (bound by restriction). Moreover, the input prefix is polyadic: this compells us to give an arity to such a construct, i.e. a number indicating how many names are bound in a receiving process (arity of agents also appears in [Mil91], for the task of the definition of sorting). For restriction, on the other hand, we have kept a monadic flavour, as suggested by the shape of rules *RES* and *OPEN* in Table 1.

The Coq inductive types for names, name lists and processes are called respectively name, l_name and pi, and are defined as follows:

```
Inductive name : Set := Ref : nat -> name.
```

```
Inductive l_name : Set := Nil : l_name | Cons : name -> l_name -> l_name.
```

```
Inductive pi : Set :=
  Skip : pi                          null process                  0
| Res : pi -> pi                     restriction (monadic)         ν
| Ban : pi -> pi                     replication                   !
| Par : pi -> pi -> pi               parallel composition          |
| Inp : name -> nat -> pi -> pi      abstraction: subject, arity,  ( )
                                     and continuation
```

```
| Out : name -> l_name -> pi -> pi.   concretion: subject, object,    [ ]
                                      and continuation
```

Let us give an example to illustrate the de Bruijn representation for names; to represent process $P \equiv a(x,y).\overline{x}[y].0$ in Coq, we make the following statement:

```
Definition P := (Inp (Ref 0) (S (S 0))
                (Out (Ref (S 0)) (Cons (Ref 0) Nil) Skip)).
```

Notice how the choice of (Ref 0) to represent $a$ is arbitrary, as $a$ is free in $P$; this point will be further discussed in Section 3.

**Actions** Actions are built the same way as processes; some remarks can be done regarding their structure within the de Bruijn framework. The side condition for output actions ($c \subseteq b$), is explained by the shape of rules *OPEN* and *RES* of the semantics, that allow a communication to carry fresh names, i.e. names that before communication are not known by the receiving process (these names correspond to list c). The great expressiveness of the $\pi$-calculus heavily relies on this phenomenon (called *name extrusion*), namely the communication of one or several private names. From the point of view of implementation, since actions may actually "carry restrictions", we have to keep track of the names that are bound inside an output action (this holds for input actions as well, because of our choice of early semantics, that forces to instantiate received names as soon as possible): since we work with de Bruijn indexes, a natural number is enough to indicate how many names among those in the transmitted name list are fresh (as for processes, names having an index less than this number are fresh, i.e. bound in the action). An input or output action thus consists of three parts: the *subject* of the action (the channel where the communication occurs), the *object* (the transmitted name list), and the number of fresh names. The type action is defined as follows:

```
Inductive action : Set :=   Ain : nat -> name -> l_name -> action
 | Aou : nat -> name -> l_name -> action  | Tau : action.
```

**Transition relation** The type commit, used to represent the transition relation, is inductively defined *à la Prolog*, each constructor expressing one of the rules of Table 1. Without stating the full definition of commit, which would require some pretty technical explanations, we will focus on a few examples, that we consider to be emblematic of the strong influence of the de Bruijn notation in our implementation.

A first immediate consequence of the use of a de Bruijn representation for names is that many side conditions in the transition rules can be discarded, by insuring their validity *within* the definitions of constructors. comm_pl, for example, implements rule $PAR_l$, and is defined as follows:

```
comm_pl : (x,p:pi)(a:action) (commit x a p) ->
   (y:pi) (commit (Par y x) a (Par (lift_pi y 0 (bound_action a)) p))
```

(recall that $(\_)\_$ is the notation for dependent product; bound_action is the function that returns the number of bound names of an action). As can be seen on this definition, the inactive process y is in some way modified by the action, by the means of function lift_pi: the latter operator adds a number (here (bound_action a)) to all indexes of free names of y, hence avoiding possible name clashes with the fresh names brought by the performed action. The advantage of such a technique is that the renaming that has to be done in order to avoid conflicts between names is *built in*, and we do not have to check for such conflicts.

Rules *OPEN*, *RES* and *CLOSE*₁ define the behaviour of the restriction constructor in a communication. Intuitively, when a process is liable to send a list l of names on a given channel $a$, then if we add a restriction to this process, either we restrict $a$, in which case no communication is possible (because no other process can listen on $a$), or we apply one of the rules *RES* and *OPEN*. If the restricted name occurs in l, then rule *OPEN* is applied (name extrusion); otherwise, rule *RES* is applied. Rule *RES* can also be used to add a restriction to a receiving process (if the restricted name is not among the names of the action) or to a process that performs an internal communication.

Within the de Bruijn framework, these rules imply some manipulation of the name that gets restricted, in order to "follow" its evolution inside the term. Indeed, as rule *RES* is applied, the restricted name is not involved in the action, and has to "pass over" those names that participate in the action. This is performed by exchanging some indexes inside the term, with an operator similar to function lift_pi discussed above, called swap (notice as well how action a becomes (lower_action a), i.e. a with all indexes lowered by 1, because in some way the restricted name "crosses" the action):

```
comm_re : (x,p:pi) (a:action) (commit x a p)
  -> ~(occ_act a)                          (* side condition *)
  -> (commit (Res x) (lower_action a)
            (Res (swap p (bound_action a) 0 0)))
```

In the implementation of rule *OPEN*, some other technical manipulations have to be done on the list of transmitted names (and hence on the processes involved in the transition). Indeed, in classical $\pi$-calculus theory, processes $P_1 = (\nu x)(\nu y)\overline{a}[x, y].0$ and $P_2 = (\nu y)(\nu x)\overline{a}[x, y].0$ are considered to be equivalent (i.e. it should be provable from the rules of Table 1 that these processes are bisimilar). If we define these processes within the de Bruijn notation, we get (informally) $P_1' = \nu\nu\overline{k}[1, 0].0$ and $P_2' = \nu\nu\overline{k}[0, 1].0$, $k$ being the index that represents free name $a$ in the translation. With a naive definition of operational semantics, we cannot hope to prove the equivalence, since the actions they are liable to perform ($\nu^2\overline{k}[1, 0]$ for $P_1'$, $\nu^2\overline{k}[0, 1]$ for $P_2'$) are different. Actually, we have to provide a kind of $\alpha$-conversion for actions, in order to relate these processes. The solution we adopt is to embed a canonical representation for actions *into the definition* of the transition relation: each time rule *OPEN* is applied, names in the transmitted list are exchanged in order to put the outermost restricted (fresh) name as close as possible to the head of the list. Without entering the technical definition of such a manipulation, let us just stress the fact that this guarantees a unique representation for actions, allowing us in particular to prove processes $P_1'$ and $P_2'$ bisimilar (intuitively, as *OPEN* rule is applied for the second time to derive the transition of $P_2'$, indexes 0 and 1 are exchanged in order to get the outermost restricted one (1) at the head of the list). Such an embedding of a canonical form for actions is reminiscent of the "de Bruijn philosophy", in that the mechanism we provide to prove transitions gives the conversion between actions for free. We do not state here the definition of constructor comm_op, that implements rule *OPEN*, as its form should need explanations of some more technical details. However, we hope that some insight onto the main ideas related to the management of restrictions in the de Bruijn framework has been given. We have not proved that the full definition of commit (that can be found in [Hir97]) actually encodes the presentation given above; however, the many classical results we have been able to prove within our framework give confidence about its correctness.

# 3 Bisimulation and Related Proof Techniques

Having described how processes are constructed and how they behave, we may want to compare them; a popular notion to describe process equivalence is *bisimulation*. Let us state its usual definition:

**Definition 3.1 (Bisimulation, bisimilarity)** *A symmetrical relation $\mathcal{R}$ over processes is a bisimulation iff, whenever $P\mathcal{R}Q$ and $P \xrightarrow{a} P'$, there exists a process $Q'$ s.t. $Q \xrightarrow{a} Q'$ and $P'\mathcal{R}Q'$. Bisimilarity (written $\sim$) is the greatest bisimulation.*

## 3.1 Sangiorgi's Theory of Progressions of Relations

Definition 3.1 contains in an essential way a certain form of circularity: two bisimilar processes perform the same action and stay "inside" the given bisimulation relation. When it comes to actually build bisimulation proofs, and *a fortiori* to mechanise these proofs, this turns out to be quite expensive in terms of the size of the relations one has to exhibit. Indeed, to prove two processes to be bisimilar, one has to exhibit a bisimulation relation that contains the whole "future" of the related processes.

Several techniques have been introduced to facilitate bisimulation proofs by reducing the size of the relation to be given. [San95b] presents a generalisation of these techniques, based on the notion of *progression of relations*. The clean mathematical presentation given in [San95b] allowed us to implement this theory quite straightforwardly in Coq, keeping the mechanised proofs remarkably close to the original ones. Therefore, we just state in a mathematical style the main results we prove, postponing the discussion of implementation issues to the proof of the main theorem of this Section, namely the up to context bisimulation Theorem 3.8.

We start by defining the notion of progression of relations:

**Definition 3.2 (Progression of relations)** *We say that a symmetrical relation $\mathcal{R}$ over processes progresses to a relation $\mathcal{S}$ (written $\mathcal{R} \to \mathcal{S}$) if, whenever $P\mathcal{R}Q$ and $P \xrightarrow{a} P'$, there exists a process $Q'$ such that $Q \xrightarrow{a} Q'$ and $P'\mathcal{S}Q'$.*

Intuitively, $\mathcal{R} \to \mathcal{S}$ means that $\mathcal{S}$ contains the "future" of $\mathcal{R}$. From such a point of view, bisimulation can be given a new definition, in terms of progression:

**Definition 3.3 (Bisimulation - new version)** *A relation is a bisimulation if it progresses to itself.*

It is easy to prove that this definition is equivalent to Definition 3.1.

We now turn to the study of functions over relations (briefly called *functions*); we introduce two properties of such objects:

**Definition 3.4 (Soundness, respectfulness)**

- *A function $\mathcal{F}$ is* sound *if for any $\mathcal{R}$, $\mathcal{R} \to \mathcal{F}(\mathcal{R})$ implies $\mathcal{R} \subseteq \sim$.*
- *A function $\mathcal{F}$ is* respectful *if $(\mathcal{R} \subseteq \mathcal{S}$ and $\mathcal{R} \to \mathcal{S})$ implies $(\mathcal{F}(\mathcal{R}) \subseteq \mathcal{F}(\mathcal{S})$ and $\mathcal{F}(\mathcal{R}) \to \mathcal{F}(\mathcal{S}))$.*

As proved below, respectfulness is a sufficient condition for soundness; moreover, it enjoys nice compositional properties, and will thus be convenient to use.

**Theorem 3.5 (Soundness of respectful functions)** *If a function $\mathcal{F}$ is respectful, then $\mathcal{F}$ is sound.*

The proof is easy, and basically reduces to build a bisimulation relation by successive iterations of $\mathcal{F}$ on a given relation $\mathcal{R}$. In the following, we shall work with respectful functions, that by Theorem 3.5 provide proof techniques to establish bisimilarities: given a respectful (hence sound) function $\mathcal{F}$, to prove that two processes $P$ and $Q$ are bisimilar, it is sufficient to exhibit a relation $\mathcal{R}$ such that $P\mathcal{R}Q$ and $\mathcal{R} \to \mathcal{F}(\mathcal{R})$. Intuitively, the rôle of $\mathcal{F}$ is to make $\mathcal{R}$ grow, by building its "future": if we find good respectful functions, we can hope to considerably reduce the size of $\mathcal{R}$, and as well to reduce the number of cases to consider in the proof of the progression relation (as will be shown in the following sections).

We have also implemented, following [San95b], some results that allow us to combine several respectful functions to obtain another respectful function. Due to lack of space, we do not describe this part of Sangiorgi's theory. Let us just mention a key result from it:

**Lemma 3.6 (up to bisimilarity proof technique)** *If $\mathcal{F}$ is respectful, then the function that associates $\sim \mathcal{F}(\mathcal{R}) \sim$ to $\mathcal{R}$ is also respectful (with $\sim \mathcal{S} \sim = \{(P,Q)$ s.t. $\exists P_1, Q_1. (P \sim P_1) \wedge (P_1 \mathcal{S} Q_1) \wedge (Q_1 \sim Q)\})$.*

## 3.2 Up to Context Proof Technique for the $\pi$-Calculus

We apply the above results to our implementation of $\pi$-calculus, in order to define the function that builds the closure under contexts of a relation, and prove its respectfulness. This will then give us a very useful technique to prove bisimilarity results, as shown in Section 4. Several questions arise when implementing this proof, that are related to the implementation choices described in Section 2. The main issue is the treatment of free names within the de Bruijn framework, as we attempt to compare processes: indeed, as seen above, transitions of processes may involve the application of operators on free names, like the *lift* function in rule $PAR_l$. These transformations, however, do not really have a strong significance, since they return another representation of the same process (in the non-de Bruijn version of $PAR_l$, process $Q$ in the conclusion of the rule is the same as $Q$ in the hypothesis), but rather do some kind of "administrative work" to keep the notation coherent. Therefore, if a pair $(P, Q)$ of processes belongs to a given relation $\mathcal{R}$, there should be no reason for $(lift^k(P), lift^k(Q))$ not to be in $\mathcal{R}$. More generally, for any substitution $f$, injective on the free names of $P$ and $Q$, $(f(P), f(Q))$ should belong to $\mathcal{R}$. We thus define a predicate over relations as follows:

```
Definition good : (pi->pi->Prop)->Prop :=
  [R: (relation pi)] (p,q:pi) (R p q) ->
  (l:l_name) (injective l) ->
  (le (max_nat (max_free_0 p) (max_free_0 q)) (l_length l)) ->
  (R (pi_subst_n p l O) (pi_subst_n q l O)).
```

The whole theory of progressions above is parametrised with the good predicate, since we work only with "good" relations over processes. Note that this predicate actually implements the respectfulness of the closure over injective substitutions (which is *proved* in [San95b]) as a built-in property of our implementation.

To describe function $\_^{\mathcal{C}}$, that builds the closure under contexts of a relation (we shall write $\mathcal{R}^{\mathcal{C}}$), we must first define contexts. Here again, the syntax of our processes dictates the shape of the contexts we use: while in [San95b] Sangiorgi could restrict his study to *monadic* contexts (contexts with one occurrence of the hole), having recursive definitions in his calculus, the presence of the replication operator compells us to work with polyadic contexts, because of the shape of the *BANG* rule (see Table 1). We then define function $\_^{\mathcal{C}}$ as follows:

**Definition 3.7 (Closure under contexts function)**
$$\mathcal{C}(\mathcal{R}) = \cup_{C \ non-guarded}\{(C[P], C[Q]) : (P, Q) \in \mathcal{R}\} \ \bigcup$$

$$\cup_{C \ guarded}\{(C[P], C[Q]) : (P\sigma, Q\sigma) \in \mathcal{R}, \ for \ all \ substitutions \ \sigma\},$$
and in Coq:

```
Inductive Close [R:pi -> pi -> Prop] : pi -> pi -> Prop :=
  Clo_cons : (c:context)(p,q:pi)(close_cons c R p q) ->
    (Close R (c2pi c p) (c2pi c q)).
```

The guardness property for polyadic contexts is defined as follows: a context is *guarded* if some occurrence of the hole is under a prefix construct; if this condition does not hold, the context is said to be *unguarded*. Guarded contexts have a special rôle in $\pi$-calculus because they can modify the process that fills the hole, through the application of a substitution. In the Coq definition, close_cons is a function that returns the requirement on objects R, p and q corresponding to the guardness of its first argument (context c), according to Definition 3.7.

Actually, function $\_^C$ alone is not respectful in our setting. To obtain a respectful function, we must consider the transitive closure of $\_^C$, written $\_^{C^T}$ (and implemented in Coq by a function named T_Close). Indeed, as we work with polyadic contexts, transitivity is needed for the parallel construct, in order to be able to use many times the inductive hypothesis. There is also a more tricky reason for which we have to consider the transitive closure of function $\_^C$; without being too technical, let us say that in the "input" case of the proof below, as the substitution propagates within the (possibly polyadic) context, we have to split in some way the polyadic context into several monadic contexts, i.e. perform an induction over the number of holes of our context, to establish the result we want to prove. This induction actually requires the transitivity property brought by the $\_^T$ function.

**Theorem 3.8 (up to context bisimulation)** *Function $\_^{C^T}$ is respectful.*

*Proof* For the nontrivial part of this proof, we consider two relations $\mathcal{R}$ and $\mathcal{S}$ such that $\mathcal{R} \subseteq \mathcal{S}$ and $\mathcal{R} \to \mathcal{S}$, and prove $\mathcal{R}^{C^T} \to \mathcal{S}^{C^T}$. We therefore consider processes $P$, $P'$ and $Q$ and an action $\lambda$ such that $P\mathcal{R}^{C^T}Q$ and $P \xrightarrow{\lambda} P'$. We first perform an elimination on the inductive function that builds the transitive closure. The transitivity case is straightforward; we thus suppose $P\mathcal{R}^C Q$ (i.e. $C[P]\mathcal{R}\,C[Q]$ for some $C$), and we have to exhibit $Q'$ such that $Q \xrightarrow{\lambda} Q'$ and $P'\mathcal{S}^{C^T}Q'$.

In [San95b], this proof is achieved by structural induction on the context $C$; we have checked that the original proof faithfully translates into the Coq system for the finite case (using monadic contexts). If we want to consider also non finite contexts, however, we have to eliminate the inductively defined proposition stating the transition relation $C[P] \xrightarrow{\lambda} P'$, otherwise an induction on $C$ would generate circularity in the proof.

Due to lack of space, we just give as an example the shape of the Coq proof for the case where the transition relation is obtained by using the comm_pl rule above. The goal to prove is the following:

```
H  : (good R)
HO : (good S)
H1 : (r_incl pi R S)                (R ⊆ S)
Hind : (q:pi)                       (induction hypothesis)
         (close_cons c R p q)
       ->(Ex [q':pi]
             (commit (c2pi c q) lambda q')/\(T_Close S p' q'))
```

```
Hclose : (close_cons (cPar c' c) R p q)    (induction hypothesis)
H3 : (commit (c2pi c p) lambda p')         (induction hypothesis)
==============================
 (Ex [q':pi]                                (goal to prove: "∃ q' ...")
    (commit (Par (c2pi c' q) (c2pi c q)) lambda q')
    /\(T_Close S
        (Par (lift_pi (c2pi c' p) O (bound_action lambda)) p') q'))
```

((c2pi c p) is the Coq translation of $C[P]$). The idea is to use the induction hypothesis Hind with process q the following way ((close_cons c R p q), which has to be proved in order to use Hind, is a direct consequence of Hclose):

```
Elim (Hind q).
Intros q0 Hfoo; Elim Hfoo; Clear Hfoo; Intros.
```

This generates the new hypotheses:

```
H4 : (commit (c2pi c q) lambda q0)
H5 : (T_Close S p' q0)
==============================
```

We can now exhibit a process satisfying the conditions of the conclusion, with the Exists tactic:

```
Exists (Par (lift_pi (c2pi c' q) O (bound_action lambda)) q0); Split.
```

The left part of the conclusion is proved using the comm_pl rule:

```
Apply comm_pl; Trivial.
```

For the right part of the conclusion, we use the transitivity property, and some basic manipulations lead us to the following goal:

```
H6 : (Close S (c2pi c' p) (c2pi c' q))
==============================
 (Close S (lift_pi (c2pi c' p) O (bound_action lambda))
    (lift_pi (c2pi c' q) O (bound_action lambda)))
```

The proof of this subgoal is carried using hypothesis H0 : (good S), which allows us to remove the lift_pi operator from the conclusion of the goal, thanks to a lemma stating that this function can be represented by an injective substitution. We conclude this way the proof for this subcase, and work similarly for the other cases. We thus show respectfulness of the $\_^{C^\tau}$ function, which means correctness for the up to context bisimulation technique.

# 4 Classical Algebraic Theory of $\pi$-Calculus

Section 2 introduced the objects we study, and Section 3 was devoted to the definition of tools to manipulate these objects in order to state equivalence properties about them. This is actually all we need, at least from a conceptual point of view, to establish the main results of classical $\pi$-calculus theory.

Indeed, the bisimilarity results stated here are obtained in a uniform way: the method is to exhibit a relation $\mathcal{R}$, and to prove that $\mathcal{R} \to \sim (\mathcal{R}^{c^T}) \sim$. The definition of $\mathcal{R}$ follows the shape of the property we want to prove. The progression relation is proved with heavy use of Coq's `Inversion` tactic, that allows one to derive all possible hypotheses from an instance of a term belonging to an inductively defined type.

For some technical lemmas, we sometimes have to perform an induction over the term stating the transition of a process, even if it would be more natural to make a structural induction over the process itself, because of the shape of the *BANG* rule (as explained above). In some cases, a structural induction can be performed on the process *resulting from the transition*, a technique that also avoids the introduction of circularity in our proofs. It should be of interest to study how these restrictions on the shape of our proofs evolve when working with coinductive types [Gim96].

We first prove congruence, stated as follows:

**Theorem 4.1 (Congruence)** $\sim$ *is a congruence relation with respect to constructors* $|$, $\nu$ *and* $!$. *To obtain congruence for all operators of $\pi$-calculus, we must consider relation* $\sim^c$, *defined by: "$P \sim^c Q$ iff for all substitution $\sigma$, $P\sigma \sim Q\sigma$".*

We then turn to the bisimilarity properties called *structural equivalence* in [Mil91], or alternatively *$\pi$-calculus equivalence* in [AM94].

**Theorem 4.2 (Structural equivalence)** *We have, for all processes $P, Q, R$ and names $x, y$:*

1. $P|0 \sim P$;
2. $P|Q \sim Q|P$;
3. $P|(Q|R) \sim (P|Q)|R$;
4. $P|(\nu x)Q \sim (\nu x)(P|Q)$ *if* $x \notin fn(P)$ *(de Bruijn: $P|\nu Q \sim \nu(lift^1(P)|Q))$;*
5. $(\nu x)(\nu y)P \sim (\nu y)(\nu x)P$ *(de Bruijn: $\nu\nu P \sim \nu\nu P_{\{0\leftrightarrow 1\}}$. $P_{\{0\leftrightarrow 1\}}$ represents process $P$ where indexes 0 and 1 are exchanged);*
6. $!P \sim !P|P$.

For lack of space, and because we always apply the same proof technique, we just give as an example the shape of the proof for relation 2 above. To prove $\forall P, Q.P|Q \sim Q|P$, without the up to context technique, one has to prove that relation

$$\mathcal{R} = \{((\nu x)(P|Q), (\nu x)(Q|P))\}$$

is a bisimulation (we have to add the restrictions for the case where a communication, which may involve name extrusion, occurs between $P$ and $Q$). The rules we have to take in account when considering the transitions of processes related by $\mathcal{R}$ are thus $PAR_l$, $PAR_r$, $CLOSE_1$, $CLOSE_2$, $RES$ and $OPEN$. With the technique we use, we can get rid of the restrictions (that in some way are brought along by the closure under contexts function), and we only have to consider rules $PAR_l$, $PAR_r$, $CLOSE_1$ and $CLOSE_2$. Notice that for this proof, work can be factorised by proving only a simulation instead of a bisimulation, because of symmetry (this also holds for relation 5, by remarking that $(P_{\{0\leftrightarrow 1\}})_{\{0\leftrightarrow 1\}} = P$).

We will not enter further the details of the proofs for Theorem 4.2. Let us just mention that their size and readability can be considerably different according to the shape of the bisimilarity property we want to prove. More precisely, it seems that the more the theorem involves names manipulations (especially properties about restriction), the bigger the amount of technical work concerned with the operators on de Bruijn indexes.

# 5 Towards Functions as Processes

The proof method that we used in the previous Section allows us to derive another important result of $\pi$-calculus theory, sometimes referred to as the "replication theorems". The "functions as processes" paradigm, namely the ability for $\pi$-calculus to encode (functional) sequential computation, is one of the many applications of these theorems. After proving the replication theorems, we discuss the verification of the operational correspondence for an encoding of lazy $\lambda$-calculus [Abr89] into $\pi$-calculus, as presented in [San95a].

## 5.1 The Replication Theorems

The results we prove here (still using, as a matter of fact, the method of Section 4) help to show the expressiveness of our implementation, or equivalently the power of Theorem 3.8. To state these results, we introduce a family of sets of processes, indexed by a name $a$, and defined as:

$$\mathcal{N}_a = \{P : a \text{ occurs in } P \text{ only in output subject position}\}$$

(the subject of a prefix is the name where the communication occurs). For the replication theorems, we will consider processes of the form $(\nu a)(P \mid !a(\mathbf{b}).Q)$, with $P, Q \in \mathcal{N}_a$. Roughly speaking, $\mathcal{N}_a$ is the set of processes that consider $a$ as a name giving access to a resource (a request to the resource is performed by sending a message along channel $a$, with parameters $\mathbf{b}$, the resource being $Q$). We prove the following bisimilarity relations (taken as they appear in [San95b]; many other papers mention them, e.g. [San95a, Mil91]):

**Theorem 5.1 (Replication theorems)** *For all $R, P_1, P_2, \alpha.P \in \mathcal{N}_a$, we have:*

*1. $(\nu a)(!a(\mathbf{b}).R \mid P \mid Q) \sim (\nu a)(!a(\mathbf{b}).R \mid P) \mid (\nu a)(!a(\mathbf{b}.R \mid Q)$;*

2. $(\nu a)(!a(\mathbf{b}).R \mid !\alpha.P) \sim !(\nu a)(!a(\mathbf{b}).R \mid \alpha.P)$.

The up to context proof technique allows us to considerably simplify the proofs given in [Mil91], especially for the second result: while Milner had to consider relation

$$\mathcal{R} = \{(\,(\nu \mathbf{x})(\nu a)(!a(\mathbf{b}).R \mid !\alpha.P \mid Q),$$
$$(\nu \mathbf{x})(!(\nu a)(!a(\mathbf{b}).R \mid \alpha.P) \mid (\nu a)(!a(\mathbf{b}).R \mid Q)))\},$$

we can restrict ourselves to the relation suggested by the property, namely:

$$\mathcal{R}' = \{(\,(\nu a)(!a(\mathbf{b}).R \mid !\alpha.P), !(\nu a)(!a(\mathbf{b}).R \mid \alpha.P))\}.$$

Thanks to a few lemmas that characterise the possible transitions of terms of the form $(P|!a(\mathbf{b}).Q)$, we get some quite simple and readable (although not small) proofs for these results.

## 5.2 λ-Calculus Encoding

At this point, an interesting subject we may want to consider is the study of the encoding of lazy λ-calculus into π-calculus. This can be seen as a benchmark for our π-calculus implementation, while being at the same time, of course, a step forward in the field of mechanisation of π-calculus theory (to our knowledge, no mechanisation of the proof of the functions as processes theorem exists by now). We have implemented the main lines of the proof of operational correspondence for the encoding, mostly following [San95a], but without giving a full proof for many technical results, and rather stating them as hypotheses. It has to be stressed that the replication theorems stated above are a key result to carry this proof, and have been fully verified. Actually, we think some work should be done to reformulate some parts of the proof in a way that would be more tractable for the task of mechanisation. We present below the main issues that arise as we try to implement the proof, stressing the notions that turned out to be awkward to handle in our Coq implementation.

To represent λ-terms, we start from Huet's work [Hue93], that also provides a de Bruijn notation for variables; the definition of the encoding supposes that the set of λ-calculus variables is a subset of π-calculus names. As we do not have a notion of subtyping in Coq, this cannot be directly formalised in our setting. Instead, the correspondence between variables in an encoded λ-term and their representation in the encoding has to be defined at meta-level, in order to guarantee the success of the proof of operational correspondence.

Another notion that is important in this proof is the *expansion* relation, a preorder over processes containing bisimilarity. Intuitively, a process $P$ expands a process $Q$ if it is liable to perform the same actions as $Q$ modulo some extra $\tau$-actions (in our case, we must actually prove that the encoding of a $\beta$-redex evolves to a process that *expands* the encoding of the reduced λ-term). The proof of [San95a] uses some quite technical reasoning to show that expansion is a congruence relation, taking advantage from the fact that processes resulting from the encoding are asynchronous (i.e. processes for which there is no continuation after an output prefix). For asynchronous processes, we have a very strong result, namely that bisimulation (and expansion as well) is preserved by any kind of substitution (see for example [ACS96]). Instead of adapting the classical proof of this result (which would be rather tedious, as it turned out from a first attempt), we may want to see if the techniques presented in Section 3 can be adapted to expansion. They cannot be straightforwardly adapted, because some nice compositional properties of respectful functions would not be true; however, the task of providing a tractable method to prove expansion relations along the ideas of the theory of progressions seems to be quite interesting and promising.

## 6  Conclusion

We have presented an implementation of $\pi$-calculus, together with an account of classical results of $\pi$-calculus theory. Proofs for these results have been carried using the up to context technique, which has turned out to be efficient in performing clear and elegant proofs. Technical work, however, still represents the biggest part of our implementation, mainly due to the managing of De Bruijn indexes: indeed, as stressed above, the De Bruijn notation, while drastically simplifying work for bound names, requires accuracy in dealing with free names. Of our 800 proved lemmas, about 600 are concerned with operators on free names; the implementation consists of 70 files of Coq specifications and proofs in Coq V6.1 [BBC+96a]. Some proofs, especially those for the tedious results involving De Bruijn indexes, are somewhat "rough", and could probably be reformulated in a uniform way, instead of deriving ad hoc results along the way. A few files contain as well proof texts that were automatically generated by CtCoq [BBC+96b], which is an user interface that allows one to perform derivations with the proof-by-pointing technique [BKT94]. This technique has turned out to be helpful for general theorems, in that the user has facilities to build a proof by controlling its general shape without entering too much into the details at first. For technical lemmas, however, a direct interaction with the Coq system is often more efficient, mostly since the results one has to prove offer no conceptual difficulty, and the derivation is only some kind of an administrative work to do.

The work that can be considered as the closest to ours has been done within the HOL system. M. Nesi has defined CCS and a modal logic for this algebra in [Nes92]; regarding $\pi$-calculus, the original formalisation by T. Melham [Mel94] has been used as a starting point for the work of O. Aït-Mohamed, which consisted in proving equivalence [AM94], and building a system to prove bisimilarities for processes interactively [AM95]. Differences with our implementation arise at the level of technical issues, as well as at the level of the general presentation. Regarding the calculus itself and the way it is implemented, our choice of the De Bruijn notation is a key issue (while in [Nes92], assumptions are made about avoiding name clashes, in [Mel94] and [AM95], renaming has to be done in order to preserve freshness for bound names). About the formal representation of bound and free names, let us mention two alternative solutions to the de Bruijn representation: [MG96] presents and axiomatisation of λ-terms up to alpha conversion, proves it sound with respect to de Bruijn terms, and suggests as one of the possible applications of this presentation the proof of semantical properties of π-terms. In [KP93], bound and free variables are distinguished syntactically, which allows one to simplify the definition of substitution, and hence the proofs. Another point of view on substitution is presented in [Sto88], where a definition by structural recursion is presented; in this work, bound variables are systematically renamed in a substitution, while in our de Bruijn setting we always rename free variables.

Miller has described in [Mil92] another interesting point of view onto π-calculus specification by the means of a translation into linear logic that allows one to define some testing equivalences for a subclass of processes.

Finally, let us mention as well Giménez work in Coq on coinductive types [Gim96], which includes an implementation of CBS; we only used coinductive types in a toy example, to prove that our notion of bisimulation coincides with a formulation in terms of a greatest fix point of a combinator (using the fact that a coinductive definition implicitly implements a greatest fixpoint).

Future work on this implementation has already been partially discussed in the previous section, regarding the full formalisation of the functions as processes theorem. Another interesting direction could be to take advantage of Coq's extraction facility in order to build a system for π-calculus verification, along the ideas of Aït-Mohamed's PIC system [AM95], but exploiting the greater generality of our theorems (especially for proofs involving the replication construct). Reflection [Bou96] could also be used to build certified tactics to manipulate our π-terms.

*Acknowledgments* We thank Davide Sangiorgi and René Lalement for enlightening discussions about this work, as well as the anonymous referees for some very useful comments.

# References

[Abr89]    S. Abramsky. The lazy lambda calculus. *Research Topics in Functional Programming*, pages 65–116, 1989.

[ACS96]    R. Amadio, I. Castellani, and D. Sangiorgi. On bisimulations for the asynchronous π-calculus. In *CONCUR '96*, number 1119 in LNCS, 1996.

[AM94]     O. Ait-Mohamed. Vérification de l'équivalence du π-calcul dans HOL. Rapport de recherche 2412, INRIA-Lorraine, November 1994. (In French).

[AM95]     O. Ait-Mohamed. PIC: A proof checker for the π-calculus in Higher Order Logic. Technical report, INRIA-Lorraine, 1995.

[Amb91]    Simon J. Ambler. A de Bruijn notation for the π-calculus. Technical Report 569, Dept. of Computer Science, Queen Mary and Westfield College, London, May 1991.

[BBC⁺96a]  B. Barras, S. Boutin, C. Cornes, J. Courant, JC. Filliâtre, E. Gimenez, H. Herbelin, G. Huet, C. Muñoz, C. Murthy, C. Parent, C. Paulin-Mohring, A. Saïbi, and B. Werner. *The Coq Proof Assistant Reference Manual*. Projet Coq, INRIA Rocquencourt / CNRS - ENS Lyon, 1996.

[BBC+96b] J. Bertot, Y. Bertot, Y. Coscoy, H. Goguen, and F. Montagnac. *User Guide to the CtCoq Proof Environment.* INRIA, Sophia-Antipolis, February 1996.

[BKT94]   Y. Bertot, G. Kahn, and L. Théry. Proof by pointing. In *Proceedings of STACS*, LNCS, Sendai (Japan), April 1994.

[Bou96]   S. Boutin.   Using reflection to build efficient and certified decision procedures.   Unpublished - available at http://pauillac.inria.fr/~boutin/publis.html, 1996.

[dB72]    N.G. de Bruijn. Lambda Calculus Notation with Nameless Dummies: a Tool for Automatic Formula Manipulation, with Application to the Curch-Rosser Theorem. In *Indagationes Mathematicae*, volume 34, pages 381–392. 1972.

[Gim96]   E. Giménez. *Un calcul de constructions infinies et son application à la vérification de systèmes communicants.* PhD thesis, E.N.S. Lyon, 1996.

[Hir97]   D. Hirschkoff. Up to context proofs for the π-calculus in the Coq system. Technical Report 97-82, CERMICS, Noisy-le-Grand, January 1997.

[Hue93]   G. Huet. Residual theory in λ-calculus: A formal development. Technical Report 2009, INRIA, Rocquencourt - France, Août 1993.

[KP93]    J. Mc Kinna and R. Pollack. Pure Type Systems Formalized. In *Proceedings of TLCA'93*, volume 664 of *LNCS*. Springer Verlag, 1993.

[Mel94]   T. F. Melham. A mechanized theory of the π-calculus in HOL. *Nordic Journal of Computing*, 1(1):50–76, 1994.

[MG96]    T. F. Melham and A. Gordon. Five Axioms of Alpha-Conversion. In *Proceedings of TPHOL'96*, volume 1125 of *LNCS*. Springer Verlag, 1996.

[Mil91]   R. Milner. The polyadic π-calculus: a tutorial. Technical Report ECS-LFCS-91-180, LFCS, Dept. of Computer Science, Un. of Edinburgh, 1991.

[Mil92]   D. Miller. The π-calculus as a theory in linear logic: Preliminary results. In E. Lamma and P. Mello, editors, *Proceedings of the Workshop on Extensions to Logic Programming*, volume 660 of *Lecture Notes in Computer Science*, pages 242–265. Springer-Verlag, 1992.

[MPW92]   R. Milner, J. Parrow, and D. Walker. A calculus of mobile processes, Parts I and II. *Information and Computation*, 100:1–77, September 1992.

[Nes92]   M. Nesi. A formalisation of the CCS process algebra in higher order logic. Technical Report 278, Computer Laboratory, University of Cambridge, December 1992.

[NP96]    U. Nestmann and B. C. Pierce. Decoding choice encodings. In *Proceedings of CONCUR '96*, number 1119, August 1996.

[Pie95]   B.C. Pierce. *Programming in the Pi-Calculus (Tutorial Notes).* Computer Laboratory, Cambridge - UK, November 1995.

[San95a]  D. Sangiorgi. Lazy functions and mobile processes. Technical Report RR-2515, INRIA - Sophia Antipolis, 1995.

[San95b]  Davide Sangiorgi. On the bisimulation proof method. Revised version of Technical Report ECS–LFCS–94–299, University of Edinburgh, 1994. An extended abstract can be found in Proc. of MFCS'95, LNCS 969, 1995.

[Sto88]   A. Stoughton. Substitution revisited. *Theoretical Computer Science*, 59:317–325, 1988.

[Wer94]   B. Werner. *Une théorie des constructions inductives.* Thèse de doctorat, Université Paris 7, 1994.

# Rewriting, Decision Procedures and Lemma Speculation for Automated Hardware Verification

## Deepak Kapur

Institute for Programming and Logics
State University of New York
Albany, NY 12222.
kapur@cs.albany.edu

**Preliminary Version**

## 1 Introduction

The use of a rewrite-based, induction theorem prover, *Rewrite Rule Laboratory* (*RRL*) [13] is discussed for verifying arithmetic circuits at the gate level. It is shown that the induction scheme generation heuristic in *RRL* based on the cover set method [18], the integration of decision procedures [7] with contextual rewriting [17], and the intermediate lemma speculation heuristics can help, with minimal user guidance, in finding verification proofs of arithmetic circuits

*RRL* has been used to verify that the ripple-carry, carry-save, and the more sophisticated carry-lookahead adders perform addition on numbers represented by bit vectors of any length [10]. While doing a proof of the carry-lookahead adder, the parallel-prefix operator, commonly used in data-parallel algorithms, is equationally axiomatized.

The verification of multiplier circuits is established generically and parametrically in *RRL*. It is shown that a family of multiplier circuits including the linear multiplier, Wallace multiplier, 7-3 multiplier as well as Dadda multiplier can all be done in the same way [9]. Intermediate lemmas, needed for verifying that the multipliers perform multiplication on numbers represented by bit vectors of any length, can be mechanically generated from the circuit structure, repetitive use of carry-save adders and the fact that bit vectors represent numbers. Such a lemma speculation heuristic is likely to be more widely applicable on a large class of circuits with regular structure [11].

Finally, it is shown that the invariant properties of an SRT division circuit described by Clarke, German and Zhao [5] can also be established automatically by *RRL* using its linear arithmetic procedure, rewriting and case analysis mechanisms [12]. This shows that verification of such a circuit does not need sophisticated capabilities of computer algebra systems such as Maple and Mathematica. This proof, in fact, turned out to be straightforward, and considerably simpler than proofs for multiplier and adder circuits.

In the rest of this extended abstract, a brief overview of our results in verifying arithmetic circuits using *RRL* is given first. Various features of *RRL* found useful for automated hardware verification are reviewed: particularly, (a) contextual rewriting that combines congruence closure on ground terms with conditional rewriting, (b) the integration of a linear arithmetic procedure with rewriting, and (c) a lemma speculation heuristic.

## 2  SRT Division

Recently, Kapur and Subramaniam used *RRL* to mechanically verify an SRT division circuit as discussed in [5]. It is generally believed that a circuit similar to this one in the Pentium chip had a bug in its table. Below, a summary of the verification of the SRT division circuit description, highlighting the main ideas, is given. A more detailed report will be available soon [12].

The SRT division circuit implements an algorithm due to Sweeney, Robertson and Tocher, essentially mimicking the third grade division algorithm with at least two major differences:

1. Quotient digit is approximately computed by considering only a first few digits in the divisor and dividend, which makes the computation faster. A predefined table is looked-up for finding the quotient digit.
2. Partial remainder is computed by adding or subtracting depending upon whether the quotient digit is guessed correctly or overestimated by 1.

In the specification below, this is done by the functions *nqsign* (for computing whether the guess is an overestimate or not) and *nqd* (for computing the next quotient digit). The function *nqd* uses a **table** for determining the next digit.

From the circuit description and the Analytica/Mathematica input given in [5], we derived an equational specification of the SRT division. Since rational numbers are not supported in *RRL*, all specifications are written using integers. This is possible in this case since the circuit uses floating point numbers with fixed precision, which can be represented as rationals with a single denominator since all denominators are powers of 2.

The functions *nquot* and *nrout* successively compute the quotient and remainder, respectively, using *nqd* and *nqsign*. Depending upon the estimate of the quotient digit, addition/subtraction is performed.

```
[nrin  :  int -> int]
nrin(xrt) := 4 * xrt

[ndiv : int -> int]
ndiv(xd1) := xd1

[nqsign : int, int -> bool]
nqsign(xrt1, xd1)  :=  32 * xrt1 < getb3(8 * xd1)

[nqd : int, int, int, int -> int]
nqd(xrt1,xd1,xw,xs) := cond(table_lookup(32*xrt1,8*xd1,xw,xs),xw,5)
```

```
[nrout : int, int, int, int, int -> int]

nrout(xrt, xrt1, xd, xd1, xw) :=
    nrin(xrt) + nqd(xrt1, xd1, xw, 1) * xd if  nqsign(xrt1, xd1)
nrout(xrt, xrt1, xd, xd1, xw) :=
    nrin(xrt) - nqd(xrt1, xd1, xw, 0) * xd if  not(nqsign(xrt1, xd1))

[nquot : int, int, int, int -> int]

nquot(xqt, xrt1, xd1, xw) :=
    4 * xqt -  nqd(xrt1, xd1, xw, 1) if nqsign(xrt1, xd1)
nquot(xqt, xrt1, xd1, xw) :=
    4 * xqt +  nqd(xrt1, xd1, xw, 0) if not(nqsign(xrt1, xd1))
```

The formalization of the subcircuit guessing the quotient digit and the sign is based on the description in [5], using functions *getbi'* to implement the boundary value list $\{b_1, b_2, b_3, b_4, b_5, b_6\}$ given in [5]. The predicate *table_lookup* formalizes the accessing of the table based on truncated divisor and dividend.

```
[table_lookup : int, int, int, int -> bool]

table_lookup(x, y, 3, 1)   := (x  < getb1(y))
table_lookup(x, y, 3, 0)   := (x >= getb6(y))
table_lookup(x, y, 2, 1)   := ((getb1(y) <= x) and (x <  getb2(y)))
table_lookup(x, y, 2, 0)   := ((getb5(y) <= x) and (x <  getb6(y)))
table_lookup(x, y, 1, 1)   := ((getb2(y) <= x) and (x < getb3(y)))
table_lookup(x, y, 1, 0)   := ((getb4(y) <= x) and (x < getb5(y)))
table_lookup(x, y, 0, 1)   := false
table_lookup(x, y, 0, 0)   := (x < getb4(y))
```

The correctness of the circuit is established by proving the invariants as discussed in [5]. The first invariant expressing that during each iteration, the quotient and remainder are correct, can be automatically verified. The second invariant,

$$-2 \text{ xd} <= 3 \text{ nrout}(xrt, xrt1, xd, xd1, xc) < 2 \text{ xd},$$

is more interesting as it expresses what part of the quotient selection table is accessed for quotient digit estimate in each iteration (in other words, the computation does not overflow). The invariant is proved by case analysis. The following formula generated by *RRL* corresponds to one of the cases.

```
minus(2) * xd  <= 3 * nrout(xrt, xrt1, xd, xd1,  1)  if
32 * xrt1 <= 32 * xrt and 64 * xrt < 64 * xrt1 + 2 and
8 * xd1 <= 8 * xd and 16 * xd < 16 * xd1  + 2 and
nqsign( xrt1, xd1) and nqd(xrt1, xd1, 1, 1) < 4 and 8 *  xd1 = 8 and
minus(2) * xd <=  3 * xrt and  3 * xrt < 2 * xd.
```

The whole proof is done easily and automatically using the contextual rewriting integrated with the linear arithmetic procedure in *RRL*. No additional mechanism is found necessary. No extensions had to be made to *RRL*. This is in contrast to a proof attempt using *Analytica* [5] built on top of *Mathematica*, a powerful computer algebra system, as well as a proof attempt on *PVS* which supports higher-order specifications, module facility, a special data type *table* as well as the linear arithmetic procedure [15]. Even the total execution time taken by *RRL* to do these proofs seems to be much less than the time taken to do such proofs on *Analytica* and *PVS*, because of the tight integration of rewriting with the linear arithmetic procedure in *RRL*.

We believe the following extensions to *RRL* would be useful for verifying properties of circuits with similar structure as the SRT division circuit. They would especially make the SRT division proof even easier to find, increasing the speed considerably.

1. Case analysis heuristics which exploit the common structure among different cases and prune out hypotheses irrelevant to a conclusion being attempted, will speed-up the proof search.
2. Efficient representation of integers and linear terms will make rewriting faster.
3. Hard-wiring the table data structure will be useful for efficiently handling definitions such as *table_lookup*.
4. A facility for identifying bugs in definitions and specifications from failed proof attempts will aid in initial attempts to getting the proper formalization of a circuit description.

## 3  Multipliers and Adders

The descriptions of adder and multiplier circuits are input to *RRL* as recursive definitions by exploiting regularity in the circuit. It is thus possible, in fact more convenient, to describe a circuit of arbitrary word size than a circuit operating on a fixed word size, say 32 bits or 64 bits. The behavioral specification of an adder circuit, for example, is given as: the adder circuit results in a bit vector that corresponds to the number obtained by adding the two numbers corresponding to the two bit vectors given as input to the circuit. The correctness is demonstrated with respect to the circuits realizing the respective number theoretic functions, and not defining boolean functions as is typically done using *OBDD* based methods [2]. Proofs are done by induction, without making any assumption about the length of the bit vectors on which a circuit operates.

## 3.1 Adders

As illustrated in [10], the ripple-carry adder can be verified automatically using *RRL* without any user guidance at all. Attempting a correctness proof of carry-lookahead adder was, however, a challenge. It is unclear whether an automatic proof can be carried out directly. We instead proved the equivalence of a carry lookahead adder with a ripple carry adder, thus indirectly establishing the correctness of a carry lookahead adder.

Carry lookahead circuit can be succinctly described using the divide and conquer strategy and the parallel prefix operator for computing the carry. We wrote its specification using Misra's powerlist data structure. The following table summarizes the complexity of the description, the level of effort and the execution time needed to do these proofs on a Sun Sparc 5 station with 64 MB memory. *RCP* stands for the ripple-carry circuit description using powerlists; this description is introduced as an intermediary to show the equivalence between the carry-lookahead (*CLA*) and ripple-carry adders. *RCL* stands for the ripple-carry circuit description using linear lists. Proofs in which 0 and 1 are represented as bits in contrast to natural numbers can be found slightly faster. For a detailed discussion, see [10].

| Adders | Definitions | Lemmas | Time (secs.) |
|---|---|---|---|
| RCP-CLA (numbers) | 15 | 2 | 14.00 |
| RCL-RCP(numbers) | 23 | 3 | 17.73 |
| RCL-RCP(bits) | 21 | 3 | 14.40 |
| RCL(numbers) | 11 | 0 | 10.25 |
| RCL(bits) | 9 | 0 | 7.75 |

## 3.2 Multipliers

In [9], a methodology for mechanically verifying a family of multiplier circuits, including the linear array, the Wallace tree and the 7-3 multiplier is discussed. A top level specification for these multipliers is obtained by abstracting the commonality in their behavior. The behavioral correctness of any multiplier in the family can be mechanically verified by a uniform proof strategy. Adders are abstracted as generic hardware components to separate their specification from the implementation, enabling verification of circuits in terms of behavioral constraints that can be realized in different ways. The use of generic components aids the reuse of proofs and helps modularize the correctness proofs, allowing verification to go hand in hand with the hardware design process in a hierarchical fashion. Such modularization of proofs is crucial for any verification methodology to effectively scale up to larger and more complex hardware circuits, especially those built from complex components for which internal details may either not be available or are, perhaps, irrelevant.

Most of these multiplier circuits are based on the grade school principle of multiplying any two given $n$ bit vectors–computing the partial sums and adding the partial sums to obtain the required result. This basic underlying principle is often not evident in commonly found descriptions of these circuits. The computation of partial sums is done in the same manner in these circuits, and these circuits differ only in the addition of partial sums. A common top level specification for the family of multiplier circuits based on this observation is developed in [9].

A linear array multiplier performs the multiplication of two $n$ bit vectors in linear time by successively adding the partial sums one by one. A Wallace multiplier, in contrast, does partial sum addition of $n$ $n$-bit vectors in logarithmic time by considering three partial sums for addition together. The multiplication scheme due to Wallace was generalized and improved upon by Dadda. In these multipliers, larger than three partial sums are taken together for addition in a single stage. Considering a larger number of partial sums does not improve the asymptotic complexity but considerably reduces the number of stages required for multiplication, resulting in reduced wiring delays. The 7-3 multiplier used in *IBM RS/6000* is based on this observation.

The specification and the correctness proofs of the Wallace tree multiplier were attempted first in *RRL*, and it took less than a week. This includes the time taken to familiarize ourselves with the multiplier itself. The other multiplier circuits were formalized, and their correctness proofs were done in a couple of days. The statistics for the various correctness proofs obtained using *RRL* are given in the following table. For each multiplier circuit, only two definitions specific to the circuit are needed.

| *Multiplier Circuits* | *Common Definitions* | *Common Lemmas* | *Specific Definitions* | *Specific Lemmas* | *Time (secs)* |
|---|---|---|---|---|---|
| Linear Array | | | 2 | 0 | 2.5 |
| Wallace Tree | 12 | 0 | 2 | 0 | 2.5 |
| 7-3 | | | 2 | 0 | 6.25 |

In [9], it is reported that the generic proof required 5 intermediate lemmas. Subsequently, we have developed a heuristic for speculating intermediate lemmas based on circuit structure and the fact that bit vectors represent numbers. This heuristic was implemented in *RRL*. It is now possible to verify the multiplier circuit descriptions automatically. All intermediate lemmas needed in the proofs are generated using this heuristic and other heuristics in *RRL*. This heuristic is discussed in more detail in a later section.

Multiplier circuits, in contrast, cannot be handled easily by OBDD based approaches because of the state explosion problem; see however [3] where OB-DDs are generalized as binary moment diagrams for multiplier circuits. Binary moment diagrams, however, cannot handle division circuits.

## 4  Interaction between Rewriting and Decision Procedures

For theorem provers to be acceptable to application experts, the theorem prover should be able to easily perform reasoning steps considered routine in an application domain. In other words, routine reasoning should not become a burden on the application expert while using a theorem prover. We have called this *reasoning in the large* and the inference steps used for such reasoning as *large* inference steps, to distinguish from *reasoning in the small* performed using *small* inference steps typically supported in most proof checkers. Many proof checkers, however, do provide a user to design tactics which can be used to combine small inference steps to have the effect of a large inference step. Every user however must define such tactics, or use tactics from the library developed by other users.

We consider the following features crucial in buildings *large* inference steps.

1. integrating decision procedures for equality, numbers, bits, bit vectors, finite sets, finite lists, and other frequently used data structures in applications,
2. performing case analyses automatically,
3. searching for appropriate instantiations of definitions and already proved lemmas, and
4. discharging conditions in conditional axioms generated from definitions and lemmas.

Currently, *RRL* supports decision procedures for (i) equality on ground terms using completion/rewriting, (ii) propositional reasoning, (iii) bits, (iv) freely generated data structures as canonical rewrite rules, as well as a linear arithmetic procedure over integers and naturals [7]. A distinguishing feature of these decision procedures is that if a formula cannot be found unsatisfiable, then equalities are generated as consequences to be used as rewrite rules for simplification.

As illustrated below, these decision procedures are tightly integrated with rewriting. The matching algorithm in *RRL* uses them for determining whether a rewrite rule is applicable on a goal. This is perhaps the main reason why we have been successful in automatically proving properties of arithmetic circuits as well as in generating readable and compact proofs.

Below, we illustrate, using an example, the desired features of large inference steps. As the reader would notice, the combination of the decision procedures for equality on ground terms, propositional calculus, and linear arithmetic interact with each other. Further, appropriate instantiations for the rules are found by establishing the conditions of the rules for those instantiations. What would take many human-guided steps in many provers and proof checkers can be done in a single step in *RRL*.[1]

Suppose the following conjecture over the integers is attempted:

$$(p(x) \wedge (x \leq max(x, y)) \wedge (z \leq f(max(x, y))) \wedge (0 < min(x, y)) \wedge (max(x, y) \leq x))$$
$$\supset (z < g(x) + y).$$

Assume that among other rules, the following rewrite rules for $max, f, g, p$ are already in the data base.

$$1.\ min(x, y) \to y \quad if \quad max(x, y) = x,$$
$$2.\ f(x) \leq g(x) \to true \quad if \quad p(x).$$

---

[1] Boyer and Moore's prover [1] may also be able to prove this conjecture without any user guidance.

In $RRL$, the conjecture is negated and Skolemized to give:

$$p(A) \wedge (A \le max(A, B)) \wedge (L \le f(max(A, B))) \wedge (0 < min(A, B)) \wedge$$

$$(max(A, B) \le A)) \wedge \neg(L < g(A) + B).$$

This goal must be shown to be unsatisfiable. Equalities on uninterpreted symbols are first made into rewrite rules, and they are normalized. These rewrite rules are used to normalize the rest of the goal. Then the linear arithmetic decision procedure is invoked on linear equalities and inequalities. If not found unsatisfiable, any new equalities deduced by the linear arithmetic procedure are made into rewrite rules and the goal is further normalized. This process is repeated until a contradiction is found or no new equality can be deduced.

In the above example, from the linear inequalities, an implicit equality $max(A, B) = A$ is derived by the linear arithmetic procedure, which is used to simplify the inequality set to:

$$-f(A) + L \le 0, -min(A, B) \le -1, g(A) + B - L \le 0.$$

The linear term $L$ is eliminated by the linear arithmetic procedure to give:

$$-min(A, B) \le -1, -f(A) + g(A) + B \le 0.$$

No new equality can be deduced by the decision procedures now.

If a goal cannot be shown to be unsatisfiable and no new equalities can be deduced from the interaction of the decision procedures, it is then checked whether a rewrite rule from the data base of definitions and lemmas applies. Literals in the goal are analyzed for matching the rewrite rules, starting with the maximal literals. If a match with the left side of some rule is found, then a proof of the condition of the rule, if any, under the match is attempted. If successful, the instance of the rewrite rule is added as a new equality, and the above process is repeated.

Continuing with the above example, rule 1 is applicable using $\{x \leftarrow A, \ y \leftarrow B\}$ since its condition follows from the known equalities. $min(A, B)$ is reduced to $B$; the equality $min(A, B) = B$ is also added to the equality set. Assuming an ordering $f > g$, $f(A)$ matches a maximal term in the linear rule 2 since $P(A)$ is true. The instance of the linear rule, $f(A) \le g(A)$, is added to the inequality set:

$$-B \le -1, -f(A) + g(A) + B \le 0, f(A) - g(A) \le 0.$$

The decision procedure detects a contradiction implying that the original conjecture is proved.

We are planning to implement in $RRL$ decision procedures for other frequently used data structures including finite arrays, bit vectors, finite sets and finite lists. Since for large circuits with complex control, OBDD based methods have been found to be more effective [2, 4] than traditional theorem proving methods for propositional reasoning and word-level reasoning, it might also be necessary to integrate an OBDD method and word-level reasoning with rewriting. Theoretical issues related to the development of decision procedures and their interaction with rewriting are under investigation [6].

# 5 Intermediate Lemma Speculation

Based on our experience in verifying arithmetic circuits, we have been developing a heuristic for speculating intermediate lemmas as guided by the circuit structure and the behavioral specification of different components in the circuit. A naive version of this heuristic has been implemented in *RRL*. Preliminary experiments are very encouraging; it is possible using this heuristic and other heuristics in *RRL* to automatically verify the multiplier circuits. No intermediate lemmas have to be supplied by the user; in that sense, *RRL* can be run in the push-button mode. Without this heuristic, the verification of the Wallace multiplier needed 5 intermediate lemmas from the user [9]. Below, we illustrate some of the main ideas of this new heuristic using the Wallace multiplier circuit below in Figure 1. A paper giving all the details is under preparation [11].

The Wallace multiplier circuit can be decomposed into four subcircuits. A detailed specification of Wallace multiplier circuit and its verification are discussed in [9].

1. circuit doing partial sum computation, *Psum-All*,
2. carry-save adder circuit, *CSA*, for performing addition, which takes three bit vectors as input, and outputs two bit vectors,
3. replication of the carry-save adders to add *n* bit vectors, considering them three at a time (relating *3-at-a-time-addrepeat* to *3-at-a-time-addonce*), and
4. ripple-carry adder, *RCA*, at the end to produce the final output.

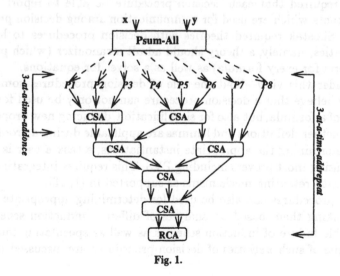

Fig. 1.

The Wallace multiplier circuit is the composition of these subcircuits. A behavioral specification of the multiplier circuit can be propagated backwards to impose constraints on the behavior of each of these subcircuits. And, this leads to speculating a lemma about the behavior of each of these subcircuits.

1. A lemma relating the number corresponding to the output of $RCA$ to the addition of numbers corresponding to its two input bit vectors.
2. A lemma stating that the number corresponding to the two output bit vectors from $CSA$ is the addition of the numbers corresponding to the three input bit vectors.
3. A lemma stating that the number corresponding to the output of a family of the $CSA$ adders is indeed the sum of numbers corresponding to the output of $Psum$-$All$.
4. A lemma stating that the number corresponding to the output generated by $Psum$-$All$ gives the result of multiplication.

In addition to these lemmas, another lemma corresponding to the loop (specified as a tail-recursive function *3-at-a-time-addrepeat*) implementing the repetitive use of $CSA$'s for adding 3 bit vectors at a time (*3-at-a-time-addonce*) is needed.

The above lemmas are expressed using two homomorphisms: *bton* relating a bit vector to the number it represents, and *btonlist*, relating a list of bit vectors to the number the list represents.

# 6 New Uses of Decision Procedures

The view taken towards the role of decision procedures in both Nelson and Oppen's approach [14] as well as Shostak's approach [16] is that of determining whether a formula is valid or not. For combining decision procedures, Nelson and Oppen required that each decision procedure be able to report equalities among constants which are used for communication among decision procedures. In contrast, Shostak required theories with decision procedures to have additional properties, namely, a theory should admit a canonizer (which produces a canonical form for every formula) as well as a solver for equations.

We consider this view about the role of decision procedures somewhat restricted. We believe that a decision procedure can not only be used for deciding the validity of a formula, but also for simplification, deducing new properties, determining whether definitions and lemmas are applicable during a proof attempt, and if so, determining the appropriate instantiations, a task a user is burdened with, while using most provers including PVS. This requires integrating decision procedures with rewriting mechanisms as supported in [1, 13].

Decision procedures can also be used for determining appropriate induction schemes, ranking them based on analyses of different induction schemes, analyzing possible failure of induction schemes as well as speculating intermediate lemmas. Some of such *new* uses of decision procedures are discussed in [8].

# 7 Concluding Remarks

Based on our limited experience, it appears that a theorem prover such as $RRL$ can be effectively used for verifying properties of (at least, simple) arithmetic circuits. The theorem prover has worked essentially in the push-button mode. It is being widely recognized now that for circuits involving data paths, OBDD based methods and their extensions are limited in their applicability. On the other hand, theorem provers provide considerable flexibility and generality, where proofs can be developed modularly and generically, exploiting the circuit structure.

For theorem provers to be more useful, it is extremely important that they be oriented to address the needs of circuit designers instead of demanding circuit designers to adapt to the needs of theorem provers. Interfaces between commonly used circuit description languages and theorem provers must be developed. Lemma speculation heuristics based on specific features of circuits should be investigated. Finally, theorem provers should be able to provide useful (even limited) feedback to a designer when a bug (in the specification or the circuit) is identified.

**Acknowledgement:** This work has been done jointly with my former student Mahadevan Subramaniam. At the time of the submission of this extended abstract, Subu was unavailable to approve it, that is why his name does not appear as a coauthor. I apologize for not citing the related work. Some of the relevant citations can be found in [10, 9, 13, 8].

# References

1. R.S. Boyer and J. Moore, *A Computational Logic Handbook.* New York: Academic Press, 1988.
2. R.E. Bryant, "Graph-based algorithms for boolean function manipulation," *IEEE trans. on Computers*, C-35(8), 1986.
3. R. E. Bryant, and Y.-A. Chen, "Verification of arithmetic functions with binary moment diagrams," Tech. Rep. CMU-CS-94-160, June 1994.
4. J. R. Burch, E.M. Clarke, K. L. Mcmillan and D.L. Dill, "Sequential circuit verification using symbolic model checking," Proc. *27th ACM/IEEE Design Automation Conference*, 1990.
5. E.M. Clarke, S.M. German and X. Zhao, "Verifying the SRT division algorithm using theorem proving techniques," Proc. *Computer Aided Verification, 8th Intl. Conf. - CAV'96*, New Brunswick, July/August 1996, Springer LNCS 1102 (eds. Alur and Henzinger), 111-122.
6. D. Kapur, "Shostak's congruence closure as completion," Proc. *Intl. Conf. on Rewriting Techniques and Applications (RTA-97)*, Barcelona, Spain, June 1997.
7. D. Kapur and X. Nie, "Reasoning about numbers in Tecton," Proc. *8th Intl. Symp. Methodologies for Intelligent Systems, (ISMIS'94)*, Charlotte, North Carolina, October 1994, 57-70.
8. D. Kapur and M. Subramaniam, "New uses of linear arithmetic in automated theorem proving for induction," *J. Automated Reasoning*, 16(1-2), 1996, 39-78.
9. D. Kapur and M. Subramaniam, "Mechanically verifying a family of multiplier circuits," Proc. *Computer Aided Verification (CAV'96)*, New Jersey, Springer LNCS 1102 (eds. Alur and Henzinger), 1996, 135-146.

10. D. Kapur and M. Subramaniam, "Mechanical verification of adder circuits using powerlists," Dept. of Computer Science Tech. Report, SUNY Albany, November 1995. Accepted for publication in *J. of Formal Methods in System Design.*

11. D. Kapur and M. Subramaniam, "Intermediate lemma generation from circuit descriptions," under preparation, State University of New York, Albany, NY, May 1997.

12. D. Kapur and M. Subramaniam, "An automatic proof of properties of an SRT division circuit," under preparation, State University of New York, Albany, NY, May 1997.

13. D. Kapur, and H. Zhang, "An overview of Rewrite Rule Laboratory (RRL)," *J. of Computer and Mathematics with Applications,* 29, 2, 1995, 91-114.

14. G. Nelson, and D.C. Oppen, "Simplification by cooperating decision procedures," *ACM Tran. on Programming Languages and Systems* 1 (2), 1979, 245-257.

15. H. Ruess, N. Shankar and M.K. Srivas, "Modular verification of SRT division," Proc. *Computer Aided Verification, 8th Intl. Conf. - CAV'96,* New Brunswick, July/August 1996, Springer LNCS 1102 (eds. Alur and Henzinger), 123-134.

16. R.E. Shostak, "Deciding combination of theories," *Journal of ACM* 31 (1), 1984, 1-12.

17. H. Zhang, "Implementing contextual rewriting," Proc. *3rd Intl. Workshop on Conditional Term Rewriting Systems,* Springer LNCS 656, (eds. Remy and Rusinowitch), 1992, 363-377.

18. H. Zhang, D. Kapur, and M.S. Krishnamoorthy, "A mechanizable induction principle for equational specifications," Proc. *9th Intl. Conf. Automated Deduction (CADE),* Springer LNCS 310, (eds. Lusk and Overbeek), Chicago, 1988, 250-265.

# Refining Reactive Systems in HOL
# Using Action Systems

Thomas Långbacka[1]* and Joakim von Wright[2]*

[1] Department of Computer Science, University of Helsinki
http://www.cs.Helsinki.FI/~tlangbac/
[2] Department of Computer Science, Åbo Akademi University
http://www.abo.fi/~jwright/

**Abstract.** Work on embedding reasoning about programs in a mechanised logic has mostly focused on meta-theoretic reasoning about programming logics or notations. This paper describes an attempt to formalise a theory of actions systems in HOL, in such a way that a tool for developing and reasoning about distributed and reactive systems can be built on top of the theory. By reducing action system refinement proofs to proofs of data refinement between sequential statements, we are able to reuse existing theories and tools for sequential programs.

## 1   Introduction

*Reactive systems* have been studied with great interest in the formal methods community during recent years. Many different formal frameworks have been suggested for dealing with such systems.

A reactive system is a program that interacts with an *environment*. Such a system observes the activities in the environment and reacts to certain types of events. Typically reactive systems are modelled as non-terminating programs, and also the environment is often described in the programming notation used. An operating system could be seen as an example of a reactive system. Its job is just to react to commands from its environment – its users. Although an operating system might be terminated and the computer shut down, it still has a state that lives on, e.g. the file system.

In this paper we document work on formalising *action systems* in HOL. Action systems can be used to model parallel and reactive programs. In [5] a *trace semantics* and a corresponding refinement relation (trace refinement) are defined for action systems and it is shown that a simulation method can be used to prove trace refinement. Furthermore, simulation reduces reasoning about action systems to reasoning about sequential programs using the framework of the *Refinement Calculus* [2,3]. Thus, in order to formalise action systems in HOL we can build directly on the existing work on formalising the refinement calculus in HOL [4,11].

---

\* **Second affiliation:** Turku Centre for Computer Science – TUCS

Reactive systems can be (and have been) treated in HOL formalisations of such formal frameworks as CSP [7], UNITY [1] or TLA [12]. We will not argue for or against the respective merits of any of the above systems (or their HOL incarnations) as compared to action systems. However, it is well known that working with HOL formalisations of programming logics is usually very difficult. Since reactive systems are often complex, this does not make the task easier.

Thus, one main motivation for our work is that it will be integrated into the *Refinement Calculator* [6], a tool for systematic development of sequential programs within the Refinement Calculus framework. By extending the Refinement Calculator with facilities for handling action systems, we get a tool that allows a user to specify and refine reactive programs using a graphical user interface and with every development step verified by a proof in the HOL theorem prover.

## 2 Background

In this section we give a brief description of those parts of the Refinement Calculus and its formalisation in HOL that are relevant to this paper.

### 2.1 The Refinement Calculus

The Refinement Calculus [2,3] extends Dijkstra's weakest precondition semantics for programs [8] by introducing a refinement relation between programs and by adding specification statements that allow specifications to be expressed within the programming notation.

The semantics of a statement $S$ is defined by the function $wp$ which given a statement $S$ and a predicate $Q$ (the postcondition) returns $wp(S, Q)$, the weakest predicate $P$ such that executing $S$ in an initial state where $P$ holds guarantees that $S$ terminates and $Q$ holds upon termination.

We will not assume a specific program notation; in the examples we use (multiple) assignments of the form $x := E$. Other constructs will be described as they are needed.

*Refinement* The refinement relation is defined in terms of the weakest preconditions of the related programs. Program $S_0$ is refined by $S_1$ iff

$$\forall P.\ wp(S_0, P) \Rightarrow wp(S_1, P)$$

Essentially, this means that program $S_1$ must satisfy all total correctness properties that program $S_0$ satisfies. The refinement relation (denoted $\leq$) is a preorder. Thus programs can be developed in a *stepwise*, linear fashion as in the following sequence

$$S_0 \leq S_1 \leq \ldots \leq S_n$$

which establishes the refinement $S_0 \leq S_n$, because of the transitivity of the relation.

An important property is that one can refine subcomponents of programs without affecting the total correctness of the whole program. Formally this means that if we have proved that $T \leq T'$ then we have in fact established the refinement $S[T] \leq S[T']$ (provided the context $S[\cdot]$ is monotonic with respect to refinement – however, all contexts that arise using ordinary specification and programming constructs are monotonic).

*Data refinement* In program development, it is often useful to specify a program using *abstract* (high-level and often unimplementable) data structures and then refine such specifications into executable programs where the abstract data structures have been replaced by *concrete* data structures.

In practice this is achieved by providing a relation (say $R$) that relates the unimplementable abstract data structure to the one used in an executable program and show that when this relation holds also refinement is achieved. In the Refinement Calculus, this is achieved using an *abstraction statement* of the form $E = \{+a - c.\ R\}$. This statement adds abstract variable(s) $a$ to the state so that the condition $R$ holds and then removes concrete variable(s) $c$ from the state. Statement $S$ over the abstract state is then *data refined* by concrete statement $S'$ if the following refinement holds:

$$E; S \leq S'; E$$

We write $S \leq_E S'$ for this data refinement.

## 2.2 Formalising The Refinement Calculus in HOL

This section briefly summarises work that have been done over several years on formalising the refinement calculus theory in HOL (see e.g. [4, 11]).

*Program state* When formalising a (state-based) programming logic in HOL an important decision to be taken is how to represent the state of a program. We will be working with a *shallow embedding*, i.e., one where we do not define new types to represent syntactic classes such as program variables, expressions or statements. In this situation, one natural way to deal with states is to represent them as tuples. On the general level, states are defined using a polymorphic type[3]. In individual programs, each program variable is represented as one component in the tuple. This means that a program can contain variables of different types. On the other hand, a slight drawback is that the global variable space is hard-wired into every statement.

*Predicates* The semantics used is a weakest precondition semantics where the meaning of programs are defined using predicates over the program state. Thus, predicates (**pred**) are functions of type **state→bool**, where the state is represented as described above. For predicates of this type a set of connectives (as well as truth values) have to be defined (lifted HOL connectives). For example, we define

---

[3] We use the convention from HOL90 for writing type variables, i.e. they are written in the form 'a etc.

$\vdash_{def}$ true $= \lambda v.\ T$

$\vdash_{inf}$ and p q $= \lambda v.\ p\ v \wedge q\ v$

$\vdash_{inf}$ implies p q $= \forall v.\ p\ v \Rightarrow q\ v$

Here the symbol "$\vdash_{inf}$" indicates that an operator is defined as an infix. Ordinary prefix operators are preceded by the symbol "$\vdash_{def}$". Theorems that have been proved in HOL will be preceded by the symbol "$\vdash_{HOL}$". Note that implies is the relation of strength on predicates.

*Predicate transformers* Program statements are defined directly as *predicate transformers*, i.e. functions of type pred→pred. Assume that f represents a state function (i.e., $f$ has type state→state) and that c1 and c2 represent statements. We then define assignment and sequential composition by the constants assign and seq, as follows:

$\vdash_{def}$ assign f q $= \lambda s.\ q(f\ s)$

$\vdash_{inf}$ seq c1 c2 q $= c1(c2\ q)$

This corresponds to the traditional definitions of weakest precondition semantics for assignment and sequential composition:

$$wp(x := E, Q) = Q[E/x]$$
$$wp(S_1; S_2, Q) = wp(S_1, wp(S_2, Q))$$

For example,

assign ($\lambda$s:num#num. (FST s,FST s $+$ 1))

represents the assignment $y := x + 1$ in a two-component state space $(x, y)$. In fact, the initial and final state spaces need not be the same, so a state function can be of the form f:state1→state2 (this feature is used when abstraction statements are defined in HOL).

*Refinement and data refinement* The refinement relation is simply implication lifted from predicates to predicate transformers:

$\vdash_{inf}$ ref c c' $= \forall q.\ (c\ q)$ implies (c' q)

To use data refinement in HOL we assume state spaces of the form 'x#'s where the first component represents the local state and the second component represents the global state. The abstraction statement is then defined as a predicate transformer in HOL:

$\vdash_{def}$ abst r q $= (\lambda w.\ \exists a.\ r(a,FST\ w,SND\ w) \wedge q(a,SND\ w))$

where r:('a#'c#'s)→bool is the abstraction relation and q:('a#'s)→bool is a predicate over the abstract state space.

Now the data refinement relation can be defined directly:

$\vdash_{def}$ dataref r c c' $= ((abst\ r)\ seq\ c)\ ref\ (c'\ seq\ (abst\ r))$

Here c is a program operating on the abstract data space ('a#'s) whereas c' operates on the state space ('c#'s).

# 3   Action Systems – Theory

Action systems [5] can be used to model reactive systems. In this paper, we use the following (ad hoc) syntax for action systems:

$$var \ v$$
$$ini \ A_0$$
$$act \ A_1 [\!] A_2 [\!] \ldots [\!] A_m$$
$$fin \ A_F$$

where $v$ is the list of *local variables*, $A_0$ is the *initialisation* predicate, $A_F$ is the *finalisation* predicate and $A_1, \ldots, A_m$ are *actions*. Each action is a *guarded command* of the form $g \to S$ where $S$ is a statement (the *body*) and $g$ is an enabling predicate (the *guard*). The semantics for the action is then given by $wp(g \to S, Q) = g \Rightarrow wp(S, Q)$. The global variables are not specified; all program variables that are not explicitly listed as local variables are considered to be global.[4]

Informally an action system behaves as follows

1. The local variables are assigned initial values that make the initialisation predicate hold.
2. Actions are chosen for execution non-deterministically over and over (an action can be chosen only if its guard evaluates to true).
3. If the finalisation predicate evaluates to true (at any point in the computation) then the action system *may* terminate.

If the finalisation and all action guards are false at the same time, then the system has *deadlocked*.[5]

*Semantics and refinement of action systems* Since reactive programs frequently are supposed to run forever, a predicate transformer semantics is not adequate. Instead, action systems are given *trace* semantics. The meaning of an action system is defined as the set of *traces* (a trace is a state sequence with the local state components filtered away and all finite stuttering removed) that its execution can generate. Thus, a trace is a (finite or infinite) sequence of global states.

An action system $\mathcal{A}$ is *trace refined* by another action system $\mathcal{C}$ (written $\mathcal{A} \sqsubseteq \mathcal{C}$ if every trace of $\mathcal{C}$ is also a possible trace of $\mathcal{A}$. Thus, trace refinement is a suitable relation for talking about refinement of action systems as closed systems. However, when considering action systems as reactive components that interact with other action systems, then we are more interested in *simulation refinement*.

---

[4] Standard notation for action systems is $|[var \ v = v_0; do \ g_1 \to S_1 [\!] \ldots [\!] g_m \to S_m \ od]|$. This corresponds to the notation used here but with a deterministic initialisation and an implicit finalisation predicate $\neg(g_1 \vee \ldots \vee g_m)$.

[5] The original theory of action systems does not include finalisation predicates – they have been introduced by Back and von Wright in (as yet) unpublished work.

Assume that the following two action systems are given

$$\mathcal{A} = var\ a$$
$$ini\ A_0$$
$$act\ A_1 [\!] \ldots [\!] A_m$$
$$fin\ A_F$$

and

$$\mathcal{C} = var\ c$$
$$ini\ C_0$$
$$act\ C_1 [\!] \ldots [\!] C_m$$
$$fin\ C_F$$

and that $E = \{+a - c.\ R\}$ is an abstraction statement. Then $\mathcal{A}$ is *simulation refined through* $E$ *by* $\mathcal{C}$ (written $\mathcal{A} \leq_E \mathcal{C}$) if the following three conditions hold:

$$C_0 \Rightarrow wp(E, A_0) \tag{1}$$
$$E; (A_1 \wedge \ldots \wedge A_m) \leq (C_1 \wedge \ldots \wedge C_n); E \tag{2}$$
$$wp(E, \neg A_F) \Rightarrow \neg C_F \tag{3}$$

where $S_1 \wedge S_2$ is the *demonic choice* between statements $S_1$ and $S_2$; its semantics is $wp(S_1 \wedge S_2, Q) = wp(S_1, Q) \wedge wp(S_2, Q)$. The above conditions are referred to as *initialisation simulation* (1), *action simulation* (2) and *finalisation simulation* (3). Note that condition (2) is a data refinement – thus simulation refinement between action systems reduces to data refinement between the actions involved. Since these actions are sequential program statements, the original Refinement Calculus for sequential programs can be used to finish the details of a proof of simulation.

An important special case of simulation refinement is when the abstraction statement is *local* (i.e., of the form $\{+a - c.\ R\}$ where $R$ does not mention any global variables). We write $\mathcal{A} \preceq \mathcal{C}$ if there exists a local abstraction statement $E$ such that $\mathcal{A} \leq_E \mathcal{C}$ holds.

Simulation is a stronger relation than trace refinement. Thus, the following rule is valid:

$$\frac{\vdash \mathcal{A} \leq_E \mathcal{C}}{\vdash \mathcal{A} \sqsubseteq \mathcal{C}} \tag{4}$$

Furthermore, local simulation is both reflexive and transitive.

*Parallel composition* Reactive programs are executed in an *environment*. For action systems, this is modelled using parallel composition $\|$. Given an action system $\mathcal{A}$, executing it in the environment $\mathcal{E}$ means executing the action system $\mathcal{A}\|\mathcal{E}$.

The parallel composition of the assumed action systems $\mathcal{A}$ and $\mathcal{C}$ is the following action system:

$$\mathcal{A}\|\mathcal{C} = var\ a, c$$
$$ini\ A_0 \wedge C_0$$
$$act\ A_1 [\!] \ldots [\!] A_m [\!] C_1 [\!] \ldots [\!] C_n$$
$$fin\ A_F \wedge C_F$$

Thus the local state of the parallel composition is the combination of the two local states, and every action is also an action of the parallel composition. Obviously, parallel composition is both associative and commutative.

The following compositionality rule can be used to refine individual action systems in a parallel context:

$$\frac{\vdash A \preceq C}{\vdash A \| \mathcal{E} \preceq C \| \mathcal{E}} \tag{5}$$

In the general case (i.e., simulation $\leq_E$ where $E$ is not local) there is an additional *noninterference condition* associated with this rule. This condition states that every action of the environment must commute with the abstraction statement $E$.

*An example* The following is an example of an action system.

$$
\begin{aligned}
A = \ &var\ g : bool, y : num \\
&ini\ \neg g \\
&act\ f \wedge \neg g \rightarrow f, g, y := false, true, x \ \| \\
&\quad\ g \rightarrow g, out := false, consume(y) \\
&fin\ \neg f \wedge \neg g
\end{aligned}
$$

Here $f : bool$, $x : num$ and $out : num$ are global variables. The behaviour of $A$ can be described as follows. Its first action moves a values from $x$ to the local variable $y$ and the second action transforms the value (the function *consume*) and moves it to the global variable $out$. The flags $f$ and $g$ make sure that no new value is taken in before the previous value is consumed (when both flags are *false* the system terminates).

In isolation, $A$ cannot do very much. But in an environment where new values are put in $x$ and the flag $f$ is reset, $A$ can go on consuming values indefinitely. The parallel composition $A \parallel B$ is a *producer–consumer system*, where

$$
\begin{aligned}
B = \ &var \\
&ini\ true \\
&act\ \neg f \rightarrow f, x := true, produce(in) \\
&fin\ f
\end{aligned}
$$

Here $B$ has no local variables at all, and *in* is an additional global variable from which variables to be consumed are taken.

## 4 Action Systems – HOL Formalisation

As described in section 3 an action system essentially consists of three separate parts: the initialisation and finalisation predicates and a list of actions. The two predicates are directly represented as boolean functions over a two-component state space, as described in Section 2.2. Actions are represented as pairs (g,c) where g is a predicate and c is a predicate transformer.

*Example* Consider the action system $\mathcal{A}$ from section 3. In HOL it looks as follows:

(not g,
[(f and (not g), assign ($\lambda$s. (T,x s),F,x s,in s,out s));
 (g, assign ($\lambda$s. (F,y s),f s,x s,in s,consume (y s)))],
(not f) and (not g))

Here the program variables have been represented as projection functions on the state. The local state is (g,y) while the global state is (f,x,in,out), so we have defined, e.g., f = FST ∘ SND and x = FST ∘ SND ∘ SND.

*Simulation* In order to define simulation we start by defining three *projection functions* to access the different components in HOL action system triples (and also to improve readability):

⊢$_{\text{def}}$ ini = FST
⊢$_{\text{def}}$ act = FST ∘ SND
⊢$_{\text{def}}$ fin = SND ∘ SND

The conditions (1) and (3) are given the following formalisation in HOL:

⊢$_{\text{def}}$ inisim r AA CC = (ini CC) implies (abst r (ini AA))
⊢$_{\text{def}}$ finsim r AA CC = (abst r (not(fin AA))) implies (not(fin CC))

Here r:('a#'c#'s)→bool is the abstraction relation, AA is an action system triple working on the state space 'a#'s and CC is an action system triple working on the state space 'c#'s

In order to formalise the action simulation (2) condition we need to define demonic choice over a list of actions. For this we use the HOL theory of lists and define the constant aldch to represent the demonic choice as follows:

⊢$_{\text{def}}$ aldch [ ] q = true ∧
    aldch (CONS a al) q = (not (FST a)) or ((SND a q) and (aldch al q))

Here FST accesses the guard (the first component) of an action while SND accesses the body.

Many things that are assumed as self-evident in a pen-and-paper treatment have to be proved explicitly in order to be used. For example, to be able to reorder actions in a list of the type above, we have proved the following HOL theorem:

⊢$_{\text{HOL}}$ ∀a b. aldch (APPEND a b) = aldch (APPEND b a)

The action simulation (2) condition is defined as follows:

⊢$_{\text{def}}$ actsim r AA CC = dataref r (aldch (act AA)) (aldch (act CC))

The general simulation relation is now easily defined:

⊢$_{\text{def}}$ rsim r AA CC = inisim r AA CC ∧ actsim r AA CC ∧ finsim r AA CC

We are (currently) interested primarily in local simulations, since the compositionality rule for local simulations has no side conditions. Thus we define a specific relation for that. First we define locality:

$\vdash_{def}$ local r = $\exists$rr. $\forall$s. r s = rr(FST s,FST(SND s))

This definition says that locality of a relation r (of the same type as above) means always being able to find a relation rr:('a#'c)$\rightarrow$bool that has the same value as r regardless of what value the global state component has.

Now we define the local simulation relation:

$\vdash_{inf}$ lsim AA CC = $\exists$r. local r $\wedge$ rsim r AA CC

and prove that it is reflexive and transitive:

$\vdash_{HOL}$ $\forall$ AA. AA lsim AA
$\vdash_{HOL}$ $\forall$ AA BB CC. AA lsim BB $\wedge$ BB lsim CC $\Rightarrow$ AA lsim CC

*Parallel composition defined in HOL* Two action systems can be composed in parallel if they work on the same global state. Our idea is to formalise parallel composition of two action systems $\mathcal{A}$ (on state space 'a#'s) and $\mathcal{C}$ (on state space 'c#'s) so that $\mathcal{A}\|\mathcal{C}$ works on the state space ('a#'c)#'s. To do this, we *adapt* the two action systems involved to the larger state space using a special adaption operator.

Before we define adaption and parallel composition, we make the following definitions:

$\vdash_{inf}$ ppar p q u = p (FST u) $\wedge$ q (SND u)
$\vdash_{inf}$ par c1 c2 q u = $\exists$ q1 q2. (q1 ppar q2 implies q) $\wedge$
$\qquad\qquad\qquad\qquad\qquad$ c1 q1 (FST u) $\wedge$ c2 q2 (SND u))

The ppar operator composes two predicates p and q that operate on disjoint state spaces (i.e., over the two components of the paired state space u). Similarly par defines a "parallel composition" operator for statements (c1 and c2) working on disjoint state spaces. Given these definitions we can define an adaption operator as follows:

$\vdash_{def}$ adapt f g c = (assign f) seq (c par skip) seq (assign g)

Using state functions f:'s$\rightarrow$'s1#'s2 and g:'s1#'s2$\rightarrow$'s that reorder the components of the state space (with g being the inverse function of f) the adaption operator has the effect that execution of adapt f g c corresponds to executing c over state space 's1 and skip over state space 's2. In what follows we write $\bar{c}$ to denote an adapted command c.

Now we define parallel composition of two action systems as follows:

$\vdash_{inf}$ apar AA BB = (inicomb AA BB,actcomb AA BB,fincomb AA BB)

where inicomb, actcomb and fincomb are defined to adapt and combine the corresponding parts of the two action systems AA and BB. We have

⊢$_{def}$ inicomb AA BB = (λs. ini AA (FST(FST s),SND s) ∧
ini BB (SND(FST s),SND s))
⊢$_{def}$ fincomb AA BB = (λs. fin AA (FST(FST s),SND s) ∧
fin BB (SND(FST s),SND s))

where the state is s:('a#'c)#'s, i.e., the space of the action system that is created using parallel composition

To combine the lists of actions we use adaption

⊢$_{def}$ actcomb AA BB = APPEND $\overline{\text{act AA}}$ $\overline{\text{act BB}}$

Here $\overline{\text{act AA}}$ is the adaption of the list of action from AA. The definition of this adaption essentially states that we map suitable adaptions into every guard and body of the list. The full definition (including type information) is fairly long and complex and therefore not included in the text.

*Properties of parallel composition* As mentioned in Section 3 parallel composition is commutative and associative. However, the formalisation of parallel composition and the way states are represented mean that AA apar BB and BB apar AA have different types. Thus commutativity (and similarly associativity) is lost. The solution to this problem is that we still have *commutativity and associativity up to simulation equivalence*; the following are theorems:

⊢$_{HOL}$ ∀ AA BB. (AA apar BB) lsim (BB apar AA)
⊢$_{HOL}$ ∀ AA BB CC. ((AA apar BB) apar CC) lsim (AA apar (BB apar CC))
⊢$_{HOL}$ ∀ AA BB CC. (AA apar (BB apar CC)) lsim ((AA apar BB) apar CC)

This is really sufficient for our purposes; since simulation is transitive, we can always commute or reassociate action systems in the middle of a sequence of simulation refinement steps.

*Compositionality as a HOL theorem* Before we can refine action systems containing parallel composition we have to prove the compositionality theorem (5). We have done this, i.e. we have proved the following HOL theorem:

⊢$_{HOL}$ ∀ AA CC BB. AA lsim CC ∧ EVERY mono (MAP SND (act AA)) ⇒
(∀b. (AA apar BB) lsim (CC apar BB))

In this theorem the term EVERY mono (MAP SND (act AA)) means that every action body of the system AA must be monotonic.[6] The definition of monotonicity is as follows:

⊢$_{def}$ mono c = ∀p q. p implies q ⇒ (c p) implies (c q)

---

[6] Monotonicity – one of Dijkstra's original "healthiness conditions" for predicate transformers – cannot be taken for granted in the HOL formalisation of program statements; it has to be proved explicitly to hold for a statement. However, monotonicity for standard statements can be proved automatically in the HOL theory of refinement.

In order to prove simulations between action systems we also need a large collection of theorems that facilitate data refinement proofs between action lists (this is the most difficult part in simulation proofs). Typical theorems deal with breaking down lists into parts etc. An example is the following theorem:

$\vdash_{\mathsf{HOL}} \forall$ r a b c d. dataref r (aldch a) (aldch b) $\wedge$
$\qquad$ dataref r (aldch c) (aldch d)
$\qquad\Rightarrow$ dataref r (aldch (APPEND a c)) (aldch (APPEND b d))

which is useful in the simple case when actions are replaced one by one in a simulation.

The definition of simulation reduces refinement between action systems to data refinement between sequential program statements. This means that we can reuse existing HOL theories of program refinement [11] to finish off refinement proofs.

*Trace refinement and HOL* The trace semantics mentioned in section 3 has not been formalised in HOL. Formalising it would be a demanding exercise in theorem proving, but it would not add any advantage from a practical point of view, since all proof efforts when working with action systems are aimed at proving simulations. Defining the trace semantics would be interesting only in order to prove the rule in equation (4). Here we treat this rule as a *meta-level axiom* that is outside the HOL theory.

# 5 An Example of a Simulation Proof

Recall the two action systems $\mathcal{A}$ (consumer) and $\mathcal{B}$ (producer) from Section 3

$$
\begin{aligned}
\mathcal{A} = \ &var\ g : bool, y : num \\
&ini\ \neg g \\
&act\ f \wedge \neg g \to f, g, y := false, true, x\ \| \\
&\qquad g \to g, out := false, consume(y) \\
&fin\ \neg f \wedge \neg g
\end{aligned}
$$

and

$$
\begin{aligned}
\mathcal{B} = \ &var \\
&ini\ true \\
&act\ \neg f \to f, x := true, produce(in) \\
&fin\ f
\end{aligned}
$$

As an example, we describe a small but complete refinement of the action system $\mathcal{A}$ by another action system $\mathcal{C}$, where the local variables $g$ and $y$ have been replaced by a list $z$ (note that $z$ is either empty or contains just one element).

$$
\begin{aligned}
\mathcal{C} = \ &var\ z : (num)list \\
&ini\ f \wedge (z = [\,]) \\
&act\ f \wedge (z = [\,]) \to f, z := false, [x]\ \| \\
&\qquad z \neq [\,] \to z, out := [\,], consume(hd\ z) \\
&fin\ \neg f \wedge (z = [\,])
\end{aligned}
$$

The refinement as such is fairly trivial, as it does not change the structure or behaviour of the system. However, it illustrates the basic principles of action system refinement: the simulation refinement of a component in a parallel composition using techniques of data refinement. In HOL the theorem proving the validity of the above simulation looks as follows:

$\vdash_{\text{HOL}}$ ((not g,
      [(f and (not g), assign ($\lambda$s. ((T,x s),F,x s,inv s,out s)));
       (g, assign ($\lambda$s. ((F,y s),f s,x s,inv s,consume (y s))))],
      (not f) and (not g))
  apar
      (true,
      [(not f, assign ($\lambda$s. (dum s,T,produce (inv s),inv s,out s)))],
      f))
  lsim
      (((($\lambda$s. z s = [ ]),
      [(($\lambda$s. f s $\wedge$ (z s = [ ])), assign ($\lambda$s. ([x s],F,x s,inv s,out s));
       ($\lambda$s.$\neg$(z s = [ ])),
        assign ($\lambda$s. (TL (z s),f s,x s,inv s,consume (HD (z s))))],
      ($\lambda$s. $\neg$(f s) $\wedge$ (z s = [ ])))
  apar
      (true,
      [(not f, assign ($\lambda$s. (dum s,T,produce (inv s),inv s,out s)))],
      f))

(here dum:one is a dummy local component, added to the action system $B$ so that its state space has the required form, i.e., a product of a local and a global state).

In order to prove this theorem one first matches the whole term against the compositionality rule. This way we get rid of the environment (in this case $B$). We then need to prove that all the actions of $A$ are monotonic (this is done using an automatic monotonicity prover) and that the lsim relation holds between the two action systems $A$ and $C$. We use the definition of lsim to rewrite the current term and then supply the abstraction relation we want to use. It is $(\neg g \wedge (z = [\ ])) \vee (g \wedge (z = [y]))$, which is represented in HOL as follows:

$\lambda$s. $(\neg$g(old s) $\wedge$ (z(new s) = [ ])) $\vee$ (g(old s) $\wedge$ (z(new s) = [y(old s)]))

where old recovers the state space of the old (abstract) action system and new recovers the state space of the new (concrete) action system from the state space of the abstraction relation (so old s = (FST(FST s),SND s) and new s = (SND(FST s),SND s)).

The proof is then continued by proving that the above relation is local (which is trivial) and that the rsim relation holds. Proving initialisation and finalisation simulation is straightforward. To prove action simulation we use the theorem for breaking down data refinement between action lists into data refinement of individual actions (see section 4) and then use the existing theories for proving data refinement.

# 6 Future Work

The HOL theory presented here shows that HOL can be used to prove refinement theorems for action systems. However, it is also clear from the presentation that the theory is not easy to use directly. We are well aware of this fact and the solution we propose is to integrate the theory into the Refinement Calculator [6], an extendable tool that supports the production of refinement calculus proofs in HOL. Working with the Refinement Calculator means selecting (using the mouse) parts of a program that one wants to refine, and executing suitable commands to carry out refinements and other transformation steps.

In order to make the action system theory usable within the Refinement Calculator there are a number of things that have to be done:

- Since the Refinement Calculator is based on the HOL Window Library [9], the theory has to be adapted so that window inference can be used. This requires proving (as we have done) that the local simulation relation is reflexive and transitive. Furthermore, a set of so called *window* rules have to be proved. These rules justify transforming a term in a context containing other terms. In our case, the main window theorem is the compositionality theorem which states that an action system can be a (local) simulation refined in any parallel context. Other window rules allow a user to select a subcomponent of an action system (e.g., a guard or a part of a body) and transform it.
- Translation and pretty printing between the action system notation presented in this paper and a suitable surface syntax must be handled. The Refinement Calculator supports using a surface syntax. This is very convenient; it allows working with named program variables (hiding the state variable), and it allows a traditional programming notation to be used. Adding parsing and pretty-printing will not be very difficult since action systems add very few new syntactic elements compared with what is alredy supported by the Refinement Calculator.
- A collection of theorems and functions that are used in almost every action system refinement have to be proved and made available to the tool, so that they can be applied automatically behind the scene whenever needed. Typical examples are the theorems saying that parallel composition is commutative and associative up to simulation equivalence. Another example is a function that automatically proves that a given abstraction relation is local.

Once these additions above have been done, working with reactive refinement in the Refinement Calculator will be more or less equivalent to working with ordinary refinement. In fact the most difficult part in proving a simulation is the action simulation part, and proving action simulation amounts to proving an ordinary data refinement.

The Refinement Calculator is currently being extended with a tool for data refinement. This tool can compute the data refinement of a given program, given the abstract program and the abstraction relation [10]. It can also be used to prove that the data refinement holds between two explicitly given statements. Since the main step in a simulation proof is data refinement, this tool can be directly used by the tool that we propose for action systems.

Finally, it should be noted that more advanced forms of action system refinement can also be handled by extending the work presented here. These include refinements that change the number of actions in an action system, e.g., by splitting existing actions or by introducing stuttering actions (a stuttering action is a concrete action that corresponds to *skip* on the abstract level).

## 7 Conclusions

Our formalisation of action systems shows that it is possible to represent a fairly complex theory of reactive systems in HOL, in a way that makes it possible to prove refinement also between nontrivial systems. Since we have used a shallow embedding and represented the state as a tuple, program variables can have any HOL type and a program can contain variables of different types.

The standard interface of the HOL system makes it hard to work with action system refinement directly. However, the aim of our formalisation of action systems is to provide a foundation for a tool that manipulates HOL terms (representing action systems) through a graphical user interface that allows easy selection and choice of transformation and that hides details that the user is not interested in at the moment (through the focusing mechanism of the HOL window Library).

Since such a tool already exists for sequential programs (the Refinement Calculator) and since the theory of action systems reduces reasoning about reactive systems to reasoning about sequential programs, the steps remaining until we have a prototype tool are few.

## References

1. F. Andersen, K.D. Petersen, and J.S. Petterson. A Graphical Tool for Proving UNITY Progress. In T.F. Melham and J. Camilleri, editors, *Higher Order Logic Theorem Proving and Its Applications – 7th International Workshop. Valletta, Malta, September 1994*, volume 859 of *Lecture Notes in Computer Science*. Springer Verlag, 1994.
2. R. Back. *Correctness Preserving Program Refinements: Proof Theory and Applications*, volume 131 of *Mathematical Center Tracts*. Mathematical Centre, Amsterdam, 1980.
3. R. Back. A calculus of refinements for program derivations. *Acta Informatica*, 25:593–624, 1988.
4. R. Back and J. von Wright. Refinement concepts formalized in higher order logic. *Formal Aspects of Computing*, 2:247–272, 1990.
5. R. Back and J. von Wright. Trace refinement of action systems. Reports on computer science and mathematics 153, Åbo Akademi, 1994.

6. M. Butler and T. Långbacka. Program derivation using the refinement calculator. In J. von Wright, J. Grundy, and J. Harrison, editors, *Theorem Proving in Higher Order Logics: 9th International Conference*, volume 1125 of *Lecture Notes in Computer Science*, pages 93–108. Springer Verlag, August 1996.
7. A. Camillieri. Mechanizing CSP trace theory in Higher Order Logic. *IEEE Transactions on Software Engineering*, 16(9):993–1004, 1990.
8. E. Dijkstra. *A Discipline of Programming*. Prentice–Hall International, 1976.
9. J. Grundy. Window inference in the HOL system. In M. Archer, J.J. Joyce, K.N. Levitt, and P.J. Windley, editors, *Proceedings of the International Tutorial and Workshop on the HOL Theorem Proving System and its Applications*, pages 177–189, University of California at Davis, August 1991. ACM-SIGDA, IEEE Computer Society Press.
10. R. Ruksenas and J. von Wright. A tool for data refinement. To appear as a TUCS Technical Report, Turku Centre for Computer Science, Lemminkäisenkatu 14A, 20520 Turku, Finland, 1997.
11. J. von Wright. Program refinement by theorem prover. In *BCS FACS Sixth Refinement Workshop – Theory and Practise of Formal Software Development. 5th – 7th January, City University, London, UK.*, 1994.
12. J. von Wright and T. Långbacka. Using a theorem prover for reasoning about concurrent algorithms. In G. von Bochmann and D.K. Probst, editors, *Computer Aided Verification – Fourth International Workshop. CAV '92. Montreal. Canada. June 29 – July 1. 1992*, volume 663 of *Lecture Notes in Computer Science*. Springer Verlag, 1993.

# On Formalization of Bicategory Theory

Takahisa Mohri

Department of Information Science, The University of Tokyo,
Hongo 7–3–1, Bunkyo-ku, Tokyo 113, Japan
E-mail: mohri@is.s.u-tokyo.ac.jp

**Abstract.** Bicategory theory is important in dealing with category theory from the categorical point of view. 2-categories and monoidal categories are special instances of bicategories. Although the Yoneda lemma for bicategories was expected to hold, it had not been rigorously proved before because its proof involves highly complex algebraic structures. The bicategorical Yoneda embedding is the most important corollary of the above lemma and it had not been rigorously proved, either. In this paper, we formalize the bicategorical Yoneda embedding directly on Extended Calculus of Constructions and report its implementation under the proof-checker LEGO. We then point out problems on our implementation and examine required functions of a proof-checker for the formalization of bicategory theory. The formalization signifies that application of a proof-checker is so effective to prove theorems which involve complex algebraic structures such as bicategories.

## 1 Introduction

Category theory is important in several areas of computer science, such as semantics of functional and imperative programming languages, specification of programs and modules, typing, etc.

In this paper, as we adopt the type-theoretical formulation of category theory, we use the following definition of categories.

**Definition 1.1 (Categories)** *A category* $C = (\mathrm{Ob}_C, \mathrm{Hom}_C, \circ, \mathrm{id})$ *consists of the following data.*

- *a collection of objects* $\mathrm{Ob}_C$,
- *for each* $a, b \in \mathrm{Ob}_C$, *the homset* $\mathrm{Hom}_C(a, b)$,
- *a composition operation* "$\circ$",
- *an identity operation* id.

*The identity and composition, moreover, must satisfy the following conditions;* **associativity law:**

- $(f \circ g) \circ h = f \circ (g \circ h)$,

**identity laws:**

- $f \circ \mathrm{id}_a = f$,
- $\mathrm{id}_b \circ f = f.\square$

Other categorical structures such as functor and natural transformation are also defined in accordance with the type-theoretical formulation.

Category theory is a meta-theory of bicategory theory in which category theory itself is used to describe categorical structures. In other words, analysis of category theory is one of the main objectives of bicategory theory. Therefore, in bicategory theory, we analyze category theory from the categorical point of view. Thus bicategory theory is concerned with the meta-theoretical aspect of category theory.

Significance of bicategory theory in computer science is increasing recently. In bicategory theory, we can analyze relations between arrows in terms of category theory. This makes it possible to distinguish between two arrows which are identical in category theory. For example, bicategory theory is useful for observing functions syntactically. In categorical semantics, denotations of $\beta$—equivalent functions are identical arrows, but these functions might be distinct syntactically.

Making one more step, we can reach tricategory theory. Recently, tricategories are said to be necessary for computer science[19].

As another application of bicategory theory for computer science, we should mention bicategories for processes[12]. For modeling processes, objects of any abstract category are thought of as states, and arrows as processes. Such processes may have internal structures and may be compared. Then 2-cells naturally arise. Bicategories for processes are related to theories of circuit design.

The Yoneda lemma is one of the greatest discoveries in category theory. We formalized the Yoneda lemma for ordinary category theory[17] based on Aczel's formalization[1]. The Yoneda embedding is the most important corollary and it is often called the Yoneda lemma. For bicategories, although the Yoneda embedding was expected to hold, it was avoided to prove the proposition with complete rigor because of its complexity. As far as we know, the formal proof reported in this paper is the first completely rigorous proof of the proposition. (In the present proof, we checked some complicated proofs omitted as the routine work in the conventional proof[13].)

The bicategorical Yoneda embedding is closely concerned with the so-called reduction-free approach to normalization proof[20, 5, 2]. For example, a proof of the coherence theorem[1] for bicategory theory essentially depends on the proposition[8, 11].

In formalized mathematics, many areas of mathematics are formalized, and category theory is not an exception. Category theory has been formalized on various formal theories. Altucher and Panangaden[3] implement it on a proof-checker Nuprl based on a Martin-Löf's type theory[6]. Aczel[1] formalizes it on Extended Calculus of Constructions (ECC) under the proof-checker LEGO[18, 14], and Huet and Saïbi translate it to Coq[7] and proceed the formalization[10].

Because, in type theory, much information is naturally represented in types and types can be checked automatically, we choose type theory out of various formal theories, on which our formalization is based. In this paper, we formalize the bicategorical version of the Yoneda embedding on a modified ECC system.

---

[1] All diagrams consist of id,$\otimes$, $\alpha$, $\rho$, $\lambda$ commute.

We construct the Yoneda pseudo-functor by defining its components directly. We then formalize the proofs of its fullness and faithfulness.

It is significant to formalize complex proofs because we should check many complex conditions which are extremely huge as terms. The more complex a proof is, the more formalized it should be.

In Section 2, definitions of basic notions in bicategory theory are introduced, and the Yoneda embedding for ordinary category and for bicategory are explained. In Section 3, we show how the proof can be formalized on ECC and mention the levels of defined notions in type universe hierarchy. In Section 4, we describe its implementation under LEGO and discuss problems on the implementation. In Section 5, we describe conclusions and future work.

## 2 Bicategorical notions

### 2.1 Basic structures

To compare bicategorical structures and categorical ones, we formulate two basic structures in bicategory theory. The formulation is based on Kinoshita's[13].

**Definition 2.1 (Bicategories)** *A bicategory $B$ is built up with seven data:* $\mathrm{ob}(B), \mathrm{Hom}_B, \otimes, 1, \alpha, \rho, \lambda$. *The types of the data are as follows.*

- *a collection $\mathrm{ob}(B)$, its element is called a 0-cell.*
- *for each $x, y \in \mathrm{ob}(B)$, a category (homcategory), $\mathrm{Hom}_B(x, y)$.*
- *for each $x, y, z \in \mathrm{ob}(B)$, a functor $\otimes^{xyz} : B(y, z) \times B(x, y) \to B(x, z)$.*
- *for each $x \in \mathrm{ob}(B)$, an object $1_x$ of $B(x, x)$.*
- *for each $w, x, y, z \in \mathrm{ob}(B)$, a natural isomorphism $\alpha^{wxyz} : (- \otimes^{xyz} -) \otimes^{wxz} - \Rightarrow - \otimes^{wyz} (- \otimes^{wxy} -) : B(y, z) \times B(x, y) \times B(w, x) \to B(w, z)$.*
- *for each $x, y \in \mathrm{ob}(B)$, a natural isomorphism $\rho^{xy} : - \otimes^{xxy} 1_x \Rightarrow I_{B(x,y)} : B(x, y) \to B(x, y)$.*
- *for each $x, y \in \mathrm{ob}(B)$, a natural isomorphism $\lambda^{xy} : 1_y \otimes^{xyy} - \Rightarrow I_{B(x,y)} : B(x, y) \to B(x, y)$.*

*The data must satisfy the two conditions called coherence equations.* □

Here, $I_C$ is the identity functor on $C$, $B(x, y)$ denotes $\mathrm{Hom}_B(x, y)$. An object and an arrow of a homcategory is called a *1-cell* and a *2-cell*, respectively.

The following table shows the correspondence between the categorical side and bicategorical side.

| category | bicategory |
|---|---|
| functor | pseudo-functor |
| natural transformation | pseudo-natural transformation |
| object | 0-cell |
| morphism | 1-cell |
| homset | homcategory |
| composition | $\otimes$ |
| identity | 1 |
| associativity law | $\alpha$ |
| right identity law | $\rho$ |
| left identity law | $\lambda$ |

**Definition 2.2 (Pseudo-functors)** *Let $B$ and $\overline{B}$ be bicategories. A* pseudo-functor $H$ *from $B$ to $\overline{B}$ consists of the following data.*

- *a function $\mathrm{ob}(H) : \mathrm{ob}(B) \to \mathrm{ob}(\overline{B})$, written just $H$,*
- *for each $x, y \in \mathrm{ob}(B)$, a functor $H^{xy} : B(x, y) \to \overline{B}(H(x), H(y))$,*
- *for each $x, y, z \in \mathrm{ob}(B)$, a natural isomorphism $H^{xyz}$ :*
  $H^{yz}(-)\overline{\otimes}H^{xy}(-) \Rightarrow H^{xz}(- \otimes -) : B(y, z) \otimes B(x, y) \to \overline{B}(H(x), H(z))$,
  *and*
- *for each $x \in \mathrm{ob}(B)$, an isomorphic 2-cell $H_x : \overline{1}_{H(x)} \Rightarrow H(1_x) : H(x) \to H(x)$ in $\overline{B}$.*

*These data are required to satisfy the three axioms for preserving the coherence conditions.*□

Bicategories and pseudo-functors correspond to categories and functors in category theory, respectively. Moreover, the axiom(or equation) parts in the categorical side are translated to the data parts in the bicategorical side. A category consists of 4 data and 3 axioms while a bicategory has just 7 data. The data parts corresponding to the axioms parts indicate existence of isomorphic 2-cells. In the bicategorical side, to preserve coherence conditions, some axioms are added.

Number of components in the definitions are shown in the below table.

| *Categorical side* | | | *Bicategorical side* | | |
|---|---|---|---|---|---|
| notion | data | axiom | notion | data | axiom |
| category | 4 | 3 | bicategory | 7 | 2 |
| functor | 2 | 2 | pseudo-functor | 4 | 3 |
| natural transformation | 1 | 1 | pseudo-natural transformation | 2 | 3 |
| | | | modification | 1 | 1 |
| | m | n | | m+n | for coherence |

A modification is like an arrow from one pseudo-natural transformation to another.

## 2.2 Bicategorical Yoneda Embedding

In ordinary category theory, the Yoneda embedding is the most famous corollary of the Yoneda lemma and then the words "the Yoneda lemma" often means the Yoneda embedding. The Yoneda embedding is significant for representation of categories as follows.

**Theorem 2.3 (the Yoneda embedding for ordinary category)** *For any bicategory $C$, the Yoneda functor*

$$Y : C \longrightarrow Funct(C^{op}, Set)$$

*is full and faithful.*□

The theorem claims that the following one-to-one correspondence exists.

$$\text{an object in } C \longleftrightarrow \text{a functor from } C^{op} \text{ to } Set$$
$$\text{an arrow in } C \longleftrightarrow \text{a natural transformation}$$

The Yoneda lemma and the Yoneda embedding for ordinary categories are formalized in [17].

On the other hand, bicategorical version of the theorem is the following.

**Theorem 2.4 (the Yoneda embedding for bicategory)** *For any bicategory $B$, the Yoneda pseudo-functor*

$$Y : B \longrightarrow Bicat(B^{op}, Cat)$$

*is full and faithful.*□

Here, *Bicat* is the bicategory of pseudo-functors, pseudo-natural transformations and modifications and *Cat* is the bicategory of categories, functors and natural transformations. The claim of the theorem is existence of the following one-to-one correspondence.

$$\text{a 0-cell in } B \longleftrightarrow \text{a pseudo-functor from } B^{op} \text{ to } Cat$$
$$\text{a 1-cell in } B \longleftrightarrow \text{a pseudo-natural transformation}$$
$$\text{a 2-cell in } B \longleftrightarrow \text{a modification}$$

Notably, the Yoneda functor embeds morphisms while the Yoneda pseudo-functor embeds not only 1-cells but also 2-cells. The following table shows the correspondence in the categorical and bicategorical Yoneda.

| Yoneda functor | Yoneda pseudo-functor |
|---|---|
| a natural transformation | a pseudo-natural transformation |
| *Funct*(the functor category) | *Bicat* |
| *Set*(the category of all sets) | *Cat* |
| hom functor | hom pseudo-functor |

# 3  Formalization

In the proof with nested algebraic structures such as our proof of the bicategorical Yoneda embedding, proof terms are extremely huge. Thus use of a proof checker is very important. We can go on constructing a proof interactively and dynamically, while types of occurring terms are machine-checked. The more complex a proof is, the more formalized it should be. This formalization signifies that this kind of theorem which treats complex algebraic structures as bicategories is an instance of application of a proof-checker.

On a proof assistant LEGO[18, 14], we formalize the proof in the previous chapter of the bicategorical Yoneda embedding based on the Extend Calculus of Constructions(ECC)[15, 16].

## 3.1  Theory: ECC+surjective paring

Existence of $\Sigma$-abstraction(the strong sum) is the strongest reason why we choose ECC as base theory. In some type theory, $\Sigma$-abstraction is used for expressing the data subject to proper conditions. An element of the type $\Sigma a : T.P(a) : Prop$ is a pair of an element $b \in \{a \in T | P(a)\}$ and a proof of $P(b)$ in ECC. In general, an algebraic notion is defined with data and the expected conditions. Thus types which denote algebraic notions can be defined as a term in ECC.

ECC was thought to have enough power to complete the formalization. But, in the way of formalizing, need for surjective pairing arose. That pairing is surjective means $(\pi_1 a, \pi_2 a)$ can be converted to $a$ (here, $\pi_1, \pi_2$ are the first and the second projections). The necessity of surjective pairing arises to unify $(\pi_1 a, \pi_2 a)$ and $a$ in the formalization of the third component of the Yoneda pseudo-functor. Fundamentally, the request is caused by introducing products of categories. They occur in types of some functors in the definition of bicategories in Section 2. We could curry those functors and define bifunctors to be distinct from unary functors. If bifunctors and functors are not be defined uniformly, we need many variant definition of natural transformations and formalization related to them. Therefore we added the surjective pairing rule: $(\pi_1 a, \pi_2 a) \rightarrow a$ as a reduction rule in ECC. It is a very natural rule for formalizing mathematics. Exactly, our formalization is not based on ECC but on new theory ECC+surjective paring. The extended theory is consistent because $(\pi_1 a, \pi_2 a)$ and $a$ are identical in the $\omega-$Set (realizability) model.

## 3.2  Formalization of category theory

Bicategory theory is formulated in terms of category theory as mentioned in Section 1. Therefore bicategory theory is formalized by using definitions in the formalization of ordinary category theory. We adopt the formalization with setoids as the formalization of category theory[17]. A setoid is a set equipped with equality on it[4]. In the formalization, a homset is not defined as a set but as a setoid.

We show a definition of the type of categories in ECC as follows.

$\Sigma$ Ob : Type$_0$ .
$\Sigma$ Hom : Ob $\to$ Ob $\to$ Setoid .
$\Sigma \circ : \Pi a$: Ob . $\Pi b$: Ob . $\Pi c$: Ob .
  elem(Map_setoid(Hom $b\ c$)(Map_setoid (Hom $a\ b$) (Hom $a\ c$))).
$\Sigma$ id : $\Pi a$: Ob . elem(Hom $a\ a$).
  $\{\Pi a$: Ob . $\Pi b$: Ob . $\Pi c$: Ob . $\Pi d$: Ob .
  $\Pi f$: elem(Hom $c\ d$). $\Pi g$: elem(Hom $b\ c$). $h$: elem(Hom $a\ b$).
  $f \circ (g \circ h) = (f \circ g) \circ h\}$
  $\times \{\Pi a$: Ob . $\Pi b$: Ob . $\Pi f$: elem(Hom $a\ b$). $f = f \circ \text{id}(a)\}$
  $\times \{\Pi a$: Ob . $\Pi b$: Ob . $\Pi f$: elem(Hom $a\ b$). $\text{id}(b) \circ f = f\}$

Type$_0$ is the lowest type universe and often used as the set of all sets. elem is the selector which selects the component of base sets from Setoid. Map_setoid is the setoid whose base set is the set of mappings.

The types of functors and natural transformations are defined in the same way. Moreover, some special members such as the functor categories of them are defined.

### 3.3 Formalization of bicategory theory

After all necessary terms in ordinary category theory are defined, we formalize bicategory theory with them. Formalization of this kind of abstract mathematics consists of definitions of types which means algebraic structures and some special members of the types. In this formalization, we started with definitions of four types of basic notions (bicategories, pseudo-functors, pseudo-natural transformations, modifications) in bicategory theory. Here we proved some auxiliary propositions to deal with the types and defined some algebraic property of the structures such as fullness of pseudo-functors.

In order to define the Yoneda pseudo-functor, we then defined the following special members of the above defined types.

- bicategory of categories *Cat*
- pseudo-functor bicategories *Bicat*
- oppositing bicategories
- hom pseudo-functors

To define a member of the type which expresses the algebraic structure, we should define some data and prove that the data satisfy the axioms for the algebraic structure. Such proofs occupy the greater part of all the formalizations.

### 3.4 Yoneda Embedding

We then formalized the Yoneda pseudo-functor and the bicategorical Yoneda embedding. As in Section 2, a pseudo-functor has 4 data components and 3 proofs of axioms. At first, we constructed the Yoneda pseudo-functor by defining its 4 data components as a pseudo-functor.

In case of the Yoneda pseudo-functor each component has nested algebraic structures, for example, the following is its second component(action on hom-categories) Ymor.

$$\text{Ymor\_ob}_0\text{\_ob} \equiv \lambda x\!: \text{ob } B.\lambda y\!: \text{ob } B.\lambda f\!: \text{Ob}(\text{hom } x\, y).\lambda z\!: \text{ob } B^{op}.$$
$$\lambda g\!: \text{Ob}(\text{hom } z\, x).f \otimes g$$

$$\vdots$$

$$\text{Ymor\_ob}_0 \equiv \lambda x\!: \text{ob } B.\lambda y\!: \text{ob } B.\lambda f\!: \text{Ob}(\text{hom } x\, y).\lambda z\!: \text{ob } B^{op}.$$
$$\{(\text{Ymor\_ob}_0\text{\_ob } x\, y\, f\, z, \cdots, \cdots, \cdots)$$
$$: \text{Funct}\,(\text{pF}_0\,(\text{Yob } x)\, z)\,(\text{pF}_0\,(\text{Yob } y)\, z)\}$$

$$\vdots$$

$$\text{Ymor\_ob} \equiv \lambda x\!: \text{ob } B.\lambda y\!: \text{ob } B.\lambda f\!: \text{Ob}(\text{hom } x\, y).$$
$$\{(\text{Ymor\_ob}_0\ x\, y\, f, \cdots, \cdots, \cdots, \cdots): \text{pNat}\,(\text{Yob } x)\,(\text{Yob } y)\}$$

$$\vdots$$

$$\text{Ymor} \equiv \lambda x\!: \text{ob } B.\lambda y\!: \text{ob } B.\{(\text{Ymor\_ob } x\, y, \cdots, \cdots, \cdots)$$
$$: \text{Funct}\,(\text{hom } x\, y)\,(\text{hom}\,(\text{Yob } x)\,(\text{Yob } y))\}$$

After defining data parts of the Yoneda pseudo-functor, we formalized proofs of 3 axioms for a pseudo-functor.

Finally, fullness and faithfulness of the pseudo-functor were formalized. In ECC, the propositions are written as follows.

**Fullness of the Yoneda pseudo-functor $Y$:**
$\Pi B\!: \text{BiCat}.$
$\Pi x\!: \text{ob } B.\Pi y\!: \text{ob } B.$
$\Pi f\!: \text{Ob}(\text{hom } B\, x\, y).\Pi g\!: \text{Ob}(\text{hom } B\, x\, y).$
$\Pi a\!: \text{elem}(\text{Hom } f\, g).\Pi b\!: \text{elem}(\text{Hom } f\, g).$
$\{(\text{pF}_2\,(Y\, B)\, a) = (\text{pF}_2\,(Y\, B)\, b)\} \to (a = b)$

**Faithfulness of the Yoneda pseudo-functor $Y$:**
$\Pi B\!: \text{BiCat}.$
$\Sigma G\!:\{\Pi x\!: \text{ob } B.\Pi y\!: \text{ob } B.$
$\quad \Pi f\!: \text{Ob}(\text{hom } B\, x\, y).\Pi g\!: \text{Ob}(\text{hom } B\, x\, y).$
$\quad \text{elem}(\text{Hom}\,(\text{pF}_1\,(Y\, B)\, f)\,(\text{pF}_1\,(Y\, B)\, g)) \to \text{elem}(\text{Hom } f\, g)\}.$
$\{\Pi x\!: \text{ob } B.\Pi y\!: \text{ob } B.$
$\Pi f\!: \text{Ob}(\text{hom } B\, x\, y).\Pi g\!: \text{Ob}(\text{hom } B\, x\, y).$
$\Pi a\!: \text{elem}(\text{Hom}\,(\text{pF}_1\,(Y\, B)\, f)\,(\text{pF}_1\,(Y\, B)\, g)).$
$((\text{pF}_2\,(Y\, B)\,(G\, x\, y\, f\, g\, a)) = a)\}$

"ob" and "hom" is the selector out of a bicategory for the set of its 0-cells and for its homcategory respectively. "pF$_1$","pF$_2$" is the selector out of a pseudo-functors for its action on 1-cells and on 2-cells respectively. This two proof are formalized easily with support of the system LEGO, but their proof terms are so huge to write out in this paper. Thus we finished formalization of the bicategorical Yoneda embedding.

To compare the formal proof to the informal one, we watch the case of definition of the Yoneda pseudo-functor. We consider the quantity of description. In the formal proof, types of all terms should be described and trivial conditions should be proved. But on type information, we only insert the information calculated by a proof-checker into a formal proof. Moreover, we can get a trivial proof from the existing proof by a bit of modification such as renaming variables and so on.

In the declaration parts, definitions are as readable as formal ones. Readability of a proof depends on the system although one can read what rules are used.

## 3.5 Type universe

In literatures, category theory was formalized by some set/type-theory with universe(s). So we are concerned with universes in our formalization. This subsection is a by-product of this formalization and is not closely connected with the main story of this paper.

The universes of ECC are types closed under $\Pi$- and $\Sigma$- abstraction. They form a cumulative hierarchy:

$$Prop \in Type_0 \in Type_1 \in Type_2 \quad Prop \subseteq Type_0 \subseteq Type_1 \subseteq Type_2 \ldots$$

Here $Prop$ means the type of all propositions.

We determined the levels of the types of the basic notions in bicategory theory and the dependency of the levels.

As for category theory, we obtained the following results[17]. Let Setoid(i) be the type of setoids whose base set inhabits Type(i), and let Cat(i,j) be the type of categories whose object inhabits Type(i) and whose homsetoid inhabits Setoid(j).
For S:Setoid(i), T:Setoid(j), C:Cat(i,j), D:Cat(k,l),
F,G:Functor(i,j,k,l),

- Setoid(i):Type(i+1)
- Map_setoid(i,j) S T:Setoid(max(i,j))
- Cat(i,j):Type(max(i,j)+1)
- Functor(i,j,k,l) C D:Type(max(i,j,k,l))
- Nattrans(i,j,k,l) C D F G:Type(max(i,j,l))
- FunctCat(i,j,k,l) C D:Cat(max(i,j,k,l),max(i,j,l)).

Besides on the above, we have the following results. Let Bicat(i,j,k) be the type of categories whose 0-cell inhabits Type(i) and whose homcategory inhabits Cat(j,k).

For B1:Cat(i,j,k), B2:Cat(l,m,n), H,K:Pfunctor(i,j,k,l,m,n),
beta,gamma:Pnattrans(i,j,k,l,m,n),

- `Bicat(i,j,k) : Type(max(i,j,k)+1)`
- `Pfunctor(i,j,k,l,m,n) B1 B2 : Type(max(i,j,k,l,m,n))`
- `Pnattrans(i,j,k,l,m,n) B1 B2 H K : Type(max(i,j,m,n))`
- `Mod(i,j,k,l,m,n) B1 B2 H K beta gamma: Type(max(i,j,n))`
- `CAT:Bicat(1,1,1)`
- `PnCat(i,j,k,l,m,n) B1 B2 H K: Cat(max(i,j,m,n),max(i,j,n))`
- `BICAT B1 B2:Bicat(max(i,j,k,l,m,n),max(i,j,m,n),max(i,j,n))`
- `Hompf B1 x:Pfunctor(i,j,k,1,1,1)`
- `Y B1:Pfunctor(i,j,k,max(i,j,k,1),max(i,j,1),max(i,j,1)).`

$i \leq j \leq k$ follows by existence of identity. However `Bicat(1,0,0)` is well-defined because `Cat(0,i)` $\subseteq$ `Cat(1,i)` from the cumulativity of hierarchy, where `Bicat(1,0,0)` is `Bicat(0,0,0)` actually.

# 4  Implementation on LEGO

In this Section, we implement the formal proof of the bicategorical Yoneda embedding on LEGO, and discuss problems on the work.

Generally, when one implements a formal proof on a proof-checker, he can select one of the two styles; 1)After completing an informal proof, he checks it by a proof-checker. 2)He builds up a whole proof while interacting to a proof-checker. Although we prefer the second approach, we took the first approach in this formalization as insurance. But associativity was proved interactively all through the formalization. Associativity is used implicitly in a manual proof, but must be proved explicitly in a formal proof.

## 4.1  LEGO

Why do we choose LEGO as the proof system? As described in Subsection 3.1, we need ECC as theory to represent types of algebraic structures naturally. LEGO is one of the valuable system which supports ECC. Moreover, we can use implicit arguments in LEGO. We can omit some logically redundant arguments of a function while writing a formal proof. It improves readability of the formal proof, too.

In this formalization, we often needed to let some type have different expression. For example, the type of objects of the functor category equals to the type of functors. The type system of LEGO are useful in such situations. The proof mode of LEGO made it possible to construct very huge proof terms easily.

LEGO syntax is as the table.

| ECC syntax | LEGO syntax |
|------------|-------------|
| $\lambda x : A.B$ | `[x:A]B` |
| $A \to B$ | `A->B` |
| $\Pi x : A.B$ | `{x:A}B` |
| $\Sigma x : A.B$ | `<x:A>B` |
| $A \times B$ | `A#B` |
| $\pi_1 a$ | `a.1` |
| $\pi_2 a$ | `a.2` |
| $(a, b)$ | `(a,b)` |

Moreover, the implicit version of `[x:A]B`, `{x:A}B` are `[x|A]B`, `{x|A}B` respectively.

For example, the following is a part of our formal definition of `BiCat`, the type of bicategories.

```
BiCat == <ob:Type>
         <hom:ob->ob->Cat>
         <tensor:{x,y,z:ob}
             Funct (Prod (hom y z) (hom x y)) (hom x z)>
         <one:{x:ob}Ob (hom x x)>
         <alpha:Alpha_Type ob hom tensor>
         <rho:Rho_Type ob hom tensor one>
         <lambda:Lambda_Type ob hom tensor one>
          (Coherence_A ob hom tensor alpha)
         #(Coherence_U ob hom tensor one alpha rho lambda);
```

## 4.2 Theory

As mentioned in Subsection 3.1, we modify LEGO to support the surjective pairing because we cannot unify $(\pi_1 a, \pi_2 a)$ and $a$ in the original ECC. We added several lines to the source code written in ML for $(\pi_1 a, \pi_2 a)$ to be reduced to $a$ in LEGO.

## 4.3 Reduction of checking time

Because checking of the proof costs much time, we tried to reduce checking time in various ways. First, we always use the **Freeze** commands to suppress expanding defined constants internally while the types are being checked. Without using **Freeze**, even a basic definition can be expanded to a rather long term as follows. In case of the constant `Cat`,

```
<Ob:Type>
<Hom:Ob->Ob->Setoid>
<o:Comp_Type Ob Hom>
<i:Id_Type Ob Hom>
  (Assoc_law Ob Hom o)
#(Idl_law Ob Hom o i)#(Idr_law Ob Hom o i);
```

it can be internally expanded up to:

```
<Ob:Type>
<Hom:Ob->Ob->
   <S:Type><R:S->S->Prop>
   {X|Prop}(({x:S}R x x)->({x,y|S}(R x y)->R y x)->
                  ({x,y,z|S}(R x y)->(R y z)->R x z)->X)->X>
<o:{a,b,c:Ob}
   <f:((Hom b c)).1->
      <f:((Hom a b)).1->((Hom a c)).1>
         {x,y:((Hom a b)).1}
               (((Hom a b)).2.1 x y)->((Hom a c)).2.1 (f x) (f y)>
      {x,y:((Hom b c)).1}
         (((Hom b c)).2.1 x y)->
            {x'10:((Hom a b)).1}
               ((Hom a c)).2.1 (((f x)).1 x'10) (((f y)).1 x'10)>
<i:{a:Ob}((Hom a a)).1>
({a,b,c,d:Ob}
  {f:((Hom c d)).1}{g:((Hom b c)).1}{h:((Hom a b)).1}
   ((Hom a d)).2.1 (((((o a c d)).1 f)).1
                       ((((((o a b c)).1 g)).1 h))
                  (((((o a b d)).1
                       ((((((o b c d)).1 f)).1 g))).1 h))
#({a,b:Ob}
   {f:((Hom a b)).1}
   ((Hom a b)).2.1 f (((((o a a b)).1 f)).1 (i a)))
#({a,b:Ob}
   {f:((Hom b a)).1}
   ((Hom b a)).2.1 (((((o b a a)).1 (i a))).1 f) f)
```

Identifiers for defined constants should be **Unfreezed** only if necessary. Importance of freezing expansion is familiar fact, but this is especially important in this kind of formalization.

Second, long proofs are divided to proofs of some lemmata. As the number of composition increases, time to check proofs increases greatly. The reason is that the associativity of composition is natural for humans, but the machine must calculate to prove the equation with nested associativity.

By each of the two improving techniques, checking time over one day is reduced to a few hours.

To prove a goal proposition, LEGO enters the proof mode. In the proof mode of LEGO, expanding terms is a very expensive operation because they are pushed on to the stack. Then we expanded some parts of the terms by hand. While executing the **Expand** command, LEGO tries to unify implicit arguments again and again. It may often happen to unify equivalent expressions represented in the low level and in the high level.

## 4.4 Universe Polymorphism

As the universe polymorphism[9] of LEGO is not the complete one which we intuitively expect, we must define `bicat0.1` and `bicat.1`. BiCat0 corresponds to `Bicat(0,j,k)` and BiCat to `Bicat(i,j,k)` ($i \geq 1$) in the list in Subsection

3.5. The level of Cat varies when the level of Ob changes. But there is only one object Cat, not a fresh instance of Cat every time it is used. That is, once the level is instantiated, the concrete level of the type Cat is determined. We can define $A = Type_n$ with the universe polymorphism in LEGO. However, once we use $A$ such as foo $= a : A$ for $a : Type_1$, $n$ is fixed to 1 from the type of $a$. After that, we cannot use $A$ polymorphically, where we cannot assert $b : A$ for $b : Type_2$.

## 4.5 Suggestions for improvement of LEGO

Many problems happened all through this formalization on LEGO because this kind of formalization goes wide of the mark of LEGO originally. This subsection is not a condemnation of LEGO, but a suggestion for improve to cope with formalizing this kind of abstract mathematics.

In the previous subsection, we described how to improve the writing style of proofs to reduce checking time. We point out some problems of LEGO in formalizing a proof such as ours, and suggest some improvement of LEGO to reduce time for completing a formal proof.

We want to use Expand and Freeze on occurrences of variables but not on variables. Given (o (apNt (o tau mu) x) (apNt nu x)) , if we execute Expand o; to unfold the composition of natural transformations in the example, then the left most o were also expanded unfortunately.

Can LEGO go back to an old state correctly? Although we can use the Undo command in the proof mode and Forget in other modes, the information of "Freezing" is not restored. Freezing of variables are important for an efficient proof check. The history of Freeze and Forget should be saved as system information. To restore the system state on Freezing, one must save the system state by using ExportState command. In execution of the command, LEGO uses a function exportML in ML. The function induces at least one major garbage collection which takes a lot of time.

In the proof mode we cannot use the ExportState command, although we can use the Undo command. This is not good for a longer proof.

On the universe polymorphism actually implemented in LEGO, once the information of the dependency of type universes is instantiated, we cannot cancel the information with Undo nor Forget.

## 4.6 Summary

Anyway, checking the proof costs a lot of memory space and time. We ran LEGO on Sun Ultra1 (UltraSPARC(167MHz), 128Mbyte memory). Finally, LEGO requires 300Mbyte as heap and a major garbage collection takes 20 minutes. Time for checking the whole proof is over four hours. To export a state of LEGO, we must wait for 45 minutes because garbage collections occur.

The following list is the LEGO files for this formalization.

| word count filename | main content |
|---|---|
| 110 setoid.l | setoids |
| 120 map.l | maps |
| 749 cat.l | categories |
| 56 catp.l | properties of categories |
| 365 func.l | functors |
| 312 NT.l | natural transformations |
| 141 natiso.l | natural isomorphisms |
| 417 PROD.l | category product |
| 1187 FPROD.l | functor product |
| 1326 bicat0.l | bicategories(level 0) |
| 1492 bicat0_aux.l | auxiliary for bicategories(level 0) |
| 1326 bicat.l | bicategories(more than level 1) |
| 1492 bicat_aux.l | auxiliary for bicategories(more than level 1) |
| 805 pfunct.l | pseudo-functors |
| 68 pfp.l | property of pseudo-functors |
| 497 pNT.l | pseudo-natural transformations |
| 168 pNT_aux.l | auxiliary for pseudo-natural transformations |
| 2828 pNT_hcomp.l | horizontal composition of pseudo-natural transformations |
| 215 mod.l | modifications |
| 254 mod_hcomp.l | horizontal composition of modifications |
| 791 bicat_op.l | opposite bicategories |
| 595 fcat.l | functor categories |
| 2359 CAT.l | *Cat* |
| 588 pcat.l | categories of pseudo-natural transformations |
| 4398 BICAT.l | *Bicat* |
| 2274 Hompf.l | Hom pseudo-functor |
| 5117 Y.l | Yoneda pseudo-functor |
| 906 YE.l | Yoneda embedding |

From ftp://nicosia.is.s.u-tokyo.ac.jp/pub/staff/mohri/BY, these files are available. See the readme-file for details.

# 5 Conclusion and future work

We proved the bicategorical Yoneda embedding which had not been proved rigorously before. Formalization of the bicategorical Yoneda embedding in ECC+surjective pairing was complex on the system LEGO. This formalization signifies that application of a proof-checker is so effective to prove theorems which involves rich algebraic structures such as bicategories.

As a result of formalization, what an absolute type universe the types of basic notions in bicategory theory inhabits were determined.

We pointed out problems and required functions for the proof system to formalize the huge algebraic proof as the bicategorical Yoneda embedding. In particular, importance of suppression of expansion of definitions were emphasized.

As our future work, we will prove that the Yoneda pseudo-functor preserves ccc-structure of category built up from of 0-cells and 1-cells and formalize it. Applying it to the reduction-free approach[20], we will get a normalization function of $\lambda\beta\eta$-calculus as an ECC term. We can try to formalize bicategories with other advanced structures.

Moreover, we will study on automation of categorical inference. The present formal proof in this paper consists of list of definitions and proofs in which only variable introductions and refinements are used. Thus inference in proof on this type is suited to automation. For example, when a complex type and its some components are given, can the rest components be calculated automatically?

## Acknowledgements

I would like to express my thanks to people who provided information for this work. I am especially thankful to Masami Hagiya and Yohji Akama for their very precious suggestions.

## References

1. P. Aczel. Galois: a theory development project. In *A report on work in progress for the Turein meeting on the Representeation of Logical Fralmeworks*. 1993.
2. T. Altenkirch, M. Hofmann, and T. Streicher. Categorical reconstruction of a reduction-free normalisation proof. In *Proc.CTCS '95*, volume 953 of *LNCS*, pages 182–199. Springer Verlag, 1995.
3. James A. Altucher and Prakash Panangaden. A mechanically assisted constructive proof in category theory. In *CADE-10*, LNAI 449, pages 500–513. Springer Verlag, 1990.
4. G. Barthe. Mathematical concepts in type theory. DRAFT, 1993.
5. I. Beylin and P. Dybjer. Extracting a proof of coherence for monoidal categories from a formal proof of normalization for monoids. In *TYPES '95*, LNCS. Springer Verlag, 1996.
6. R.L. Constable et al. *Implementing Mathematics with the Nuprl Proof Development System*. Prentice-Hall, Inc., Englewood Cliffs, New Jersey 07632, 1986.
7. G. Dowek, A. Felty, H. Herbelin, G. Huet, P. Paulin-Mohring, and B. Werner. *The Coq Proof Assistant User's Guide*. INRIA-Rochuencourt, CNRS-ENS Lyon, 1991.
8. R. Gordon, A. Power, and R. Street. Coherence for tricategories. In *Memoirs of the American Mathematical Society*. 1996.
9. R. Harper and R. Pollack. Universe polymorphism. *Theoretical Computer Science*, 89, 1991.
10. Gérard Huet and Amokarane Saïbi. Constructive category theory. In Peter Dybjer and Randy Pollack, editors, *Informal proceedings of the joint CLICS-TYPES workshop on categories and type theory*. 1995.
11. A. Joyal and R. Street. Braided tensor categories. In *Advances in Mathematics*, volume 102, pages 20–79. June 1993.

12. P. Kartis, N. Sabadini, and R. F. C. Walters. Bicategories of processes. *Journal of Pure and Appled Algebra*, November 1995.
13. Yoshiki Kinoshita. A bicategorical analysis of e-categories. Technical Report TR97-1, Electrotechnical Laboratory, 1997.
14. Z. Luo, R. Pollack, and P. Taylor. How to use LEGO:a preliminary user's manual. LFCS Techincal Notes LFCS-TN-27, Dept. of Computer Science, University of Edinburgh, 1989.
15. Zhaohui Luo. ECC, an extended calculus of constructions. In *Proceedings, Fourth Annual Symposium on Logic in Computer Science*, pages 386–395, Asilomar, California, U.S.A., June 1989. IEEE Computer Society Press.
16. Zhaohui Luo. *An Extended Calculus of Constructions*. PhD thesis, University of Edinburgh, 1990.
17. Takahisa Mohri. On formaliztion of category theory. BSc.thesis, The University of Tokyo, 1995.
18. R. Pollack. *The theory of LEGO*. PhD thesis, University of Edinburgh, 1994.
19. John Power. Why tricategories? *Information and Computation*, 120:251–262, 1995.
20. Djordje Čubrič, Peter Dybjer, and Philip Scott. Normalizaton and the yoneda embedding. October 1996.

# Towards an Object-Oriented Progification Language

Wolfgang Naraschewski

Technische Universität München
Institut für Informatik
Arcisstraße 21
D-80290 München, Germany
narasche@informatik.tu-muenchen.de
http://www4.informatik.tu-muenchen.de/~narasche/

**Abstract.** To support formal verification of object-oriented programs
we have proposed elsewhere an encoding in the type-theoretic proof-
checker Lego. By treating programs and proofs uniformly, the encoding provides object-oriented proving principles — including inheritance
of proofs — as analogues to object-oriented programming principles.
Though the encoding is suitable for implementing ideas, it is not convenient for developing large verified programs.
Here we propose a portmanteau language hopefully better suited to
both ends: *programming* and *verification*. Although the language could
be translated rigorously to λ-terms of the Lego-encoding we sketch the
translation informally. We shall argue, along the way, that object oriented
verification can be regarded as a kind of generalized object-oriented programming.

## 1 Introduction

In earlier work [HNSS96] object-oriented structuring mechanisms for verification
were presented and rigorously formalized in the type-theoretic proof checker Lego
[LP92]. Using the Curry–Howard isomorphism, which establishes a direct, formal correspondence between programs and proofs, the object-model of Pierce,
Turner, and Hofmann [PT94] [HP94] was extended with a proof component.
Since the object model, which is based on the higher order λ-calculus $F_{\leq}^{\omega}$, is
encoded straightforwardly in Lego, the proof checker can be used as a basis for
extending the object model to deal with verification. The uniform treatment of
methods and proofs gives rise in a natural way to object-oriented proof principles — including inheritance, late binding, and encapsulation of proofs — as
analogues to object-oriented programming principles.

Since programming and proving are performed simultaneously, we freely use
the expression *progification*[1] to emphasize that programs and proofs are both
first class citizens in our language.

---

[1] Progification = Programming + Verification

Though Lego is a suitable tool for testing and implementing ideas, it is *not tailored* for object-oriented progification. The generality provided by the theorem prover is mere ballast when performing even small progifications, as we demonstrated in a case-study dealing with Smalltalk-like collections in [Nar96]. To be practically useful, it is necessary to design a language that provides not only syntactic sugar, but specific support for object-oriented verification. Although our experiments with Lego made extensive use of the underlying type system's properties, notably dependent types and the Curry-Howard correspondence, much of the encoding could be adapted to other theorem provers implementing higher-order logic. Furthermore it seems premature to be smithing tools before we have tested these ideas first on a number of case-studies. The aim of this paper is to propose an object-oriented progification language to demonstrate the practical feasibility of the approach presented in [HNSS96]. This language could, in principle, be implemented by translating it into Lego. We discuss the main features of the translation without presenting it in detail. The Lego-definitions corresponding to the definitions of the informal language of this paper can be accessed at http://www4.informatik.tu-muenchen.de/~narasche/publications.html.

The reader who is looking for theorems is asked to forbear; we propose instead a notation whose aim it is to make it easier to program 'objectively' and to develop, hand in hand, fully formal verifications. The central idea behind this approach is that step-by-step verified hierarchies of classes are developed. When relying on a class from the library, a user inherits not only the code but the correctness proofs as well, which may be used in the next layer of verification. The crucial point about inheritance of proofs is that the proofs are not just simply duplicated. The progification language provides the means to modify programs and to inherit proofs which are then adapted to fit the case by the computer.

This paper is not intended to show how object-oriented progification can be encoded in a theorem prover since detailed definitions can be found in [HNSS96]. In contrast to our earlier paper, the focus of this paper is on the *usage* of object-oriented progification. In particular we want to demonstrate that object-oriented progification can be understood as generalized object-oriented programming.

In the next section we explain briefly the object-oriented terminology we use. The following section illustrates progification using the canonical example of points and coloured points. We conclude by discussing prospective work.

## 2 The object model

Before turning to the constructs of the object-oriented progification language, we briefly recapitulate the object-oriented terminology we apply. An *object* is a collection of *methods*, working on an internal *state* together with a collection of *correctness proofs*. The state as well as the methods and the correctness proofs are *encapsulated* or hidden inside the object and access is controlled by the interface. Getting access to the encapsulated methods or proofs is called *method invocation* or *proof invocation* respectively.

We call the type of the internal state the *representation type* and the type of the methods the *signature*. The behavior of an object is formally characterized by its *specification* which, due to the Curry-Howard isomorphism, is the same as the type of the correctness proofs.

A *class* serves as a blueprint for objects and can be used in two ways: First, to create new objects, the class *instances*, sharing the representation, implementation and correctness proofs common to the class. Second, to define new subclasses incrementally by *inheritance*, where (parts of) the definitions of the superclass may be used. By inheritance, some methods may be re-implemented and overridden or new methods may be added to unchanged, inherited ones. Likewise, it is possible to inherit already existing proofs from the superclass and to add new proofs. Note that when inheriting a proof, the proof is in general not simply duplicated but adapted according to the re-implementation of the methods.

An important intricacy are the so-called *self-methods* and *self-proofs*. The self-methods, popular since Smalltalk, permit methods to be defined in terms of other methods of the same class. What makes it difficult to model is that *self* does not refer statically to the methods implemented by the class. If a method refers via *self* to another method and gets inherited by a subclass, then *self* no longer refers to the methods of the superclass, from which it was inherited, but dynamically to the ones of the new class; in case one of the methods is re-implemented, all others referring to it via *self* are modified as well. This is known as dynamic binding of methods or *late binding*. Since we treat programs and proofs uniformly in our model, the described late-binding applies to proofs that are defined in terms of *self* as well.

The last ingredient we mention is *subtyping*. Subtyping constitutes an order relation on types, where $S \leq T$ means that an element of type $S$ can be regarded as an element of $T$ and thus safely be used when an inhabitant of $T$ is expected. This is known as *substitutability* or *subsumption*. Subtyping must not be confused with inheritance: Inheritance is the *construction* of a new subclass, whereas subtyping is concerned with the *use* of objects — or terms in general. Although inheritance and subtyping are different in this model, there is a connection between them: the type of any instance of a subclass is a subtype of the type of any instance of the superclass. Subclasses and superclasses themselves, however, are not related by subtyping.

# 3   Towards an object-oriented progification language

In this section we use the canonical example of points and coloured points as a thread to align the constructs of the progification language. As we go along, we informally discuss intricacies of the translation to the λ-terms of Lego.

We start by defining the type of point-objects and then implement and verify a concrete point-object. In the second part of the section we present classes. As for the points, we have to define the type of point-classes first before implementing and verifying a concrete point-class. Subsequently we show how point-objects can be generated from this particular point-class by instantiation. Finally, we demonstrate on a class of coloured points how subclasses can be inherited from superclasses.

In contrast to [HNSS96], where the aim was to *encode rigorously* an object-oriented progification language in Lego, this paper focuses on the *usage* and *design* of such a language. We are convinced that object-oriented progification is a natural generalization of object-oriented programming in the sense that progification looks very much like ordinary object-oriented programming. As we build upon an interactive theorem prover, not only the proofs but also the programs are constructed interactively.

To make the language suggestive we use a notation close to common object-oriented programming languages. In particular, we have tried to keep close to the pseudo-notation used in [AC96]. The language — as presented here — has not been implemented yet, but doing so would be straightforwad following the Lego-encoding. The mock system interactions we describe below are meant to make the basic steps of the system comprehensible. Many of these trivial steps could be automated by tactics.

## 3.1 Objects

We embark by defining the type of a point. The point is intended to comprise methods *getX* and *getY* to inquire about the coordinates, *setX* and *setY* to overwrite them and *incX* to increment the $x$-coordinate by one.

In the following, we suggest how an interactive session would look. Initially, the system should expect an expression to be evaluated. Our notation > for a prompt is meant to suggest that the system is ready.

To keep our definitions modular, we define the types of the methods and the types of the correctness-proofs separately (recall that in type-theory the specification can be seen as the type of the correctness-proofs).

**Types of objects** First, we define the types of the methods which we call collectively the *signature* of the object. Due to our particular object model (see [PT94]) we have to make explicit in the signature how the methods work on the state. To ensure hiding, the signature is defined for an abstract representation type (= type of state) *Rep*. The method *setX*, for example, has type $Rep \to Nat \to Rep$. The type of *setX* indicates that *setX* updates the state with its second argument. Consequently, the signature *SigPoint* of points is defined as follows:

> **Signature** *SigPoint*(*Rep*) **is**
>     **method** *getX*, *getY* : $Rep \to Nat$
>     **method** *setX*, *setY* : $Rep \to Nat \to Rep$
>     **method** *incX* : $Rep \to Rep$
>   **end**;
> **val** *SigPoint* : **Signature**

Now we want to specify the methods of signature *SigPoint*. For simplicity, we only postulate two elementary equations:

> **Specification** *SpecPoint*(*Rep*) **of Signature** *SigPoint* **is**
>     **proof** *getX_setX* : *getX* (*setX r n*) = *n*
>     **proof** *getX_incX* : *getX* (*incX r*) = (*getX r*) + *1*
> **end**;
> **val** *SpecPoint* : **Specification** (*SigPoint*)

Finally, we are ready to define the type of point-objects:

> **ObjectType** *Point* **is**
>     **Signature**     *SigPoint*
>     **Specification** *SpecPoint*
> **end**;
> **val** *Point* : **ObjectType**

Note that we have defined the type of points independently of any specific representation type. This ensures that no information about the actual implementation of the state is anticipated in the type.

Before defining a concrete object of type *Point* we show how these definitions are translatable into Lego-terms of the encoding presented in [HNSS96]. The signature *SigPoint* is mapped to the type-constructor[2]

$$\lambda\, Rep : \star .\ \{\ getX : Rep \to Nat,$$
$$setX : Rep \to Nat \to Rep,\ ...\}$$

which given a representation type *Rep* constructs a record type for *getX*, *setX*, *incX*, *getY* and *setY*. Accordingly, the type of signatures **Signature** is simply an abbreviation for $\star \to \star$.

The specification *SpecPoint* is translated into the type-constructor

$$\lambda\, Rep : \star .\ \lambda\, meths : (SigPoint\ Rep).$$
$$\{getX\_setX : \forall\, r : Rep .\ \forall\, n : Nat .\ meths.getX\ (meths.setX\ r\ n) = n,$$
$$getX\_incX : \forall\, r : Rep .\ meths.getX\ (meths.incX\ r) = (meths.getX\ r) + 1\}$$

which has type $\forall\, Rep : \star .\ (SigPoint\ Rep) \to \star$.

To understand the type of point-objects *Point* we have to say a word about the encoding in [HNSS96]. In this encoding, encapsulation is achieved by existential quantification; encapsulation by existential quantification was first proposed by [MP88], though for abstract data types rather than objects. The object-type *Point* is translated to the term

$$\exists\, Rep : \star .\ \{state : Rep, meths : (SigPoint\ Rep), prfs : (SpecPoint\ Rep\ meths)\}$$

which means that **ObjectType** — which is the type of object-types — simply stands for $\star$. Note that we have to use dependent records for this definition since the specification — which is the type of the correctness proofs — depends on the methods.

---

[2] Types and propositions both have type $\star$. See [HNSS96] for a discussion of this issue.

**Implementing objects** Having defined the type of point-objects we implement a concrete point-object *MyPoint*. The first thing to do is to determine the representation type of *MyPoint*. It is natural to choose two fields $x : Nat$ and $y : Nat$ for the coordinates resulting in the representation type

> **RepresentationType** *RepPoint* **is**
>     **var** $x : Nat$
>     **var** $y : Nat$
>   **end**;
> **val** *RepPoint* : **RepresentationType**

As we have said, the interactive theorem prover allows us to define the object step by step. The prompt ≫ hereby indicates that the definition is still incomplete.

Rather than giving a definition of *MyPoint* at once, we instruct the system that we want to create an object of type *Point*:

> **create object** *MyPoint* **of ObjectType** *Point*;

The system inquires for a specific representation type for *MyPoint*.

   $Rep = ?$  ≫  *RepPoint*;

Since we have chosen *RepPoint* as representation type for our point, the system expects initial values for the $x$ and $y$-coordinate:

   $x = ?$  ≫  5;
   $y = ?$  ≫  3;

In the signature we have determined that points have five methods: *getX*, *setX*, *getY*, *setY* and *incX*. Accordingly, we are asked to implement these methods. As we are implementing the point for representation type *RepPoint*, the type of the methods to be implemented is *SigPoint RepPoint*. This implies that the method *getX*, for example, has type $RepPoint \to Nat$. We implement *getX* by record projection $getX = \lambda r . \; r.x$. The implementation of the remaining methods is similar:

   $getX = ?$  ≫  $\lambda r . \; r.x$;
   $setX = ?$  ≫  $\lambda r . \lambda n . \; r.x := n$;
   $getY = ?$  ≫  $\lambda r . \; r.y$;
   $setY = ?$  ≫  $\lambda r . \lambda n . \; r.y := n$;
   $incX = ?$  ≫  $\lambda r . \; r.x := r.x + 1$;

Since our aim is to verify the objects hand in hand with their implementation, we have to prove the correctness of these methods relative to the specification *SpecPoint*. Again, the system serves as guideline:

   $getX\_setX = ?$  ≫

It is helpful to display the goal by the command **prf**:

$getX\_setX$ = ?  $\gg$ **prf**;
  $\forall\, r : RepPoint\,.\, \forall\, n : Nat\,.\, (r.x := n).x = n$
$getX\_setX$ = ?  $\gg$

This goal expresses (as demanded in *SpecPoint*) the well-behavior of the implementation of *getX* on the implementation of *setX*. After introducing the quantifiers (command **Intros** $r\,n$)[3] the term $(r.x := n).x$ reduces to $n$ and hence the goal is proved by reflexivity of equality (command **Refine** $refl_=$).

$getX\_setX$ = ?  $\gg$ **Intros** $r\,n$; **Refine** $refl_=$;
  $getX\_setX$ **q.e.d.**
$getX\_incX$ = ?  $\gg$ **prf**;
  $\forall\, r : RepPoint\,.\, (r.x := r.x + 1).x = r.x + 1$

The second equation is provable by reflexivity of equality as well.

$getX\_incX$ = ?  $\gg$ **Intros** $r$; **Refine** $refl_=$;
  $getX\_incX$ **q.e.d.**

Now we are done, which is acknowledged by the system:

**val** *MyPoint* : *Point*
$>$

**Method invocation** So far we have means to introduce objects, but we have not said a word about how to invoke methods. Since we use the existential quantifier to account for encapsulation, method invocation cannot simply be achieved by record selection. To get access to the methods, we have to eliminate the existential quantifier first. In [HP94] it was shown that — for positive occurrences of the representation type in the signature — elimination functions can be generated automatically. These functions work not only on objects of type *Point* but also on objects whose signatures and specifications are subtypes of *SigPoint* and *SpecPoint*. For our point example the system could infer elimination functions $Point'getX_<$, $Point'setX_<$ and $Point'incX_<$ where $Point'setX_<$, for example, has type[4]

$\forall\, Sig \,|\, \textbf{Signature}\,.\forall\, Spec \,|\, \textbf{Specification}\,(Sig)\,.$
$(Sig \leq SigPoint) \rightarrow (Spec \leq SpecPoint) \rightarrow$
  $(Object\ Sig\ Spec) \rightarrow Nat \rightarrow (Object\ Sig\ Spec)$

---

[3] Note that for the verification it is absolutely inessential which theorem-prover our language is based on. We arbitrarily choose to conduct the proofs in Lego-style.

[4] The Lego proof-checker and thus our language can infer the signature *Sig* and the specification *Spec* from the following subtyping proofs. This is indicated by using | instead of : in the type.
Given a signature *Sig* and a specification *Spec*, the type constructor *Object* constructs the type of objects with signature *Sig* and specification *Spec*.

Since subtypes are not build in to Lego, we have to represent the statement $S \leq T$ by a coercion function from $S$ to $T$. Defining subtypes this way, the polymorphic identity function ensures reflexivity and function composition transitivity of the subtype relation. Applying $Point'setX_{\leq}$ to the reflexivity proofs $refl_{=SigPoint}$ of type $SigPoint \leq SigPoint$ and $refl_{=SpecPoint}$ of type $SpecPoint \leq SpecPoint$ yields an elimination function tailored for points only:[5]

> $Point'setX = Point'setX_{\leq}$ $refl_{=SigPoint}$ $refl_{=SpecPoint}$;
val $Point'setX : Point \rightarrow Nat \rightarrow Point$

Losing structural subtyping is the price we have to pay for dealing with proofs. Though it is, at least in principle, possible to represent subtyping by coercion-functions, this approach is not very practicable. Furthermore, the proofs are redundant when executing programs; even worse they are ballast. Therefore we propose to develop verified programs in a progification language and thereafter to jettison the proofs. The resulting programs can be executed in a programming language with structural subtyping (e.g. in $F^{\omega}_{\leq}$ [Pie92]).

**Proof invocation** Objects in our object model do not only comprise method-implementations but also correctness proofs. Just as we want to invoke the methods, we want to get access to the proofs by so called *generic proofs*. Again, functions are used to eliminate the existential quantifier. We conjecture that — under similar positiveness conditions as above — these functions can be generated automatically. As shown in [HNSS96] the elimination function $Point'getX\_setX$ for the proof $getX\_setX$ has type[6]

$$\forall p : Point . \forall n : Nat . Point'getX (Point'setX \, p \, n) = n$$

Note that this proposition holds for any object of type $Point$ regardless of its representation, implementation or correctness proofs.

## 3.2 Classes

In the second part of this section we want to step beyond objects and define classes. Recall that classes are introduced as blueprints for objects. Although a class summarizes in some sense objects, classes should not be confused with the type of objects. Classes can be used for *instantiation* and *inheritance*, though classes themselves are not executable. In the definition of classes the progifier can refer to the methods and proofs of the same class by the keyword *self* and to those of the superclass by the keyword *super*. The methods and proofs refered to by *self*, though, do not refer statically to the methods and proofs of the present

---

[5] Strictly speaking the system would infer type $(Object\ SigPoint\ SpecPoint) \rightarrow Nat \rightarrow$ $(Object\ SigPoint\ SpecPoint)$. To shorten the presentation, we freely pretend that the system infers type $Point$ rather than $Object\ SigPoint\ SpecPoint$.

[6] The definition of generic proofs for subtypes of points is similar to the definition of generic methods.

class, but dynamically to the ones of the relative subclass. This *late-binding* of *self* provides flexible reuse of code at the price of complicating the verification. A solution to the problem of verifying late-bound methods was proposed in [HNSS96] and is only sketched shortly here.

When constructing a class *MyPointClass* of points we might want to implement the method *incX* as follows:

$$incX\ r = self.setX\ r\ (self.getX\ r) + 1$$

No matter which implementation $Impl_{getX}$ we choose for *getX*, it is not possible to prove the second equation of the specification which reduces to:

$$\underbrace{Impl_{getX}}_{getX}\ \underbrace{(self.setX\ r\ (self.getX\ r + 1))}_{incX\ r} = \underbrace{Impl_{getX}\ r + 1}_{getX\ r}$$

Due to the late-binding of *self*, the method *self.setX* can be overridden arbitrarily in subclasses as long as the specification is met. The implementations of *setX* in subclasses then need not necessarily be well behaved together with the current implementation $Impl_{getX}$ of the method *getX*. In each subclass, though, the methods *self.getX* and *self.setX* are related as demanded by the specification. To take advantage of this observation, we bind the method *getX* late in our specification. The second equation of the specification *SpecPoint* then becomes:

$$self.getX\ (incX\ r) = self.getX\ r + 1$$

which is provable as we will see now. For the above implementation of *incX* and an *arbitrary* implementation of *getX* this equation reduces to

$$\underbrace{self.getX}_{self.getX}\ \underbrace{(self.setX\ r\ (self.getX\ r + 1))}_{incX\ r} = \underbrace{self.getX\ r + 1}_{self.getX\ r}$$

which is an instance of the self-proof

$$self.getX\_setX\ :\ \forall r : Rep\ .\ \forall n : Nat\ .\ self.getX\ (self.setX\ r\ n) = n$$

by taking the bound variable $r$ to be $r$ and $n$ to be $self.getX\ r + 1$. To shorten the presentation we overline methods or specifications to indicate that they are late-bound. After these preliminary remarks we are ready to define a class *MyPointClass* of points. As for the point-objects we define the type of point-classes first.

**Types of classes** The representation type *RepPoint* and the signature *SigPoint* of the point *MyPoint* remain unchanged. As we have seen, we have to use a late-bound specification $\overline{SpecPoint}$ to deal with late-bound methods.

> **Specification** $\overline{SpecPoint}(Rep)$ **of Signature** *SigPoint* **is**
>     **proof** $getX\_setX : getX\ (setX\ r\ n) = n$
>     **proof** $getX\_incX : \overline{getX}\ (incX\ r) = \overline{getX}\ r + 1$
>     **end;**

**val** $\overline{SpecPoint}$ : **Specification** $(SigPoint)$
**val** $SpecPoint$ : **Specification** $(SigPoint)$

Beyond the generalized specification $\overline{SpecPoint}$, the system defines an ungeneralized version by taking the late-bound methods to be ordinary methods. In doing so, the ungeneralized specification *SpecPoint* is identical with the specification of the same name defined earlier. This definition may look a bit mysterious. Therefore we present its translation.

$$\lambda\,Rep : \star.\ \lambda\,meths : (SigPoint\ Rep).\ \lambda\,self : (SigPoint\ Rep).$$
$$\{getX\_setX : \forall\,r : Rep.\ \forall\,n : Nat.\ meths.getX\ (meths.setX\ r\ n) = n,$$
$$getX\_incX : \forall\,r : Rep.\ self.getX\ (meths.incX\ r) = (self.getX\ r) + 1\}$$

With this representation type, signature and specification we define the type of our class as

> **ClassType** *PointClass* **is**
  **RepresentationType** *RepPoint*
  $\overline{\textbf{Signature}}$  *SigPoint*
  $\overline{\textbf{Specification}}$  *SpecPoint*
  **end;**
  **val** *PointClass* : **ClassType**

**Implementing classes** Just as we defined *MyPoint* interactively, we define *MyPointClass* step-by-step. First, we instruct the system that we want to create a class:

> **create class** *MyPointClass*(*Rep*) **of ClassType** *PointClass*;

To be flexible for changes of the representation type in subclasses, the class is not implemented for the fixed representation type *RepPoint* but for an abstract representation type *Rep* which is a subtype of *RepPoint* in the following sense (assume $r : Rep$ and $m,n : Nat$ arbitrarily; $s$ and $s'$ stand for selectors):

– We can *select* from $r : Rep$ the fields of *RepPoint* (e. g. $r.x$).
– We can *update* in $r : Rep$ the fields of *RepPoint* (e. g. $r.x := n$).

Additionally, we can rely on the satisfaction of the equations *GetPutLaws* (see [HP95] for a detailed discussion of this particular interpretation of subtyping):

$$(r.s := n).s = n \tag{1}$$
$$(r.s := n).s' = r.s' \tag{2}$$
$$(r.s := r.s) = r \tag{3}$$
$$((r.s := n).s := m) = (r.s := m) \tag{4}$$
$$((r.s := n).s' := m) = ((r.s' := m).s := n) \tag{5}$$

In our definition of *MyPointClass* we are again guided by the system.

$$x = ? \qquad \gg 3;$$
$$y = ? \qquad \gg 5;$$
$$getX = ? \qquad \gg \lambda r \,.\, r.x;$$
$$setX = ? \qquad \gg \lambda r \,.\, \lambda n \,.\, r.x := n;$$
$$getY = ? \qquad \gg \lambda r \,.\, r.y;$$
$$setY = ? \qquad \gg \lambda r \,.\, \lambda n \,.\, r.y := n;$$
$$incX = ? \qquad \gg \lambda r \,.\, self.setX\, r\, (self.getX\, r) + 1;$$
$$getX\_setX = ? \quad \gg \mathbf{prf};$$
$$\forall r : Rep \,.\, \forall n : Nat \,.\, (r.x := n).x = n$$

To solve this goal we first eliminate the quantifiers and then solve the resulting goal by unification with *GetPutLaws.1* (command **Refine** *GetPutLaws.1*):

$$getX\_setX = ? \quad \gg \textbf{Intros } r\, n;\ \textbf{Refine } GetPutLaws.1;$$
$$getX\_setX \ \textbf{q.e.d.}$$
$$getX\_incX = ? \quad \gg \mathbf{prf};$$
$$\forall r : Rep \,.\, self.getX\,(self.setX\, r\,(self.getX\, r + 1)) = self.getX\, r + 1$$

Finally, we introduce the universal quantifier and unify the goal with the self-proof *self.getX_setX* of type $\forall r : Rep \,.\, \forall n : Nat \,.\, self.getX\,(self.setX\, r\, n) = n$:

$$getX\_incX = ? \quad \gg \textbf{Intros } r;\ \textbf{Refine } self.getX\_setX;$$
$$getX\_incX \ \textbf{q.e.d.}$$
$$\textbf{val } MyPointClass : PointClass$$

**Instantiation** Classes are introduced as blueprints for objects. Hence, we want to derive objects — the *instances* — from the class *MyPointClass*. A particular point-object *MyPointInstance* is instantiated by the following definition:

> **object** *MyPointInstance* **is instance of** *MyPointClass*
> **end**;
> **val** *MyPointInstance* : *Point*

Implementing instantiation is not as simple as this definition might suggest. At instantiation time the *self*-methods and *self*-proofs get replaced by true implementations. If there are circular self-dependencies (e. g. a method is defined by self-reference to itself), the replacement algorithm and thus the instantiation itself will not terminate (see [HNSS96] for a discussion of this problem).

**Inheritance** It is commonly agreed that object-oriented programming languages support flexible reuse of programming code. In class-based languages the reuse is achieved by constructing new classes from existing ones by *inheriting* methods. We claim that object-oriented progification languages support — besides flexible reuse of programs — flexible reuse of proofs, too. In this section, we illustrate the reuse of proofs only on the toy example *MyCPointClass* — a class of coloured points which we inherit from *MyPointClass*. As for the definition of *MyPointClass*, we start with defining the type of the coloured point class.

The representation type of coloured points extends the representation type of points *RepPoint* by a component for the colour.

> **RepresentationType** *RepCPoint* **extends** *RepPoint* **by**
>     **var** *colour* : *Colour*
>   **end**;
> **val** *RepCPoint* : **RepresentationType**

Coloured points possess, in addition to the methods of points, a method *setC* to set the colour and *getC* to interrogate it.

> **Signature** *SigCPoint*(*Rep*) **extends** *SigPoint* **by**
>     **method** *setC* : *Rep* → *Colour* → *Rep*
>     **method** *getC* : *Rep* → *Colour*
>   **end**;
> **val** *SigCPoint* : **Signature**

For sake of illustrating the dynamic binding of *self*, we add two artificial equations to the specification of points. Our intention is to re-define the method *setX* such that it artificially sets the colour to *blue*. Due to the late-binding of *self* the method *incX*, which was defined in terms of *setX*, will set the colour to *blue* as well.

> $\overline{\text{Specification}}$ $\overline{SpecCPoint}$(*Rep*) **extends** $\overline{SpecPoint}$ **by**
>     **proof** *getC_incX* : $\overline{getC}$ (*incX r*) = *blue*
>     **proof** *getC_setX* : *getC* (*setX r n*) = *blue*
>   **end**;
> **val** $\overline{SpecCPoint}$ : **Specification** (*SigCPoint*)
> **val** *SpecCPoint* : **Specification** (*SigCPoint*)

Analogous to *PointClass* we define the type of coloured point classes:

> **ClassType** *CPointClass* **is**
>     **RepresentationType** *RepCPoint*
>     **Signature**           *SigCPoint*
>     **Specification**       *SpecCPoint*
>   **end**;
> **val** *CPointClass* : **ClassType**

Now we are ready to construct the class *MyCPointClass* by inheritance from class *MyPointClass*. When inheriting a method or field from the superclass, we do not want to have to declare this explicitly. Therefore we decide on which methods or fields we want to override and expect the remaining methods and fields to be inherited without saying so.

> **create class** *MyCPointClass*(*Rep*) **of ClassType** *CPointClass*
>     **by inheritance from** *MyPointClass*
>     **override var** *x*
>     **override method** *setX*
>   **end**;

According to the representation type *RepCPoint* and the signature *SigCPoint* we have to implement the fields and methods that are either new for coloured points or determined to be overridden.

$x = ?$ $\quad \gg 0$;
$\quad y$ **inherited**
$colour = ?$ $\quad \gg red$;
$\quad getX$ **inherited**
$setX = ?$ $\quad \gg \lambda r . \lambda n . (super.setX\ r\ n).colour := blue$;
$\quad getY, setY, incX$ **inherited**
$setC = ?$ $\quad \gg \lambda r . \lambda c . r.colour := c$;
$getC = ?$ $\quad \gg \lambda r . r.colour$;

In the implementation of the method *setX* we have referred to the implementation of the superclass by the key-word *super*. Note that the behavior of *incX* changes in the coloured point-class — although *incX* has been inherited without alteration — since it invokes the method *self.setX* which constantly sets the colour to blue. Hence, we expect the same behavior for *incX* and we shall see shortly how to establish this formally. Beforehand, we have to prove the goals arising from the point's specification. The first proof *getX_setX* cannot be inherited directly since we have overridden the method *setX*.

$getX\_setX = ?$ $\quad \gg$ **prf**;
$\quad \forall r : Rep . \forall n : Nat . super.getX ((super.setX\ r\ n).colour := blue) = n$
$getX\_setX = ?$ $\quad \gg$ **Intros** $r\ n$;

To solve this goal we apply *GetPutLaws.2*. Thereafter the goal becomes

$\quad super.getX (super.setX\ r\ n) = n$

This goal, finally, is unified with the inherited proof *super.getX_setX* that has type $\forall r : Rep . \forall n : Nat . super.getX (super.setX\ r\ n) = n$

$getX\_setX = ?$ $\quad \gg$ **Refine** $super.getX\_setX$;
$\quad getX\_setX$ **q.e.d.**
$\quad getX\_incX$ **inherited q.e.d.**

The system proves *getX_incX* automatically by inheriting the corresponding proof from the superclass. Note that it is possible to inherit the proof although the method *incX* (which is specified by *getX_incX*) has been altered in the coloured point class due to late-binding of *self*. This is only feasible since the self-proofs themselves are late-bound.

At last we have arrived at the verification of the equations specific to coloured points. The first of these equations is immediate by the *self*-proof *self.getC_setX* which has type $\forall r : Rep . \forall n : Nat . self.getC (self.setX\ r\ n) = blue$.

$getC\_incX = ?$ $\quad \gg$ **prf**;
$\quad \forall r : Rep . \underbrace{self.getC}_{self.getC} \underbrace{(self.setX\ r\ (self.getX\ r) + 1)}_{incX\ r} = blue$
$getC\_incX = ?$ $\quad \gg$ **Intros** $r$; **Refine** $self.getC\_setX$;
$\quad getC\_incX$ **q.e.d.**

The proof of the last equation is an instance of *GetPutLaws.1*.

$getC\_setX = ?$ $\gg$ **prf**;
$\quad \forall\, r : Rep\,.\, \forall\, n : Nat\,.\; \underbrace{((super.setX\; r\; n).colour := blue)}_{setX\; r\; n}.colour = blue$

$getC\_setX = ?$ $\gg$ **Intros** $r\; n$; **Refine** *GetPutLaws.1*;
$\quad getC\_setX$ **q.e.d.**
**val** *MyCPointClass* : *CPointClass*

In the definition of *MyCPointClass* we refrained from discussing the critical issue of subtyping. In subclasses we are free to modify the representation type, signature and specification which gives rise to flexible reuse of programs and proofs. Of course we cannot expect to get this flexibility for free. To get inherited methods working in a modified framework we have to make our modifications explicit. This is achieved by proving that the modified representation type, signature or specification is a subtype of the one in the superclass. As mentioned already, there are no subtypes built in Lego, which entails that we have to supply coercion functions explicitly. For record-extensions the coercion functions can be found by a tactic, since we can prove in general that record-extension induces a subtype-relation. In our example of *MyCPointClass* we have only extended records. Therefore we can assume that a tactic solves the proof-obligations arising due to subtyping. The system would of course not only provide a proof for record-extension but a set of subtyping proofs. Using a tactic to prove the subtyping property means mimicing structural subtyping as for example in [Pie92]. Having to renounce structural subtyping is the price we have to pay for our decision to work in a logical rather than a purely computational framework. The loss of structural subtyping might be an obstacle for the practical work but it provides additional flexibility not present in languages with structural subtyping. Consider the following examples:

- We have implemented our point-example based on cartesian coordinates. In a subclass it might be advantageous to use polar coordinates for the implementation. In this case the coercion functions are conversion functions between polar and cartesian coordinates.
- In a hierarchy of Smalltalk-style collections one could think of two methods *remove* and *removeAll* which remove one or all occurrences of an element from a collection respectively. In a subclass that implements sets the behavior of these methods is identical. It would be convenient to meld them to a method *removeSet*. This can be achieved by a coercion function that maps *removeSet* to both *remove* and *removeAll*.
- Having unified the two methods *remove* and *removeAll* to *removeSet* in a class implementing sets it does not make sense to take over all equations from *remove* and *removeAll* into the specification of *removeSet* since some of them will express the same thing. The specification can be slimmed to a specification fitting for *removeSet*. The coercion function then has to show that the specification of the set-class logically implies the specification of the superclass.

In all these cases the programs and proofs of the superclass can be inherited without explicit change by the progifier. The necessary adaptions are performed by the system according to the given coercion functions.

# 4 Conclusions

In this paper we presented a language for object-oriented progification. We aimed to show that object-oriented progification can be understood as generalized object-oriented programming. However, refrained from justifying our assertion that the object-oriented verification mechanisms really allow flexible reuse of proofs. In our opinion this can only be achieved by means of case-studies. Some experience has been gained in Lego already by performing a small case study concerned with Smalltalk-style collections [Nar96]. We want to sketch briefly how the late-binding of self-proofs can be used to account for flexible reuse of proofs.

To structure the hierarchy of collections we introduce *virtual classes*, which are not meant to be instantiated into objects. In our setting, those are classes that contain methods or proofs which are referring to themselves via the variable *self* and which we call *virtual methods* or *virtual proofs*. Hence virtual classes do not denote a new concept, but refer to a special usage of the already encountered mechanism *self-reference*.

To understand how virtual classes allow reuse of methods, consider a class *Collection*, which forms the root of the hierarchy of collection classes. It provides methods common to all collections. We just focus on four operations: *length*, *add*, *empty*, and *fold*, with the usual meaning. In the class *Collection*, the method *length* is defined straightforwardly in terms of *fold* and the methods *fold*, *add* and *empty* are virtual i. e. *fold* = *self.fold*, *add* = *self.add*, *empty* = *self.empty*. No matter which implementation of *fold* we choose in subclasses, the corresponding operation *length* will always be defined.

An analogous mechanism — *virtual proofs* — supports flexible reuse of proofs. Consider the following induction principle

$$(P \; empty) \to (\forall a.\forall c'.(P \; c') \to (P \; (add \; a \; c'))) \to \forall c.(P \; c)$$

In the root class *Collection* we cannot provide a proof of such an induction principle yet, since *empty* and *add* are merely virtual. Instead of proving this rule directly, we use a *virtual proof* defined as *induction* = *self.induction*. Nevertheless, we can prove many results in the class *Collection* already relying on the induction principle. For subclasses, constructed by inheritance, these proofs are adapted automatically, depending on the specific implementation of the representation type, on the operations and on the correctness proofs.

**Acknowledgements** I am grateful to Markus Wenzel and Thorsten Altenkirch for their comments on drafts. Furthermore, I sincerely want to thank Terry Stroup for his suggestions. Finally, I want to thank the anonymous referees for their constructive comments.

# References

[AC96]     Martín Abadi and Luca Cardelli. *A Theory of Objects*. Monographs in
           Computer Science. Springer, 1996.

[HNSS96]   Martin Hofmann, Wolfgang Naraschewski, Martin Steffen, and Terry
           Stroup. Inheritance of proofs. Technical Report IMMDVII-5/96, Informatik
           VII, Universität Erlangen-Nürnberg, June 1996. presented at the Third In-
           ternational Workshop on Foundations of Object-Oriented Languages (FOOL
           96), submitted to a special issue of Theory and Practice of Object-oriented
           Systems (TAPOS), January 1997.

[HP94]     Martin Hofmann and Benjamin Pierce. A unifying type-theoretic frame-
           work for objects. In P. Enjalbert, E. W. Mayr, and K. W. Wagner, editors,
           *STACS '94*, volume 775 of *Lecture Notes in Computer Science*, pages 251–
           262. Springer, 1994.

[HP95]     Martin Hofmann and Benjamin Pierce. Positive subtyping. In *Proceedings
           of Twenty-Second Annual ACM Symposium on Principles of Programming
           Languages*, pages 186–197. ACM, January 1995. Full version in *Information
           and Computation*, volume 126, number 1, April 1996. Also available as Uni-
           versity of Edinburgh technical report ECS-LFCS-94-303, September 1994.

[LP92]     Zhaohui Luo and Randy Pollack. LEGO proof development system: User's
           manual. Technical Report ECS-LFCS-92-211, Laboratory for Foundations
           of Computer Science, University of Edinburgh, May 1992.

[MP88]     John Mitchell and Gordon Plotkin. Abstract types have existential type.
           *ACM Transactions on Programming Languages and Systems*, 10(3):470–502,
           July 1988.

[Nar96]    Wolfgang Naraschewski. *Object-Oriented Proof Principles using the Proof-
           Assistant Lego*. Diplomarbeit, Universität Erlangen, 1996.

[Pie92]    Benjamin Pierce. *F-Omega-Sub User's Manual*, version 1.0 edition, October
           1992.

[PT94]     Benjamin Pierce and David Turner. Simple type-theoretic foundations
           for object-oriented programming. *Journal of Functional Programming*,
           4(2):207–247, April 1994. A preliminary version appeared in Principles of
           Programming Languages, 1993, and as University of Edinburgh technical
           report ECS-LFCS-92-225, under the title "Object-Oriented Programming
           Without Recursive Types".

# Verification for Robust Specification

Doron Peled

Bell Laboratories, 700 Mountain Ave., Murray Hill, NJ, 07974, USA
email: doron@research.bell-labs.com

**Abstract.** The choice of a specification formalism for describing properties of concurrent systems is influenced by several factors. Two of them are adequate expressiveness and the availability of verification tools. A factor that is less often taken into consideration is the ability to provide *robust* specification. Informally, robust specifications cannot distinguish between behaviors that are essentially the same. The use of robust specifications can also provide some more practical advantages such as more manageable proof systems or more efficient automatic verification algorithms. We will present a formal definition for robustness in the framework of linear temporal logic, describe an algorithm for deciding robustness, and demonstrate how the knowledge of robustness can be exploited for verifying program correctness.

## 1 Introduction

Choosing the right specification for describing properties of concurrent systems is related to various criteria. This includes:

- *Expressiveness.* The specification formalism must be rich enough to formulate all the necessary properties of the modeled system.
- *Availability of validation tools.* The mathematical theory of verification (manual or automatic) and testing should be available, preferably supported by some implementation.
- *Abstractness.* The specification formalism should not overspecify the behavior by including unnecessary details. These may not only be confusing, but also make verification harder.

Of the above conditions, we will focus on one criterion of abstractness, which will be termed *robustness*. A specification is robust if, informally, it cannot distinguish between behaviors that are essentially the same. One example is *stutter equivalence* [6] which does not distinguish between behaviors that differ from each other only by the number of consecutive repetition of states. Two such equivalent sequences can be resulted in by the occurrence of some environment transition that does not affect the system properties. Another example is *trace equivalence* [8], which does not distinguish between behaviors that are resulted in from shuffling the order of concurrently executed transitions. The occurrences of concurrently executed transitions are put in an arbitrary order only to create a totally ordered behavior. Thus distinguishing between equivalent sequences is largely artificial.

We will define a robust specification as one that cannot distinguish between two behaviors that are equivalent, with respect to some given equivalence relation. In particular, we will concentrate on behaviors that are described using *sequences of states*. As a specification formalism, we will use *linear temporal logic (LTL)* [14].

Usually, the benefits of certain specification formalisms, including LTL, with respect to expressiveness and verification machinery outweight certain robustness considerations. Returning to the previous examples of behavior equivalences, LTL does allow non robust specifications. Similar specification formalisms, e.g., first and second order monadic logic, share a similar situation. Thus, the following questions follow naturally:

1. How can we exploit the knowledge that a given specification is robust? We are interested to take advantage of robustness for improving proof systems, or making model checking algorithms become more efficient.
2. Is there a specification formalism that expresses *exactly* all the robust properties of some class of properties? For example, we would be interested to limit the expressiveness of LTL to include exactly all the properties that are robust under the above equivalences.
3. Can we algorithmically recognize the robust specifications of some specification formalism? For example, we would like to have an algorithm that decides whether a given LTL formula is stutter or trace robust.

We will address here these three questions in the context of LTL, and in particular with respect to the above examples of equivalences. However, the treatment is quite general and can be easily applied to other specification formalisms and equivalences.

## 2  A Formal Definition of Robustness

A *behavior* of a concurrent system is a finite or infinite *sequence* of either *states* or *transitions*. Let $\Xi$ be the set of all sequences over some appropriate domain $\Sigma$. A *specification* is a formula $\varphi$ of some (temporal) logic $\mathcal{L}$.

Let $R$ be an equivalence (namely, reflexive, symmetric and transitive) relation.

**Definition 1.** A set of sequences $\Delta \subseteq \Xi$ such that for every equivalence class $C$ of $\sim$, either $\Delta \supseteq C$ or $\Delta \cap C = \phi$, is said to be *closed* under $\sim$. Similarly, a specification $\varphi \in \mathcal{L}$ is *robust* with respect to $R$ when $\forall \sigma, \sigma' \in \Xi : \sigma R \sigma' \Rightarrow (\sigma \models \varphi \Leftrightarrow \sigma' \models \varphi)$.

Thus, a robust specification $\varphi$ does not distinguish between any two equivalent sequences. Stated differently, the set of behaviors $L\varphi$ that satisfy the specification $\varphi$ is closed under $\sim$.

We will use two examples of equivalences on sequences. It will be easier to define them first for finite sequences and later move to the infinite case.

## Stutter equivalence

The stutter removal operator $\sharp : \Sigma^+ \mapsto \Sigma^+$ is defined inductively, using the following rewriting rules:

$$\sharp(a) = a$$
$$\sharp(vabw) = \sharp(va)\sharp(bw)$$
$$\sharp(vaaw) = \sharp(vaw)$$

where $a, b \in \Sigma$, $a \neq b$, $v, w \in \Sigma^*$.

**Definition 2.** $u$ and $w$ are *stutter equivalent*, denoted $u \sim_{st} v$, when $\sharp(u) = \sharp(v)$.

Thus, $u \sim_{st} v$ when $u$ and $v$ differ only by the number of adjacent repetitions of letters. It is easy to check that the above is indeed an equivalence relation.

## Trace equivalence

A *dependency relation* is a reflexive and symmetric relation $D \subseteq \Sigma \times \Sigma$.

**Definition 3.** Two words $u, v$ are *trace equivalent*, denoted $u \sim_{tr} v$, if there exists a sequence of words $u = w_0, w_1, \ldots, w_n = v$, such that for each $0 \leq i < n$, there exist $x, y \in \Sigma^*$, $a, b \in \Sigma$ such that $w_i = xaby$, $w_{i+1} = xbay$ and $(a, b) \notin D$.

Thus, $u \sim_{tr} v$ when one can transform $u$ to $v$ by permuting adjacent independent transitions. It is easy to check that the above is indeed an equivalence relation.

Stutter and trace equivalences are extended to infinite sequences as follows.

**Definition 4.** The *limit extension* of a relation $\sim^{fin}$ on finite strings is defined as follows: $v \sim v'$ iff

- for each finite prefix $u$ of $v$, there exists a finite prefix $u'$ of $v'$ and a finite string $w$ such that $uw \sim^{fin} u'$, and
- for each finite prefix $u'$ of $v'$, there exists a finite prefix $u$ of $v$ and a finite string $w'$ such that $u'w' \sim^{fin} u$.

We will use $\sim_{st}$ and $\sim_{tr}$ for both the finite and infinite versions of the stutter and trace equivalences, respectively. Let $\text{fst}(v)$ and $\text{lst}(v)$ be the first and last letter of a nonempty string $v$. The following generalization of *left cancellativeness* will be used in the sequel.

**Definition 5.** Let $g$ be a function $\Sigma \times \Sigma \mapsto \mathcal{F}$, where $\mathcal{F}$ is some finite set. A congruence relation $\sim$ is called *flexible with respect to $g$* if the following conditions hold for all $v, v', w, w' \in \Sigma^+$, $a \in \Sigma$:

1. If $v \sim v'$, $vw \sim v'w'$ and $g(\text{lst}(v), \text{fst}(w)) = g(\text{lst}(v'), \text{fst}(w'))$, then $w \sim w'$.
2. If $v \sim v'$, then $g(\text{lst}(v), a) = g(\text{lst}(v'), a)$.

If $\sim$ is flexible with respect to some function $g$, then we say that $\sim$ is *flexible*.

It is easy to see that stutter equivalence is flexible, with $g(a, b) = 0$ and $g(a, a) = 1$, for each distinct $a, b \in \Sigma$. Trace equivalence is flexible, with $g$ an arbitrary constant function.

## Linear Temporal Logic

Let $\Gamma$ be the set of formulas of some given logic. LTL over the state assertions $\Gamma$ has the following syntax:

$$\varphi ::= \bigcirc\varphi \,|\, (\varphi U \varphi) \,|\, (\varphi \wedge \varphi) \,|\, \neg\varphi \,|\, \Gamma$$

Let $\sigma^i$ be the suffix of $\sigma$ starting from the $i$th state and $\sigma(i)$ be the $i$th element of $\sigma$. The semantics of the modal operator *nexttime* '$\bigcirc$' is $\sigma \models \bigcirc\varphi$ iff $\sigma^1 \models \varphi$. For the operator *until* '$U$', $\sigma \models \varphi U \psi$ iff for some $i \geq 0$, $\sigma^i \models \psi$, and for each $0 \leq j < i$, $\sigma^j \models \varphi$. The usual boolean operators can be defined using '$\neg$' and '$\wedge$' in a standard way. We also use the notation $\varphi \Rightarrow \psi$ as an abbreviation for $\Box(\varphi \rightarrow \psi)$.

## 3  Exploiting Robustness

There are several methods to exploit the robustness of specification. A general principle is *verification using representatives*.

**Definition 6.** Let $L_P \subseteq \Xi$ be the set of behaviors of the verified system $P$ and $L\varphi$ be the set of behaviors that satisfy the specification $\varphi$. Then, $P$ *satisfies* $\varphi$ when $L_P \subseteq L\varphi$.

The verification using representatives is based on the following Lemma.

**Lemma 7.** *Let $\sim$ be an equivalence relation such that $L\varphi$ is closed under $\sim$ (i.e., $\varphi$ is robust w.r.t. $\sim$). Further, let $\Delta \subseteq L_P$ be a set of sequences such that for each equivalence class $C$ of $\sim$ such that $L_P \cap C \neq \phi$, it holds that $\Delta \cap C \neq \phi$. Then, $L_P \subseteq L\varphi$ iff $\Delta \subseteq L\varphi$.*

Thus, one needs an effective way of generating or reasoning about an appropriate subset $\Delta$ of the system behavior $L_P$. Two examples of how this can be done are given below for program verification and model checking.

## Program Verification

Manna and Pnueli, in a series of papers, presented a proof system for LTL properties. The verified programs are represented using a finite set of transitions. In [7], several examples are given of translation from various concurrent programming languages into such a notation. The proof rules in these methods are based on using invariants and parametrized intermediate assertions. The proof rules establish the invariant claims, or the progress achieved from states satisfying one intermediate assertion to another. We will present here a variant of such a proof system that can take advantage of trace robustness. In particular, the invariants and intermediate assertions need only be satisfied by a subset of the program states, namely those on some sequences *representing* the trace equivalence class.

**Definition 8.** A *state space* of a system $P$ is a triple $\langle S, T, I \rangle$, where

- $S$ is a finite or infinite set of *states*,
- $T$ is a finite set of deterministic *transitions*. For each transition $a \in T$ we associate a partial function $S \mapsto S$,
- $I \subseteq S$ is the set of *initial states*.

The set of transitions enabled (executable) at a state $s$ is denoted by $enabled(s)$. When $a$ is enabled from $s$, executing $a$ from $s$ results in the state $t = a(s)$. With each program transition $\tau \in T$ there is a predicate transformer $wp_\tau$; $wp_\tau(\varphi)$ is a predicate satisfied exactly by states from which, by executing $\tau$, a state that satisfies $\varphi$ is obtained. The enabling condition $en_\tau \overset{\Delta}{=} wp_\tau(\text{TRUE})$ holds for states where $\tau$ is enabled. The predicate $\Theta$ is the *initial condition*, i.e., $s \models \Theta$ iff $s \in I$.

Dependency between transitions must adhere to the following constraints: for each $s \in S$, when $(\alpha, \beta) \notin D$,

- If $\alpha \in enabled(s)$ then $\beta \in enabled(s)$ iff $\beta \in enabled(\alpha(s))$.
- If $\alpha, \beta \in enabled(s)$ then $\alpha(\beta(s)) = \beta(\alpha(s))$.

**Definition 9.** A *transitions sequence* is a finite or infinite sequence of transitions $a_0 a_1 a_2 \ldots$ such that there exists a sequence of states $s_0 s_1 s_2 \ldots$ satisfying

- $s_0 \in I$
- for each $i \geq 0$, $\alpha_i \in enabled(s_i)$ and $\alpha_i(s_i) = s_{i+1}$.
- The sequence is *weakly fair* in the following sense: if some transition $\alpha \in T$ is enabled at some state $s_i$, then for some state $s_j$, $j \geq i$, and some transition $\beta$ dependent on $\alpha$, $s_{j+1} = \beta(s_j)$.

We call the sequence $s_0 s_1 s_2 \ldots$ a *behavior*.

Weak fairness captures the intuition that if a transition is enabled, it cannot be indefinitely prevented from being executed by an infinite sequence of independent (concurrent) transitions. (Recall that an enabled transition will remain enabled unless a dependent transition, including itself, is executed.)

In order to perform verification using representatives, we first limit the state space and behaviors of the verified system $P$. This is done by restricting the set of transitions that can be taken from each state $s$ to $ample(s) \subseteq enabled(s)$. By replacing $enabled(s)$ with $ample(s)$ in Definition 9, we obtain a smaller set of transition sequences and behaviors. Only the states that appear on these sequences are relevant for the verification. We call this subset of states $S' \subseteq S$ the *reduced* set of states. Notice that since this set can be infinite, we do not explicitly construct it, but merely reason about these states using the invariants and intermediate assertions of formal proofs.

The choice of $ample(s)$ is motivated by Lemma 7: we want the reduced set of behaviors to include at least one behavior that corresponds to a transition sequences for each trace equivalence class that includes system behaviors. One way to achieve this is as follows: let $\mu_i$ be a parametrized predicate, where $i$ ranges over some finite domain. For each $i$, let $T_i \subseteq T$ be a subset of transitions, such that $\mu_i \models s$ for $s \in S'$ when $ample(s) = T_i$.

Let $G$ be a finite graph, with each node $g_i$ marked with a formula $\mu_i$. The successors of node $g_i$ are the set of nodes $suc(g_i)$. Then, the following conditions guarantee at least one representative behavior for each trace equivalence class:

A1 $\Theta \rightarrow \bigvee_i \mu_i$
A2 for each $i$, $\mu_i \rightarrow \bigwedge_{\alpha \in T_i} wp(\bigvee_{g_j \in suc(g_i)} \mu_j)$
A3 for each $i$, $\mu_i \rightarrow \delta_i$
A4 for each $i$, $\delta_i \rightarrow \bigwedge_{\alpha \notin T_i}(\bigwedge_{\beta \in T_i}(\alpha, \beta) \in D \rightarrow \neg en_\alpha)$
A5 for each $i$, $\tau \notin T_i$, $\delta_i \wedge en_\tau \rightarrow wp_\tau(\delta)$
A6 for each cycle $g_{i_1} g_{i_2} \ldots g_{i_n}$, and $\alpha \in T \setminus \bigcup_{j=i_1 \ldots i_n} T_j$,
$\qquad$ there exists $j \in i_1 \ldots i_n$, such that $\mu_j \rightarrow \neg en_\alpha$.

Clauses A1 and A2 maintain that transition sequences that start with from an initial state and are limited to choosing the set of successors $ample(s) = T_i$ when $s \models \mu_i$, contain only states satisfying $\bigvee_i \mu_i$. Clauses A3–A5 (see [5]) maintain that for each state $s \models \mu_i$, before a transition from $T_i$ is taken, only transitions independent of it can be taken. $\delta_i$ is a predicate that holds in states that are reachable from $s \models \mu_i$ using transitions that are independent of those in $T_i$. By weak fairness and the constraints on dependency, at least one transition of $T_i$ must eventually be taken.

This allows constructing for each transition sequence $\xi$ a sequence $\xi' \sim_{st} \xi$ that passes only through states satisfying $\bigvee_i \mu_i$. Consider the case where the construction of $\xi'$ reaches a state $s$ and some occurrence of a transition $\alpha \in enabled(s) \setminus ample(s)$ appears in $\xi$ and was not yet taken in $\xi'$. Then some transition $\beta \in ample(s)$, which is independent of $\alpha$, and also occurs in $\xi$ will be taken in $\xi'$ first. Nevertheless, after taking $\beta$, $\alpha$ is still enabled and can be taken.

There is still one problem: it can happen that this construction will always ignore some transition of the simulated sequence $\xi$. For example, for a sequence $\alpha(\beta\gamma)^\omega$, were $\alpha$ is independent of both $\beta$ and $\gamma$, it can happen that we keep delaying the selection of $\alpha$, constructing the sequence $(\beta\gamma)^\omega$. This is taken care of by A6: it disallows a transition $\alpha$ that is enabled at some point, yet only independent transitions participate on the selected subsets.

It should be observed that the predicate $\delta_i$ may need to describe (i.e., be satisfied by) states that are not in the reduced state space $S'$. Yet $\delta_i$ may be simple to formulate. In particular, conditions A3–A5 may, in many cases, be replaced by a syntactic procedure, based on the dependency relation and the type of program transitions enabled and disabled. For example, when $\mu_i$ asserts that one of the autonomous agents (processes) of the system must take a local transition that does not involve other agents, then $T_i$ can be a singleton set containing that transition. In some cases, A6 can be greatly simplified, e.g., by requiring that each cycle of the graph $G$ includes all the transitions.

For a system where the above conditions A1–A6 are proved, it is possible to *relativize* the proof system such that we only reason about the representative sequences. The relativized assertions will be written inside square brackets, to indicate that the proof holds within some given context. Consider for example the following proof rule for invariance.

$$\frac{\begin{array}{l} \Theta \rightarrow \varphi \\ \varphi \Rightarrow q \\ \text{for each } \alpha \in T, \ (\varphi \wedge en_\alpha) \Rightarrow wp_\alpha(\varphi) \end{array}}{\Box q}$$

Its relativized version is:

$$\frac{\begin{array}{l} \Theta \rightarrow \varphi \\ [\varphi \Rightarrow q] \\ \text{for each } i, \ \alpha \in \mathcal{T}_i, \ [(\varphi \wedge \mu_i \wedge en_\alpha) \Rightarrow wp_\alpha(\varphi)] \end{array}}{[\Box q]}$$

Thus, $\varphi$ need not be an invariant, satisfied by all the reachable states of the system. It only needs to be satisfied by states in the reduced state space. Similar relativization can be done for other proof rules. If the verified property is known to be trace robust[1], one can use Lemma 7 and remove the square brackets. Notice that the proof may involve many properties that are not trace robust (e.g., the above relativized invariant may only be needed by some other relativized proof rules); it is only the verified property itself which needs to be robust.

Albeit the apparent growth in the number of proof clauses, the use of the relativized proof rules may simplify the proof. Relativized inviariants and intermediate assertions may capture better the intuition about the way the verified system works. Another variant of verification using representatives and a more comprehensive discussion can be found in [5].

## Model Checking

Model checking, i.e., automatic verification, is usually restricted to finite state systems. For model checking algorithms, a method very similar in concept to the previously presented verification technique can be used. This method, called *partial order reduction*, is aimed at reducing the number of states used in the verification to those that appear on some representative sequences. Since most model checking algorithms work by explicitly enumerating the verified system states, the reduction of states can directly be measured by speedup and memory consumption improvement.

One of the most common algorithms used for model checking is based on depth first search. From each state $s$, the set of enabled transitions $enabled(s)$ are used to generate the successors of $s$. The version of partial order reduction

---

[1] In fact, we have here a variant of trace robustness: the specification must not distinguish between *behaviors* that correspond to *trace equivalent transition sequences* (but the behaviors themselves need not be equivalent). See [13] for how to handle this case.

that will be presented here will not assume weak fairness. It attempts to reduce the number of transitions taken from $s$ in such a way that the sequences of the resulted graph contain at least one representative for each equivalence class of $\sim_{st}$ that contain some system behaviors.

For model checking, the property is restricted to a propositional versions of temporal logic. Thus, there is a mapping $L : S \mapsto 2^{\mathcal{P}}$ from each one of the system states $S$ to a subset of the *state propositions* $\mathcal{P}$. State properties in $\Gamma$ are expressed using the propositions $\mathcal{P}$ and the boolean operators. The following definition is useful for the reduction:

**Definition 10.** A transition $\alpha$ of $P$ is *invisible* iff when applied to any state $s$ and generating a successor $s'$, $L(s) = L(s')$.

Thus, an invisible transition does not change the value of the state propositions. Checking visibility is in general not simpler than doing the original model checking. However, simple syntactic conservative approximations, which allow transitions to be considered visible even if it is actually not, are usually very efficient.

The reduction principle can now be explained in the following way: consider the state $s$ with two independent enabled transitions $\alpha$ and $\beta$. The immediate $\alpha$ successor of $s$ is $s'$ and the immediate $\beta$ successor of $s$ is $s''$, and $\hat{s}$ is the mutual (due to the independence conditions) successor of $s'$ and $s''$ (see Figure 1). Consider now the case where at least (w.l.o.g.) transition $\beta$ is invisible. Then $L(s) = L(s'')$ and $L(s') = L(\hat{s})$. Thus, the sequence $L(s)L(s')L(\hat{s})$ is stutter equivalent to $L(s)L(s'')L(\hat{s})$. Hence, at least one of the states $s'$ and $s''$ are redundant.

Generalizing this idea to more complicated cases, where $s$ has more than two successors, some of them independent of others and some are not, is systematically dealt with using the following conditions. They restrict the set of transitions $ample(s) \subseteq enabled(s)$ that can be effectively taken from a state $s$. These conditions guarantee that the generated reduced state space contains at least one representative sequence for each stutter equivalence class that contains sequences of $L_P$. We say that a node $s$ is *fully expanded* when $ample(s) = enabled(s)$.

**C0** [Non-emptiness condition] $ample(s)$ is empty iff $enabled(s)$ is empty.
**C1** [Faithful decomposition [5, 17, 9, 3, 4]] For every sequence that starts from the state $s$ and does not contain a transition from $ample(s)$, only transitions independent of those in $ample(s)$ can appear.
**C2** [Cycle condition [9, 10]] If $s$ is not fully expanded, then no transition $\alpha \in ample(s)$ closes a cycle.
**C3** [Non-visibility condition [10]] If $s$ is not fully expanded then none of the transitions in it is visible.

Conditions **C0** and **C3** are easily checked. Condition **C1** can be strengthened and then be replaced by an efficient decision procedure as was explained in the verification case. Condition **C2** can be checked by observing that in depth first search a cycle is closed when the newly generated successor already appears on

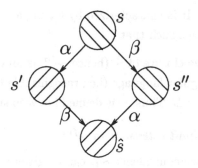

**Fig. 1.**

the search stack. It is not surprising that these conditions are related to the proof clauses A1–A6. In particular, condition C1 correspond to A3–A5, while C2 has a role similar to A6.

## 4  Fully Robust Specification Formalisms

One way to enforce robustness is to develop a specification formalism that can express exactly the robust properties among a given class of properties. We say that a logic $\mathcal{L}$ is *fully robust* if every formula of $\mathcal{L}$ is robust. Some examples of common classes of properties used in specification and verification are those expressible using first and second order monadic logic [15]. LTL has exactly the same expressive power as first order monadic logic, but its syntax seem to be more suited to reason about system behavior.

Restricting LTL to stutter closed properties can be done by simply removing the nexttime operator '◯' [6]. Although LTL stutter closed properties can be written with the nexttime operator, any such property can be rewritten without it [12]. The example of the stutter closed first order subset of LTL is in particular encouraging, since a fully robust first order expressible formalism is obtained by a simple syntactic restriction of an existing formalism.

The logic ISTL [5] (whose expressive power is uncomparable with that of first order monadic logic) is robust for trace equivalence. A verification system [11] and a model checking algorithm [1] were developed for subsets of ISTL. Another trace robust temporal logic with a model checking algorithm is TLC [2]. Recently, a temporal logic similar to ISTL that expresses exactly the trace closed first order monadic properties was introduced [16].

## 5  Deciding Robustness

In [13], an algorithm is given for deciding the closure of an LTL specification for a given class of equivalence relations. This class includes in particular trace and stutter equivalence. It is characterized by having a symmetric and reflexive relation $\overset{1}{\sim}$ on finite strings such that

- $\sim^{fin}$ is the transitive closure of $\overset{1}{\sim}$ (hence $\sim^{fin}$ is an equivalence relation).
- $\overset{1}{\sim} \subseteq \Sigma^* \times \Sigma^*$ is a regular language (i.e., recognizable by a finite automaton) over the alphabet $\Sigma \times \Sigma$. Thus, $\overset{1}{\sim}$ is defined between strings of equal lengths.
- $\sim^{fin}$ is flexible.
- $\sim$ is defined as the *limit extension*. of $\sim^{fin}$

The definition of trace equivalence $\sim_{tr}$ can be given as the transitive closure of a relation $\overset{1}{\sim}_{tr}$, which allows commuting at most a single pair of adjacent independent transitions. Similarly, stutter equivalence can be defined based on a predicate that allows two words to differ by at most one adjacent repetition of a letter.

Enforcing string related by $\overset{1}{\sim}_{st}$ to have the same length can be achieved by extending the alphabet into $\Sigma \cup \{\$\}$. Then, we can relate $u$ with itself, and $uav\$$ with $uaav$, where $u, v \in \Sigma^*$ and $a \in \Sigma$.

Checking that a temporal logic specification $\varphi$ is closed under an equivalence relation $\sim$ that satisfies the above conditions can be done using the following algorithm. The algorithm checks the emptiness of the intersection of the following three languages over the alphabet $\Sigma \times \Sigma$ (or $(\Sigma \cup \{\$\}) \times (\Sigma \cup \{\$\})$). Hence, each infinite word $\mathbf{w} = (w_1, w_2)$ over this alphabet has a left component $w_1$ and a right component $w_2$. The three languages are:

1. The language where the left component $w_1$ of the input is in $L\varphi$ (after removing the $\$$ symbols, respectively).
2. The language where the right component $w_2$ of the input is not in $L\varphi$, i.e., in $L_{\neg\varphi}$ (after removing the $\$$ symbols, respectively).
3. The language of words that can be decomposed into infinitely many finite factors that belong to $\overset{1}{\sim}$.

The algorithm can be implemented in PSPACE [13]. The idea is that there is no need to fully construct the automata for the language $L\varphi$ and $L_{\neg\varphi}$ (each can be exponential in the size of $\varphi$). Instead, one can use a binary search through the combined state space of these automata [18].

## 6 Conclusion

We presented the notion of robustness of specification and gave examples for ways it can be exploited. Achieving robustness thus not only provides a cleaner specification, but also presents some practical benefits for program verification.

Robustness can be enforced by using a logic which captures exactly the robust properties among a given class. Sometimes such a logic might be difficult to formulate, or carries a difficult proof system or a high complexity decision procedure. In these cases, a decision procedure for robustness can be used for enforcing robustness on existing formalisms.

# References

1. R. Alur, K. McMillan, D. Peled, Deciding Global Partial-Order Properties, submitted for publication.
2. R. Alur, D. Peled, W. Penczek, Model-Checking of Causality Properties, *10th Symposium on Logic in Computer Science*, IEEE, 1995, San Diego, USA, 90–100.
3. P. Godefroid, D. Pirottin, Refining dependencies improves partial order verification methods, *5th Conference on Computer Aided Verification*, LNCS 697, Elounda, Greece, 1993, 438–449.
4. P. Godefroid, P. Wolper, A Partial Approach to Model Checking, *6th Annual IEEE Symposium on Logic in Computer Science*, 1991, Amsterdam, 406–415.
5. S. Katz, D. Peled, Verification of Distributed Programs using Representative Interleaving Sequences, *Distributed Computing* 6 (1992), 107–120. A preliminary version appeared in Temporal Logic in Specification, UK, 1987, LNCS 398, 21–43.
6. L. Lamport, What good is temporal logic, *Information Processing 83*, Elsevier Science Publishers, 1983, 657-668.
7. Z. Manna, A. Pnueli, How to Cook a Temporal Proof System for Your Pet Language. Proceedings of the $10^{th}$ ACM Symposium on Principles on Programming Languages, Austin, Texas, 1983, 141-151.
8. A. Mazurkiewicz, Trace Theory, *Advances in Petri Nets 1986*, Bad Honnef, Germany, LNCS 255, Springer, 1987, 279–324.
9. D. Peled, All from one, one for all, on model-checking using representatives, *5th Conference on Computer Aided Verification*, Greece, 1993, LNCS, Springer, 409–423.
10. D. Peled. Combining partial order reductions with on-the-fly model checking. *Formal Methods in System Design* 8 (1996), 39–64.
11. D. Peled, A. Pnueli, Proving partial order properties. *Theoretical Computer Science* 126, 143–182, 1994.
12. D. Peled, Th. Wilke, Stutter-Invariant Temporal Properties are Expressible without the Nexttime Operator, submitted for publication.
13. D. Peled, Th. Wilke, P. Wolper, An Algorithmic Approach for Checking Closure Properties of $\omega$-Regular Languages, to appear in *CONCUR'96, 7th International Conference on Concurrency Theory*, Piza, Italy, August 1996.
14. A. Pnueli, The temporal logic of programs, *18th FOCS, IEEE Symposium on Foundation of Computer Science*, 1977, 46–57.
15. W. Thomas, Automata on Infinite Objects, in J. Van Leeuwen (ed.), *Handbook of Theoretical Computer Science*, Vol. B, Elsvier, 1990, 133–191.
16. P.S. Thiagarajan, I. Walukiewicz, An Expressively Complete Linear Time Temporal Logic for Mazurkeiwicz Traces, Logic in Computer Science, 1997, Warsaw, Poland.
17. A. Valmari, Stubborn sets for reduced state space generation, *10th International Conference on Application and Theory of Petri Nets*, Bonn, Germany, 1989, LNCS 483, Springer Verlag, 491–515.
18. A.P. Sistla, M.Y. Vardi, P. Wolper, The Complementation Problem for Büchi Automata with Applications to Temporal Logic, *Theoretical Computer Science*, 49 (1987), 217—237.

# A Theory of Structured Model-Based Specifications in Isabelle/HOL

Thomas Santen

GMD FIRST
Rudower Chaussee 5, D-12489 Berlin, Germany
email: santen@first.gmd.de

**Abstract.** We represent the concept of a class as it is proposed by object-oriented dialects of the specification language Z in Isabelle/HOL. Representing classes involves introducing different types for schemas describing states and operations, which are distinguished only by conventions in plain Z. Classes can be used in predicates to describe sets of objects. This leads us to define a trace semantics of classes, which is a basis to formally define behavioral relations between classes. The semantics of recursive classes is captured by a fixpoint construction. The representation of classes is a shallow encoding that orthogonally extends the encoding $\mathcal{HOL}\text{-}\mathcal{Z}$ of plain Z in Isabelle/HOL. The extended encoding provides a well-integrated environment that is suitable to abstractly define properties of classes and to reason about concrete specifications as well.

## 1 Introduction

A frequent criticism of most model-based formal specification languages, such as VDM-SL [7] and Z [15,20], is the lack of structuring mechanisms for specifying-in-the-large. For example, the only structuring mechanism of Z is the concept of a *schema*, which is used to model fundamentally different entities such as predicates, sets, state descriptions, and operations.

A general trend in software engineering, however, is to exhibit more and more of the structure of software artifacts, e.g. by encapsulating state spaces in classes in object-orientation, capturing the relationships between such structures in design patterns, and describing the general design of software in architectures. In response, a number of — in particular object-oriented — extensions to model-based specification languages have been proposed [4,8,10,11,21].

The acceptance of theorem proving — and formal techniques in general — in the process of software construction crucially depends on the way in which structural properties are supported: theorems and proofs must be stated at the level of abstraction at which software engineers are used to think. Although an ambitious goal to achieve, deduction support at this level of abstraction also gives the chance to *exploit* the structure that is made explicit, and thus to keep the complexity of theorem proving tasks manageable. Our experience with exploiting even the weak structure of Z specifications in practical applications [6] supports this claim.

This paper extends the encoding $\mathcal{HOL}\text{-}\mathcal{Z}$ [9] of Z in Isabelle/HOL [17] by a concept of a *class* similar to the one of Object-Z [4]. A class encapsulates a state description, its initialization, and a number of operations (*methods*) on this state. Because it is possible to refer to the objects denoted by classes in a class definition, classes become first-class citizens. This distinguishes the concept of a class from a pure modularization facility, such as the "abstract machines" known in the specification language B [1]. Furthermore, it is very common to have self-referring class definitions, e.g., to have methods combining an object with another one of the same class. As a consequence, the semantics of such classes has to be captured by a fixpoint construction. The objectives of this work are:

- to introduce explicit semantics for concepts, such as "state" and "operation", that are dealt with in plain Z by notational conventions only, and
- to take a first step toward deduction support for software development based on object-oriented formal specification languages.

From a logical point of view, the most challenging aspect of this work is to obtain the advantages of a deep embedding for defining meta-concepts and reasoning about specifications "in-the-large" while extending $\mathcal{HOL}$-$\mathcal{Z}$ in a way that preserves the character of a shallow embedding, which is most suitable when reasoning "in-the-small". Both characteristics play a vital role in keeping the complexity of proofs about concrete specifications manageable in practice. A shallow embedding allows the proof engine to exploit the strong type system of higher-order logic in proofs about the predicates in a class. Coding common ways of inference about classes in uniform proof procedures would lead to an enormous proof load in practical applications where classes may have dozens of components. If the embedding is sufficiently deep, however, these ways of inference can be captured in abstract theorems, which can be proved once and for all.

The theory presented here lays the basis to formally define a mechanically supportable notion of behavioral subtyping of object-oriented extensions of Z. It contributes to the research on semantics of object-oriented specification languages from the perspective of theorem proving and theory construction in the framework of higher-order logic. The ultimate goal is to provide mechanized deduction support for reasoning about libraries of reusable components, like the Eiffel Base Libraries [14], and develop a logic-based approach to a software design process that in particular supports re-using such components.

The next section briefly introduces Isabelle and $\mathcal{HOL}$-$\mathcal{Z}$. Section 3 motivates our work by way of an example specification that describes one class of the Eiffel Base Libraries. An overview over the rest of the paper is given at the end of Sect. 3.

## 2 Background: $\mathcal{HOL}$-$\mathcal{Z}$ and Isabelle

We assume some familiarity with the specification language Z, higher-order logic, and the theorem prover Isabelle. We only introduce the notation and summarize the basic features of $\mathcal{HOL}$-$\mathcal{Z}$.

Isabelle [17] is a generic tactic-based theorem prover. Its inference mechanism combines resolution with higher-order unification on meta-variables. We use Isabelle/HOL, the instance of the prover for polymorphic higher-order logics with type classes. All formulas in this paper are direct graphical representations of Isabelle's ASCII input format.

We use the usual notation for logical connectives and quantifiers. Set membership is denoted $x : S$. The basic type constructors are function space $\rightarrow$ and product types

\*. Multiple applications of $\rightarrow$ can be abbreviated using square brackets, i.e. $[\alpha, \beta] \rightarrow \gamma$ is the same as $\alpha \rightarrow (\beta \rightarrow \gamma)$. Tuples and patterns of products are written $(a, b, c)$. Type variables are denoted by greek letters, i.e. $(\alpha, \beta)$ $ty$ is a polymorphic type in the type parameters $\alpha$ and $\beta$. Constant declarations and type annotations are written $x :: t$; constant definitions $c == e$.

The choice operator $\epsilon\, x.(P\, x)$ denotes some $x$ satisfying $P$, if $P$ is satisfiable, and an arbitrary member of the type of $x$ otherwise. We will use the polymorphic constant $\underline{a} == \epsilon\, x.False$ to model "don't care" values in Sections 5 and 6.

Type synonyms and type abstractions are defined using $\overset{\text{syn}}{=}$ and $\overset{\text{abs}}{=}$, respectively. The difference is that type synonyms are just abbreviations, while a type abstraction introduces a *new* type by exhibiting a nonempty set that is isomorphic to the type. Abstraction and representation functions establishing the isomorphism are also defined by a type abstraction.

The basic idea of the encoding $\mathcal{HOL}\text{-}\mathcal{Z}$ [9] is to represent schemas by "uncurried" boolean functions. This is realized by *schema binders* that form functional abstractions over product types. The types of all schemas have the form

$$\alpha_1 * \ldots * \alpha_n \rightarrow bool$$

such that $\alpha \rightarrow bool$ is a general type-scheme for schemas. The various ways of Z to reference schemas — as predicates, as sets, or in the schema calculus — and the syntax-oriented way of Z to construct bindings are not dealt with at the logical level of the encoding. A parser constructs the appropriate arguments to functions representing schemas, and introduces explicit conversions, e.g., when schemas are referred to as sets. Figure 1 illustrates the semantic representation of a schema.

$$
\begin{array}{ll}
\underline{\quad S \quad\rule{2cm}{0pt}} & \\
\quad x : A & S == SB\, f\, x\, y.\, (x : A \wedge \\
\quad y : B & \qquad\qquad y : B \wedge \\
\quad f : A \rightarrowtail B & \qquad\qquad f : A \rightarrowtail B \\
\underline{\quad\rule{3cm}{0pt}} & \qquad\qquad |\text{ - - -} \\
\quad x \in \mathrm{dom}\, f & \qquad\qquad x : \mathrm{dom}\, f \wedge \\
\quad f\, x = y & \qquad\qquad f\, x = y)
\end{array}
$$

**Fig. 1.** Representation of a schema in $\mathcal{HOL}\text{-}\mathcal{Z}$

The schema $S$ is represented by a constant definition. The schema binder $SB$ abstracts over products, i.e. $SB\, f\, x\, y.\, e$ is semantically equivalent to $\lambda\, (f, x, y).\, e$. The body of the abstraction is a boolean term, where $|$ - - - is used to provide more syntactic similarity to the Z notation. Semantically, it denotes a conjunction. Set constructors such as $\rightarrowtail$ are defined in an Isabelle theory that represents the Mathematical Tool-Kit of Z.

A second distinguishing feature of the encoding is to preserve the structure of specifications, because constants are defined for schema representing functions, and schema references refer to these constants. Other encodings expand all schema references to the defining predicates, thereby flattening specifications, which makes structured reasoning about specifications impossible. A detailed comparison of $\mathcal{HOL}\text{-}\mathcal{Z}$ with other encodings of Z in given in [9].

# 3 An Example Specification: Collections

The specification of one class of a practically used software product — the Eiffel Base Libraries [14] — serves us as a running example. The Eiffel Base Libraries cover several hundred classes designed for reuse. One cluster of the Base Libraries, the data structure library, contains implementations of fundamental data structures and algorithms. These are organized in a hierarchy of abstractions described by abstract classes that are related by inheritance. One of the most abstract of these classes describes *collections*. They are a common abstraction of container structures, such as sets, bags, and lists. We use a slightly simplified version of this class to illustrate the problems of specifying classes in a model-based way and representing such specifications in higher-order logic.

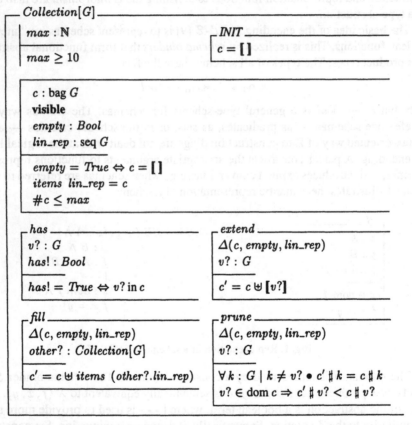

**Fig. 2.** Specification of class *Collection*.

Figure 2 shows a specification of the class *Collection* in an object-oriented extension of Z. The syntax of the specification is similar to the one of Object-Z [4], but we do not attempt to construct an encoding of that language. Instead, we concentrate on concepts that are common to most object-oriented extensions of Z. Semantic intricacies distinguishing between these are of no importance for this paper. Furthermore, we consider only value semantics, i.e. we do not introduce object identities and references to objects in our encoding.

A collection is a mutable container structure storing a number of items of a set $G$. It can be tested whether a collection is empty and whether it contains a given item. A collection can be extended by a single item or the items of another collection, and conversely, items can be removed from a collection. The attribute *lin_rep* gives access to a representation of the collection as a sequence.

The constituents of the class specification are gathered in a *class schema* called *Collection[G]*. The parameter indicates that the class is generic in a set $G$ of items.

The first component of the class schema is an axiomatic box, introducing a constant *max*, which is a natural number greater than or equal to 10. The large, unnamed schema below the axiomatic box is a *state schema*. It describes the valid states of the objects of the class, including attributes of the objects that are accessible from the outside. The first component $c$ of the state is the mathematical model of a collection, a bag.

Bags are defined relationally in the Z Mathematical Tool-Kit [20] by partial functions from the set of items $G$ to the positive natural numbers, bag $G == G \nrightarrow \mathbb{N}_1$. Bags are formed using double brackets, $[v_1, \ldots, v_n]$, the membership test for bags is ($v$ in $c$), $b \uplus d$ is the union of two bags, and $b \sharp v$ is the number of $v$'s in $b$. The function *items* maps sequences to bags.

In contrast to $c$, which is not accessible from outside of the class, the state components below the keyword **visible** are externally visible attributes of collection objects. Visible state components are a notational abbreviation for methods returning values that depend only on the internal state of an object. The predicate below the horizontal line of the state schema is the *state invariant*. It describes the relationship between the state components of valid objects.

The state of an object consists of the hidden and visible parts of the signature of the state schema, and it also contains the constants defined in an axiomatic box. Each object of class *Collection* contains a component *max*. This component cannot be changed by method applications, but the values of *max* may be different for different objects.

The schema *INIT* describes the valid initial states of objects: the container $c$ is initially empty, and, because the state invariant is implicitly required by *INIT*, *empty* = *True* and *lin_rep* = $\langle \rangle$.

The other schemas of *Collection* specify the methods of the class. Like in plain Z, input and output variables are decorated with question marks and exclamation marks, respectively. Undecorated variables refer to the state of the object before executing the method (*pre-state*), primed variables to the state after executing the method (*post-state*). Unlike operation schemas of plain Z, the method schemas of a class *implicitly* refer to the state schema, and the notation $\Delta(x, y, z)$ is used to indicate that the method may change only the state components $x$, $y$, and $z$.

Method schemas denote *relations* between the input values and pre-state, and the output values and post-state, which are, in general, nondeterministic. For example, *prune* is specified to remove a positive number of $v?$'s from the collection, $c' \sharp v? < c \sharp v?$, but nothing is said about the exact number of removed items, and each invocation of *prune* may behave differently in this respect.

In plain Z, schemas describe sets of bindings, i.e. named tuples. The interpretation of certain schemas as describing a system state or operations upon it, and the interpretation of variable decorations are merely notational conventions. There is no semantic notion of a "system description" in Z. Which schema of a specification describes a state, and which schemas describe the possible operations on that state, has to be made clear at an informal level of description. Consequently, there is no truly formal definition of relations between systems, such as refinement.[1]

Extending Z by the concept of a class offers a more economic notation. On the other hand, it also forces us to give explicit semantics to these conventions:

1. Different types of schemas have to be distinguished in the semantics. Operation schemas refer to two copies of the system state, the pre- and the post-state, and to input and output variables, which must also be reflected semantically. Operation schemas are defined in Sect. 4.
2. Grouping state and operation schemas into a class schema allows us to formally define the behavior described by a class specification. We describe the problems of introducing a modularization concept in a shallow encoding and propose a pragmatic solution in Sect. 5.
3. Interpreting class schemas as describing sets of objects (not just "abstract machines") makes them first-class citizens: classes can be referred to in declarations as describing sets of objects with associated behavior. A trace semantics of classes is defined in Sect. 6, from which the set of objects described by a class is derived.
4. Methods combining an object with another of the same class frequently occur in object-oriented designs. Their specification leads to recursively defined class schemas. The input parameter *other*? of method *fill* in Fig. 2 is meant to be an object of class *Collection*, which in turn is defined using *fill*. A fixpoint construction is used to describe the semantics of recursive class definitions in Sect. 7.

Related work is discussed in Sect. 8. In Sect. 9 we draw some conclusions, and mention open problems and further research.

## 4  Types of schemas

We first introduce type synonyms to distinguish between the different components of a class schema. The basic idea here is to partition the signature of a schema according to the role of its components. Like the entire signature of a schema in $\mathcal{HOL}\text{-}\mathcal{Z}$, the members of each partition are gathered in a product type.

The distinction between the hidden and the visible components of a state is realized by providing methods to read the visible components when encoding the class. The encoding of the state schema does not reflect the roles of state components. It is just an ordinary schema, and its type is a function to boolean values.

$$\sigma \ stateschema \stackrel{\text{syn}}{=} \sigma \rightarrow bool$$

The signature of an operation schema has four components: the pre- and post-states, and the input and output parameters.

$$(\sigma, \iota, \omega) \ opschema \stackrel{\text{syn}}{=} [\sigma, \sigma, \iota, \omega] \rightarrow bool \tag{1}$$

Based on these definitions, it is possible to define operators of the schema calculus, e.g., the $\Delta$-operator producing a relation between pre- and post-states, which is not

---

[1] In books about Z, e.g. [20], a notion of data refinement is described, but it refers to extra-logical quantifications like "for each operation" that are not reflected in the semantics of Z.

$$State\ G\ ==\ SB\ max.\ SB\ c\ empty\ lin\_rep.$$

$$c : bag\ G \wedge empty : Bool \wedge lin\_rep : seq\ G$$

$$|\ ---$$

$$empty = True \Leftrightarrow c = [\ ] \wedge$$

$$items\ lin\_rep = c \wedge$$

$$\#c \leq max$$

**Fig. 3.** Representation of the state schema of *Collection*.

possible in $\mathcal{HOL}$-$\mathcal{Z}$.

$$\Delta\ ::\ \sigma\ stateschema \rightarrow [\sigma, \sigma] \rightarrow bool$$
$$\Delta\ S\ ==\ \lambda\ s\ s'.\ (S\ s) \wedge (S\ s')$$

We can now define representations of constant definitions, state, initialization, and simple operation schemas. Figure 3 shows the representation of the state schema of *Collection*. The schema is parameterized with the parameter $G$ of the class and the constant $max$. These parameters are used to ensure that schemas of a class definition refer to the same constants and class parameters.

## 5 Modularization

The transition from single, unrelated schemas to a collection of schemas in a class schema contradicts our wish to stay with a shallow encoding and exploit the strong type system of higher-order logic. The representation of a class schema should basically be a quadruple $(C, S, I, M)$, where $C$, $S$, and $I$ are the constant definition, state and initialization schemas, respectively. The last component $M$ should be a collection of the operation schemas specifying the methods of the class.

Although all operation schemas have a common type scheme, $(\sigma, \iota, \omega)opschema$, the concrete types of different operations, in general, differ in the types of inputs, $\iota$, and outputs, $\omega$. An ad hoc solution could be to make $M$ a tuple of operation schemas, similar to the construction of schema signatures in $\mathcal{HOL}$-$\mathcal{Z}$. This representation would immediately give a shallow encoding of modules. Unfortunately, important concepts on classes would not be definable in such an encoding. Examples are the set of traces induced by a class (which we will define in Sect. 6), or the refinement of a class by another one. Definitions of these concepts must refer to each single operation of a class or even relate the operations of two classes.

A theoretically elegant solution would probably use a type theory that is more expressive than HOL and use dependent types, or, loosing the supporting effect of a type system in proofs, it could resort to an untyped theory, such as Zermelo-Frænkel set theory. However, we wish to practically work with concrete specifications using the tool Isabelle/HOL and build on the work invested in $\mathcal{HOL}$-$\mathcal{Z}$. Therefore, we adopt the following pragmatic approach:

In a concrete software development, only a finite number of classes has to be considered. For these, we can construct a sum type incorporating all types of inputs and outputs of all defined operations of all classes.[2] We can then transform an operation schema to a *method schema* by injecting the inputs and outputs of the operation into the sum type. The method schemas of a class can be collected in an algebraic data type, because they have identical types. To distinguish applications of a method schema to valid input and output values from applications to values that are not in the range of the injection, i.e. "impossible" arguments to the transformed operation, the result type of method schemas is an *optional* boolean. More specifically, we use a type of optional values

$$\text{datatype } \alpha \text{ option} = None \mid Some \; \alpha$$

that comes with the standard distribution of Isabelle/HOL. Based on this type, we define a type of pseudo-partial functions whose domains are described by predicates.

$$\alpha \rightarrowtail \beta \stackrel{\text{syn}}{=} \alpha \rightarrow (\beta \text{ option})$$

$$Opt \;::\; [\alpha \rightarrow \beta, \alpha \rightarrow bool] \rightarrow \alpha \rightarrowtail \beta$$

$$Opt == (\lambda f \; P \; x. \; if \; (Px) \; then \; Some \; (f \; x) \; else \; None)$$

$$Def \;::\; [\alpha \rightarrowtail \beta, \alpha] \rightarrow bool$$

$$Def == (\lambda f \; x.(f \; x) \neq None)$$

$$Val \;::\; [\alpha \rightarrowtail \beta, \alpha] \rightarrow \beta$$

$$Val == (\lambda f \; x.case \; f \; x \; of \; None => \underline{a} \mid Some(y) => y)$$

The expression $(Val \; (Opt \; f \; P) \; x)$ is equal to $(f \; x)$ if $(P \; x)$ holds. Otherwise, it denotes an arbitrary value. The function $(Def \; g)$ describes the "domain" of $g$, i.e., $(Def \; (Opt \; f \; P)) = P$. A method schema is a partial function mapping *pairs* of inputs and outputs to relations on states

$$(\sigma, \iota, \omega) methodschema \stackrel{\text{syn}}{=} (\iota * \omega) \rightarrowtail ([\sigma, \sigma] \rightarrow bool)$$

A pair of input and output parameters is the first argument of a method schema. This models that definedness[3] of the predicate relating input, output, pre- and post-states depends on input and output parameters simultaneously, and that it is independent of the pre- and post-states. The structure of this type considerably simplifies reasoning about method schemas, e.g., compared with the type $[\sigma, \sigma, \iota] \rightarrowtail \omega \rightarrowtail bool$, which would directly correspond to the type of operation schemas (1).

The function *LiftIO* transforms an operation schema into a method schema using two injection functions *InjI* and *InjO*. The domain of the method schema is the product of the ranges of the two injection functions.

$$LiftIO \;::\; [(\sigma, \iota, \omega) opschema, \iota \rightarrow \hat{\iota}, \omega \rightarrow \hat{\omega}]$$
$$\rightarrow (\sigma, \hat{\iota}, \hat{\omega}) methodschema$$
$$LiftIO \; OP \; InjI \; InjO == Opt \; (\lambda \; (inp, out) \; s \; s'. \; OP \; s \; s' \; inp \; out)$$
$$(\lambda \; (inp, out). \; inp : (range \; InjI) \wedge out : (range \; InjO))$$

If the parameters to *LiftIO* are proper injection functions, i.e., if they are injective, then a method application is equivalent to the corresponding operation application, where *ValMeth* is the obvious extension of *Val* to method schemas.

---

[2] Constructing a different sum type for each class looses too much information to define refinement, which relates the types of input and output parameters of methods of different classes.

[3] Not to be confused with membership in the domain of a Z function.

$inj\ InjI \wedge inj\ InjO \Rightarrow$
$ValMeth\ (LiftIO\ OP\ InjI\ InjO)\ s\ s'\ (InjI\ inp)\ (InjO\ out) = (OP\ s\ s'\ inp\ out)$

This lemma guarantees that the intended conversion to method schemas, where the input and output parameters are injected into a sum type, does not loose information.

## 5.1 Class Schemas

We define *class schemas* by a type abstraction. A class schema consists of four components: the constant definition $C$, state schema $S$, initialization schema $I$, and a finite mapping $M$ from some type $\alpha$ of identifiers to method schemas. The initialization and all methods of a class must establish the state invariant $S$.

$$(\alpha, \kappa, \sigma, \hat{\iota}, \hat{\omega})\ classschema \stackrel{abs}{=}$$
$$\{(C, S, I, M)\ |$$
$$C :: \kappa \rightarrow bool$$
$$S :: [\kappa, \sigma] \rightarrow bool$$
$$I :: [\kappa, \sigma] \rightarrow bool \qquad\qquad (2)$$
$$M :: (\alpha, (\kappa, \sigma, \hat{\iota}, \hat{\omega})\ cmethodschema)\ finmap.$$
$$(\forall c\ s.\ (C\ c) \wedge (I\ c\ s) \Rightarrow (S\ c\ s)) \wedge$$
$$(\forall n : (dom_m\ M).\forall c\ s\ s'\ i\ o.\ (C\ c) \wedge DefMeth\ ((M \uparrow_m n)\ c)\ i\ o\ \wedge$$
$$ValMeth\ ((M \uparrow_m n)\ c)\ s\ s'\ i\ o \Rightarrow (S\ c\ s) \wedge (S\ c\ s'))\}$$

Isabelle forces us to prove that the type is well-defined, i.e., that the representing set is non-empty.

Given the sum type of all relevant input and output types, it is possible to collect operation schemas in a container type by lifting them to method schemas. Since is it notationally convenient to have identifiers of some type $\alpha$ for methods, e.g. to define "signature morphisms" between classes, we use the type *finmap* of finite mappings.

Based on the pair of functions embedding the type *classschema* in its representing set, functions to construct class schemas and to select components of them are easily defined: $(primclass\ C\ S\ I)$ is a class schema without methods, and $Cls \boxplus (id, (OP, InjI, InjO))$ transforms an operation $OP$ via $InjI$ and $InjO$ into a method schema, and adds the result under name $id$ to the class schema $Cls$. The selector functions $cma$, $sma$, $ima$, and $mths$ return the constant definition, state and init schemas, and the mapping to method schemas, respectively, which is illustrated by the following theorem:

$$Rep\_classschema\ Cls = (cma\ Cls, sma\ Cls, ima\ Cls, mths\ Cls)$$

The construction so far allows us to represent all but the method *fill* of *Collection* by the class schema *Coll*, which is shown in Fig. 4. This class schema is built from the primitive class containing the constant definition, state and init schemas, by successively adding the operation schemas. The operator $\boxplus$ takes a pair of an identifier — we use strings — and operation schemas with the appropriate injections into the sum type used as a uniform representation of input and output values. The methods *empty* and *lin_rep* represent the visible attributes of *Collection* (cf. Sect. 4). The corresponding operations take no input and do not change the state. They only copy a state component to their output.

$$Coll\ G == (primclass\ (Const\ G)\ (State\ G)\ (Init\ G))$$
$$\boxplus\ ("empty", empty\ G, iounit, iobool)$$
$$\boxplus\ ("lin\_rep", lin\_rep\ G, iounit, ioseq)$$
$$\boxplus\ ("has", has\ G, iopoly, iobool)$$
$$\boxplus\ ("extend", extend\ G, iopoly, iounit)$$
$$\boxplus\ ("put", put\ G, iopoly, iounit)$$
$$\boxplus\ ("prune", prune\ G, iopoly, iounit))$$

**Fig. 4.** Representation of *Collection* without *fill* by a class schema.

# 6 Traces and Objects

In the example specification of Fig. 2, the name of the class *Collection* is used in the definition of the method *fill*. This raises two questions: first, what does a reference to a class identifier in a predicate mean? Second, what is the semantics of a recursive class definition where the class is used to define the predicates of its methods? In this section, we address the first question. Section 7 is concerned with recursive classes.

Informally, a membership proposition like *other*? : *Collection*[*G*] in *fill* means that *other*? denotes an *object* of the class *Collection*[*G*]. Objects have a state consisting of the constants and the state components of the corresponding class definition. In addition to fulfilling the properties specified for the constants and the state invariant, the state of an object must be reachable from a valid initial state by a finite number of method applications. This leads us to interpret references to class identifiers in predicates as the sets of object states consisting of the last items of all finite traces induced by the methods of the class.

The traces of objects induced by a class schema are sequences of object states that, starting with a state satisfying the initialization schema, are obtained by a finite number of method applications. The states in the trace are annotated with the name of the method and the input and output parameters used to reach that state. The type of traces is therefore a list of tuples describing such "messages" to an object and the resulting states.

$$(\alpha, \kappa, \sigma, \hat{\imath}, \hat{\omega})\ trace \stackrel{\text{syn}}{=} (\alpha * (\kappa * \sigma) * \hat{\imath} * \hat{\omega})\ list$$

The function *Traces* yields the set of traces induced by a class schema.

$$Traces :: (\alpha, \kappa, \sigma, \hat{\imath}, \hat{\omega})\ classschema \rightarrow (\alpha, \kappa, \sigma, \hat{\imath}, \hat{\omega})\ trace\ set \qquad (3)$$

We use Isabelle's package for inductive definitions [16] to define the set of traces (*Traces Cls*) for a class schema *Cls*.

```
inductive (Traces Cls)
intrs
initr   [[ cma Cls c; ima Cls c s ]] ⟹ [(a, (c, s), a, a)] : (Traces Cls)
methtr [[ tr : (Traces Cls); n : dom_m (mths Cls);
          DefMeth (((mths Cls) ↑_m n) (const_tr tr)) inp out;
          ValMeth (((mths Cls) ↑_m n) (const_tr tr)) (state_tr tr) s' inp out ]]
        ⟹ tr ⌢ [(n, (const_tr tr, s'), inp, out)] : (Traces Cls)
```

$$fill\ G == \lambda\ OBJ.\ SB\ max.$$

$$SB\ c\ empty\ lin\_rep.\ SB\ c'\ empty'\ lin\_rep'.\ SB\ otherI.SB\ outO.$$
$$(\Delta\ (State\ G\ max)(c, empty, lin\_rep)(c', empty', lin\_rep'))\ \wedge$$
$$otherI : OBJ$$
$$|\ ---$$
$$c' = c \uplus items\ (lin\_rep\ otherI)$$

$$CollectR\ G == \lambda\ OBJ.\ (Coll\ G)\ \boxplus\ ("fill", fill\ G\ OBJ, iocollection, iounit)$$
$$CollectObj\ G == lfp\ (Objects \circ Traces \circ (CollectR\ G))$$
$$Collection\ G == CollectR\ G\ CollectObj$$

**Fig. 5.** Fixpoint construction to represent *Collection*.

Two introduction rules define this set. The first, *initr*, states that all singleton traces with constants $c$ satisfying the constant definition and states $s$ satisfying the init schema are traces of *Cls*.

The second rule, *methtr*, defines how traces are extended: a trace $tr$ can be extended by a new item $(n, (const\_tr\ tr, s'), inp, out)$ provided that $n$ is the name of a method of *Cls*, that this method, $(mths\ Cls) \uparrow_m n$, is defined for input $inp$ and output $out$, and that it relates the last state reached by $tr$, $state\_tr\ tr$, to state $s'$ via input $inp$ and output $out$.

Processing this definition, Isabelle automatically converts the introduction rules to a fixpoint definition of $(Traces\ Cls)$, establishes the existence of the fixpoint and derives an induction rule for this set.

The object states reachable by a set of traces are the pairs of constants and states contained in the last item of a trace.

$$Objects\ ::\ (\alpha, \kappa, \sigma, \hat{\imath}, \hat{\omega})\ trace\ set \to (\kappa * \sigma)\ set$$
$$Objects\ tr == \{(const\_tr\ t, state\_tr\ t)\ |\ t.\ t : tr\}$$

With these definitions, the set of objects defined by a class schema *Cls* is given by

$$(Objects\ (Traces\ Cls)) \tag{4}$$

# 7 Recursive Class Definitions

The class schema representing *Collection* and the induced set of objects depend on each other, because the method *fill* refers to the set of objects defined by *Collection*. It is therefore not possible to follow the construction described in the preceeding sections sequentially, building a class schema for *Collection* first, and constructing the induced set of objects afterwards. Instead, the fixpoint construction shown in Fig. 5 leads to a representation of *Collection*:

Functions in the set *OBJ* of object states model the component schemas that recursively refer to the class, *fill* in our case. Combining these functions leads to a class schema $(CollectR\ G)$ that is parameterized with a set of object states. Using the construction (4), we obtain a function on object states. The least fixpoint $(CollectObj\ G)$ of this function is the set of object states defined by *Collection*. Finally, the class schema representing *Collection*[G] is given by $(CollectR\ G\ CollectObj)$.

The fixpoint construction succeeds if the component schemas are monotonic in the sets of objects they depend on. This condition does not restrict the practical use of the construction because classes are naturally referred to in membership propositions representing Z declarations, which occur only at positive positions in schema predicates.

The rest of this section describes the fixpoint semantics of recursive classes in detail. We will first introduce orders on method schemas and class schemas. In Sect. 7.2, the general fixpoint construction is described.

## 7.1 Orders

The construction of the fixpoint semantics of classes relies on two powerful tools provided by Isabelle/HOL: the package of inductive set definitions [16], and axiomatic type classes [24].

Inductive set definitions are realized by fixpoint constructions on the lattice of powersets. The package relies on a theory of monotonic functions on *sets*, with respect to the subset ordering, and a derivation of the Knaster-Tarski fixpoint theorem. Unfortunately, this theory is specialized for the set theoretic case, and no general theory of orders and monotonic functions is developed. To construct on order on method schemas, we have complemented the order theory on sets by a more general theory of orders based on axiomatic type classes.

Isabelle's type classes allow one to restrict the instantiation of type variables to types of a particular class. *Axiomatic* type classes associate axioms with type classes. Consequently, instantiating an axiomatic type class with a type is only possible if the associated axioms can be proven for all members of the type. Furthermore, abstract reasoning about the relations between type classes is possible.

The standard distribution of Isabelle/HOL contains a theory of orders defining the axiomatic type class *order*. It turned out to be remarkably simple to combine this theory with the fixpoint theory on sets: identifying the two different symbols for orders of the two theories and proving that the subset relation satisfies the order axioms was all we had to do.

The theories of the standard distribution also define the canonical extension of orders to function spaces and prove abstractly that these are indeed orders. Using these type classes, it only remains to show how orders are induced on optional types.

$$x \leq y == case \ x \ of \ None \ => \ True \ | \\ Some(a) \ => \ (case \ y \ of \ None \ => \ False \ | \ Some(b) \ => \ a \leq b)$$

Isabelle's type checker derives that there exists an order on method schemas, i.e. $(\sigma, \iota, \omega) \ methodschema \ :: \ order$ for arbitrary types $\sigma$, $\iota$, and $\omega$. The induced order is made explicit by the following theorem:

$$M \leq M' = \forall inp \ out. \ Def \ M \ (inp, out) \Rightarrow \\ Def \ M' \ (inp, out) \land \\ (\forall s \ s'. \ ValMeth \ M \ s \ s' \ inp \ out \Rightarrow ValMeth \ M' \ s \ s' \ inp \ out)$$

Finally, an order on class schemas is defined componentwise, additionally requiring that the sets of method names in both classes are equal.

## 7.2 Fixpoints

Given a class schema $(Cls\ OBJ)$ that is parameterized with a set of objects, we wish to construct a solution to the equation

$$OBJ = ((Objects \circ Traces \circ Cls)\ OBJ$$

By the Knaster-Tarski theorem,

$$mono\ f \Rightarrow (lfp\ f) = f\ (lfp\ f) \tag{5}$$

where

$$lfp\ ::\ (\alpha\ set \to \alpha\ set) \to \alpha\ set$$
$$lfp\ f\ ==\ \bigcap\{u \mid (f\ u) \subseteq u\}$$

the set of objects induced by $Cls$ is given by $(lfp\ (Objects \circ Traces \circ Cls))$, provided that the argument to $lfp$ is monotonic.[4]

Since $Objects$ is trivially monotonic, and the monotonicity of $Traces$ can be shown by induction, the following theorems show that the monotonicity of the components of a class schema is sufficient to guarantee that our fixpoint construction succeeds:

$$mono\ f \Rightarrow mono\ (Objects \circ Traces \circ f)$$
$$mono\ C \wedge mono\ S \wedge mono\ I \Rightarrow mono\ (\lambda\ x.\ primclass\ (C\ x)\ (S\ x)\ (I\ x))$$
$$mono\ Cls \wedge mono\ Op \Rightarrow mono\ (\lambda\ x.\ (Cls\ x) \boxplus (n, Op\ x, injI, injO))$$

A tactic uses these theorems to reduce the monotonicity requirement to monotonicity conditions on predicates, which it proves using rules about orders. For typical class schemas, such as $Collection$, the tactic works fully automatically.

The fixpoint construction presented here can be extended to deal with systems of mutually recursive classes in the usual way. Logically, a general fixpoint theory of complete lattices has to be introduced to establish that products of complete lattices (powersets in our application) are complete lattices, and to define the least fixpoint for product lattices. This extension of the theory is based on an axiomatic type class of complete lattices that is part of the Isabelle distribution.

## 8 Related Work

Few proof tools for formal specification languages support both abstract reasoning about properties of modules, and working with concrete modules at same time. The theorem prover ERGO [22] is based on Zermelo-Frænkel set theory. It supports the specification language $Sum$ that extends Z by a module concept in the spirit of classes in Object-Z, but these modules are not first-class citizens and the language is not object-oriented. The language of the prover contains features to express relations between modules, e.g. refinement, but these are expanded at the implementation level of the tool. They are not defined in the logical framework of the prover.

Smith [19] introduced the first version of Object-Z, which has a value semantics and does not deal with object identity in the language. He defined a fully abstract model of classes based on a trace semantics. He allows infinite traces to capture liveness properties, which we are not interested in.

---

[4] For a well-written account of fixpoint theory, see [3].

The semantics of full-fledged object-oriented specification languages are a very active research area. Partial solutions exist, e.g. [5,10], but especially mastering the interference of object identity models (using reference semantics), method applications, and recursive class definitions is still an open problem. This is why we chose a value semantics for our encoding.

Sekerinski [18] describes a semantic framework for object-oriented specification languages that is based on the refinement calculus. Objects consist of attributes and methods. They are members of an existential type. A class is described by a pair of the initial values of attributes and predicate transformers representing methods. Thus, classes are no new types but are values of universal types, which is an approach similar to ours. Defining meets and joins of classes, Sekerinski extends the refinement calculus to classes, but he does not consider recursive class definitions, and his work is not aimed at machine support.

In expressive type theories like the *Extended Calculus of Constructions* [13], it is not necessary to construct a uniform type of all operations of a module as we did in Sect. 5. Instead, modules can be represented by existential types. This approach, however, does not allow one to reason abstractly about the components of modules, because this would mean to reason about the object language in the object language itself. Consequently, concepts like signature morphisms and traces cannot be defined at the same level of language at which concrete modules are expressed. Approaches encoding modules by existential types may use reflection principles to develop an abstract theory of module relations [23]. This indicates that some meta-level argument is necessary when dealing with structuring concepts in a strongly typed theory.

# 9 Conclusions

After a general assessment of the encoding, we discuss experience with Isabelle at the technical level and point out directions of future research.

## 9.1 Assessment

To our knowledge, this work is the first attempt to integrate the concept of a class into a shallow encoding of a model-based specification language. The definitions of class schemas and their semantics form an orthogonal extension to the encoding of plain Z in $\mathcal{HOL}$-$\mathcal{Z}$: the language Z can be used in the usual way, and only the operation schemas of a class and schemas derived from them, e.g., operation preconditions, are represented differently. This is not surprising, because the distinction between state and operations is not treated semantically in Z at all. First experiments show that, as one would expect, reducing propositions about concrete classes to proof obligations about predicates in plain Z works quite smoothy. We therefore believe that the theory and the tactical support for Z, which is currently being developed in $\mathcal{HOL}$-$\mathcal{Z}$, can profitably be used to reason about classes.

The tight integration of $\mathcal{HOL}$-$\mathcal{Z}$ with classes is possible, because the theory of classes adheres to the principles of a shallow encoding, using the strong type system of Isabelle/HOL at the object level. The price to pay is the need to construct — at the meta-level — a suitable sum type for the inputs and outputs of each concrete collection of classes one wants to work with (cf. Sect. 5). Because this point is clearly localized in the overall theory, we believe that the practical advantages of working with a shallow encoding in a strong type system, which have already proved valuable for $\mathcal{HOL}\text{-}\mathcal{Z}$, clearly outweigh a theoretical dissatisfaction this approach may leave.

The definition of class schemas is abstract enough to define properties, semantics, and relations on classes in the logic itself. It is therefore possible to relate axiomatic descriptions of such properties, e.g. the "proof obligations" described for data refinements in [20], to semantic models in the same logical framework. In this way, these concepts are *definable* in the logic and do not have to be introduced as meta-predicates that are handled at the level of tactics only.

## 9.2 Technical Experiences

At the technical level, the theory is built so as to rely as much as possible on the standard distribution of Isabelle/HOL. This is possible because the semantic domain of traces is a powerset, and the fixpoint theory of powersets is supported well in the system. In particular, no reasoning about continuity is needed to establish the fixpoints [3].

Combining the powerset theory with the abstract theory of orders, realized as type classes, provides a means to construct a non-trivial theory in an elegant way. Having orders "in the type system", together with the type abstraction of class schemas, avoids explicit assumptions about orders and monotonicity at the logical level. This leads to more compact and readable theorems, and to shorter proofs.

Carrying out the proofs with Isabelle revealed some unexpected problems related to product types: reasoning about patterns and tuples is not supported very well. It is often necessary to instantiate variables for tuples explicitly, and, when dealing with 5-tuples, even this only works by increasing the search bound for higher-order unification. This experience suggests to develop specialized proof support for product types, because reasoning about concrete classes can easily involve products with dozens of components.

## 9.3 Future Work

The theory of classes presented in this paper is a first step toward proof support for object-oriented features in specification languages. To support reasoning about systems of classes, subtyping and behavioral equivalence of classes has to be defined based on the trace semantics presented here. As Liskov and Wing have shown [12], a notion of subtyping based only on the traces induced by the methods of a class is too restrictive to take "extra methods" into account. Future work will extend, and provide tactics to prove subtyping relations.

**Acknowledgments.** I thank Maritta Heisel for comments on several of this paper. The constructive and detailed comments of the referees helped improve the presentation. This work has been supported by the German Federal Ministry of Education, Science, Research and Technology (BMBF), under grant 01 IS 509 C6 (ESPRESS).

# References

1. J.-R. Abrial. *The B-Book: Assigning programs to meanings.* Cambridge University Press, 1996.
2. M. Broy and S. Jähnichen, editors. *KORSO: Methods, Languages, and Tools to Construct Correct Software.* LNCS 1009. Springer Verlag, 1995.

3. B. A. Davey and H. A. Priestley. *Introduction to Lattices and Order*. Cambridge University Press, 1990.
4. R. Duke, G. Rose, and G. Smith. Object-Z: A specification language advocated for the description of standards. *Computer Standards & Interfaces*, 17:511–533, 1995.
5. A. Griffiths. An extended semantic foundation for Object-Z. In *Asia-Pacific Software Engineering Conference*, pages 194–205. Springer Verlag, 1996.
6. S. Helke, T. Neustupny, and T. Santen. Automating test case generation from Z specifications with Isabelle. In J. Bowen, M. Hinchey, and D. Till, editors, *ZUM '97: The Z Formal Specification Notation*, LNCS 1212, pages 52–71. Springer Verlag, 1997.
7. C. B. Jones. *Systematic Software Development using VDM*. Prentice Hall, 2nd edition, 1990.
8. Ed. Kazmierczak, P. Kearney, O. Traynor, and Li Wand. A modular extension to Z for specification, reasoning and refinement. SVCR, Dept. of Computer Science, The University of Queensland, 1995.
9. Kolyang, T. Santen, and B. Wolff. A structure preserving encoding of Z in Isabelle/HOL. In J. von Wright, J. Grundy, and J. Harrison, editors, *Theorem Proving in Higher-Order Logics*, LNCS 1125, pages 283–298. Springer Verlag, 1996.
10. K. Lano. *Formal Object-Oriented Development*. Springer Verlag, 1995.
11. K. Lano and H. Haughton, editors. *Object-Oriented Specification Case Studies*. Prentice Hall, 1993.
12. B. Liskov and J. Wing. A behavioral notion of subtyping. *ACM Transactions on Programming Languages and Systems*, 16(6):1811–1841, 1994.
13. Zhaohui Luo. Program specification and data refinement in type theory. In S. Abramsky and T. S. E. Maibaum, editors, *Int. Joint Conference on Theory and Practice of Software Development (TAPSOFT)*, LNCS 493, pages 143–168, 1991.
14. B. Meyer. *Reusable Software*. Prentice Hall, 1994.
15. J. Nicholls. Z Notation – version 1.2. Draft ISO standard, 1995.
16. L. C. Paulson. A fixedpoint approach to implementing (co)inductive definitions. In A. Bundy, editor, *Proc. 12th Conference on Automated Deduction*, LNAI 814, pages 148–161. Springer Verlag, 1994.
17. L. C. Paulson. *Isabelle – A Generic Theorem Prover*. LNCS 828. Springer Verlag, 1994.
18. E. Sekerinski. *Verfeinerung in der objektorientierten Programmkonstruktion*. PhD thesis, Universität Karlsruhe, 1994.
19. G. P. Smith. *An Object-Oriented Approach to Formal Specification*. PhD thesis, University of Queensland, 1992.
20. J. M. Spivey. *The Z Notation – A Reference Manual*. Prentice Hall, 2nd edition, 1992.
21. S. Stepney, R. Barden, and D. Cooper, editors. *Object-Orientation in Z*, Workshops in Computing. Springer Verlag, 1992.
22. M. Utting and K. Whitewell. Ergo user manual. Technical Report 93–19, Software Verification Research Centre, Dept. of Computer Science, University of Queensland, 1994.
23. F. W. von Henke, A. Dold, H. Rueß, D. Schwier, and M. Strecker. Construction and deduction methods for the formal development of software. In Broy and Jähnichen [2], pages 239–254.
24. M. Wenzel. Using axiomatic type classes in Isabelle. Distributed with the Isabelle system, 1995.

# Proof Presentation for Isabelle

Martin Simons

GMD Research Institute for
Computer Architecture and Software Technology
and
Technische Universität Berlin
Forschungsgruppe Softwaretechnik*

**Abstract.** We present an approach to the intelligible communication of formal proofs. Observing a close correspondence between the activities of formal-proof development and program development, and using this as a guideline, we apply well-known principles from program design to proof design and presentation, resulting in formal proofs presented in a literate style, that are hierarchically structured and emphasize calculation. We illustrate the practicability of this approach by describing its instantiation to the case of the interactive theorem prover Isabelle and by presenting a proof of the Church-Rosser theorem.

## 1 Introduction

Formal-proof systems have long been studied as part of mathematical logic, but they were not originally intended for actual use in carrying out standard mathematical proofs. With the advent of powerful and sophisticated implementations of logics, formal reasoning in general and formal proofs in particular are becoming relevant and accessible to other fields that use and rely on mathematical reasoning techniques. Though the use of formalisms enables formal proofs to be found and checked with the help of the computer, such proofs have one serious defect: they are overburdened by large amounts of technical detail and by the idiosyncrasies of the underlying formal systems. This *formal noise* obscures the basic line of reasoning and hinders human comprehension. There is evidently a wide gap, then, between formal proofs and conventional mathematical proofs, whose essential purpose — in addition to establishing the truth of propositions — is to provide insight and understanding. One may argue that it is not worthwhile trying to understand a formal proof at all, once it has been machine-checked for correctness. This is certainly the case where proofs are technical and tedious and fail to offer any insights; and we would be happy to leave the verification of such arguments to the machine. But in other cases, a formal proof — just as its informal counterpart — carries important information that we would like to communicate. Our approach to proof presentation is guided by an analogy relating the activities of proving and programming[1]: developing a program from a specification is very much like developing a proof for a theorem. By following this analogy, we apply techniques and principles known from

---

\* TU Berlin, Forschungsgruppe Softwaretechnik (FR5-6), Franklinstr. 28/29, D-10587 Berlin.
e-mail: simons@cs.tu-berlin.de

[1] Not to be confused with the "propositions-as-types" and "proofs-as-objects" principle underlying the use of type theories as logical frameworks and the extraction of programs from proofs.

program design to proof design and presentation. Most important, we apply the principle of refinement to proofs. Refinement has been used as both an informal and a formal abstraction principle to control complexity and to structure and guide the process of programming. By transferring the refinement paradigm to formal proof design, we show how we arrive at *literate* and *hierarchically structured* formal proofs, which are presented at different levels of abstractions.

We outline in Section 2 our general approach to presenting formal proofs. We then describe in Section 3 its instantiation to Isabelle, and the architecture of the tool support we developed. We assume that the reader is familiar with the generic theorem prover Isabelle (Paulson 1994) and with expressing proofs in higher-order logic. In Section 4, we present selected parts of a proof of the Church-Rosser theorem formalized in Isabelle, and we contrast the key formal proof with a proof taken from a journal publication. We conclude the paper with a brief discussion and an overview of related work.

## 2 A General Approach to Presenting Formal Proofs

The metaphor underlying our approach is that developing formal proofs is like developing programs. We should expect methods and techniques developed for the presentation of programs to be adaptable to formal proofs. The approach can best be described by distinguishing three aspects that influence proof presentation. The first relates to the local and global structure of a proof; the second to the underlying language in which formal proofs are expressed; and the third to human-oriented issues in the presentation of proofs, which we should not attempt to formalize, but which can still be machine-supported. Note that we are attempting to narrow the gap between formal and informal proofs, while retaining the ability to have the correctness of the formal proof checked by a machine. This accounts for some of the compromises we have been forced to make. Furthermore, note that presenting a proof — formal or informal — implies having already found it. In other words, we are not concerned with documenting the discovery and production of a proof, including every failed attempt or dead-end encountered — although, in certain situations, this may make sense for didactic purposes.

*Structure.* The global organization and structure of a formal development has a decisive influence on comprehensibility. The technique of stepwise refinement has been proposed to break down the complexity of large programs and keep them intellectually manageable. The situation with proofs is similar: a proof is a hierarchically structured argument. The hierarchical structure makes explicit dependencies between the arguments in a proof. In fact, one of the major difficulties with badly structured arguments in informal essay-like proofs is untangling the dependencies, i.e. understanding which hypotheses are valid at which points in the argument. Not infrequently, confusing these dependencies during proof development is the cause of faulty proofs. This observation has led to the emergence of more rigorous and disciplined proof styles. Notable examples include Jones' (1990) "boxed proofs" or Lamport's (1994) "structured proofs". These styles emphasize the hierarchical structure of an argument and make its structure explicit in the presentation. They can be seen as implementing Gentzen's *natural* deduction on a rigorous and nonformal level. A key element of a hierarchical proof style is a method for decomposing a proof step into substeps, and an accompanying numbering scheme for labeling and referencing substeps.

We contend that hierarchical structuring can be adapted to the presentation of formal proofs: on the highest level, a formal proof can remain sketchy, with more detail being added the lower one gets in the hierarchy. Hierarchical structuring, besides structuring the proof process for the developer of a proof, also helps the reader, who can only cope with a limited amount of detail at any one time. The only difference between a good informal and formal proof should be that the formal one requires more levels of detail. In fact, with advances in automated theorem-proving technology, it will become increasingly possible to leave proofs of lower levels entirely to the machine. A mechanical check of the remaining structured decomposition of the proof then guarantees that the decomposition is valid, providing additional assurance to the reader of the proof.

We regard hierarchical structuring as a way to provide the *global* organization of a proof. At the local level, we propose applying, wherever possible, the calculational method of proving. The merits of this simple and compact — yet powerful — form of mathematical reasoning have been recognized and advocated elsewhere (Gasteren 1987, Dijkstra & Scholten 1990, Gries & Schneider 1993, Backhouse 1995). The linear structure of a calculation is easily grasped and understood, and the hints that are interspersed throughout the proof enable the reader to check the argumentation. The effort involved in designing a calculus for a given problem domain always pays off in terms of a better understanding of the problem domain and proofs that are easier to understand. Unlike Gries and Schneider, we contend that calculational reasoning blends easily and naturally with the variants of natural deduction such as the boxed or structured proofs. An analysis of larger calculational proofs from the literature reveals that natural deduction is used — albeit between the lines — to decompose the proof into subproofs, which then, further down the line, are tackled by calculation. When such a proof is formalized, the decomposition must be formalized, too, and structured hierarchical decomposition as outlined above is a natural choice for presenting the resulting proof. Moreover, the hints given in a calculational proof involve further subproofs if the proof is formalized. This further decomposition is in keeping with hierarchical decomposition as it also leads to more detail at lower levels of abstraction.

*Language.* We call a language in which we express formal developments a *proof programming language*. Just as the technical detail contained in a program written in an assembly language hinders comprehensibility, the technical detail contained in a formal proof expressed in a (low-level) formal system does the same. The goal, then, should be to design a *high-level* proof programming language. In order to abstract from uninteresting proof details, a suitable proof programming language should, in our view, offer high-level constructs for the specification and composition of (possibly very complex) proof steps. One way of accomplishing this is to integrate the notion of *proof refinement* into the proof programming language, reflecting the concept of structured proofs at the language level. Integrating refinement into the language would also allow a controlled treatment of *incomplete proofs* with possibly unproven parts. At the very least, a machine would be able to check the refinement down to the parts left unproven. Users should be able to choose incrementally the level of machine-verified certainty they wish to attain for a certain amount of effort. This liberal approach to formal reasoning is, in our view, justified by experience. The success of VDM and Z, for instance, can be attributed, in part at least, to the fact that they do not enforce the discharge of all proof obligations. Their major advantage is that they provide adequate means for formally specifying and developing a system, and for formally reasoning about the system and the development. But it is up to the user to decide if and when the necessary proofs should be carried out. Most current systems for interactive proof construction support the abstraction from proof details via *tactics* and *tacticals*, which can be thought of as forming the elementary building blocks and composition operators of a proof programming language. Integrating refinement into the proof programming language would also enable us to *specify* the effects of tactics in terms of how they behave when applied to a proof state, i.e. a partially refined proof.

*Presentation.* We know from programming that the way we explain something to a machine is probably not the best way to explain it to a human being. Computer programs are quite hard to understand if read or explained from the first to the last line. It makes much more sense to begin by explaining the central component, and then go on to its dependent components, and so forth. In order to reconcile human and machine requirements, Knuth (1984) designed and implemented his WEB system of structured documentation. In his motivation, he states: "Instead of imagining that our main task is to instruct a *computer* what to do, let us concentrate rather on explaining to *human beings* what we want a computer to do." A similar statement should be made with regard to formal proofs: "Instead of imagining that our main task is to explain to a computer why a formal proof is correct, let us concentrate rather on explaining to human beings why it is correct." Such an explanation may — and usually does — use means and devices that are employed in the process of human understanding. Language and notation are used to explain the reasoning; pictures or diagrams provide helpful insights; intuition, association and metaphor may be used to help the reader. As in literate programming, this explanation is locally close to the formal code and may directly relate to it. We therefore propose a literate approach to the presentation of formal proofs that integrates a formal proof and its explanation into a single document. The support of mathematical notation deserves special attention. Well-designed notation plays an important role in the communication of mathematical understanding (Backhouse 1989). There are numerous examples of notation helping to keep complex reasoning concise and abstracting from inessential detail. Besides the integral calculus, the quantifier calculus (Dijkstra & Scholten 1990) is an example of a mathematical calculus with which we are all familiar and which provides essential notational conventions for expressing and manipulating operations over finite and infinite sequences of values. Consequently, a proof programming language must provide means for expressing and dealing with notation, and this notation must be rendered in a familiar style when a proof is presented.

## 3   Presenting Isabelle Proofs

To support the presentation of backward-style Isabelle proofs in accordance with the principles set out in the previous section, we have developed a prototypical set of WEB tools for Isabelle. The overall architecture of the tool support is shown in Figure 1. The tool support consists basically of two components: WEB support built around noweb, and a set of special Isabelle tactics aiding presentation. In order not to interfere with the basic principles for using Isabelle, we have attempted to maintain independence from this system as far as possible, i.e. we have tried to avoid the need to change the source code.

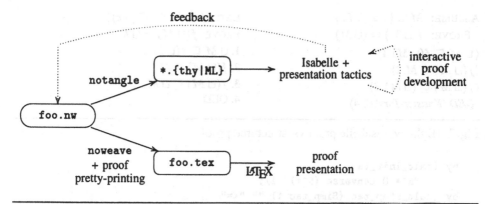

**Fig. 1.** The architecture of the Isabelle support tools

Ramsey's (1994) noweb is a language-independent suite of literate-programming tools. This set of tools realizes only the essential, language-independent parts of a WEB tool, i.e. it allows a document to be structured into code and documentation chunks, and provides means for generating index and cross-reference information. There are no built-in pretty-printing mechanisms. Noweb is, however, designed to be extendible by means of its pipeline architecture. Both of its main components, noweave and notangle, are realized as pipelines of stages, each responsible for a different task. These pipelines can be extended by user-defined stages, as we have done for noweave in order to selectively pretty-print parts of the Isabelle code chunks.

*Structure.* The type of backward Isabelle proof we wish to be able to present is a sequence of top-level tactic applications that transform an initial proof state to a state without any remaining subgoals. Such a backward proof is started by a command that sets up the initial proof state, and terminated by a command that enters the proven theorem and its user-given name into Isabelle's database of theorems. These two commands enclose the sequence of tactic applications that constitute the actual proof. Following the discipline suggested in Section 2, we construct a hierarchical backward proof using WEB's chunking mechanism. For instance, the Isabelle code chunk

```
by (assume_and_prove_tac (all_tac) [(["M=={x.x<=f x}"],"")]
                              "f(Union M) = Union M" 1);
<<"Union M <= f(Union M)">>
<<"f(Union M) : M">>
<<"f(Union M) <= Union M">>
<<QED (Knaster-Tarski)>>
```

— when woven and typeset — is rendered as the Isabelle display shown in Figure 2. Chunks are numbered consecutively for easy reference; cross-reference tables of these sections can be generated automatically. Global structuring is useful when the application of a tactic to the proof state produces multiple new subgoals. Local structuring is applicable when tactics transform single subgoals. General techniques that make the effects of tactics on the proof state visible are discussed below. To present calculational-style reasoning, we have implemented a small set of tactics allowing fairly general calculations. For example, the sequence of tactic applications

ASSUME: $M \equiv \{x.x \sqsubseteq fx\}$
  PROVE: $f(\sqcup M) = (\sqcup M)$
$\langle \sqcup M \sqsubseteq f(\sqcup M) \ 1 \rangle$
$\langle f(\sqcup M) \in M \ 2 \rangle$
$\langle f(\sqcup M) \sqsubseteq (\sqcup M) \ 3 \rangle$
$\langle QED \ (Knaster\text{-}Tarski). \ 4 \rangle$

LET: $M \triangleq \{x : x \sqsubseteq f(x)\}$
PROVE: $f(\sqcup M) = \sqcup M$
1. $\sqcup M \sqsubseteq f(\sqcup M)$.
2. $f(\sqcup M) \in M$.
3. $f(\sqcup M) \sqsubseteq \sqcup M$.
4. QED.

**Fig. 2.** High-level Isabelle proof vs. structured proof

```
by (calc_init_tac
        "R^* O converse (R^*)" 1);
by (calc_step_tac (Simp_tac 1) "" "<="
        "(R^* O converse R^*)^*" 1);
by (calc_step_tac
      (simp_tac ((!simpset) addsimps [Un_rtrancl RS sym]) 1) "" "="
      "(R Un converse R)^*" 1);
by (calc_step_tac
      (asm_full_simp_tac ((!simpset) addsimps [Un_commute]) 1) "" "<="
      "converse (R^*) O R^*" 1);
by (calc_finish_tac 1);
```

which is part of the proof that the Church-Rosser property is equivalent to confluence (see below), is typeset as the calculation in Figure 3.

In general, the tactics operate on the conclusion of a subgoal of the proof state, which is assumed to be of the form *lhs R rhs* for a transitive relation $R$ and terms *lhs* and *rhs*. Two tables of laws — reflexivities and transitivities, indexed by transitive-relation operators — are used to construct the calculation:

$$t \, R \, t \qquad\qquad (\texttt{reflexivities}(R))$$

$$\frac{r \, R' \, s; \quad s \, R \, t}{r \, R \, t} \qquad\qquad (\texttt{transitivities}(R, R'))$$

calc_init_tac *lhs′ i* initiates a calculational proof of subgoal $i$. It generates an auxiliary subgoal *lhs = lhs′* and tries to resolve it with the reflexivity law of equality.

calc_step_tac *tac hint R′ lhs′ i* produces a new step in the calculation of subgoal $i$. It generates an auxiliary subgoal *lhs R′ lhs′* and tries to solve it with *tac*; then, by transitivities$(R, R')$, it yields *lhs′ R rhs* as the new subgoal. The string *hint* is used, if nonempty, as a replacement for *tac* in the pretty-printing of this step.

calc_finish_tac *i* completes the calculation of subgoal $i$. It tries to discharge subgoal $i$ by resolving it with the reflexivity law associated with $R$.

Variants of these three tactics are provided for situations in which it is either not possible or not desirable to extract automatically the main relation operator $R$ from the proof state. These tactics take the intended main relation operation as an additional argument.

*Language.* Isabelle is traditionally theorem-oriented: once a theorem is proven, it is stored and its proof is forgotten. The facilities for constructing new theorems from old ones in a forward manner, and the tactics and tacticals used primarily in backward

$$R^* \circ R^* \cup$$
$\sqsubseteq$   by (Simp_tac 1)
$$(R^* \circ R\cup^*)^*$$
$=$   by (simp_tac ((!simpset) addsimps [Un_rtrancl RS sym]) 1)
$$(R \cup R\cup)^*$$
$\sqsubseteq$   by (asm_full_simp_tac ((!simpset) addsimps [Un_commute]) 1)
$$R^* \cup \circ R^*$$

**Fig. 3.** Calculational Isabelle proof

proofs, are implicit in the sense that they do not explicitly represent the proof. These imperative commands tell Isabelle how to construct a proof, but do not allow conclusions to be drawn about the progress of the deduction or the state of the proof at a particular point. We will describe a partial remedy for this in the next section. Nevertheless, we see the combination of these facilities of Isabelle as an approximation to the higher-order proof programming language envisioned in Section 2. It allows complex reasoning to be expressed concisely and at a quite abstract level. We thus argue — and hope to demonstrate in this paper — that our presentation approach is applicable.

*Presentation.* The Isabelle WEB tools allow Isabelle formalizations to be developed together with their documentation. They generate cross-reference information on code chunks and on the variables used. For pretty-printing Isabelle terms, we have constructed a pretty-printing filter that exploits Isabelle's own pretty-printing mechanism: for each Isabelle theory, we defined a TEX pretty-printing syntax in the form of an associated TEX theory file. When the filter recognizes an Isabelle term, it calls Isabelle's pretty-printing routine with respect to the appropriate TEX theory. The filter also recognizes sections of an Isabelle theory file and typesets them accordingly. Furthermore, it recognizes special directives to typeset lists of theorems stored in Isabelle's database.

Tactic applications typically operate on one of the proof state's subgoals. For interactive use, this is economical and appropriate, since the user is constantly presented with the complete proof state in the form of a numbered list of subgoals. However, no information about the proof state's exact nature is retained, and the sequence of tactic applications that make up a proof is relatively unintelligible to human readers. To present Isabelle proofs, we must therefore make relevant parts of the state visible. To this end, we implemented simple tactics that verify that a subgoal contains certain hypotheses and a certain goal formula, and that are pretty-printed in a certain form.

assume_and_prove_tac *tac assums concl i* verifies that, after applying *tac*, subgoal
  *i* is implied by $\llbracket assums \rrbracket \implies concl$. It is pretty-printed as
  ASSUME: *assums*
    PROVE: *concl*

  *tac* being concealed as it only serves to reorganize the proof state by, say, renaming
  variables. Typically, this tactic initiates a new level of a hierarchical proof.

transform_assum_tac *tac assums i* verifies that, after applying *tac*, subgoal *i* contains each assumption in *assums*. It is pretty-printed as
  by *tac*
  DEDUCE: *assums*

`prove_by_induction_tac` *tac concl txt i* verifies that the conclusion of subgoal *i* is *concl*, and then applies *tac* to the proof state. It is pretty-printed as

PROVE: *concl*

PROOF: *txt*

*tac* being intentionally concealed, since its action is assumed to initiate an induction, the nature of which is explained by *txt*.

# 4 The Church-Rosser Theorem

The Church-Rosser property is one of the fundamental notions of term-rewriting systems. In essence, it captures the uniqueness of normal forms of terms. When implementing rewriting systems, such as functional languages, this property allows us to select the most appropriate of various reduction strategies, such as lazy or strict evaluation, while guaranteeing deterministic behavior. Huet (1980) gives a good overview of results pertaining to Church-Rosser theorems for rewriting systems. This theorem has received wide attention from the theorem-proving community and has served as the subject of various formalization experiments based on different formal frameworks. The main concern of these experiments was, however, the formalization as such, and not its presentation. The proof we are about to present is broadly based on an early version of Nipkow's (1996) Isabelle formalization. The proof itself is a formalization of a proof that was recently given by Takahashi (1995) as a variation on the classic proof that uses the Tait-and-Martin-Löf method (Barendregt 1984). The development of the proof is structured as follows: we first define, in the abstract setting of binary relations, the Church-Rosser property and the equivalent — but easier to prove — notion of confluence. We then go on to define the terms of the lambda calculus and $\beta$-reduction. The proof of the Church-Rosser theorem is finally presented in more or less the same style and order as Takahashi's. We will only present selected parts of the proof. The complete development, which forms the basis of this paper and from which a set of Isabelle theories can be automatically extracted, is given by Simons (1996).

## 4.1 Abstract Definitions and Properties

Let $R$ and $S$ be binary relations. The composition of $R$ and $S$ is denoted by $R \circ S$ and is defined as the set $\{(x, z) . \exists y . (x, y) \in S \wedge (y, z) \in R\}$. The converse of $R$ is denoted by $R\cup$, and its reflexive and transitive closure, closure for short, by $R^*$. Recall that converse commutes with the reflexive transitive closure: $R\cup^* = R^*\cup$. Moreover, let id denote the identity relation; then $R^*$ satisfies the domain equation $R^* = \text{id} \cup (R \circ R^*)$. More precisely, we have the following induction principle for reflexive transitive closures $[\![\text{id} \sqsubseteq S; R \circ S \sqsubseteq S]\!] \implies R^* \sqsubseteq S$ This induction rule is, for example, helpful when proving the distribution law $(R \cup S)^* = (R^* \circ S^*)^*$, which allows us to distribute the closure over a join by turning the join into a composition. Another important law of the relational calculus states that, whenever two relations weakly commute, their reflexive transitive closures also weakly commute: $R \circ S \sqsubseteq S \circ R \implies R^* \circ S^* \sqsubseteq S^* \circ R^*$. Properties of rewriting relations are traditionally expressed as individual rewritings $(x, y) \in R$, commonly read as $y$ is an $R$-*successor* of $x$, or $x$ is an $R$-*predecessor* of $y$. An $R^*$-successor is an $R$-*descendant*, and an $R^*$-predecessor an $R$-*ancestor*. The pointwise notation is appropriate when studying specific rewriting relations such as $\beta$-reduction (see below), but when studying abstract properties of rewriting relations, the abstract setting of the relational calculus is more suitable and leads to simpler proofs. In this setting, we interpret $R$ merely as "an $R$ rewriting step"; $R\cup$ is interpreted as the reverse rewriting; $R^*$ as a succession (possibly empty) of $R$-rewritings; $R \circ S$ as an $S$-rewriting followed by an $R$-rewriting, and $R \cup S$ as the choice between an $R$-rewriting and an $S$-rewriting. An inclusion $R \sqsubseteq S$ means that any $R$-rewriting is also an $S$-rewriting. The smallest equivalence generated by $R$ is determined by $(R\cup \cup R)^*$, and this expression nicely reflects the operational intuition. Furthermore, the expression $R\cup \circ R$ characterizes all those pairs that have a common $R$-successor; and, conversely, $R \circ R\cup$ characterizes those pairs that have a common $R$-predecessor. The reader can check these interpretations by unfolding the definitions of composition and converse.

**Definition.** A binary relation $R$ is *Church-Rosser* if equivalence wrt. $R$ implies having a common $R$-descendant. It satisfies the *diamond property* if a common $R$-predecessor implies a common $R$-successor. It is *confluent* if $R^*$ satisfies the diamond property.

$\langle$*Definition of Church-Rosser, diamond, and confluence* $1\rangle\equiv$

$$\text{Church\_Rosser } R \equiv (R\cup \cup R)^* \sqsubseteq R\cup^* \circ R^* \qquad \text{(Church\_Rosser\_def)}$$
$$\text{diamond } R \equiv R \circ R\cup \sqsubseteq R\cup \circ R \qquad \text{(diamond\_def)}$$
$$\text{confluent } R \equiv \text{diamond}(R^*) \qquad \text{(confluent\_def)}$$

Confluence thus expresses the fact that, no matter how an $R$-path diverges from a common ancestor, it will eventually converge at a common descendant. ☐

**Lemma** (`diamond_confluence`) *A relation that satisfies the diamond property is confluent:* diamond $R \implies$ confluent $R$. ☐

**Lemma** (`Church_Rosser_equivales_confluence`) *A binary relation is Church-Rosser if and only if it is confluent:* Church\_Rosser $R = $ confluent $R$. ☐

These lemmas are the basis of the proof method underlying both the Tait-and-Martin-Löf proof and Takahashi's proof for showing that $\beta$-reduction is Church-Rosser: in order to show that some relation $R$ is Church-Rosser, we seek a relation $R'$ that satisfies the diamond property and whose reflexive transitive closure is equal to that of $R$. More specifically, $R'$ is chosen such that $R \sqsubseteq R'$ and $R' \sqsubseteq R^*$. Then, we may calculate:

$\langle$*Proof of* `diamond_to_Church_Rosser` $2\rangle\equiv$

$$\text{diamond } R' \wedge R \sqsubseteq R' \wedge R' \sqsubseteq R^*$$
$\Rightarrow$ { monotonicity of star }
$$\text{diamond } R' \wedge R^* \sqsubseteq R'^* \wedge R'^* \sqsubseteq R^{**}$$
$=$ { idempotence of star }
$$\text{diamond } R' \wedge R^* \sqsubseteq R'^* \wedge R'^* \sqsubseteq R^*$$
$=$ { anti-symmetry }
$$\text{diamond } R' \wedge R^* = R'^*$$
$\Rightarrow$ { Lemma `diamond_confluence` }
$$\text{confluent } R' \wedge R^* = R'^*$$
$\Rightarrow$ { definition of confluence }
$$\text{confluent } R$$

= { Lemma Church_Rosser_equivales_confluence }
    Church_Rosser $R$

In this display, we have given comments describing the action of the tactics used to prove each step, instead of printing the tactics themselves. The calculation then more or less coincides with the proof script we prepared on paper before attempting a proof with Isabelle. If one is used to the calculational proof style, the tactics for calculational reasoning also help to guide Isabelle through the proof. Moreover, they are valuable for less sophisticated users of Isabelle, because they allow interaction with Isabelle in a more natural way, the user being the one who defines the path along which the interaction with the prover moves. From a methodological point of view, this is a more satisfying mode of working with Isabelle, because the user is in better control of how the proof state changes. To summarize, we have derived the following proof principle

$$\frac{\text{diamond } R'\,;\, R \sqsubseteq R'\,;\, R' \sqsubseteq R^*}{\text{Church\_Rosser } R} \qquad \text{(diamond\_to\_Church\_Rosser)}$$

and we apply this strategy to the case of $\beta$-reduction in Section 4.3.

## 4.2 Lambda Terms

Before looking at $\beta$-reduction, we first define the lambda terms. To avoid dealing explicitly with renaming, we choose the nameless notation introduced by de Bruijn (1972).

**Definition.** The set $db$ of lambda terms is defined inductively as follows:

⟨*Definition of lambda terms* 3⟩≡  db = Var nat |  · db db | $\lambda$ db

where application is written infix and has weaker binding strength than the variable constructor and stronger binding strength than the abstraction constructor.  □

**Definition.** The *substitution* of $s$ for $k$ in $t$ is denoted by $[s/k]t$. Incrementing by one in term $s$ all free indices greater than or equal to $k$ is denoted by lift $k$ $s$.  □

The following law expresses interaction between lifting and substitution. Let $i \leq j$:

$$[[v/j]u/i] \circ [\text{lift}\, i\, v/\, \text{Suc}\, j] = [v/j] \circ [u/i] \qquad \text{(subst\_subst)}$$

## 4.3 $\beta$-Reduction

**Definition.** A term $s$ $\beta$-reduces to term $t$, written $s \to t$, if $(s,t)$ is an element of the binary relation beta defined inductively by the following axioms:

⟨*Definition of $\beta$-reduction* 4⟩≡

$$(\lambda s) \cdot t \to [t/0]s \qquad \text{(beta)} \qquad s \to t \Longrightarrow s \cdot u \to t \cdot u \qquad \text{(appL)}$$

$$s \to t \Longrightarrow \lambda s \to \lambda t \qquad \text{(abs)} \qquad s \to t \Longrightarrow u \cdot s \to u \cdot t \qquad \text{(appR)}$$

for all terms $s$, $t$ and $u$. The fact that $(s,t)$ is an element of the reflexive and transitive closure beta$^*$ will be denoted by $s \overset{*}{\to} t$.  □

**Theorem** (Church_Rosser_beta) *$\beta$-reduction is Church-Rosser.*  □

**Proof Sketch.** We prove this theorem by the principle we derived at the end of Section 4.1. For this, we define an auxiliary relation par_beta, such that beta $\sqsubseteq$ par_beta and par_beta $\sqsubseteq$ beta$^*$, and which satisfies the diamond property. Thus, by the rule diamond_to_Church_Rosser, $\beta$-reduction is Church-Rosser.  □

## 4.4 Parallel $\beta$-Reduction

The relation known as "parallel $\beta$-reduction" is the key idea of what has become known as the Tait-and-Martin-Löf proof method.

**Definition.** A term $s$ $\beta$-reduces in parallel to $t$, written $s \Rrightarrow t$, if the pair $(s, t)$ is an element of the binary relation par_beta. This reduction relation is defined inductively by the following axioms:

$\langle$*Definition of parallel $\beta$-reduction 5*$\rangle\equiv$

$$\text{Var}\, n \Rrightarrow \text{Var}\, n \qquad \textbf{(var)} \qquad\qquad s \Rrightarrow t \Longrightarrow \lambda s \Rrightarrow \lambda t \qquad \textbf{(abs)}$$

$$\frac{s \Rrightarrow s' ; t \Rrightarrow t'}{s \cdot t \Rrightarrow s' \cdot t'} \qquad \textbf{(app)} \qquad\qquad \frac{s \Rrightarrow s' ; t \Rrightarrow t'}{(\lambda s) \cdot t \Rrightarrow [t'/0]s'} \qquad \textbf{(beta)}$$

for all indices $n$ and all terms $s$, $s'$, $t$ and $t'$. $\qquad\qquad\square$

It is easy to see that any $\beta$-reduction can be cast into a parallel $\beta$-reduction, beta $\sqsubseteq$ par_beta, since every axiom of beta corresponds to an axiom of par_beta. Similarly, every parallel $\beta$-reduction can be turned into a sequence of $\beta$-reductions, par_beta $\sqsubseteq$ beta$^*$, by serializing the simultaneous reductions. Now we can turn to proving that parallel $\beta$-reduction satisfies the diamond property. Recall that this means that, whenever $t \Rrightarrow t_1$ and $t \Rrightarrow t_2$, we must construct a common successor $s$ of $t_1$ and $t_2$. A first important step toward this goal is the following observation.

**Lemma** *Parallel $\beta$-reduction is compatible with lifting and substitution, i.e.*

$$t \Rrightarrow t' \Longrightarrow \text{lift}\, n\, t \Rrightarrow \text{lift}\, n\, t' \qquad\qquad \frac{t \Rrightarrow t' ; s \Rrightarrow s'}{[s/l]t \Rrightarrow [s'/l]t'} \quad \textbf{(par\_beta\_subst)}$$
$$\textbf{(par\_beta\_lift)}$$

*for all indices $n$ and all terms $s$, $s'$, $t$ and $t'$.* $\qquad\qquad\square$

The classic Tait-and-Martin-Löf proof now proceeds by proving directly that parallel $\beta$-reduction satisfies the diamond property. The typical proof (e.g. Barendregt's (1984) proof of Lemma 3.2.6) constructs the successor $s$ inductively along $t \Rrightarrow t_1$ for all $t \Rrightarrow t_2$. Such a successor $s$ is, by construction, as close to $t_1$ and $t_2$ as possible. However, we do not need this much information: since we are free to choose the successor, we might as well take a canonical one. The canonical choice $t^*$ as a successor of $t$ is obtained by contracting simultaneously *all* $\beta$-redexes in $t$. Intuitively, we expect

$$t \Rrightarrow t' \Longrightarrow t' \Rrightarrow t^* \qquad\qquad \textbf{(par\_beta\_cd)}$$

since we can contract in $t'$ those remaining $\beta$-redexes that are inherited from $t$ and are not newly introduced. A corollary is the diamond property of parallel $\beta$-reduction.

**Theorem** (`diamond_par_beta`) *Parallel $\beta$-reduction satisfies the diamond property.*

Before proving `par_beta_cd` we must make the definition of $t^*$ precise.

**Definition.** The *complete development* $t^*$ of a term $t$ is obtained by simultaneously contracting all $\beta$-redexes. This operation is defined inductively as follows:

$$\text{Var}\, n^* = \text{Var}\, n \qquad \textbf{(cd\_Var)} \qquad (\text{Var}\, n \cdot t)^* = \text{Var}\, n \cdot t^* \qquad \textbf{(cd\_App\_Var)}$$
$$(\lambda s)^* = \lambda s^* \qquad \textbf{(cd\_Fun)} \qquad ((r \cdot s) \cdot t)^* = (r \cdot s)^* \cdot t^* \qquad \textbf{(cd\_App\_App)}$$
$$((\lambda s) \cdot t)^* = [t^*/0]s^* \qquad \textbf{(cd\_App\_Fun)}$$

for indices $n$ and terms $r$, $s$ and $t$. $\qquad\qquad\square$

**Lemma** (par_beta_cd) *For all terms $t$ and $t'$: $t \Rrightarrow t' \Longrightarrow t' \Rrightarrow t^*$.*  □

⟨*Proof of* par_beta_cd 6⟩≡
goal ParRed.thy "∀t'.t ⇒ t' ⇒ t' ⇒ t*";
PROVE: $\forall t'. t \Rrightarrow t' \Rightarrow t' \Rrightarrow t^*$
PROOF: by structural induction on $t$

⟨*Case* $t = \text{Var}\, n$ 7⟩              ⟨*Case* $t = \underline{\lambda} t_1$ 8⟩
⟨*Case* $t = t_1 \cdot t_2$ *is not a* $\beta$-*redex* 9⟩       ⟨*Case* $t = t_1 \cdot t_2$ *is a* $\beta$-*redex* 11⟩
qed_spec_mp "par_beta_cd";

The variable and the abstraction case are straightforward.

⟨*Case* $t = \text{Var}\, n$ 7⟩≡                    ⟨*Case* $t = \underline{\lambda} t_1$ 8⟩≡
ASSUME: $\text{Var}\, n \Rrightarrow t'$                         ASSUME: $\forall t'. t_1 \Rrightarrow t' \Rightarrow t' \Rrightarrow t_1^*$
  PROVE: $t' \Rrightarrow \text{Var}\, n^*$                          $t' = \underline{\lambda} t_1', t_1 \Rrightarrow t_1'$
                                                        PROVE: $t' \Rrightarrow (\underline{\lambda} t_1)^*$

                $t'$                                     $t'$
        =  { $t$ is a variable }               =  { $t$ is an abstraction }
                $\text{Var}\, n$                                     $\underline{\lambda} t_1'$
        ⇒  { par_beta.var }                   ⇒  { ind. hyp., par_beta.abs }
                $\text{Var}\, n$                                     $\underline{\lambda} t_1^*$
        =  { cd_Var }                          =  { cd_Fun }
                $\text{Var}\, n^*$                                   $(\underline{\lambda} t_1)^*$

If $t = t_1 \cdot t_2$ is not a $\beta$-redex, then $t' = t_{11}' \cdot t_{12}'$ for some $t_{11}'$ and $t_{12}'$. Moreover, $t_1$ is either a variable $\text{Var}\, n$ or an application $t_{11} \cdot t_{12}$.

⟨*Case* $t = t_1 \cdot t_2$ *is not a* $\beta$-*redex* 9⟩≡       ⟨*Case* $t = t_1 \cdot t_2$ *is not a* $\beta$-*redex* 9⟩+≡
ASSUME: $\forall t'. \text{Var}\, n \Rrightarrow t' \Rightarrow t' \Rrightarrow \text{Var}\, n^*$  ASSUME: $\forall t'. t_{11} \cdot t_{12} \Rrightarrow t' \Rightarrow t' \Rrightarrow (t_{11} \cdot t_{12})^*$
        $\forall t'. t_2 \Rrightarrow t' \Rightarrow t' \Rrightarrow t_2^*$                 $\forall t'. t_2 \Rrightarrow t' \Rightarrow t' \Rrightarrow t_2^*$
        $t' = t_1' \cdot t_2', \text{Var}\, n \Rrightarrow t_1', t_2 \Rrightarrow t_2'$       $t' = t_1' \cdot t_2', t_{11} \cdot t_{12} \Rrightarrow t_1', t_2 \Rrightarrow t_2'$
  PROVE: $t' \Rrightarrow (\text{Var}\, n \cdot t_2)^*$                PROVE: $t' \Rrightarrow ((t_{11} \cdot t_{12}) \cdot t_2)^*$

                $t'$                                     $t'$
        =  { $t$ is a variable }               =  { $t_1$ is an application }
                $t_1' \cdot t_2'$                                   $t_1' \cdot t_2'$
        ⇒  { ind. hyp., par_beta.app }        ⇒  { ind. hyp., par_beta.app }
                $\text{Var}\, n^* \cdot t_2^*$                          $(t_{11} \cdot t_{12})^* \cdot t_2^*$
        =  { cd_Var, cd_App_Var }             =  { cd_App_App }
                $(\text{Var}\, n \cdot t_2)^*$                         $((t_{11} \cdot t_{12}) \cdot t_2)^*$

If $t = t_1 \cdot t_2$ is a $\beta$-redex, we distinguish two further subcases, depending on whether the redex is contracted during the parallel reduction or not.

⟨*Case* $t = t_1 \cdot t_2$ *is a* $\beta$-*redex* 11⟩≡
ASSUME: $\forall t'. \underline{\lambda} t_{11} \Rrightarrow t' \Rightarrow t' \Rrightarrow (\underline{\lambda} t_{11})^*, \forall t'. t_2 \Rrightarrow t' \Rightarrow t' \Rrightarrow t_2^*$
        $(\underline{\lambda} t_{11}) \cdot t_2 \Rrightarrow t'$
  PROVE: $t' \Rrightarrow ((\underline{\lambda} t_{11}) \cdot t_2)^*$
by (etac (par_beta.mk_cases db.simps "$(\underline{\lambda} t_{11}) \cdot t_2 \Rrightarrow t'$") 1)

Then property (5) $[M \Rightarrow N \implies N \Rightarrow M^*]$ can be verified by induction on $M$, as follows.

*Case* 1. If $M = x \Rightarrow N$, then $N = x \Rightarrow x = M^*$.

*Case* 2. If $M = \lambda x.M_1 \Rightarrow N$, then $N = \lambda x.N_1$ for some $N_1$ with $M_1 \Rightarrow N_1$. Since $M_1$ is a subterm of $M$, by the ind. hypothesis we get $N_1 \Rightarrow M_1^*$. This implies $\lambda x.N_1 \Rightarrow \lambda x.M_1^* = M^*$.

*Case* 3. If $M = M_1 M_2 \Rightarrow N$ and $M$ is not a $\beta$-redex, then $N = N_1 N_2$ for some $N_i$ with $M_i \Rightarrow N_i$ $(i = 1, 2)$. Then we have $N_1 N_2 \Rightarrow M_1^* M_2^* = M^*$.

*Case* 4. If $M = (\lambda x.M_1)M_2 \Rightarrow N$, then either $(N = \lambda x.N_1)N_2$ or $N = [x := N_2]N_1$ both for some $N_i$ with $M_i \Rightarrow N_i$ $(i = 1, 2)$. Here we have $N_i \Rightarrow M_i^*$ $(i = 1, 2)$ by the induction hypothesis.

*Subcase* 4.1. If $N = (\lambda x.N_1)N_2$, then $N \Rightarrow [x := M_2^*]M_1^* = M^*$.

*Subcase* 4.2. If $N = [x := N_2]N_1$, we also have $N \Rightarrow [x := M_2^*]M_1^* = M^*$ by property (3) [par_beta_subst] above.

This completes the proof of (5) [...].

---

**Fig. 4.** Takahashi's (1995) original proof of `par_beta_cd`

PROOF: by case analysis

$\langle$*Case* $t = (\underline{\lambda} t_{11}) \cdot t_2$ *is not contracted* 12$\rangle$   $\langle$*Case* $t = (\underline{\lambda} t_{11}) \cdot t_2$ *is contracted* 13$\rangle$

| $\langle$*Case* $t = (\underline{\lambda} t_{11}) \cdot t_2$ *is not contracted* 12$\rangle \equiv$ | $\langle$*Case* $t = (\underline{\lambda} t_{11}) \cdot t_2$ *is contracted* 13$\rangle \equiv$ |
|---|---|
| ASSUME: $t' = t_1' \cdot t_2', t_1' = \underline{\lambda} t_{11}'$ | ASSUME: $t' = [t_2'/0]t_{11}'$ |
| $t_{11} \Rightarrow t_{11}', t_2 \Rightarrow t_2'$ | $t_{11} \Rightarrow t_{11}', t_2 \Rightarrow t_2'$ |
| PROVE: $t' \Rightarrow ((\underline{\lambda} t_{11}) \cdot t_2)^*$ | PROVE: $t' \Rightarrow ((\underline{\lambda} t_{11}) \cdot t_2)^*$ |

| | | | | |
|---|---|---|---|---|
| | $t'$ | | | $t'$ |
| $=$ | { $t$ is not contracted } | | $=$ | { $t$ is contracted } |
| | $(\underline{\lambda} t_{11}') \cdot t_2'$ | | | $[t_2'/0]t_{11}'$ |
| $\Rightarrow$ | { ind. hyp., `par_beta.beta` } | | $\Rightarrow$ | { ind. hyp., `par_beta_subst` } |
| | $[t_2{}^*/0]t_{11}{}^*$ | | | $[t_2{}^*/0]t_{11}{}^*$ |
| $=$ | { `cd_App_Fun` } | | $=$ | { `cd_App_Fun` } |
| | $((\underline{\lambda} t_{11}) \cdot t_2)^*$ | | | $((\underline{\lambda} t_{11}) \cdot t_2)^*$ |

This completes the proof of `par_beta_cd`.                                    □

The proof of `par_beta_cd` also completes the verification of the Church-Rosser property of $\beta$-reduction. From this literate presentation of the proof, `notangle` can extract an Isabelle proof script that can then be checked by Isabelle for correctness. The proof we have given follows the same line of reasoning as the proof by Takahashi (1995), which we reproduce in Figure 4. Even without the accompanying explanatory text, this example of a formal structured calculational proof can be easily understood by readers who are not familiar with Isabelle.

Our formalization is based on a precursor of Nipkow's (1996) paper, which was circulated via the Isabelle-user mailing list. Except for minor cosmetic changes, we have reused all of Nipkow's definitions. We have also reused several of his lower-level theorems and their proofs. Our presentation of abstract rewriting systems differs significantly from Nipkow's presentation, he preferring a diagrammatic — or geometric —

style to our calculational style: Nipkow's notion of a square, square $RSTU$, corresponds to the statement $R \circ S^\cup \sqsubseteq T^\cup \circ U$ in the relational calculus. Although we had to develop the proofs of this chapter again in order to prepare them for presentation in our style, we benefited a lot from Nipkow's work and the techniques for using Isabelle contained in the files of the official distribution. We therefore wish to see our work as yet another step in this line of case studies, leading toward the goal of bringing formalized mathematics closer to textbook mathematics. A comprehensive survey of earlier formalizations of the Church-Rosser theorem is given by Simons (1996).

# 5  Discussion

We have described an approach to formal-proof presentation and illustrated how it was adapted to the presentation of Isabelle developments. We conclude by discussing some of the merits and shortcomings of this instantiation as we see them. The discussion is followed by a brief review of related work on proof presentation.

*Structure.* The proof of the Church-Rosser theorem illustrates convincingly that we are able to present backward-style Isabelle proofs in a structured hierarchical manner. This is not really surprising, since backward-style tactic-driven Isabelle proofs can themselves be regarded as an instance of this general proof development paradigm. However, Isabelle is geared to *interactive* development, and not *static* presentation. Of course, the proofs presented differ significantly in structure from the sort of Isabelle proofs one is used to. After all, most of the effort expended during an Isabelle development is directed to achieving as high as possible a degree of automation. For instance, Nipkow's proof of Lemma `par_beta_cd` comprises only the following 5 tactic applications:

$\langle Nipkow's\ proof\ of\ \texttt{par\_beta\_cd}\ 14\rangle\equiv$
```
goal ParRed.thy "∀t'.t ⇉ t' ⇒ t' ⇉ t*";
by (db.induct_tac "t" 1);
by (Simp_tac 1);
be rev_mp 1;
by (db.induct_tac "db1" 1);
by (ALLGOALS (fast_tac (parred_cs addSIs [par_beta_subst]
                                  addss (!simpset))));
qed_spec_mp "par_beta_cd";
```

We are quite satisfied with the calculations, which we are able to present in the conventional style and, at the same time, have them checked by Isabelle. We are not aware of the existence of any similar formal presentations. More experiments with this style of proof using Isabelle are needed. We also intend to investigate whether the "window inference" technique (Robinson & Staples 1993, Grundy 1996) can be suitably adapted or combined with our style of hierarchical calculations.

*Language.* Isabelle's language of theorem-constructing operations, which is used to express forward proofs, and the tactic language, which is used to construct backward proofs, are very powerful tools for interactive proof development. One construct however, we found to be lacking — which could serve the dual purpose of documenting the progress in a deduction *and* constraining the search space during proof search. Isabelle provides no direct means for supplying hints to a proof-search procedure, but it is possible to simulate such an effect by inserting additional subgoals into the proof state using `subgoal_tac`. We made frequent use of this tactic, which receives very little attention in Isabelle's documentation, when programming the presentation tactics. It would be interesting to explore the possibility of giving direct hints to search procedures, which could also serve documentation purposes. As we have mentioned earlier, proof refinement as such cannot be expressed in Isabelle, because proofs are not treated as first-class objects. With the advent of proof objects in Isabelle, it would appear natural to investigate how we can view them as a testbed for practical experiments with proof refinement, an issue raised in (Simons 1996, Simons & Sintzoff 1997).

*Presentation.* When implementing the prototypical set of tools described in Section 3, we deliberately refrained from interfering too much with Isabelle's source code. This was of no concern to us, since the experiment merely served as a proof of concept, which we think we have successfully given. A closer integration of our tools with the Isabelle system, and the user interfaces currently being designed for it, would, however, improve the usability of the tools.

*Related Work.* Coscoy et al. (1995) describe how a pseudo-natural-language proof description can be extracted automatically from proof objects, which are in their case $\lambda$-terms of the Calculus of Construction encoding a natural-deduction proof. They use techniques that are similar to the ones employed to extract programs from proofs. Questions such as hierarchical structuring are not addressed, nor is the treatment of special proof styles. This technique would therefore appear — thus far — to be usable for small proofs only. Kalvala (1994) investigates, for the case of HOL, the potential for equipping proof terms with *annotations* that carry extraformal information explaining and guiding the proof development. To this end, she augments the term structure of HOL's meta logic by an additional annotation attribute. Moreover, she introduces annotated *proof trees* for recording backward-style tactic-driven proofs. Kalvala (1995) reports on work in progress to adapt her approach to Isabelle. She provides only simple examples and no complete proofs. So, it is therefore difficult to judge whether her approach scales up in practice, and what proof styles are best suited for documentation by annotations. It is also unclear whether, in her framework, an annotated proof tree actually represents the proof, in the sense that it can be stored for later reuse, while at the same time serving as its own documentation. Issues such as refinement, hierarchical structuring or hiding unwanted detail are not addressed. Wong (1994) has developed `mweb`, a set of WEB tools for HOL that can be used to present HOL developments in a literate style. He uses HOL's built-in pretty-printing mechanism to typeset HOL formulas, but does not provide any means to structure the presentation of proofs. In particular, `mweb` does not implement the chunking mechanism. Carrington et al. (1996) discuss the presentation of formal program development in the refinement calculus. They propose presenting refinements, as well as the associated proof obligations, in a hierarchical and calculational manner, and state requirements for adequate tool support. They suggest that hierarchical calculations are naturally obtained by carrying out the deductions according to the window-inference paradigm. Along similar lines, Back et al. (1996) propose a structured calculational proof format for writing proofs. They extend the conventional form of calculations by a very attractive and concise set of notational means for structuring calculations and for including contextual information similar to window inferences. Moreover, they stress the fact that, through the structuring they introduce, calculations can be presented at various levels of detail. Thus, these two approaches are, in essence, very close to our approach to formal proof presentation in general. It would be interesting to see, once tools are available, whether they can be adapted to create an integrated environment for the composition of literate, hierarchically structured and calculational proofs, expressed, for example, in Isabelle.

*Acknowledgments.* I wish to thank Thomas Santen, Michel Sintzoff and Matthias Weber for valuable discussions and for their continued interest in this work. My thanks also go to Phil Bacon for polishing up the English.

# References

Back, R., Grundy, J. & von Wwright, J. (1996), Structured calculational proof, Technical Report TR-CS-96-09, Department of Computer Science, The Australian National University.

Backhouse, R. C. (1989), 'Making formality work for us', *Bulletin of the EATCS* (38), 219–249.

Backhouse, R. C. (1995), 'The calculational method', *Information Processing Letters* **53**.

Barendregt, H. P. (1984), *The Lambda Calculus: Its Syntax and Semantics*, Vol. 103 of *Studies in Logic and the Foundations of Mathematics*, revised edn, North Holland.

Carrington, D., Hayes, I., Nickson, R., Watson, G. & Welsh, J. (1996), Structured presentation of refinements and proofs, *in* K. Ramamohanarao, ed., 'Nineteenth Australasian Computer Science Conference (ACSC'96)', pp. 87–96.

Coscoy, Y., Kahn, G. & Théry, L. (1995), Extracting text from proof, *in* M. Dezani & G. Plotkin, eds, 'International Conference on Typed Lambda Calculi and Applications (TLCA'95)', LNCS 902, Springer.

de Bruijn, N. G. (1972), 'Lambda calculus notation with nameless dummies, a tool for automatic formula manipulation, with application to the Church-Rosser theorem', *Indigationes Mathematicae* **34**(5), 381–392.

Dijkstra, E. W. & Scholten, C. (1990), *Predicate Calculus and Predicate Transformers*, Springer.

Gasteren, A. J. M. v. (1987), *On the Shape of Mathematical Arguments*, LNCS 445, Springer.

Gries, D. & Schneider, F. B. (1993), *A Logical Approach to Discrete Math*, Springer.

Grundy, J. (1996), 'Transformational hierarchical reasoning', *The Comp. Jour.* **39**(4), 291–302.

Huet, G. (1980), 'Confluent reductions: Abstract properties and applications to term rewriting systems', *Journal of the ACM* **27**(4), 797–821.

Jones, C. B. (1990), *Systematic Software Development Using VDM*, Prentice Hall International.

Kalvala, S. (1994), 'Annotations in formal specifications and proofs', *Formal Methods in Systems Design* **5**, 119–144.

Kalvala, S. (1995), Proof annotation issues in Isabelle, *in* L. C. Paulson, ed., 'First Isabelle Users Workshop', Technical Report number 379, Cambridge University Computer Laboratory.

Knuth, D. (1984), 'Literate programming', *The Computer Journal* **27**(2), 97–111.

Lamport, L. (1994), 'How to write a proof', *American Mathematical Monthly* **102**(7), 600–608.

Nipkow, T. (1996), More Church-Rosser proofs (in Isabelle/HOL), *in* M. McRobbie & J. K. Slaney, eds, 'Automated Deduction — CADE-13', LNCS 1104, Springer, pp. 733–747.

Paulson, L. C. (1994), *Isabelle*, LNCS 828, Springer.

Ramsey, N. (1994), 'Literate programming simplified', *IEEE Software* **11**(5), 97–105.

Robinson, P. J. & Staples, J. (1993), 'Formalizing a hierarchical structure of practical mathematical reasoning', *Journal of Logic and Computation* **3**(1), 47–61.

Simons, M. (1996), The Presentation of Formal Proofs, PhD thesis, TU Berlin.

Simons, M. & Sintzoff, M. (1997), Algebraic composition and refinement of proofs. In prep.

Takahashi, M. (1995), 'Parallel reductions in λ-calculus', *Inf. and Comp.* **118**(1), 120–127.

Wong, W. (1994), mweb: proof script management utilities. Manual for the HOL contrib package.

# Derivation and Use of Induction Schemes in Higher-Order Logic

Konrad Slind

kxs@cl.cam.ac.uk

Cambridge University Computer Lab

**Abstract.** We discuss how to formally derive induction schemes for recursively defined functions in higher order logic. The functions are able to be defined using ML-style pattern-matching, and the induction schemes are also phrased in terms of these patterns. As part of the TFL system, this facility is portable: it has been incorporated into both the HOL and Isabelle systems.

## 1 Introduction

In a previous paper [12], we argued that the built-in functions of higher-order logic provide a convenient, albeit ultimately limited, representation of pure functional programs. We also showed how total recursive functions, described by pattern-matching style recursion equations, could be defined by using a well-founded recursion operator, with the input recursion equations being re-derived as logical consequences of the definition. Here our intent is to examine the other side of the coin: how can one reliably produce a customized induction theorem for each recursive definition?

Our approach to induction follows that of Boyer and Moore [3], in which the structure of the recursive definition is used as a basis on which to construct the induction theorem. This is in contrast to the *structural induction* approach, which has been used with success in many applications [9]. At times, however, structural induction is insufficient, and our examples include some illustrative instances. Having more than one kind of applicable induction can mean confusion: which induction theorem to use when? We do not have anything conclusive to say about this issue, but we will at least discuss our experiences with this.

One aspect of our work is that the induction scheme is derived by inference. In TFL, the derivation happens as a composition of the inference mechanisms of the host logic implementation. The derived induction theorem can thus be seen as a kind of conservative extension: it can be trusted to the same extent as the host mechanisms used in the derivation.

### 1.1 Acknowledgements

This work was performed at the Technische Universität in Munich.

## Notation and basic definitions

We use $\equiv$ to show that a definition is being made and $\overline{x}$ denotes a finite sequence of distinct syntactic objects. In parsing logical expressions, earlier members of the following list of infixes have stronger binding power than later members: $=, \wedge, \vee, \supset, \equiv$. All infixes associate to the right. The list-processing functions ::, *mem, filter, exists,* and @ (an infix version of *append*) are used; we assume the reader is familiar with their definitions. $\forall(M)$ denotes the universal quantification of all free variables in $M$. The notation $\Gamma, . \vdash M$ is equivalent to $\Gamma, M \vdash M$. Finally, we will need the following consequence of a logical datatype $ty$ with constructors $C_1, \ldots, C_n$ :

$$\vdash \forall x : ty. \ (\exists \overline{y}.x = C_1 \overline{y}) \vee \ldots \vee (\exists \overline{y}.x = C_n \overline{y}).$$

## 2 Wellfoundedness and induction

The notion of wellfoundedness is a basic one in set theory. There are a variety of equivalent formulations [11]; we choose the following, which is pleasant to work with.

**Definition 1 Wellfoundedness.**

$$WF(R) \equiv \forall P. \ (\exists w. \ P \ w) \supset \exists min. \ P \ min \wedge \forall b. \ R \ b \ min \supset \neg P \ b.$$

Wellfoundedness serves as a means of identifying when induction is valid, ensuring that the inductive hypothesis is not, in effect, what is to be proved. From the definition, one can quickly prove a general induction theorem, which epitomizes a useful proof construction.

**Theorem 2 Wellfounded induction.**

$$\forall P \ R. \ WF(R) \supset (\forall x. \ (\forall y. \ R \ y \ x \supset P \ y) \supset P \ x) \supset \forall x. \ P \ x.$$

*Proof.* Assume $R$ is wellfounded. Assume $P$ $x$ holds when $P$ $y$ holds for all $y$ $R$-less than $x$. Towards a contradiction, assume there's a $z$ such that $\neg P$ $z$. By wellfoundedness, there's an $R$-minimal element $min$ such that $\neg P$ $min$. Hence, for all $y$ $R$-less than $min$, $P$ $y$ holds. Hence $P$ $min$ holds, a contradiction. $\square$

Theorem 2 generalizes the usual mathematical induction in two ways: it can be instantiated to any predicate, not just predicates on numbers; and it allows the assumption of a strong induction hypothesis, *i.e.*, one gets to assume that the property holds for *all* $R$-smaller elements, not just the $R$-predecessor. Many useful forms of induction, *e.g.*, mathematical, course-of-values, structural, simultaneous, mutual, transfinite, and recursion induction, can be obtained as instantiations of this one general result. In the remainder of this paper, we will focus on the automatic derivation of recursion induction.

# 3  The derivation of induction schemes

In [12], we described how termination conditions are extracted automatically from definitions. From a function definition

$$f(pat_1) = rhs_1[f(a_{11}), \ldots, f(a_{1k_1})]$$

$$\vdots$$

$$f(pat_n) = rhs_n[f(a_{n1}), \ldots, f(a_{nk_n})]$$

the extraction process from [12] returns the termination conditions

$$WF(R),$$
$$\forall(\Gamma(a_{11}) \supset R\ a_{11}\ pat_1), \quad \ldots, \forall(\Gamma(a_{1k_1}) \supset R\ a_{1k_1}\ pat_1),$$

$$\vdots$$

$$\forall(\Gamma(a_{n1}) \supset R\ a_{n1}\ pat_n), \ldots, \forall(\Gamma(a_{nk_n}) \supset R\ a_{nk_n}\ pat_n)$$

where $\Gamma(a_{ij})$ represents the *context* of the recursive call $f\ a_{ij}$ and $R$ is the termination relation. (The notion of context is explained in [12]; roughly, it is a collection of facts that are true at the occurrence of $a_{ij}$ in the HOL formula.) The termination conditions can be used to generate the form of a useful induction theorem for $f$ (displayed in Figure 1). The essence of the theorem is that, for each case in the definition, the property in question is assumed to hold for each argument to a recursive call of the function, provided that the context requirements can be satisfied. Thus the shape of the induction theorem follows that of the function definition. This style supports the user in that the case analysis of the proof will follow that of the function definition. Therefore, goals emerging from an application of the induction theorem should be more readily understood and related to the source program being reasoned about.

$$\left( \forall \left( \begin{array}{c} (\forall(\Gamma(a_{11}) \supset P\ a_{11})) \quad \wedge \\ \vdots \\ (\forall(\Gamma(a_{1k_1}) \supset P\ a_{1k_1})) \end{array} \right) \wedge \supset P(pat_1) \right) \wedge$$

$$\vdots$$
$$\wedge$$

$$\left( \forall \left( \begin{array}{c} (\forall(\Gamma(a_{n1}) \supset P\ a_{n1})) \quad \wedge \\ \vdots \\ (\forall(\Gamma(a_{nk_n}) \supset P\ a_{nk_n})) \end{array} \right) \wedge \supset P(pat_n) \right) \supset \forall v.\ P\ v.$$

Fig. 1. Shape of target induction theorem

**Example.** From the following version of Euclid's algorithm

$$gcd(0, y) = y$$
$$gcd(\text{Suc } x, 0) = \text{Suc } x$$
$$gcd(\text{Suc } x, \text{Suc } y) = \text{if } (y \leq x) \text{ then } gcd(x - y, \text{Suc } y) \text{ else } gcd(\text{Suc } x, y - x).$$

we obtain the following induction principle:

$$\forall P.$$
$$(\forall y.\ P(0, y)) \land$$
$$(\forall x.\ P(\text{Suc } x, 0)) \land$$
$$(\forall x\ y.$$
$$\quad (y \leq x \supset P(x - y, \text{Suc } y)) \land$$
$$\quad (\neg(y \leq x) \supset P(\text{Suc } x, y - x)) \supset P(\text{Suc } x, \text{Suc } y))$$
$$\supset \forall v\ v_1.\ P(v, v_1)$$

□

The mechanized derivation of the induction theorem proceeds by establishing that the antecedent of the target induction theorem implies the antecedent of wellfounded induction (theorem 2):

$$\left( \left( \forall \begin{pmatrix} (\forall(\Gamma(a_{11}) \supset P\ a_{11}))\ \land \\ \vdots \\ (\forall(\Gamma(a_{1k_1}) \supset P\ a_{1k_1})) \end{pmatrix} \supset P(pat_1) \right) \land \\ \vdots \\ \land \\ \left( \forall \begin{pmatrix} (\forall(\Gamma(a_{n1}) \supset P\ a_{n1}))\ \land \\ \vdots \\ (\forall(\Gamma(a_{nk_n}) \supset P\ a_{nk_n})) \end{pmatrix} \supset P(pat_n) \right) \right) \supset \forall x.(\forall y.\ R\ y\ x \supset P\ y) \supset P\ x.$$

Then by transitivity, we will have established the target induction theorem. In full detail, the proof proceeds according to the following algorithm.

1. Assume the antecedent of the target theorem.

$$.\vdash \left( \forall \begin{pmatrix} (\forall(\Gamma(a_{11}) \supset P\ a_{11}))\ \land \\ \vdots \\ (\forall(\Gamma(a_{1k_1}) \supset P\ a_{1k_1})) \end{pmatrix} \supset P(pat_1) \right) \land$$

$$\vdots$$
$$\land$$

$$\left( \forall \begin{pmatrix} (\forall(\Gamma(a_{n1}) \supset P\ a_{n1}))\ \land \\ \vdots \\ (\forall(\Gamma(a_{nk_n}) \supset P\ a_{nk_n})) \end{pmatrix} \supset P(pat_n) \right)$$

2. Consider cases on $pat_1, \ldots, pat_n$.

   (a) For case $pat_i$, assume $P$ holds of any $y$ that is $R$-smaller than $pat_i$:

$$\forall y.\; R\, y\, pat_i \supset P\, y \vdash \forall y.\; R\, y\, pat_i \supset P\, y.$$

      We will abbreviate the term $\forall y.\; R\, y\, pat_i \supset P\, y$ by $hyp_i$.

   (b) Specialize (a) to each recursive argument in the clause, getting

$$(hyp_i) \vdash R\, a_{i1}\, pat_i \supset P\, a_{i1}$$

$$\vdots$$

$$(hyp_i) \vdash R\, a_{ik_i}\, pat_i \supset P\, a_{ik_i}.$$

   (c) Prove each antecedent of the theorems from (b): first, assume the corresponding termination condition

$$\forall(\Gamma(a_{i1}) \supset R\, a_{i1}pat_i) \vdash \Gamma(a_{i1}) \supset R\, a_{i1}pat_i$$

$$\vdots$$

$$\forall(\Gamma(a_{ik_i}) \supset R\, a_{ik_i}pat_i) \vdash \Gamma(a_{ik_i}) \supset R\, a_{ik_i}pat_i\; ;$$

      then use transitivity of $\supset$ (or just *modus ponens*, when context is empty), to eliminate $R\, a_{i1}\, pat_i, \ldots, R\, a_{ik_i}\, pat_i$ to get

$$(hyp_i), \forall(\Gamma(a_{i1}) \supset R\, a_{i1}pat_i) \vdash P\, a_{i1}$$

$$\vdots$$

$$(hyp_i), \forall(\Gamma(a_{ik_i}) \supset R\, a_{ik_i}pat_i) \vdash P\, a_{ik_i}.$$

   (d) Now discharge the context of each recursive call from the theorems from (c) and quantify the local variables. Quantification is only over the variables in $FV(\Gamma(a_{ij}) \supset P\, a_{ij}) - FV(pat_i)$. This allows for the proper quantification of variables local to the right-hand side of a clause in a function definition, *e.g.*, those introduced by a let binding.

$$(hyp_i), \forall(\Gamma(a_{i1}) \supset R\, a_{i1}pat_i) \vdash \forall(\Gamma(a_{i1}) \supset P\, a_{i1})$$

$$\vdots$$

$$(hyp_i), \forall(\Gamma(a_{ik_i}) \supset R\, a_{ik_i}pat_i) \vdash \forall(\Gamma(a_{ik_i}) \supset P\, a_{ik_i}).$$

   (e) By *modus ponens* with the $i$th conjunct of theorem 1 and the conjunction of the theorems from (d) we have

$$\left\{ \begin{array}{c} (hyp_i), (1)\; \forall(\Gamma(a_{i1})\; \supset R\, a_{i1}pat_i), \\ \vdots \\ \forall(\Gamma(a_{ik_i}) \supset R\, a_{ik_i}pat_i) \end{array} \right\} \vdash P\, pat_i$$

and by discharging $(hyp_i)$, we obtain

$$\left\{ \begin{array}{c} (1), \forall(\Gamma(a_{i1})\; \supset R\, a_{i1}pat_i), \\ \vdots \\ \forall(\Gamma(a_{ik_i}) \supset R\, a_{ik_i}pat_i) \end{array} \right\} \vdash (\forall y.\; R\, y\, pat_i \supset P\, y) \supset P\, pat_i$$

(f) Replace $pat_i$ by $x$:

$$\left\{\begin{array}{l} x = pat_i,\ (1),\\ \forall(\Gamma(a_{i1}) \supset R\,a_{i1}pat_i),\\ \qquad \vdots\\ \forall(\Gamma(a_{ik_i}) \supset R\,a_{ik_i}pat_i) \end{array}\right\} \vdash (\forall y.\ R\,y\,x \supset P\,y) \supset P\,x$$

3. We've done steps $a$ to $f$ for each case, so we have proved $n$ theorems

$$\left\{\begin{array}{l} x = pat_1,\ (1),\\ \forall(\Gamma(a_{11}) \supset R\,a_{11}pat_1),\\ \qquad \vdots\\ \forall(\Gamma(a_{1k_1}) \supset R\,a_{1k_1}pat_1) \end{array}\right\} \vdash (\forall y.\ R\,y\,x \supset P\,y) \supset P\,x$$

$$\vdots$$

$$\left\{\begin{array}{l} x = pat_n,\ (1),\\ \forall(\Gamma(a_{n1}) \supset R\,a_{n1}pat_n),\\ \qquad \vdots\\ \forall(\Gamma(a_{nk_n}) \supset R\,a_{nk_n}pat_n) \end{array}\right\} \vdash (\forall y.\ R\,y\,x \supset P\,y) \supset P\,x$$

4. We now need a *pattern completeness* theorem

$$\vdash \forall x.\ (\exists \overline{y_1}.\ x = pat_1) \vee \ldots \vee (\exists \overline{y_n}.\ x = pat_n)$$

where the free variables of $pat_i$ in disjunct $i$ comprise the vector $y_i$. We will consider the production of this theorem separately.

5. By applying a disjoint cases rule scheme to (3) and (4) and then generalizing $x$, we obtain

$$\left\{\begin{array}{l} (1),\ \forall(\Gamma(a_{11})\ \supset R\,a_{11}pat_1),\\ \qquad \vdots\\ \forall(\Gamma(a_{1k_1})\ \supset R\,a_{1k_1}pat_1),\\ \qquad \vdots\\ \forall(\Gamma(a_{n1})\ \supset R\,a_{n1}pat_n),\\ \qquad \vdots\\ \forall(\Gamma(a_{nk_n}) \supset R\,a_{nk_n}pat_n) \end{array}\right\} \vdash \forall x.\ (\forall y.\ R\,y\,x \supset P\,y) \supset P\,x.$$

6. Now by *modus ponens* with the wellfounded induction theorem and (5), we have derived $WF(R), \ldots, (1) \vdash \forall x.\ P\,x$, which is what we want. Discharge the assumption (1) and then generalize to get the target theorem:

$$
\left[
\begin{array}{l}
WF(R), \\
\forall(\Gamma(a_{11}) \supset R\, a_{11} pat_1), \ldots, \forall(\Gamma(a_{1k_1}) \supset R\, a_{1k_1} pat_1), \\
\qquad\qquad\qquad \vdots \\
\forall(\Gamma(a_{n1}) \supset R\, a_{n1} pat_n), \ldots, \forall(\Gamma(a_{nk_n}) \supset R\, a_{nk_n} pat_n)
\end{array}
\right]
$$

$$\vdash$$

$$
\left( \forall \left( \begin{array}{ll} (\forall(\Gamma(a_{11}) \supset P\, a_{11})) & \wedge \\ \vdots & \\ (\forall(\Gamma(a_{1k_1}) \supset P\, a_{1k_1})) & \wedge \end{array} \right) \supset P(pat_1) \right) \wedge
$$

$$
\vdots
$$

$$
\wedge
$$

$$
\left( \forall \left( \begin{array}{ll} (\forall(\Gamma(a_{n1}) \supset P\, a_{n1})) & \wedge \\ \vdots & \\ (\forall(\Gamma(a_{nk_n}) \supset P\, a_{nk_n})) & \wedge \end{array} \right) \supset P(pat_n) \right) \supset \forall v.\ P\ v.
$$

□

The assumptions of this theorem are just the termination conditions of the recursive definition. The theorem can be used to perform inductive proofs, regardless of whether or not the termination of the function has been proven. Unproven termination conditions will simply propagate via the inference mechanisms of the logic until the termination conditions have been eliminated. Thus no special 'proof obligation' support is required for unsolved termination conditions.

## 3.1 Pattern completeness

The proof of pattern completeness is not trivial to automate: patterns can be arbitrarily nested, and can occur in any order. The author was stymied in his efforts to automate this class of proofs until he realized that an adaptation of the standard pattern matching algorithm can be used to drive the proof. Augustsson's translation of patterns to case expressions [1] *implicitly* establishes the completeness of pattern sets: if the algorithm completes successfully, one knows that the patterns are complete and non-overlapping. We take advantage of this and re-use the control structure of Augustsson's algorithm to *explicitly* prove the completeness of patterns.

To be specific, in the following we present an algorithm which is an adapted version of the one presented in section 4.1 of [12]. The algorithm presented here has the same general control structure, but manipulates different data (theorems *versus* case expressions). To emphasize the similarity, we re-use the presentation of [12] as much as possible.

Loosely, the algorithm operates by traversing the patterns from top to bottom, re-building each pattern (in the form of a theorem) along the way. When the recursion bottoms out, the variables in a pattern are existentially quantified. As the recursion unwinds, the exhaustion theorems for datatypes are used to combine the theorems coming from subcases. The end result is a single theorem expressing the completeness of the given patterns.

The algorithm cpat takes two arguments: a stack of variables and a list of *rows*. A row is a triple: a list of the patterns still to be traversed, a theorem representing the pattern, and a list of variable bindings. Assume we are given the patterns $pat_1, \ldots, pat_n$. The algorithm starts by building the rows. The stack is initialized to a variable $z$, which does not equal $x$ and does not occur in any of the patterns. The variable $x$ also does not occur in any of the patterns.

$$\vdash \forall x.\ \text{cpat} \left( [z], \begin{bmatrix} ([pat_1], (.\vdash x = z), []), \\ \vdots \\ ([pat_n], (.\vdash x = z), []) \end{bmatrix} \right)$$

The algorithm is controlled by analyzing the column formed by taking the head of each pattern list. There are 3 rules that apply: one when each term in the column is a variable; one when each term in the column is built from a constructor, and the last, which applies when the column is empty.

**Variable.**

The current subterm (denoted by $z$) is identified with the head pattern. In this case, the notation $\langle u, v \rangle$ denotes a binding, which is deferred until the **End** case is encountered.

$$\begin{aligned} &\text{cpat}(z :: stack, [(v :: pats, th, \theta)_1 \quad \ldots, (v :: pats, th, \theta)_n]) \\ &= \text{cpat}(stack, \quad [(pats_1, th_1, \langle z, v_1 \rangle :: \theta_1), \ldots, (pats_n, th_n, \langle z, v_n \rangle :: \theta_n)]) \end{aligned}$$

**Constructor.**

Now suppose the current sub-pattern being examined in all patterns is a constructor for a type $ty$. The system requires that the exhaustion theorem for this type

$$\forall x : ty.\ (\exists \overline{y}.x = C_1\overline{y}) \vee \ldots \vee (\exists \overline{y}.x = C_n\overline{y})$$

is available. TFL maintains an internal database of these theorems (each of which is easily derived from the structural induction theorem for a datatype). We begin in the following situation:

$$\text{cpat} \left( \begin{array}{l} z :: stack, \\ \begin{bmatrix} (C_1\overline{p} :: pats, (\Gamma \vdash x = N), \theta)_1, \ldots, (C_1\overline{p} :: pats, (\Gamma \vdash x = N), \theta)_{k_1}, \\ \vdots \\ (C_n\overline{p} :: pats, (\Gamma \vdash x = N), \theta)_1, \ldots, (C_n\overline{p} :: pats, (\Gamma \vdash x = N), \theta)_{k_n} \end{bmatrix} \end{array} \right)$$

The problem is partitioned into $n$ subproblems of size $k_1 \ldots k_n$. In subproblem $i$, supposing the constructor $C_i$ has type $\tau_1 \to \ldots \to \tau_j \to \beta$, $j$ new variables $v_1 : \tau_1, \ldots, v_j : \tau_j$ are pushed onto the stack. This vector of variables is denoted $\overline{v : \tau_i}$. We make a case split over the type and recurse, also building an extra level on the pattern. The $\overline{y}$ are fresh variables.

$$
\begin{aligned}
&\text{cpat} \left( \overline{v : \tau_1}@stack, \begin{bmatrix} (\overline{p}@pats, (\Gamma, z = C_1\overline{y} \vdash x = [z \mapsto C_1\overline{y}]N), \theta)_{11}, \\ \vdots \\ (\overline{p}@pats, (\Gamma, z = C_1\overline{y} \vdash x = [z \mapsto C_1\overline{y}]N), \theta)_{1k_1} \end{bmatrix} \right) \\
&\quad\vdots \\
&\text{cpat} \left( \overline{v : \tau_n}@stack, \begin{bmatrix} (\overline{p}@pats, (\Gamma, z = C_n\overline{y} \vdash x = [z \mapsto C_n\overline{y}]N), \theta)_{n1}, \\ \vdots, \\ (\overline{p}@pats, (\Gamma, z = C_n\overline{y} \vdash x = [z \mapsto C_n\overline{y}]N), \theta)_{nk_n} \end{bmatrix} \right)
\end{aligned}
$$

The recursive calls return the following theorems.

$$
\begin{aligned}
\Gamma, z = C_1\overline{y} &\vdash (\exists \overline{y}. \ x = M_{11}[\overline{y}]) \vee \ldots \vee (\exists \overline{y}. \ x = M_{1k_1}[\overline{y}]) \\
&\quad\vdots \\
\Gamma, z = C_n\overline{y} &\vdash (\exists \overline{y}. \ x = M_{n1}[\overline{y}]) \vee \ldots \vee (\exists \overline{y}. \ x = M_{nk_n}[\overline{y}])
\end{aligned}
$$

The cases can be existentially quantified on the left and disjoined:

$$
\begin{aligned}
\Gamma, \exists \overline{y}. \ z = C_1\overline{y} \vdash \ &(\exists \overline{y}. \ x = M_{11}[\overline{y}]) \vee \ldots \vee (\exists \overline{y}. \ x = M_{1k_1}[\overline{y}]) \vee \\
&\qquad\qquad \vdots \qquad\qquad\qquad\qquad \vee \\
&(\exists \overline{y}. \ x = M_{n1}[\overline{y}]) \vee \ldots \vee (\exists \overline{y}. \ x = M_{nk_n}[\overline{y}]) \\
&\quad\vdots \\
\Gamma, \exists \overline{y}. \ z = C_n\overline{y} \vdash \ &(\exists \overline{y}. \ x = M_{11}[\overline{y}]) \vee \ldots \vee (\exists \overline{y}. \ x = M_{1k_1}[\overline{y}]) \vee \\
&\qquad\qquad \vdots \qquad\qquad\qquad\qquad \vee \\
&(\exists \overline{y}. \ x = M_{n1}[\overline{y}]) \vee \ldots \vee (\exists \overline{y}. \ x = M_{nk_n}[\overline{y}])
\end{aligned}
$$

To this, we apply a disjoint cases rules scheme with the exhaustion theorem, giving

$$\Gamma \vdash (\exists \overline{y}. \; x = M_{11}[\overline{y}]) \vee \ldots \vee (\exists \overline{y}. \; x = M_{1k_1}[\overline{y}]) \vee$$
$$\vdots$$
$$\vee$$
$$(\exists \overline{y}. \; x = M_{n1}[\overline{y}]) \vee \ldots \vee (\exists \overline{y}. \; x = M_{nk_n}[\overline{y}])$$

**End.**

At this point we existentially quantify the theorem. The binding list controls the order in which quantification occurs (this matters because the disjoint cases rules scheme applied in the **Constructor** step is not operating modulo the commutativity of $\exists$).

$$\text{cpat}([\,], ([\,], (\Gamma \vdash x = M[x_1, \ldots, x_j]), [\langle x_1, y_1 \rangle, \ldots, \langle x_j, y_j \rangle]))$$
$$= \; \Gamma \vdash \exists y_1 \ldots y_j. \; x = M[y_1, \ldots, y_j].$$

## 3.2 Incomplete and overlapping patterns

There is a question as to what happens when the function has been defined by incomplete and/or overlapping patterns. In TFL, these are expanded at function definition time into a complete and non-overlapping set of patterns. The criteria used to resolve such ambiguities is that of ML: the resulting set is equivalent to choosing the first pattern that matches in a top-to-bottom and left-to-right scan. Thus, the proof of pattern completeness does not need to deal with overlapping and incomplete patterns, since they have been translated away. [1]

## 4 Examples

In this section we consider some small but illustrative examples.

### 4.1 Variant

The following non-structural recursion, described in [12] increments a variable until its value no longer lies in a fixed list.

$$variant(x, l) = \text{if } mem \; x \; l \text{ then } variant(\text{Suc } x, l) \text{ else } x.$$

The derived induction theorem

$$\forall P. \; (\forall x \; l. \; (mem \; x \; l \supset P(\text{Suc } x, l)) \supset P(x, l)) \supset \forall v \; v_1. \; P(v, v_1)$$

---

[1] After developing the translation, the author discovered that it had already been nicely described in [8].

proves the principal correctness property of *variant*

$$\neg mem \ (variant(x, l)) \ l$$

almost immediately. An attempt at structural induction on either or both of the two arguments to *variant* will lead to frustration.

## 4.2 Quicksort

This example displays the effect of local *let* bindings on induction theorems. Special proof support is needed to manipulate the *let* bindings in the goal resulting from an application of the induction theorem. Given the following definitions:

$$part(P, [\,], l_1, l_2) = (l_1, l_2)$$
$$part(P, h :: t, l_1, l_2) = \text{if } P \ h \ \text{then } part(P, t, h :: l_1, l_2)$$
$$\text{else } part(P, t, l_1, h :: l_2)$$

$$qsort(R, [\,]) = [\,]$$
$$qsort(R, h :: t) = \text{let } (l_1, l_2) = part(\lambda y. \ R \ y \ h, t, [\,], [\,])$$
$$\text{in}$$
$$qsort(R, l_1) \ @ \ [h] \ @ \ qsort(R, l_2)$$

we obtain the following principle of recursion induction for *qsort*.

$$\forall P.$$
$$(\forall R. \ P(R, [\,])) \ \wedge$$
$$(\forall R \ h \ t.$$
$$(\forall l_1 l_2. \ ((l_1, l_2) = part((\lambda y. \ R \ y \ h), t, [\,], [\,])) \supset P(R, l_2)) \ \wedge$$
$$(\forall l_1 l_2. \ ((l_1, l_2) = part((\lambda y. \ R \ y \ h), t, [\,], [\,])) \supset P(R, l_1)) \supset P(R, h :: t))$$
$$\supset \forall v \ v_1. \ P(v, v_1)$$

Now suppose we attempt to prove the correctness of quicksort. There are 2 theorems to prove: that the output is a permutation of the input, and that the output is sorted in accordance with the relation parameter $R$. We will only discuss the first. Permutation is defined as follows (equality is being used twice as a curried prefix):

$$perm \ l_1 l_2 \equiv \forall x. filter \ (= \ x) \ l_1 = filter \ (= \ x) \ l_2.$$

The permutation property is written as

$$perm \ L \ (qsort(R, L)).$$

To prove this, we apply the induction theorem. We obtain the inductive case as the following goal: [2]

$$perm(x :: rst)$$
$$\quad (\text{let } (l_1, l_2) = part((\lambda y.R\ y\ x), rst, [\,], [\,])$$
$$\quad \text{in}$$
$$\quad \quad qsort(R, l_1)@[x]@qsort(R, l_2))$$

1. $\forall l_1 l_2.\ ((l_1, l_2) = part((\lambda y.Ryx), rst, [\,], [\,])) \supset perm\ l_2\ (qsort(R, l_2))$
2. $\forall l_1 l_2.\ ((l_1, l_2) = part((\lambda y.R\ y\ x), rst, [\,], [\,])) \supset perm\ l_1\ (qsort(R, l_1))$

In order to use the inductive hypotheses, the entire *let* binding must somehow be brought to the top of the goal. Applying the following higher order rewrite rule

$$P(\text{let } (x, y) = M \text{ in } N\ x\ y) = (\text{let } (x, y) = M \text{ in } P(N\ x\ y))$$

will achieve this, giving the equivalent goal where the binding has been lifted to the top-level:

$$\text{let } (x', y) = part((\lambda y.\ R\ y\ x), rst, [\,], [\,])$$
$$\text{in}$$
$$perm(x :: rst)\ (qsort(R, x')@[x]@qsort(R, y)).$$

Then it is straightforward to apply a *let* introduction rule[3]

$$\frac{\Gamma, (vstruct = M) \vdash N}{\Gamma \vdash \text{let } vstruct = M \text{ in } N}$$

which liberates the former binding $(x', y) = part((\lambda y.R\ y\ x), rst, [\,], [\,])$ so that it can be used to liberate the inductive hypotheses. After this (and ignoring used hypotheses), we have the goal

$$perm\ (x :: rst)\ (qsort(R, x')@[x]@qsort(R, y))$$

4. $perm\ y\ (qsort(R, y))$
5. $perm\ x'\ (qsort(R, x'))$

Use of a simple lemma about permutations finishes the proof.

An alternative to the use of higher-order rewriting would be to rewrite with the definition of *let* then do beta conversion (*let* expressions are represented as suspended beta redexes in HOL). This approach has several drawbacks, among them being: the goal size can explode; the user's intuition is not supported; and the inductive hypotheses must be altered in order for them to be used, which may involve tedious mucking about in the hypotheses.

---

[2] In HOL, a horizontal line is used to differentiate the goal (above the line) from assumptions (below).

[3] A *vstruct* is an arbitrary tuple built up from (non-repeated) variables.

## 4.3 Nested recursion

A *nested recursion* is one where the result of a recursive call to the function depends on the results of another recursive call to the the function. For a running example, we use the following description of a convoluted way to compute the function that, given a number, always returns zero:

$$g\ 0 = 0$$
$$g(\text{Suc } x) = g(g\ x).$$

The main difficulty with nested recursion is that establishing the totality of the function (proving all the termination conditions) is dependent on knowing values of the function. However, if the function has not been defined, *i.e.*, been shown to terminate on all arguments, why should it be sound to use values of the function in the proof of totality? There is an apparent cyclic dependency between definition and valuations. However, this cycle can be broken by appeal to wellfoundedness: breaking cycles is what wellfoundedness is for!

The wellfoundedness of the termination relation can be used in the following way in our example: the value of the inner call to the function ($g\ x$) must be $R$-smaller than the initial call ($g(\text{Suc } x)$)—this is one of the termination conditions. At the time of termination condition extraction, this property can not in general be established, so it is maintained as a constraint on the nested recursive call in the recursion equations, and also as a constraint on using the nested induction hypothesis in the induction theorem. Thus, the above definition, using the termination relation $<$ yields the recursion equations (ARB denotes an arbitrary number)

$$g\ 0 = 0$$
$$g\ (\text{Suc } x) = \text{if } g\ x < \text{Suc } x \text{ then } g(g\ x) \text{ else ARB}$$

and the induction theorem

$$\forall P.\ P\ 0\ \land (\forall x.\ (g\ x < \text{Suc } x \supset P\ (g\ x)) \land P\ x \supset P(\text{Suc } x)) \supset \forall v.\ P\ v,$$

which are both constrained. The constraint $g\ x < \text{Suc } x$ can now be (manually) proved by using the constrained induction theorem. Although this application of induction may be surprising at first sight, it is just a consequence of wellfoundedness: the inductive hypothesis is only usable at $R$-smaller instances of the constraint. The final induction theorem in this case is

$$\forall P.\ P\ 0 \land (\forall x.\ P\ (g\ x) \land P\ x \supset P(\text{Suc } x)) \supset \forall v.\ P\ v.$$

With some kinds of nested recursion the above approach works well: termination constraints on nested calls can be proven by the constrained induction theorem. We have tested the methodology on a large test case: a re-verification of the unification algorithm presented by Manna and Waldinger, as re-done by Paulson[10]. In the example, the constraint on the nested recursive call to *Unify* was proved by constrained induction and then eliminated; after that, the correctness properties of *Unify*, namely that the returned unifier is most general and idempotent, were straightforward to prove using the unconstrained induction theorem.

However, not all our experiments with nested functions were able (by us anyway) to fit this methodology. In a verification of McCarthy's 91 function, we had to resort to wellfounded induction on the termination relation to prove termination of the nested call, *i.e.*, application of the custom induction theorem led to seemingly hopeless goals. We suspect that this has something to do with the fact that the 91 function is phrased in the destructor style. Further work is needed to clarify the situation.

## 4.4  Higher order recursion

Functions defined by so-called *higher order recursion* feature recursive calls with the function only partially applied. For example, the following defines the *occurs check* for a simple term language:

> **datatype** $\alpha$ *term* = Var of $\alpha$
> | Const of $\alpha$
> | App of $(\alpha\ term)(\alpha\ term)$

$$Occ\ (v_1, \text{Var}\ v_2) = (v_1 = v_2)$$
$$Occ\ (v, \text{Const}\ x) = \text{False}$$
$$Occ\ (v, \text{App}\ M\ N) = exists\ (\lambda x.\ Occ(v, x))\ [M; N]$$

This form of recursion requires the TFL definition mechanism to be set up with the following congruence theorem:

$$(L = L') \wedge (\forall y.\ mem\ y\ L' \supset (P\ y = P'\ y)) \supset (exists\ P\ L = exists\ P'\ L').$$

The returned induction theorem is

$$\forall P.\ (\forall v_1 v_2.\ P(v_1, \text{Var}\ v_2)) \wedge$$
$$(\forall v\ x.\ P(v, \text{Const}\ x)) \wedge$$
$$(\forall v\ M\ N.\ (\forall x.\ mem\ x\ [M; N] \supset P(v, x)) \supset P(v, \text{App}\ M\ N))$$
$$\supset \forall v\ v_1.P(v, v_1).$$

One can prove properties of *Occ* using this induction theorem, but it turns out that structural induction on terms is easier. It seems that the higher-order nature of the recursion is not as important as the data objects being recursed over. For *Occ*, this is merely the elements of the list $[M; N]$, and these are immediate subterms of the pattern at the head of the recursive case of the definition.

## 4.5  Mutual functions

One area where we have not yet devoted much effort is functions defined by mutual recursion. Many common algorithms are naturally expressed in this manner, *e.g.*, recursive descent parsers and algorithms on expressions in formalized programming languages. It is well-known that mutual recursion can be reduced to ordinary recursion, at the cost of some encoding and decoding. In our experience, many mutual recursions are really just structurally recursive; when this is so, the structural induction theorems provided by packages for mutually-declared datatypes are a good choice.

# 5 Related research

The system of Boyer and Moore [3] is based around induction schemes of the sort that we have described here. Related work has also been done in the RRL system with their notion of *cover set induction* [7] and in the Clam system [4]. Holger Busch has written a detailed description of how induction schemes can be synthesized by higher-order unification in the LAMBDA system [6]. Juergen Giesl has recently proposed a method for automatically solving nested termination conditions [5]. Currently, Richard Boulton of Edinburgh University and the author are collaborating on an interface [2] between the Clam and HOL systems. One aim of ours is to enable Clam to use the induction schemes created by TFL.

# 6 Conclusion

In this paper, we have shown how a useful induction scheme can be automatically derived from a recursive definition and its termination conditions. Since termination condition extraction has been automated [12], the whole process is automatic. Thus the act of defining a terminating function in higher-order logic is analogous to defining it in ML. In an ML compiler the function has its type inferred and is also compiled; in TFL the function has its type inferred, its recursion equations are derived, and an induction theorem for it is derived. This is fully automatic: the user only needs to supply recursion equations and a termination relation (and for non-nested recursive definitions, no termination relation need be immediately given).

In deriving the induction theorem, a valuable piece of static analysis has been performed: the customized induction theorem tells, for any property, what cases must hold and what assumptions can be made in each case in trying to prove the property. Put another way, the induction theorem gives an abstract enumeration of all paths through the program. Furthermore, the induction theorems are relatively general (in that many different functions will have the same induction theorem) and thus perhaps might be useful as a means of classifying functions.

The customized induction theorems presented here are not the full picture, because a further stage of customization can happen when a particular goal is known: the induction schemes of functions involved in the goal can be *merged* to build a perhaps more suitable induction scheme. This approach was developed by Boyer and Moore [3]. We have not, as yet, implemented this facility.

Finally, one should question whether recursion induction of the form that we derive is worth the trouble. After all, we are passing from strong induction to a weaker form: instead of being able to assume the property for *all R*-smaller terms, we are assuming it for only the recursive arguments in the body of the function. In many cases, the latter form suffices, but perhaps a high degree of automation could allow just the use of the strong form? This would be simpler, in that only one induction scheme would be needed, and also potentially allow more proofs to go through.

# References

1. Lennart Augustsson. Compiling pattern matching. In J.P. Jouannnaud, editor, *Conference on Functional Programming Languages and Computer Architecture (LNCS 201)*, pages 368–381, Nancy, France, 1985.
2. Richard Boulton, Alan Bundy, Mike Gordon, and Konrad Slind. A prototype interface between Clam and HOL. Participants Proceedings of TPHOLs97, May 1997.
3. Robert S. Boyer and J Strother Moore. *A Computational Logic*. Academic Press, 1979.
4. Alan Bundy. The use of explicit plans to guide inductive proofs. In R. Lusk and R. Overbeek, editors, *Proceedings of the Ninth International Conference on Automated Deduction*, pages 111–120. Springer-Verlag, 1988.
5. Juergen Giesl. Termination of nested and mutually recursive algorithms. *Journal of Auotmated Reasoning*, page ??, 1996. to appear.
6. H. Busch. Unification based induction. In L.J.M. Claesen and M.J.C. Gordon, editors, *International Workshop on Higher Order Logic Theorem Proving and its Applications*, pages 97–116, Leuven, Belgium, September 1992. IFIP TC10/WG10.2, North-Holland. IFIP Transactions.
7. Deepak Kapur and M. Subramaniam. Automating induction over mutually recursive functions. In *Proceedings of AMAST'96*, Munich, 1996.
8. Luc Maranget. Two techniques for compiling lazy pattern matching. Technical Report 2385, INRIA, October 1994.
9. Tom Melham. Automating recursive type definitions in higher order logic. In Graham Birtwistle and P.A. Subrahmanyam, editors, *Current Trends in Hardware Verification and Automated Theorem Proving*, pages 341–386. Springer-Verlag, 1989.
10. Lawrence Paulson. Verifying the unification algorithm in LCF. *Science of Computer Programming*, 3:143–170, 1985.
11. Piotr Rudnicki and Andrzej Trybulec. On equivalents of well-foundedness. Technical report, University of Alberta, March 1997. http://www.cs.ualberta.ca/ piotr/Mizar/Wfnd/wfnd.ps.
12. Konrad Slind. Function definition in higher order logic. In *Theorem Proving in Higher Order Logics*, number 1125 in Lecture Notes in Computer Science, Abo, Finland, August 1996. Springer Verlag.

# Higher Order Quotients
# and their Implementation in Isabelle HOL

Oscar Slotosch*

Technische Universität München
Institut für Informatik, 80290 München, Germany
http://www4.informatik.tu-muenchen.de/~slotosch/
slotosch@informatik.tu-muenchen.de

**Abstract.** This paper describes the concept of higher order quotients
and an implementation in Isabelle. Higher order quotients are a generalization of quotients. They use partial equivalence relations (PERs)
instead of equivalence relations to group together different elements. This
makes them applicable to arbitrary function spaces. Higher order quotients are conservatively implemented in the Isabelle logic HOL with a
type constructor and a type class for PERs. Ordinary quotients are a
special case of higher order quotients. An example shows how they can
be used in Isabelle.

## 1 Introduction

Quotients are used in mathematics to group together different elements. This is
done by defining an equivalence relation relating different elements. The quotient
is a structure (type) consisting of groups (sets) of equivalent elements, called
*equivalence classes*. Equivalent elements are in the same equivalence class. In
formal system and software engineering quotients are used in many ways. For
example to abstract from irrelevant details in the modelling of systems.

Due to the high complexity of systems and software, formal methods are
used to support the correctness proof of realizations of systems with respect to
the specification. Theorem provers are very useful in formal software development since they are tools to prove the correctness of the realization with respect
to the specification. To prove abstract requirements we need theorem provers
supporting quotients.

Functional languages are well suited for the development of systems, since
they allow us to program in a clean and modular way. An important concept
of functional languages is λ-abstraction which supports the formalization of abstract and higher order programs, which are highly reusable (a small example is
the map functional). A higher order logic supports an adequate formalization of
higher order programs.

* This work is partially sponsored by the German Federal Ministry of Education and
Research (BMBF) as part of the compound project "KorSys".

Isabelle is a generic theorem prover. One logic for Isabelle is HOL, a higher order logic which goes back to [Chu40] and includes some extensions like polymorphism and type constructors of [GM93]. Isabelle HOL supports the definition of higher order functions, but a quotient construction is not yet available. In this work we define quotients and higher order quotients and give an implementation in Isabelle HOL.

This papers is structured as follows: First a short overview over the relevant concepts of Isabelle is given. It is described in Section 3 how quotients could be implemented in Isabelle HOL. Section 4 defines PERs (partial equivalence relations) and higher order quotients and describes an implementation of them in Isabelle HOL. This implementation includes the simple quotients as a special case. Theorems for higher order quotients are derived and compared to those for quotients. In Section 5 a method is presented for the definition of different quotients over the same type and an example is performed. Section 6 concludes with a summary, future work and comparisons to some related work.

## 2 Isabelle HOL

This section shortly presents the used concepts of Isabelle, especially of the logic HOL. For a more detailed description see [Pau94].

### 2.1 Defining Types

The logic HOL is strongly typed. Every type has to be non-empty[2]. The axiomatic declaration of types with the **types** section and some rules cannot ensure non-emptyness and therefore it can lead to inconsistent specifications[3]. Therefore we use the following definition form of Isabelle HOL to define types conservatively (like types in Gordon's HOL system [GM93]).

```
PNAT = Nat +
typedef pnat = "{p::nat.0<p}"     (PosNE)
end
```

In this example we introduce the type of positive natural numbers in a theory called PNAT which uses the theory Nat. The type of positive natural numbers (pnat) is defined to be (isomorphic to) the set of elements p of type nat (written p::nat) which fulfil the predicate $0<p$. The witness that the new type is not empty ($\exists x.x \in \{p::nat.0<p\}$) is proved in a theorem over natural numbers before the type pnat is defined. This theorem is called PosNE. The typedef construct introduces the type only if the representing subset can be proved to be non-empty. With the given witness (PosNE) this proof is trivial.

---

[2] For example this is ensured by the **datatype** construct for the definition of free inductive data types (see [Völ95]).

[3] Inconsistent in the sense that it does not allow us to deduce **False**.

Isabelle HOL has no "real" subtyping, but subtypes may be introduced with coercion functions *abs* and *rep*. These coercion functions can be used to define functions on the subtype. For example `pnat_plus` $= \lambda$`x y.Abs_pnat(Rep_pnat x + Rep_pnat y)`. The `typedef` construct in the example `PNAT` is equivalent to the following theory with explicit coercion functions:

```
PNAT = Nat + (* expanded typedef *)
consts  (* signature of functions / constants *)
        pnat      :: "nat set"
        Abs_pnat :: "nat set ⇒ pnat"
        Rep_pnat :: "pnat ⇒ nat set"

defs    (* definition of the subset *)
        pnat_def      "pnat ≡ {p.0<p}"

rules   (* coercion rules *)
        Rep_pnat              "Rep_pnat x ∈ pnat"
        Abs_pnat_inverse  "y ∈ pnat ⟹ Rep_pnat(Abs_pnat y) = y"
        Rep_pnat_inverse  "Abs_pnat(Rep_pnat x) = x"
end
```

Axioms (names and rules) are declared in Isabelle after the keyword `rules`. Definitions are special rules (with the defining equality ≡). The keyword `defs` causes Isabelle to check whether a rule is a definition. Using only `defs` and `typedef` we cannot introduce inconsistencies.

In Isabelle HOL we may also use polymorphic types and type constructors. Type constructors can be seen as functions on types. For example `list` takes a type $\alpha$ and maps it into the type $\alpha$ `list`. Type constructors can also be defined using `typedef`.

## 2.2 Axiomatic Type Classes

Type classes are used to control polymorphism. For example in ML there are two main type classes ($\alpha$ and $\alpha_=$) to distinguish arguments of polymorphic functions that do not permit equality tests from those that do. As in other type systems (Haskell/Gofer [HJW92, Jon93]) Isabelle allows type classes to be defined with a subclass hierarchy.

In Isabelle there are different possibilities to introduce type classes[4]. We focus here on the defining form. This form is called *axiomatic type classes* in Isabelle (see [Wen94, Wen95, Wen97] for more details).

Axiomatic type classes characterize a type class by some axioms. Instantiating a type into a type class requires to prove that these axioms hold for the type. We explain the axiomatic type classes on the example of equivalence relations.

---

[4] Type classes are also called "sorts".

```
ER = HOL +   (* theory of equivalence relations *)

consts  (* polymorphic (infix) constant *)
        "~~"    :: "α::term ⇒ α ⇒ bool" (infixl 55)

axclass er < term
        (* axioms for equivalence relations *)
        ax_er_refl    "x ~~ x"
        ax_er_sym     "x ~~ y ⟹ y ~~ x"
        ax_er_trans   "[x ~~ y; y ~~ z] ⟹ x ~~ z"
```

To characterize the type class er of equivalence relations we introduced a constant ~~, available on all types of the class term[5]. A type belongs to the class er, if ~~ on that type satisfies the axioms ax_er_refl, ax_er_sym and ax_er_trans. To show the instantiation of a type into a type class we define now a theory to instantiate the type pnat into the class er (with the total equivalence relation True).

```
PNAT2 = PNAT + ER +
defs   (* concrete definition of ~~ on pnat *)
       er_pnat_def    "(op ~~) ≡ (λx y::pnat.True)"
end
```

For this theory we can trivially derive the following theorems:

```
        er_refl_pnat    "(x::pnat) ~~ x"
        er_sym_pnat     "(x::pnat) ~~ y ⟹ y ~~ x"
        er_trans_pnat   "[ (x::pnat) ~~ y; y ~~ z ] ⟹ x ~~ z"
```

These theorems ensure that the type pnat belongs to the class er. The instantiation of pnat needs these theorems as witnesses:

```
PNAT3 = PNAT2 +        (* instance of pnat into er *)
instance pnat::er      (er_refl_pnat,er_sym_pnat,er_trans_pnat)
end
```

This instantiation makes all theorems for α::er applicable to pnat.

Using axiomatic type classes is a conservative form to introduce type classes and instances into the specifications. In contrast to the introduction of type classes with the constructs classes and arities (see for example [Reg94]) axiomatic type classes do not require to provide an instance as witness that the type class is not empty[6]. However using axiomatic type classes in this way has a small disadvantage: type checking cannot ensure that equivalence relations are only applied to terms of types belonging to the class er. For example we are

---

[5] term is the universal class in Isabelle HOL to which all HOL types automatically belong.

[6] In [Reg94] the correctness of instantiations is justified by extra-logical arguments and therefore it is not checked by Isabelle.

allowed to write the term (n::nat) ~~ n, even if we fail to prove it, if **nat** is not instantiated into **er**.

Therefore we introduce an additional constant into the specification ER, which is only available on types of class **er**.

```
(* ER (continued) *)
consts  (* characteristic constant for er *)
        "~"      :: "α::er ⇒ α ⇒ bool"    (infixl 55)
defs
        er_def       "(op ~) ≡ (op ~~)"
end
```

We call those constants *characteristic constants* and we can easily derive the *characteristic axioms* for it.

```
        er_refl       "x ~ x"
        er_sym        "x ~ y ⟹ y ~ x"
        er_trans      "[x ~ y; y ~ z] ⟹ x ~ z"
```

We can use ~ in all general proofs about equivalence relations. The constant ~~ is only used for the correct instantiation of types. To expand the definition of ~ on pnat we derive the following *instantiation rule*:

```
        inst_pnat_er    "(op ~) = (λx y::pnat.True)
```

With this rule we do not need the overloaded constant ~~ on **pnat** any more.

Using ~ instead of ~~ has the advantage that the type checker can prohibit us from writing strange terms (like n::nat~~n if on **nat** no concrete definition of ~~ is given). Trying to prove (n::nat) ~ n would result in a type error, if **nat** is not instantiated into the class **er**.

Since HOL has also type constructors for higher order types, the instantiation rule allows us to describe the class of the result of a type constructor, provided the arguments of the type constructor are of certain classes[7]. The statement:

```
instance list::(er)er     (er_refl_list,er_sym_list,er_trans_list)
```

Instantiates all types α::er list into the class **er**[8]. In other words: If we have a concrete type with a concrete definition of the equivalence relation ~~, then we also have a concrete definition of equivalence relation on the lists over this type. Type constructors and type definitions are illustrated on the example in the following section with more details.

---

[7] With the same restrictions as the **arity** declaration of Isabelle (see [Nip91] for more details on Isabelle's type system).

[8] We omitted the definition of the equivalence ~~ on lists and the witnesses here for brevity.

# 3 Quotients in Isabelle HOL

This section shows how type definitions, type constructors and type classes can be used to define a quotient constructor in Isabelle. The used techniques are the same as in Section 4 for higher order quotients.

First we recall the definitions of equivalence relations and quotients:

**Definition 1.** Equivalence Relation
A relation $\sim$ on a type $R$ ($\sim \subseteq R \times R$) is called *equivalence relation*, iff

- REFLEXIVE: $\forall x \in R. x \sim x$
- SYMMETRIC: $\forall x, y \in R. x \sim y$ implies $y \sim x$
- TRANSITIVE: $\forall x, y, z \in R. x \sim y$ and $y \sim z$ implies $x \sim z$

Equivalence relations are formalized in Isabelle HOL in the theory ER in Section 2.2.

**Definition 2.** Quotient
Let $\sim$ be an equivalence relation on $S$. Then the *quotient* (of $S$ with respect to $\sim$) is the set of all *equivalence classes*, defined by:

- QUOTIENT: $S_{/\sim} := \{[x]_\sim \mid x \in S\}$ where
- EQUIVALENCE CLASS: $[x]_\sim := \{y \in S \mid x \sim y\}$ for all $x \in S$

To implement quotients in Isabelle we define a type constructor quot which is defined on elements of the class er. This is done in the following theory:

```
QUOT = ER +
typedef α quot = "{s.∃r.∀y.y∈s=y~r}" (QuotNE)
```

With this typedef the quotient type constructor quot is defined. The representing set of elements is defined as set of equivalence classes. It contains such elements s for which a (representative) element r exists, such that all elements in s are equivalent to this element r. The theorem QuotNE states that this set is not empty. The non-emptyness does not depend on properties of $\sim$.

As was mentioned in Section 2.1 the typedef construct introduces abstraction and representation functions (Abs_quot and Rep_quot), for quotients. With these functions we can define the equivalence class operator and the operator which picks a single element out of an equivalence class by[9]:

```
(* QUOT (continued) *)
consts
        eclass          :: "α::er ⇒ α quot"
        any_in          :: "α::er quot ⇒ α"
defs
        eclass_def      "<[x]> ≡ Abs_quot {y.y~x}"
        any_in_def      "any_in f ≡ @x.<[x]>=f"
end
```

---

[9] For readability we omit here the definitions which cause Isabelle to use <[ ]> as mixfix syntax.

For these operators we can derive a lot of useful theorems[10], which make it easy to use quotients in Isabelle HOL. The types of x and y are inferred automatically to be $\alpha::$er.

```
(* theorems for equality *)
        er_class_eqI  "x~y⟹<[x]>=<[y]>"
        er_class_eqE  "<[x]>=<[y]>⟹x~y"
        er_class_eq   "<[x]>=<[y]>=x~y"
(* theorems for inequality *)
        er_class_neqI "¬x~y⟹<[x]>≠<[y]>"
        er_class_neqE "<[x]>≠<[y]>⟹¬x~y"
        er_class_neq  "<[x]>≠<[y]>=(¬x~y)"
(* theorems for exhaustiveness and induction *)
        er_class_exh  "∃x.q=<[x]>"
        er_class_all  "∀x.P<[x]> ⟹ P q"
(* theorems for any_in *)
        any_in_class  "any_in <[x]> ~ x"
        class_any_in  "<[any_in q]> = q"
```

The theorem er_class_eqI states that equivalent elements are in the same equivalence class. With the quotient construction, the defined operations, and these theorems we can lift theorems and operations from the representations to the quotients easily. Using quotient types in Isabelle is now as easy as in mathematics:

1. Define a relation on the representing type.
2. Prove that it is an equivalence relation and instantiate the representing type into the class er.
3. Build the quotient type with the quotient constructor
4. Define functions on the quotient with <[ ]> and any_in.

A more detailed example is the construction of rational numbers in Section 5.

## 4  Higher Order Quotients in Isabelle

This section defines higher order quotients, a generalization of quotients, and gives an implementation in Isabelle HOL. Higher order quotients are called higher order, since they can be applied to higher order functions, without explicitly defining an (partial) equivalence relation for this higher order types.

Quotients can be used on every type which belongs to the class er. Therefore using quotients requires to have an equivalence relation on every representing type. At the end of Section 2.2 we mentioned the possibility to define an equivalence relation for lists, based on an equivalence relation of the elements. This

---

[10] We present them here to show how quotients may be used. We will not apply all of them in the rest of this paper.

instance is quite nice, since it allows us to build quotients over specific lists, without explicitly defining the equivalence relation (for example with an equivalence relation on pnat we can define types like types PLQ = pnat list quot).

In functional languages we have λ-abstraction and we can program functions of arbitrary higher order types. However we cannot build quotients over these functions unless we defined an equivalence relation for every function type. The reason is that, in contrast to lists, we cannot define an equivalence relation for arbitrary functions, because in general equivalence relations on functions are not reflexive (since $x \sim y \not\rightarrow f(x) \sim f(y)$).

Higher order quotients use partial equivalence relations (PERs) instead of equivalence relations to group together different elements. For PERs we can give a general PER on functions, which defines a PER on the function space, provided that domain and range of the functions belong to the class PER. It was already observed in [Rob89] that PERs are closed under functional composition. With higher order quotients we can also define types like types FQ = (pnat list ⇒ pnat) quot.

## 4.1 PERs

Partial equivalence relations (PERs) are the basis for higher order quotients. PERs are not necessarily reflexive. PERs have a domain on which they are reflexive. Therefore they are called *partial* equivalence relations.

**Definition 3.** Partial Equivalence Relation
A relation $\sim$ on a type $R$ ($\sim \subseteq R \times R$) is called *partial equivalence relation*, iff

- SYMMETRIC: $\forall x, y \in R . x \sim y$ implies $y \sim x$
- TRANSITIVE: $\forall x, y, z \in R . x \sim y$ and $y \sim z$ implies $x \sim z$

The domain $D$ of a PER is the set of values from $R$, on which $\sim$ is reflexive:

- $D := \{x \in R . x \sim x\}$

PERs are called partial equivalence relations, since they are, in contrast to equivalence relations, reflexive only on the domain $D$.

From these axioms we can derive (by symmetry and transitivity) that all values not in the domain $D$ are not partially equivalent.

- $x \sim y$ implies $x, y \in D$
- $x \notin D$ implies $x \not\sim y$

The formalization of PERs in Isabelle HOL is similar to the formalization of equivalence relations in Section 2.2. It uses a polymorphic definition and an axiomatic type class. This definition includes equivalence relations as a special case. This is expressed with the subclass relation. The advantage of this hierarchy is that all theorems derived for types with partial equivalence relations are also available on types with equivalence relations. Furthermore we can derive all theorems of Section 3 by restricting the polymorphism to the types which have an equivalence relation defined.

```
PER0 = Set + (* PERs and ER *)

consts   (* polymorphic constant *)
         "~~"      :: "α::term ⇒ α ⇒ bool" (infixl 55)

axclass per < term   (* PERs *)
         ax_per_sym      "x ~~ y ⟹ y ~~ x"
         ax_per_trans    "⟦x ~~ y; y ~~ z⟧ ⟹ x ~~ z"

axclass er < per     (* ERs are a subclass of PERs *)
         ax_er_refl     "x ~~ x"

consts  (* characteristic constant and Domain for per *)
         "~"      :: "α::per ⇒ α ⇒ bool" (infixl 55)
         D        :: "α::per set"
defs
         per_def          "(op ~) ≡ (op ~~)"
         Domain           "D ≡ {x.x~x}"
(* define ~~ on function type ⇒ *)
         fun_per_def      "f~~g ≡ ∀x y.x∈D∧y∈D∧x~y ⟶ f x~g y"
end
```

This theory contains the definition of a PER on the function space. The following theorems can be derived for PERs:

```
(* characteristic axioms for ~ *)
         per_sym         "x ~ y ⟹ y ~ x"
         per_trans       "⟦x ~ y; y ~ z⟧ ⟹ x ~ z"
(* some theorems for ~ and the Domain D *)
         sym2refl1       "x ~ y ⟹ x ~ x"
         sym2refl2       "x ~ y ⟹ y ~ y"
         DomainD         "x ∈ D ⟹ x ~ x"
         DomainI         "x ~ x ⟹ x ∈ D"
         DomainEq        "x ∈ D = x ~ x"
         DomainI_left    "x ~ y ⟹ x ∈ D"
         DomainI_right   "x ~ y ⟹ y ∈ D"
         notDomainE1     "x ∉ D ⟹ ¬ x ~ y"
         notDomainE2     "y ∉ D ⟹ ¬ x ~ y"
(* theorems for equivalence relations *)
         er_refl         "(x::α::er) ~ x"
         er_Domain       "(x::α::er) ∈ D"
(* witnesses for "⇒" ::(per,per)per *)
         per_sym_fun     "(f::α::per ⇒ β::per)~~g ⟹ g~~f"
         per_trans_fun   "⟦(f::α::per⇒β::per)~~g;g~~h⟧⟹f~~h"
```

The last two theorems allow us to instantiate the function space into the class per in the following theory:

```
PER = PER0 +   (* instance for per *)

instance fun  :: (per,per)per   (per_sym_fun,per_trans_fun)

end
```

To expand the PER on functions without using $\sim\sim$ we deduce the instantiation rule:

$$\text{inst\_fun\_per} \quad \text{"f} \sim \text{g} = (\forall x \ y . x \in D \wedge y \in D \wedge x \sim y \longrightarrow f \ x \sim g \ y)\text{"}$$

## 4.2  Higher Order Quotients

This section defines higher order quotients and gives an implementation in Isabelle HOL which generalizes the quotient implementation. The goal is that we can derive similar theorems for higher order quotients as for quotients and to apply them to quotients as a special case[11].

**Definition 4.** Higher Order Quotient Let $\sim$ be an partial equivalence relation on $S$. Then the *higher order quotient* is the set of all *partial equivalence classes*, defined by:

- HIGHER ORDER QUOTIENT: $S_{/\sim} := \{[x]_\sim \mid x \in S\}$ where
- PARTIAL EQUIVALENCE CLASS: $[x]_\sim := \{y \in S \mid x \sim y\}$ for all $x \in S$

In contrast to the definition of equivalence classes, partial equivalence classes may be empty sets. To implement higher quotients is Isabelle we define a type constructor quot which is defined on elements of the class per. This is done in the following theory:

```
HQUOT = PER +
typedef α quot = "{s.∃r.∀y.y∈s=y~r}" (QuotNE)
```

With this **typedef** the quotient type constructor quot is defined. This type is not empty, even if the PER is always false. In this case the type contains the empty set as only element.

As in the example of quotients we define the partial equivalence class operator and the function any_in by:

```
(* HQUOT (continued) *)
consts
        peclass         :: "α::per ⇒ α quot"
        any_in          :: "α::per quot ⇒ α"
defs
        peclass_def     "<[x]> ≡ Abs_quot {y.y~x}"
        any_in_def      "any_in f ≡ @x.<[x]>=f"
end
```

---

[11] Of course we can derive all theorems for quotients also for reflexive (higher order) quotients.

Of course we can derive all theorems for quotients (see Section 3) also for reflexive (higher order) quotients. The only difference is that we have to use the class **er** for the type variables. For example:

**er_class_eq** $<[(x::\alpha::er)]>=<[y]>=x{\sim}y$

Some theorems for higher order quotients are like those for quotients, but others need an additional premise, since the concept is more general.

```
(* theorems for equality *)
        per_class_eqI   "x~y ⟹ <[x]>=<[y]>"
        per_class_eqE   "[x∈D; <[x]>=<[y]>] ⟹ x~y"
        per_class_eq    "x∈D ⟹ <[x]>=<[y]>=x~y"
(* theorems for inequality *)
        per_class_neqI  "[x∈D;¬x~y] ⟹ <[x]>≠<[y]>"
        per_class_neqE  "<[x]>≠<[y]> ⟹ ¬x~y"
        per_class_neq   "x∈D ⟹ <[x]>≠<[y]>=(¬x~y)"
(* theorems for exhaustiveness and induction *)
        per_class_exh   "∃x.q=<[x]>"
        per_class_all   "∀x.P<[x]> ⟹ P q"
(* theorems for any_in *)
        per_any_in_class "x∈D ⟹ any_in <[x]> ~ x"
        per_class_any_in "∀x::α::per.x∈D ⟹
                                <[any_in(q::α::per quot)]>=q"
```

The additional premise $x{\in}D$ is required, since there may be different elements which are not in relation to each other. All those elements would be represented by the empty partial equivalence class. Therefore we cannot deduce from the equality of equivalence classes that the elements are equivalent. This problem can be solved, if we define the PER such that it is reflexive for all elements, except for one element. Using $\bot$ as the only element which is not reflexive integrates our concept of PERs with the Scott-domains (see [Slo97] for more details).

With these polymorphic theorems we can transform theorems from representations to quotients without schematically proving them again. The reason for this is that the axiomatic type classes allow us to tailor the polymorphism to our constructions. With axiomatic type classes we can justify the use of type classes without extra-logical arguments and they allow us to prove all necessary theorems within the system.

Comparing our construction with the schematic construction of quotients shows us, beside the fact that we use PERs and higher order quotients, the argument, that we can instantiate a type only once into a type class and we can therefore have at most one quotient over every type. This drawback is overcome by an embedding method, presented in the following section. The method allows us to *reuse* a basic type for multiple quotient definitions by schematically constructing another type for the definition of the PER[12].

---

[12] Note that we do not aim at the construction of value dependent (quotient) types, like the integers modulo $n$ which would exceed Isabelle's type system. Therefore the presented method suffices for "static types".

## 5  Example: Rational Numbers

This section presents the application of (higher order) quotients on the fractional representation of rational numbers. The intended quotient is to identify terms like $\frac{1}{2}$ with $\frac{2}{4}$. This example could also be treated with ordinary quotients, however we selected it, since it is small, well-known, and suffices to illustrate the method for using quotients. The emphasis lies not only in the simple task of dealing with fractions, but also in the embedding method which allows us to reuse a type as basis for several quotients. Higher order quotients can be applied in the same way, for example to identify observational equivalent functions.

Our quotient constructor builds the quotient with respect to a fixed (partial) equivalence relation. This relation is fixed for each type by the instance of this type into the class **per**. Encoding the PER into the type class has the advantage, that the operation <[ ]> does not need an additional parameter for the PER and that we may have a general type constructor for the construction of quotient types. The drawback of this encoding is that on every type we have at most one PER.

In our example we represent rational numbers by pairs of natural numbers and positive natural numbers. However, if we have PERs on positive and natural numbers, and a general PER for pairs (p $\sim\sim$ q = (fst p $\sim$ fst q $\wedge$ snd p $\sim$ snd q)), then we have already a PER defined on pairs of natural numbers. We could build quotients over it, but this is not the PER we need to identify terms like $\frac{1}{2}$ with $\frac{2}{4}$. In addition the Isabelle type system does not allow us to instance the type (nat * pnat) directly into the class **per**, since it permits only some special forms of arities[13].

To avoid these problems, we need an embedding. We define a new representing type with the **typedef** construct.

```
NPAIR = Arith + Prod + PER + PNAT +
(* embedded representation: *)

typedef NP = "{n::nat*pnat.True}"

end
```

With this representing type we define the equivalence relation by:

```
(* NPAIR (continued) *)
defs     per_NP_def " (op ~~) ≡
                   (λx y.fst(Rep_NP x) * Rep_pnat(snd(Rep_NP y)) =
                          fst(Rep_NP y) * Rep_pnat(snd(Rep_NP x))) "
```

This definition might look quite technical, but with the theorems from the **typedef** construction with the predicate True the embedding functions for NP are isomorphisms and therefore they disappear in the proofs using the simplifier.

---

[13] Arities are a very restricted form of schematic properties about type constructors.

Since we have no special multiplication for natural numbers with positive numbers, we use the representation function Rep_pnat, defined in Section 2.1. Eliminating this representation function with the corresponding abstraction function Abs_pnat requires that the argument is a positive natural number (see the following proof).

The next step is to prove that this relation is a PER. We prove:

$$\text{per\_sym\_NP} \quad \text{"(x::NP)} \sim\sim y \implies y \sim\sim x\text{"}$$
$$\text{per\_trans\_NP} \quad \text{"[(x::NP)} \sim\sim y; \ y \sim\sim z] \implies x \sim\sim z\text{"}$$

We do not need to prove reflexivity, since we are using the higher order quotient construct, which requires only a PER. To prove transitivity of this equivalence relation was the only non-trivial task in this example.

After the instantiation of our representation into the class per we define the the type fract as quotient of our representation.

```
FRACT = NPAIR + HQUOT +
instance NP::per          (per_sym_NP,per_trans_NP)
        (* now define fractions *)
types   fract = NP quot
        (* example for fractions *)
consts  half       :: "fract"
defs    half_def     "half ≡ <[Abs_NP(1,Abs_pnat 2)]>"
end
```

We derive the instantiation rule for the representation:

```
inst_NP_per "(op ~)=(λx y.fst(Rep_NP x)*Rep_pnat(snd(Rep_NP y))=
                     fst(Rep_NP y)*Rep_pnat(snd(Rep_NP x)))"
```

As an example for an application consider the proof of the following theorem:

```
> val prems = goalw thy [half_def]
        "0<n ⟹ half = <[ Abs_NP(n,Abs_pnat(2*n)) ]>";
> by (cut_facts_tac prems 1);

Level 1
half = <[ abs_NP (n, 2 * n) ]>
  1. 0 < n ⟹
        <[ Abs_NP (1, Abs_pnat 2) ]> =
        <[ Abs_NP (n, Abs_pnat (2 * n)) ]>

(* derive that 0<n+n (=2*n) *)
> by (dres_inst_tac [("m","n")] trans_less_add2 1);

Level 2
half = <[ Abs_NP (n, Abs_pnat (2 * n)) ]>
  1. 0 < n + n ⟹
```

```
        <[ Abs_NP (1, Abs_pnat 2) ]> =
        <[ Abs_NP (n, Abs_pnat (2 * n)) ]>

> fr per_class_eqI;

Subgoal 1 selected
Level 3
half = <[ Abs_NP (n, Abs_pnat (2 * n)) ]>
 1. 0 < n + n ⟹
     Abs_NP (1, Abs_pnat 2) ~
     Abs_NP (n, Abs_pnat (2 * n))

> by (simp_tac (!simpset addsimps [inst_NP_per]) 1);
Level 4
half = <[ Abs_NP (n, Abs_pnat (2 * n)) ]>
No subgoals!
```

This proof shows how the equality between quotients is reduced to the equivalence of the representations and that the embedding functions for the PER do not harm. The embedding of positive natural numbers requires a proof step. With the instantiation rule and some arithmetic knowledge the proof is completed automatically.

This example shows how easy quotients can be applied, even if an embedding is used for the representation.

## 6 Conclusion

In this work we used axiomatic type classes and type constructors to build a quotient construction for Isabelle HOL. Using PERs instead of equivalence relations allows us to build quotients over arbitrary functions and saves us from proving reflexivity. Quotients can be used as a special case of higher order quotients. Axiomatic type classes are applied to tailor the use of polymorphism to a polymorphic construction which requires neither schematic proofs nor any extra-logical justification.

Because partial equivalence classes can be empty, some theorems for higher order quotients are not as general as those for quotients. However a combination with Scott-domains provides a solution [Slo97]. The problem that type classes do not allow us to have multiple PERs on one type is methodically avoided with the embeddings presented in the example.

PERs are a very general concept in theoretical computer science. They are used for example as models in type theory [BM92]. In the field of algebraic specifications PERs are used for the implementation of ADTs. The implementation of ADTs consists of a restriction to a subtype, followed by a quotient step. Both can be expressed by PERs (for a formalization of implementation of ADTs in first order logic with PERs see for example [BH95]). PERs can also be used to

305

define a predicate to characterize observer functions and observability in a higher order logic (see [Slo97]). There has also been some work on quotients in theorem provers (for example in [Har96], or some work from T. Kalker presented at the 1990 HOL workshop without proceedings), but these approaches do not use the advantages of polymorphism in combination with the axiomatic type classes and they cannot build quotients over arbitrary function spaces.

An interesting application of quotients is to formalize the concept of states. Consider a functional description of a software module. From an observational point of view the module receives a stream of inputs and answers with a stream of outputs. The variables in the specification and realization of this module can be expressed as quotients over input histories. If the quotient over these possibly infinite input streams is finite, model checking can be used to prove the correctness of the module. So quotients can combine functional system descriptions with states and model checking. The integration of quotients into a functional development method is described in [Slo97], the combination with model checking is ongoing work in our research project KorSys.

With this work we integrated PERs and quotients into Isabelle HOL and can use Isabelle now for formal development with quotients over arbitrary types.

**Acknowledgments:** I thank Tobias Nipkow for discussions on quotients and their implementation in Isabelle. For many comments on draft versions of this paper I thank Markus Wenzel and Jan Philipps. Furthermore I thank the anonymous referees for their constructive comments.

# References

[BH95]   Michel Bidoit and Rolf Hennicker. Behavioural Theories and The Proof of Behavioural Properties. Technical report, Paris, 1995.

[BM92]   Kim Bruce and John C. Mitchell. PER models of subtyping, recursive types and higher-order polymorphism. In *Principles of Programming Languages 19*, pages 316–327, Albequerque, New Mexico, 1992.

[Chu40]  Alonzo Church. A formulation of the simple theory of types. *J. Symbolic Logic*, 5:56–68, 1940.

[GM93]   M. Gordon and T. Melham. *Introduction to HOL: A Theorem Proving Environment for Higher Order Logic*. Cambridge University Press, 1993.

[Har96]  John Robert Harrison. *Theorem Proving with the Real Numbers*. PhD thesis, University of Cambridge Computer Laboratory, New Museums Site, Pembroke Street, Cambridge, CB2 3QG, UK, 1996. Technical Report No 408.

[HJW92]  P. Hudak, S. Peyton Jones, and P. Wadler, editors. *Report on the Programming Language Haskell, A Non-strict Purely Functional Language (Version 1.2)*. ACM SIGPLAN Notices, May 1992.

[Jon93]  M. P. Jones. *An Introduction to Gofer*, August 1993.

[Nip91]  T. Nipkow. Order-Sorted Polymorphism in Isabelle. In G. Huet, G. Plotkin, and C. Jones, editors, *Proc. 2nd Workshop on Logical Frameworks*, pages 307–321, 1991.

[Pau94]  Lawrence C. Paulson. *Isabelle: A Generic Theorem Prover*, volume 828 of *LNCS*. Springer, 1994.

[Reg94]  Franz Regensburger. *HOLCF: Eine konservative Erweiterung von HOL um LCF*. PhD thesis, Technische Universität München, 1994.

[Rob89]  Edmund Robinson. How Complete is PER? In *Fourth Annual Symposium on Logic in Computer Science*, pages 106–111, 1989.

[Slo97]  Oscar Slotosch. *Refinements in HOLCF: Implementation of Interactive Systems*. PhD thesis, Technische Universität München, 1997.

[Völ95]  Norbert Völker. On the Representation of Datatypes in Isabelle/HOL. Technical Report 379, University of Cambridge Computer Laboratory, 1995. Proceedings of the First Isabelle Users Workshop.

[Wen94]  Markus Wenzel. Axiomatische Typklassen in Isabelle. Master's thesis, Institut für Informatik, TU München, 1994.

[Wen95]  M. Wenzel.
*Using axiomatic type classes in Isabelle — a tutorial*, 1995. Available at http://www4.informatik.tu-muenchen.de/~nipkow/isadist/axclass.dvi.gz.

[Wen97]  M. Wenzel. Type Classes and Overloading in Higher-Order Logic. In *Proceedings of Theorem Proving in Higher Order Logics*, 1997. in this volume.

# Type Classes and Overloading
# in Higher-Order Logic

Markus Wenzel*

Technische Universität München
Institut für Informatik, Arcisstraße 21, 80290 München, Germany
http://www4.informatik.tu-muenchen.de/~wenzelm/
wenzelm@informatik.tu-muenchen.de

**Abstract** Type classes and overloading are shown to be independent concepts that can both be added to simple higher-order logics in the tradition of Church and Gordon, without demanding more logical expressiveness. In particular, model-theoretic issues are not affected. Our meta-logical results may serve as a foundation of systems like Isabelle/Pure that offer the user Haskell-style order-sorted polymorphism as an extended syntactic feature. The latter can be used to describe simple abstract theories with a single carrier type and a fixed signature of operations.

## 1 Introduction

Higher-order logic (HOL) dates back to Church's 1940 formulation of the "simple theory of types" [2], originally intended as foundation of mathematics.

Gordon later extended the system by an object-level first-order language of types (by including type variables and type constructors), and — most importantly — definitional mechanisms that guarantee safe theory extensions. Various implementations of theorem provers based on Gordon's HOL [4] proved to be very successful for many applications in computer science and mathematics.

Paulson's generic theorem proving environment Isabelle is based on an (intuitionistic) version of HOL since Isabelle-89 [11]. In Isabelle-91, a Haskell-like type system with ordered type classes has been added [9], though without investigating logical foundation issues very much.

Somewhat later, a conceptual bug concerning the handling of empty classes was discovered that actually made Isabelle's meta-logic implementation inconsistent. Embarrassing slips of this kind illustrate why mechanized proof assistants should be based on well-understood logical frameworks only, lest the "formal" proofs conducted by users inherit any uncertainty.

The present paper aims to close this foundational gap of Isabelle. Our main contributions are:

---

* Research supported by DFG SPP "Deduktion".

- An interpretation of type classes in higher-order logic.
- A definitional mechanism for axiomatic type classes.
- A generalization of constant definitions admitting overloading and recursion over types.

In particular, we will see that type classes have already been implicitly present in Gordon-like HOL systems all the time. So the seeming extensions of Isabelle/Pure over basic HOL can be explained just as additional syntactic features offered for the user's convenience. What really goes beyond Gordon's HOL (extra-logically, though) are overloaded constant definitions.

While the concepts of type classes and overloading can be explained independently in HOL, they are closely related in practice: Without type classes as a syntactic device, overloading tends to become undisciplined. Without overloaded definitions, type classes could be defined but not instantiated in useful manners.

Although the initial motivation arose in the Isabelle setting, the subsequent presentation is more general. Our results can be easily applied to similar HOL systems.

A note on terminology: HOL shall refer to the abstract logical system used to explain the concepts in this paper. The concrete incarnations are Isabelle/Pure (Isabelle's meta-logic), Isabelle/HOL (an object-logic within Isabelle/Pure), and Gordon/HOL. As a quite harmless simplification, HOL can also be identified directly with Isabelle/Pure.

The paper is structured as follows: Section 2 starts with some examples of using type classes, without giving any formal background. Section 3 sketches the syntax and deductive system of the HOL logic. Section 4 discusses the issue of safe theory extension in general and concludes with generalized constant definitions including overloading and recursion over types. Section 5 introduces type classes and their interpretation in HOL. Section 6 concludes with safe mechanisms for definition and instantiation of axiomatic type classes.

## 2 Examples of Using Type Classes

### 2.1 Type Classes in Programming Languages

We quickly review some aspects of type classes in languages like Haskell [6].

Within a setting of this kind, classes are supposed to describe collections of types that provide (or *implement*) operations of certain names and types. For example, consider the following **class** definition (modulo concrete Haskell-syntax):

**class** *ord*
$\leq :: \alpha_{ord} \rightarrow \alpha_{ord} \rightarrow bool$

Class *ord* requires of its instances $\tau$ to provide some relation $\leq :: \tau \to \tau \to bool$. This is witnessed in the **instance** construct by a suitable definition. For example:

> **instance** *nat* :: *ord*
> $x_{nat} \leq y_{nat} \equiv nat\_le$

Nothing more specific is required of $\leq :: nat \to nat \to bool$ than its type. From the chosen name $\leq$, everyone will think of it as some order, of course. This shall be implemented appropriately by above program text *nat_le*.

So we observe that Haskell type classes can be viewed as the *signature* part of simple algebraic *structures* consisting of one carrier type and associated operations (or *member functions*). Additional semantic properties (or *class axioms*) may come in as mere convention.

Speaking in terms of the example above, the concrete instance can be understood as a poset structure $(nat, \leq^{nat})$.

## 2.2 Type Classes in HOL

The Haskell notion that instances of type classes provide operations of certain names and types is *not* amenable to logical systems like HOL. One just cannot express within the logic if objects are *declared* or *meaningful*.

Even from an extra-logical point of view, such notions are not very appropriate. The HOL world is total in the sense that everything of any type is always meaningful. Even constants of arbitrary type can be safely declared at any time, without changing very much. In the worst case it may happen that no useful theorems can be derived about some objects. Consider the latter just as a boundary case of loose specification.

We argue that a straightforward interpretation of classes should be simply as set-theoretic predicates: type classes denote classes of types. A view of classes as abstract algebras can be still recovered from this frugal interpretation. As an example consider the following class of orders in HOL:

> **consts** $\leq :: \alpha \to \alpha \to prop$
> **class** *ord*
>> *reflexive* $\quad x_\alpha \leq x_\alpha$
>> *transitive* $\quad x_\alpha \leq y_\alpha \wedge y_\alpha \leq z_\alpha \Rightarrow x_\alpha \leq z_\alpha$
>> *antisymmetric* $x_\alpha \leq y_\alpha \wedge y_\alpha \leq x_\alpha \Rightarrow x_\alpha = y_\alpha$

Note that **consts** above is not actually part of the class definition. The declaration of $\leq$ just ensures that the class axioms are syntactically well-formed.

The meaning of *ord* is a type predicate stating that $\leq :: \alpha \to \alpha \to prop$ is an order relation. It does not express anything like "$\leq$ is available on a type" — this would be trivially true in HOL anyway.

Concrete instances $\tau$ :: *ord* are required to have the corresponding $\leq ::$ $\tau \to \tau \to prop$ specified in such a way, that the order properties are derivable.

This is typically achieved by means of a constant definition[2] prior to the actual instantiation. As an example consider:

**defs** $x_{nat} \leq y_{nat} \equiv nat\_le$
**instance** $nat :: ord$

Again observe that **defs** is not part of our **instance** construct, just as **consts** had been independent of **class**. Assuming that the term $nat\_le$ expresses a suitable relation, we are able to derive *reflexive, transitive, antisymmetric* for type $nat$ in the theory. Thus the instantiation $nat :: ord$ is justified within the logic.

Note that in concrete system implementations the user will have to provide the witness theorems for **instance** explicitly.

Our version of HOL definitions not only admit overloading, but also primitive recursion over types. The latter can be used to mimic lifting of polymorphic operations. For example, consider the following definition:

**defs** $x_{\alpha \times \beta} \leq y_{\alpha \times \beta} \equiv fst\ x_{\alpha \times \beta} \leq fst\ y_{\alpha \times \beta} \wedge snd\ x_{\alpha \times \beta} \leq snd\ y_{\alpha \times \beta}$

enabling us to derive the order properties of $\leq$ on $\alpha \times \beta$, under the assumption that these already hold on $\alpha$ and $\beta$. This justifies an instantiation of the form:

**instance** $\times :: (ord, ord)\ ord$

Thus the type operator $\times$ can be understood as a functor for direct binary products of order structures.

Note that overloaded definitions must not overlap. In particular, there may be at most one equation for the same type scheme. For example, having already defined $\leq$ on $\alpha \times \beta$ component-wise rules out to redefine it later as lexicographic order.

Thus the signature part of the abstract theories that can be described is *fixed*. Type classes only have the carrier type as a parameter, but not the operations.

This drawback is not specific to HOL, though. Type classes may be only instantiated once in current Haskell-like languages, too.

More examples and applications of type classes as a light-weight mechanism of simple abstract theories can be found in the Isabelle library [7], especially in the HOL and HOL/AxClasses directories. There is also a tutorial on axiomatic type classes available as part of the Isabelle documentation [15].

Above examples should have illustrated to some extend how the two concepts of overloaded definitions and type classes can be joined into a practically useful mechanism. Both can be understood independently in HOL, though. The logical foundations of **defs** will be explained in §4, especially §4.5. The exact meaning of **class** and **instance** will be given in §6.

---

[2] Which is overloaded in general, because there may be many different instantiations.

# 3 The HOL Logic

We briefly sketch the syntax and deductive system of our version of HOL. The presentation is somewhat reminiscent of [13], but differs in many details.

## 3.1 HOL Syntax

**Types and Terms** The syntax of HOL is just that of simply-typed $\lambda$-calculus with a first order language of types.

*Types* are either variables $\alpha$, or applications $(\tau_1, \ldots, \tau_n) t$ of an $n$-place constructor $t$ applied to types $\tau_i$. We drop the parentheses for $n \in \{0, 1\}$. Binary constructors are often written infix, e.g. function types as $\tau_1 \to \tau_2$ (associate to the right).

*Terms* are built up from explicitly typed atomic terms (constants $c_\tau$ or variables $x_\tau$) through application $tu$ (of type $\tau_2$, provided that $t : \tau_1 \to \tau_2$ and $u : \tau_1$) and abstraction $\lambda x_{\tau_1}.t$ (of type $\tau_1 \to \tau_2$, provided that $t : \tau_2$). As usual, application associates to the left and binds most tightly. An abstraction body ranges from the dot as far to the right as possible. Nested abstractions like $\lambda x. \lambda y.t$ are abbreviated to $\lambda x\, y.t$.

Note that atomic terms $a_\tau$ actually consist of two components: name $a$ and type $\tau$. In particular, variables $x_{\tau_1}$ and $x_{\tau_2}$ with the same name but different types are treated as different.

Furthermore we assume suitable functions TV (on types or terms) and FV (on terms), yielding the type variables and free term variables of their respective arguments.

**Type Substitutions and Instances** Type substitutions $[\tau_1/\alpha_1, \ldots, \tau_n/\alpha_n]$ shall be defined as usual. Their application (to types or terms) is written postfix.

For types or terms $T$, $U$, we call $T$ a *type instance* of $U$ (written $T \leq U$) iff there is some substitution $\delta$ such that $T = U\delta$. Given any set $A$ of types or terms, let $A{\downarrow}$ denote the downwardly closed set of all of its type instances.

**Theories** consist of a *signature* part (constants and types) together with *axioms*. We use a notation like:

$$\Theta_2 = \Theta_1 \ \cup \ (\alpha_1, \ldots, \alpha_n) t \ \cup \ c :: \sigma \ \cup \ \vdash \Phi$$

meaning that theory $\Theta_2$ is the extension of $\Theta_1$ by declaring type constructor $t$ of arity $n$, constants $c :: \sigma$ (representing the set $c_\sigma{\downarrow}$), and asserting all axioms of the set $\Phi$.

We always assume that theories contain at least the following signature:

| | |
|---|---|
| *prop* | propositions |
| $\alpha \rightarrow \beta$ | functions |
| $\Rightarrow :: prop \rightarrow prop \rightarrow prop$ | implication |
| $\equiv :: \alpha \rightarrow \alpha \rightarrow prop$ | equality |
| $\forall :: (\alpha \rightarrow prop) \rightarrow prop$ | universal quantification |

As usual, $\forall(\lambda\, x_\tau.t)$ is written as $\forall x_\tau.\ t$. Nested $\forall$'s are abbreviated like nested $\lambda$'s. Other logical operators (*True*, *False*, $\wedge$, etc.) could be introduced in an obvious way. They sometimes simplify our presentation, without being really necessary.

Any term of type *prop* is a *formula*. Our type of propositions is sometimes called $o$ in the literature, in Gordon/HOL the analogous type is *bool*.

## 3.2 The HOL Deductive System

Due to space limitations, we do not give a full calculus for HOL here. It suffices to say that given some theory $\Theta$, we have some inductively defined relation $\Gamma \vdash_\Theta \varphi$ of *derivable sequents* (where antecedents $\Gamma$ are *finite* sets of formulas).

We use the usual abbreviations: $\Gamma \vdash \varphi$ for $\Gamma \vdash_\Theta \varphi$ if $\Theta$ is clear from context, $\vdash \varphi$ for $\{\} \vdash \varphi$, and $\Gamma_1, \Gamma_2 \vdash \varphi$ for $\Gamma_1 \cup \Gamma_2 \vdash \varphi$, and so on. The full set of inference rules for $\vdash_\Theta$ consists of about 15 schemas. As an example we present only two:

$$\frac{\Gamma \vdash \psi}{\Gamma \setminus \{\varphi\} \vdash \varphi \Rightarrow \psi}\ (\Rightarrow\mathrm{I}) \qquad \frac{\Gamma_1 \vdash \varphi \Rightarrow \psi \quad \Gamma_2 \vdash \varphi}{\Gamma_1, \Gamma_2 \vdash \psi}\ (\mathrm{MP})$$

Thus we get a single-conclusion sequent calculus, similar to the one presented in [13] for Gordon/HOL. If the rules are chosen suitably, the system may also be read as natural deduction (which is preferred in the Isabelle literature [12]). This and other details (e.g. classical vs. intuitionistic HOL) do not matter here. Subsequently, some general idea of what theorems are derivable in higher-order logic will be sufficient for the level of abstraction of this paper.

## 4 Meta-level Definitions

The most important contribution of Gordon/HOL [4] over the original formulation of Church [2] are disciplined mechanisms of theory extension. Using only these instead of unrestricted axiomatizations guarantees that certain nice properties of theories are preserved.

Such extensions are usually called *conservative*, *definitional*, *sound* etc., often with some confusion about the exact meaning of these phrases. So before introducing our generalized constant definitions (cf. §4.5), we set out to discuss what qualifies extension mechanisms as safe in our HOL setting.

## 4.1 Consistency Preservation

A theory is called *(syntactically) consistent* iff not all formulas are derivable. An inconsistent theory certainly does not have any models, since every formula is a theorem (including $\vdash$ *False*). A theory extension mechanism is called *consistency preserving* iff any extension of consistent theories is also consistent.

Although being a nice concept, consistency preservation is certainly not the key property that qualifies theory extensions as safe in the HOL setting:

Syntactic consistency of theories is not a very strong property. In particular it does not necessarily imply existence of suitable models. This would require *completeness* of the deductive system wrt. the underlying model theory, which does not generally hold in higher-order logic.

More surprisingly, some kinds of safe extensions do not necessarily preserve consistency in general — notably Gordon/HOL type definitions, see below.

## 4.2 Syntactic conservativity

**Definition 1.** An extension $\Theta_2$ of some theory $\Theta_1$ is called *(syntactically) conservative* iff for any formula $\varphi$ of signature $\Theta_1$ it holds that $\vdash_{\Theta_2} \varphi \Rightarrow \vdash_{\Theta_1} \varphi$.

Syntactic conservativity is traditional [1]. It ensures that extensions do not change derivability of formulas that do not contain any of the newly introduced syntactic objects (constants and types). It is also very easy to see that syntactic conservativity implies consistency preservation.

We consider syntactic conservativity as a minimum requirement for well-behaved extension mechanisms within purely deductive logical frameworks.

## 4.3 Model Preservation

We briefly review Gordon/HOL's extension mechanisms and the way they are justified as *conservative* [13]. Basically, the system features two kinds of theory extensions:[3]

**Constant definition** $\Theta_2 = \Theta_1 \cup c :: \sigma \cup \vdash c_\sigma \equiv t$ provided that $c$ is new and does not occur in $t$, also $FV(t) = \{\}$ and $TV(t) = TV(\sigma)$.

**Type definition** $\Theta_2 = \Theta_1 \cup (\alpha_1, \ldots, \alpha_n) t \cup \vdash (\alpha_1, \ldots, \alpha_n) t \approx A$, where $t$ is an $n$-ary type constructor and $A$ is a term representing some set, and the notation $\tau \approx A$ shall abbreviate some suitable formula stating that $\tau$ is isomorphic to $A$. The definition shall be well-formed, provided $t$ is new and does not occur in $A$, also $FV(A) = \{\}$, $TV(A) \subseteq \{\alpha_1, \ldots, \alpha_n\}$, and non-emptiness of $A$ is derivable in $\Theta_1$.

---

[3] Actually, Gordon/HOL admits more general forms of (loose) specifications than presented here. We can ignore this without loss of generality, at the level of abstraction of this paper.

Both these mechanisms are justified as being safe extensions because they preserve Gordon/HOL standard models: If $\Theta_1$ has such a model, so does $\Theta_2$. These models are specifically tailored for the Gordon/HOL logic [13] and are quite special in at least the following ways:

- They are classical.
- They are standard[4].
- Types are interpreted from subset-closed universes.

In particular, the last property is the crucial one for type definitions being safe. We quickly sketch a counterexample where Gordon/HOL type definitions do not preserve syntactic consistency.

Consider some base theory $\Theta_0$ and some formula $three^\alpha$ expressing that $\alpha$ has cardinality 3. Now let $\Theta_1 = \Theta_0 \cup \vdash (three^\alpha \Rightarrow False)$. It is easy to see that $\Theta_1$ is consistent: For example one can give a very simple model (non-standard in the Gordon/HOL-sense) where all interpretations of types are sets of some cardinality $2^k$, for $k \in \mathbb{N}_0$. Finally let $\Theta_2 = \Theta_1 \cup thr \cup \vdash thr \approx \{0,1,2\}$, and observe that $\vdash_{\Theta_2} three^{thr}$ is derivable, and thus $\vdash False$. So this theory is inconsistent!

Furthermore, type definitions are not necessarily syntactically conservative, even if the theories involved have a Gordon/HOL standard model.

The counterexample is a simple modification of the previous one: Basically, just substitute some proper constant definition $c \equiv t$ for $False$. Then it is relatively easy to see that $\Theta_0$, $\Theta_1$, $\Theta_2$ all have standard models. An argument similar to the one above shows that $\vdash c \equiv t$ is not derivable in $\Theta_1$, but is so in $\Theta_2$. That is, the definition of type $thr$ changed derivability on existing formulas — it is not syntactically conservative!

Of course nothing is wrong with Gordon/HOL type definitions, as long as one does not leave the dedicated model theory. The above examples should illustrate, though, why we cannot justify our extensions in this setting:

Our HOL should serve as a *meta-logical framework* for expressing many different kinds of deductive systems (or *object-logics* in Isabelle parlance). In other words, results about safeness of extensions should be applicable to Isabelle/Pure, not just to particular object-logics like Isabelle/HOL.

Focusing solely on the Gordon/HOL standard model theory here would basically restrict object-logics to what is known as *shallow embeddings* in the HOL community. Then justifying for example full Zermelo-Fränkel set theory in this framework [3] would be much more difficult than if encoded as a purely deductive system the Isabelle way.

---

[4] *Standard* in the sense of [1] which also treats a certain kind of *non-standard* models. The latter may interpret $\tau_1 \rightarrow \tau_2$ as proper subsets of the full function space $[\tau_1] \rightarrow [\tau_2]$. Interestingly, the deductive system of classical HOL is *complete* wrt. this class of *general* models [5].

## 4.4 Meta-safe Extensions

We now introduce a notion of safe theory extensions that is more appropriate for our meta-logical HOL setting:

**Definition 2.** Any extension $\Theta_2$ of some theory $\Theta_1$ is called *meta-safe* iff:

- It is syntactically conservative.
- Introduced objects are *(syntactically) realizable*:
  For all new $c$ there is some function $r$ from types to terms, such that $r(\tau) : \tau$ and $\vdash_{\Theta_2} \varphi \Rightarrow \vdash_{\Theta_1} \varphi[r/c]$, for all $\varphi$. Here the notation $[r/c]$ shall denote replacement of any $c_\tau$ by $r(\tau)$.

First observe that because of syntactic conservativity, object-logics are free to *ignore* meta-safe extensions, by just not referring to them syntactically.

Syntactic realizability can be seen as a generalized counterpart of model preservation, always staying within the deductive system of HOL, though. Newly introduced names can be seen as just an abbreviation for pre-existent syntactic objects that have the same properties (because the same theorems are derivable).

So there are two ways for object-logics to *cooperate* with meta-safe extensions[5]: Either just consider all object-level formulations modulo expansion of all meta definitions, without changing the semantics, or adjust your model theory to interpret defined objects according to $[r/c]$, utilizing the realization function.

## 4.5 Overloaded Constant Definitions

Having provided enough preliminaries, we can now present our generalization of constant definitions:

**Overloaded constant definition** $\Theta_2 = \Theta_1 \cup c :: \sigma \cup \vdash \Delta_c$, where $\Delta_c$ is some set of equations $c_\tau \equiv t$. The definition shall be well-formed, provided that $c$ is new, all $\mathrm{FV}(t) = \{\}$ and $\mathrm{TV}(\tau) = \mathrm{TV}(t)$; furthermore all $c_\tau$ have to be instances of $c_\sigma$, no two different $c_{\tau_1}, c_{\tau_2}$ may have common instances, and recursive occurrences of any $c_{\tau'}$ in some $t$ may be only at such types $\tau'$ that are strictly simpler than $\tau$ in a well-founded sense.

In practice, the strictly simpler notion above will be just structural containment. Thus we get constant definitions with general *primitive recursion over types*. As an example, consider:

$$0 :: \alpha$$
$$\vdash 0_{nat} \equiv zero$$
$$\vdash 0_{\alpha \times \beta} \equiv (0_\alpha, 0_\beta)$$
$$\vdash 0_{\alpha \to \beta} \equiv \lambda x_\alpha . 0_\beta$$

---

[5] Think of Gordon/HOL type definitions, where the representing sets may contain meta-safely introduced constants, for example.

which defines $0$ on *nat*, also lifting it to binary products and function spaces. $0_\tau$ is still unspecified on types $\tau$ that are not instances of *nat* or $\alpha \times \beta$ or $\alpha \to \beta$.

Note that this extension mechanism requires that all defining equations are given at the same time (right after the constant declaration). One might want to relax this in concrete system implementations, allowing the user to augment theories by additional equations for constants on new type instances in an incremental way. The system will then have to keep track of all the partial definitions, ensuring that the resulting jumble of equations can be sorted out into proper overloaded constant definitions at any time.

We now briefly sketch why overloaded constant definitions are indeed meta-safe. Due to space limitations, we have to gloss over various technical lemmas about HOL deductions (most importantly freeness of unspecified constants and the deduction theorem).

The key property of our generalized constant definitions is:

**Lemma 3.** *Given any overloaded constant definition* $\Theta_2 = \Theta_1 \cup c :: \sigma \cup \vdash \Delta_c$. *Then there is some partial function* $f$ *from types to terms of* $\Theta_1 \cup c :: \sigma$, *such that* $f(\tau) : \tau$, *and* $f$ *establishes all type instances of* $\Delta_c$:

$$\vdash_{(\Theta_1 \cup c::\sigma)} \Delta_c{\downarrow}[f/c]$$

The proof exploits the well-formedness restrictions on the set of equations $\Delta_c$ in straightforward ways: Some canonical $f^{\Delta_c}$ is constructed by well-founded recursion over types such that the given equations hold. Mainly this works, because no two different $c_{\tau_1}, c_{\tau_2}$ on the l.h.s. have common instances, and recursive occurrences on the r.h.s. are well-foundedly simpler. Also $TV(\tau) = TV(t)$ plays an important rôle.

Note that $f^{\Delta_c}$ is really partial in general, i.e. $[f^{\Delta_c}/c]$ does not necessarily eliminate all type instances of $c :: \sigma$. If one views $\Delta_c$ as a convergent term rewriting system, it leaves exactly those $c_\tau$ unchanged that are normal wrt. $\Delta_c$.

One can easily extend $f^{\Delta_c}$ to some total $F^{\Delta_c}$ that also eliminates leftover $c_\tau$ (replacing them by any term of type $\tau$), such that $\vdash \Delta_c{\downarrow}[F^{\Delta_c}/c]$ in $\Theta_1$.

Our main result on the issue of meta-level definitions is:

**Theorem 4.** *Overloaded constant definitions are meta-safe.*

The proof exploits $f^{\Delta_c}$ and $F^{\Delta_c}$ as constructed above. Then both syntactic conservativity and realizability are relatively simple consequences of lemma 3. Unfortunately, we cannot give more details (which are rather technical) at the level of abstraction of this paper.

# 5 Type Classes

## 5.1 An Order-sorted Type System

The HOL language as presented in §3 provides two syntactic layers: higher-order *terms* that are annotated by first-order *types*. We now conceptually add a third level of ordered *type classes* (or *sorts*) that qualify types. Thus the algebra of types becomes an order-sorted structure that is amenable to well-known techniques like order-sorted unification [14]. In particular, ML-style type inference can be easily generalized to the order-sorted system [9, 10].

**Order-sorted Type Signatures** consist of three basic components: a finite set $C$ of *type classes*, a *class inclusion* relation $\preceq$, and a set of *type arities*.

The initial class structure $(C, \preceq)$ is canonically extended to a quasi-ordered sort structure $(S, \sqsubseteq)$ such that sorts are finite sets of classes: Any sort $s = \{c_1, \ldots, c_n\}$ is supposed to represent the intersection $c_1 \sqcap \ldots \sqcap c_n$. Inclusion is extended from classes to sorts accordingly:

$$s_1 \sqsubseteq s_2 \quad :\Longleftrightarrow \quad \forall c_2 \in s_2.\, \exists c_1 \in s_1.\, c_1 \preceq c_2$$

Note that there is always a greatest sort, namely the empty intersection $\{\}$, which shall be subsequently written as $\top$.

Type arities are declarations of the form $t :: (s_1, \ldots, s_n)\, s$, where $t$ is an $n$-place type constructor, and $s_1, \ldots, s_n, s$ are sorts. This is supposed to be a partial specification of how $t$ acts on certain subsets of the universe of types.

**Sort Assignment** We assume that type variables $\alpha_s$ carry globally fixed sorting information. One can think of variables as actually consisting of two components: base name $\alpha$ and sort $s$.

Now given some order-sorted type signature, sorts are assigned to types via the following set of rules:

$$\frac{}{\alpha_s : s} \qquad \frac{\tau_1 : s_1 \quad \cdots \quad \tau_n : s_n \quad t :: (s_1, \ldots, s_n)\, s}{(\tau_1, \ldots, \tau_n)\, t : s} \qquad \frac{\tau : s_1 \quad s_1 \sqsubseteq s_2}{\tau : s_2}$$

While there may be many type arities for the same constructor, this introduces neither overloading nor partiality to the level of types. In fact, type arity declarations do not change the well-formedness of types (as defined in §3) at all. They only influence sort assignment — via the second rule above. Even having no arities for some constructor is no problem, then one just cannot derive interesting sort assignments.

In general, there may be many sorts assigned to any given type. The literature [14] calls a type signature *regular* iff for all types, the set of assigned sorts has some least element (modulo sort equivalence). This always holds in our setting, because sort structures are closed wrt. intersection. Another nice property is *co-regularity* which guarantees unitary order-sorted unification of types [14] and principal type schemes for arbitrary terms [9].

Such technical issues do not matter here. We will be more interested in the logical content of order-sorted type signatures (see §5.3).

## 5.2 Representing Type Classes in HOL

Expressing type predicates in HOL might seem difficult at first sight: We cannot have objects $c$: "$type$" $\to$ $prop$, as for good reasons there is no type of all types.

Type predicates are not needed as first class objects, though. A kind of *propositional language of types* that is capable to express class membership "$\tau \in c$" will be sufficient. Now HOL obviously provides this sort of thing: Any formula $\varphi[\alpha]$ that (potentially) contains some type variable $\alpha$ may be viewed as a proposition about types. As an example consider $\forall x_\alpha\, y_\alpha.\ x_\alpha \equiv y_\alpha$ that describes the class of all singleton types.

Remains the problem to encode *class constants* (in a way that admits some meta-safe mechanism for *class definitions*). There are probably many ways to accomplish this, the one presented now seems to be particularly easy to motivate.

**The Encoding** First, we augment our basis theory by simply adding unspecified types $\alpha\ itself$ and constants $TYPE$ :: $\alpha\ itself$.

Now for any type class $c$ introduced by the user, we declare a polymorphic constant $c$ :: $\alpha\ itself$ $\to$ $prop$. Applications of the form $(c_{\tau\ itself\to prop}\ TYPE_{\tau\ itself})$, which are of type $prop$, shall be considered to represent the proposition "$\tau$ is member of $c$". Subsequently, the telling notation $\langle\!\langle \tau : c \rangle\!\rangle$ will be used to abbreviate these terms.

This encoding seems to be an elaboration of a folklore technique from the LCF community, used to express flatness of domains.

**A Motivation** So far, we have just introduced abbreviations $\langle\!\langle \tau : c \rangle\!\rangle$ for some terms $(c_{\tau\ itself\to prop}\ TYPE_{\tau\ itself})$. How can we understand this as a representation of "$\tau$ is a member of $c$"?

The following motivation is based on a simple set-theoretic semantics of HOL, where types denote sets and type constructors functions that operate on sets.

We choose to interpret $[itself]$ as the function $A \mapsto \{A\}$, then $[\tau\ itself] = \{[\tau]\}$ for all types $\tau$. In other words, type constructor *itself* builds singleton sets containing the argument itself only. The sole element of any $[\tau\ itself]$ will be $[TYPE_{\tau\ itself}]$, so we see also that $TYPE_{\tau\ itself}$ has to represent type[6] $\tau$.

Next consider $[\tau\ itself \to prop]$. This is interpreted as $\{[\tau]\} \to \{0,1\}$, assuming that $[\to]$ is set-theoretic function space, and $[prop]$ just the boolean values. Observe that in general, function spaces $\{a\} \to B$ with singleton domain set $\{a\}$ may be viewed as just an isomorphic copy of $B$ marked (or parameterized) by $a$. So $[\tau\ itself \to prop]$ are propositions parameterized by types and objects $c_{\tau\ itself\to prop}$ can already be understood as expressing type membership. Their formal application to the canonical elements $TYPE_{\tau\ itself}$ is strictly speaking redundant, but then $\langle\!\langle \tau : c \rangle\!\rangle$ also has type $prop$ syntactically.

---

[6] There is nothing wrong with some terms ("objects") representing types ("collections of objects") in higher-order logic.

Note that above interpretation of $\alpha$ *itself* and *TYPE* :: $\alpha$ *itself* could have been *enforced* by means of Gordon/HOL-style definitions:

$$\vdash \alpha \; itself \approx \{\lambda x_\alpha . \; True\} \qquad \text{and} \qquad \vdash TYPE_{\alpha \; itself} \equiv \lambda x_\alpha . \; True$$

Unfortunately, the first one is an object-level type definition, which is unavailable at our more abstract meta-level of HOL. This is why we prefer to leave $\alpha$ *itself* and $TYPE_{\alpha \; itself}$ unspecified in the first place.

It is important to note that there are no HOL terms representing type classes *per se*. For that we would have to leave HOL and conceptually abstract over the first position of $\langle\!\langle \tau : c \rangle\!\rangle$. Thus contexts of the form $\langle\!\langle \_ : c \rangle\!\rangle$ could be viewed as extra-logical representations of actual type predicates.

## 5.3 Interpreting the Order-sorted Type System

We are now ready to explain the order-sorted concepts of §5.1 in terms of HOL: The meaning of primitive type signature components will be defined in a quite obvious manner. Derived notions that depend on these (e. g. sort assignment) are shown to be consistent with appropriate logical counterparts.

**Order-sorted Type Signatures** have the following logical content:

**Classes** $c$ appear as polymorphic constant declarations $c :: \alpha$ *itself* $\rightarrow$ *prop* in the theory's signature (cf. §5.2). Recall that class membership is encoded via some terms written $\langle\!\langle \tau : c \rangle\!\rangle$.

**Class inclusion** $c_1 \preceq c_2$ is simply expressed point-wise using logical implication as formula $\langle\!\langle \alpha : c_1 \rangle\!\rangle \Rightarrow \langle\!\langle \alpha : c_2 \rangle\!\rangle$.

**Sorts** $s = \{c_1, \ldots, c_n\}$ are supposed to represent intersections of finitely many classes. Thus sort membership $\tau : \{c_1, \ldots, c_n\}$ can be expressed using conjunction as $\langle\!\langle \tau : c_1 \rangle\!\rangle \wedge \cdots \wedge \langle\!\langle \tau : c_n \rangle\!\rangle$. The latter term shall be abbreviated as $\langle\!\langle \tau : \{c_1, \ldots, c_n\} \rangle\!\rangle$. Note that this interpretation is well-defined, independently of order (or repetition) of $c_1, \ldots, c_n$.

**Sort inclusion** $s_1 \sqsubseteq s_2$ has been defined in terms of class inclusion in §5.1. To show that this is compatible with $\langle\!\langle \alpha : s_1 \rangle\!\rangle \Rightarrow \langle\!\langle \alpha : s_2 \rangle\!\rangle$ in the logic one has to demonstrate that this formula can be derived in HOL under the assumption of the class inclusions taken from the corresponding relation $\preceq$ of the type signature. The proof of this fact just relies on some basic deductive properties of $\wedge$.

**Type arities** $t :: (s_1, \ldots, s_n) \; s$ are simple schematic statements about the image of type constructors. We express this point-wise as follows:

$$\langle\!\langle \alpha_1 : s_1 \rangle\!\rangle \wedge \cdots \wedge \langle\!\langle \alpha_n : s_n \rangle\!\rangle \Rightarrow \langle\!\langle (\alpha_1, \ldots, \alpha_n) \, t : s \rangle\!\rangle$$

So in ordinary mathematical notation, arity declarations would be something like $f(A_1, \ldots, A_n) \subseteq A$ and not $f : A_1 \times \cdots \times A_n \rightarrow A$.

**Sort Contexts** Sorted type variables $\alpha_s$ are supposed to express some implicit restriction to types of certain sorts. Thus formulas $\varphi[\alpha_{s_1}, \beta_{s_2}, \ldots]$ have to be interpreted actually under additional assumptions $\langle\!\langle \alpha_{s_1} : s_1 \rangle\!\rangle, \langle\!\langle \beta_{s_2} : s_2 \rangle\!\rangle, \ldots$.

In general, given any term or type $T$, let $C(T)$ denote its set of implicit sort constraints, which shall be also called *sort context* of $T$.

**Sort Assignment** $\tau : s$ has been defined §5.1 relatively to a given type signature via a certain set of inference rules. We show compatibility with a corresponding logical notion: If $\tau : s$ holds syntactically, then $C(\tau) \vdash \langle\!\langle \tau : s \rangle\!\rangle$ is derivable in HOL (having the implicit sort constraints appear as explicit assumptions).

In order to prove this, simply mimic the syntactic sort assignment rules of §5.1 by suitable logical counterparts. For example, the last rule would become:

$$\frac{C(\tau) \vdash \langle\!\langle \tau : s_1 \rangle\!\rangle \quad s_1 \sqsubseteq s_1}{C(\tau) \vdash \langle\!\langle \tau : s_2 \rangle\!\rangle}$$

These rules are either logical trivialities or just variants of modus-ponens combined with instantiation, recalling from above the meaning of $s_1 \sqsubseteq s_2$ and $t :: (s_1, \ldots, s_n) \, s$ as certain implications.

Putting all these results together, we see that syntactic operations performed at the type signature level (e. g. during order-sorted unification or type inference) can be understood as a *correct approximation* of logical reasoning.

Seen the other way round, a simple fragment of the propositional logic of types within HOL is reflected at the type signature level, thus automating some portions of logical reasoning behind the scenes, to the user's benefit.

# 6 Class Definitions and Instantiations

We finally give the logical meanings of **class** and **instance** that have already been sketched in §2.2.

First the basic mechanism that introduces type classes in a disciplined way:

**Class definition** $\Theta_2 = \Theta_1 \cup c :: \alpha \, itself \to prop \cup \vdash \langle\!\langle \alpha : c \rangle\!\rangle \equiv \varphi$ provided that $c$ is new and does not occur in $\varphi$, also $FV(\varphi) = \{\}$ and $TV(\varphi) \subseteq \{\alpha\}$.

**Theorem 5.** *Class definitions are meta-safe.*

The proof is very simple: Class definitions are already *almost* well-formed definitions of constants $c :: \alpha \, itself \to prop$. Just the equation $\vdash \langle\!\langle \alpha : c \rangle\!\rangle \equiv \varphi$ looks odd at first sight, but is actually equivalent to a proper definition $\vdash c_{\alpha \, itself \to prop} \equiv \lambda x_{\alpha \, itself} . \varphi$.

We can now explain the **class** construct, which has the general form:

**class** $c \preceq c_1, \ldots, c_n$
$\varphi_1 \cdots \varphi_m$

where $c_1, \ldots, c_n$ are the superclasses of $c$ and $\varphi_1, \ldots, \varphi_m$ the class axioms (with $TV(\varphi_j) \subseteq \{\alpha\}$ for all $j = 1, \ldots, m$). This shall be just considered concrete user interface syntax for the following proper class definition:

$$c :: \alpha \; itself \to prop$$
$$\vdash \langle\!\langle \alpha : c \rangle\!\rangle \equiv \langle\!\langle \alpha : c_1 \rangle\!\rangle \wedge \cdots \wedge \langle\!\langle \alpha : c_n \rangle\!\rangle \wedge \varphi_1' \wedge \cdots \wedge \varphi_m'$$

where the $\varphi_i'$ are the $\forall$-closures of $\varphi_i$ (thus ensuring $FV(\varphi_i') = \{\}$).

The following theorems are derivable from this definition (simply by taking the equivalence apart and stripping some $\forall$'s): The class inclusions $c \preceq c_i$ (or $\vdash \langle\!\langle \alpha : c \rangle\!\rangle \Rightarrow \langle\!\langle \alpha : c_i \rangle\!\rangle$), the *abstract class axioms* $\varphi_j[\alpha_c]$ (or $\vdash \langle\!\langle \alpha : c \rangle\!\rangle \Rightarrow \varphi_j$), and the *class instantiation rule* $\vdash (\ldots \Rightarrow \langle\!\langle \alpha : c \rangle\!\rangle)$.

Next is the **instance** construct which comes in two variants:

|  |  |
|---|---|
| **instance** $c_1 \preceq c_2$ | called *abstract instantiation* |
| **instance** $t :: (s_1, \ldots, s_n)\, s$ | called *concrete instantiation* |

provided that the class inclusion, or type arity is derivable in the corresponding theories: $\vdash \langle\!\langle \alpha : c_1 \rangle\!\rangle \Rightarrow \langle\!\langle \alpha : c_2 \rangle\!\rangle$, or $\vdash \langle\!\langle \alpha_1 : s_1 \rangle\!\rangle \wedge \cdots \wedge \langle\!\langle \alpha_n : s_n \rangle\!\rangle \Rightarrow \langle\!\langle (\alpha_1, \ldots, \alpha_n)\, t : s \rangle\!\rangle$.

The effect of instantiations is to augment the current order-sorted type signature by the stated inclusion $c_1 \preceq c_2$ or type arity $t :: (s_1, \ldots, s_n)\, s$.

**Theorem 6.** *Class instantiations are meta-safe.*

For a proof just note that **instance** is logically almost vacuous: The (axiomatic) additions to the type signature have already been derivable beforehand.

# 7 Conclusion

We have seen that simple traditional HOL systems (providing object-level type variables) implicitly contain some propositional language of types that may serve as an interpretation of type classes, type arities and related notions from Haskell-like type systems. We could even have supported more general *qualified types* [8], notably $n$-ary type relations, as does the programming language Gofer and recently proposed extensions of Haskell. Thus the whole order-sorted type system turns out to be just an addition to user convenience, without really changing expressiveness of the logic.

We have also introduced three new safe theory extension mechanisms: overloaded constant definitions with possible recursion over types, class definitions and class instantiations. These have been justified at the purely deductive meta-logical level, without referring to model theory.

One of the most surprising results of this work is *simplicity*. We did not have to leave the seemingly old-fashioned HOL in favour of full-blown theories of dependent types. The sort of abstract theories that type classes are capable of can be offered in HOL at no additional cost, apart from implementation efforts.

**Acknowledgments** I would like to thank Tobias Nipkow for many controversial and encouraging discussions about this topic. Olaf Müller, Wolfgang Naraschewski, David von Oheimb and Oscar Slotosch commented draft versions of the paper.

# References

1. P. B. Andrews. *An Introduction to Mathematical Logic and Type Theory: To Truth Through Proof.* Academic Press, 1986.
2. A. Church. A formulation of the simple theory of types. *Journal of Symbolic Logic*, pages 56–68, 1940.
3. M. J. C. Gordon. Set theory, higher order logic or both? In *Proc. 9th TPHOLs*, volume 1125 of *Lecture Notes in Computer Science*, pages 191–201. Springer-Verlag, 1996.
4. M. J. C. Gordon and T. F. Melham (editors). *Introduction to HOL: A theorem proving environment for higher order logic.* Cambridge University Press, 1993.
5. L. Henkin. Completeness in the theory of types. *Journal of Symbolic Logic*, 15(2):81–91, 1950.
6. P. Hudak, S. L. P. Jones, and P. Wadler (editors). Report on the programming language Haskell, a non-strict purely functional language (Version 1.2). *SIGPLAN Notices*, March, 1992.
7. The Isabelle library. http://www4.informatik.tu-muenchen.de/~nipkow/isabelle/.
8. M. P. Jones. *Qualified Types: Theory and Practice.* PhD thesis, University of Oxford, 1992.
9. T. Nipkow. Order-sorted polymorphism in Isabelle. In G. Huet and G. Plotkin, editors, *Logical Environments*, pages 164–188. Cambridge University Press, 1993.
10. T. Nipkow and C. Prehofer. Type checking type classes. In *20th ACM Symp. Principles of Programming Languages*, 1993.
11. L. C. Paulson. The foundation of a generic theorem prover. *Journal of Automated Reasoning*, 5(3):363–397, 1989.
12. L. C. Paulson. *Isabelle: A Generic Theorem Prover*, volume 828 of *Lecture Notes in Computer Science*. Springer-Verlag, 1994.
13. A. Pitts. The HOL logic. In Gordon and Melham [4], pages 191–232.
14. M. Schmidt-Schauß. *Computational Aspects of an Order-Sorted Logic with Term Declarations*, volume 395 of *Lecture Notes in Artificial Intelligence*. Springer-Verlag, 1989.
15. M. Wenzel. *Using axiomatic type classes in Isabelle — a tutorial.* Available at http://www4.informatik.tu-muenchen.de/~nipkow/isadist/axclass.dvi.gz.

# A Comparative Study of Coq and HOL

Vincent Zammit

Computing Laboratory, University of Kent, Canterbury, Kent, UK

**Abstract.** This paper illustrates the differences between the style of theory mechanisation of Coq and of HOL. This comparative study is based on the mechanisation of fragments of the theory of computation in these systems. Examples from these implementations are given to support some of the arguments discussed in this paper. The mechanisms for specifying definitions and for theorem proving are discussed separately, building in parallel two pictures of the different approaches of mechanisation given by these systems.

## 1 Introduction

This paper compares the different theorem proving approaches of the HOL [10] and Coq [5] proof assistants. This comparison is based on a case study involving the mechanisation of parts of the theory of computation in the two systems. This paper does not illustrate these mechanisations but rather discusses the differences between the two systems and backs up certain points by examples taken from the case studies.

One motivation of this work is that many users of theorem provers lack the perspective of knowing more than one such system, mainly due to the amount of time needed to master any such system. Having a single text which builds up pictures of two different systems in parallel allows users of one system to grasp better how the different approach of the other system affects the way theories are mechanised. As a result, knowing the main differences beforehand facilitates the process of learning the other system, and gives a better perspective of the system the user is familiar with.

The case studies are illustrated separately in [26] and in [27]. The mechanisation in HOL is based on the Unlimited Register Machine (URM) model of computation [7], and the main result of the formalisation is a proof that partial recursive functions are URM computable. The mechanisation in Coq is based on a model of computation similar to the partial recursive function model and includes a constructive proof of the $S_n^m$ theorem. Both implementations are in the order of 10,000 lines of code. HOL90 version 7 and Coq version 5.10 were used for the mechanisations.

The two systems are introduced in the next section where a brief overview of each of them is given. Since we are considering the differences between how actual mechanisations of theories are performed in practice, this comparative study treats the mechanisms for definitions (section 3) and theorem proving (section 4) separately. Other considerations are then discussed in section 5 and the last section gives some concluding remarks.

It is noted in this comparative study that the strongest point of the Coq system is the power of the logic it is based on. The HOL logic is much more simple but users can rely on a greater flexibility offered by the metalanguage. As a result HOL theorem proving is much more implementation oriented, while in Coq unnecessary implementation is avoided and discouraged by having a specification and proof language which bridges the user from the metalanguage. These points are built gradually in the following sections and are discussed in the conclusion.

## 2 An Overview of Coq and HOL

Both systems are based on the LCF [9] style of theorem proving, where all logical inferences are performed by a simple core engine. A metalanguage is provided so that users can extend the system by implementing program modules applying the operations of the core engine. The systems differ from each other however by implementing quite different logics and through the flexibility by which users are allowed to extend the system.

### 2.1 Coq

The Coq system is an implementation in CAML of the Calculus of Inductive Constructions (CIC) [4], a variant of type theory related to Martin-Löf's Intuitionistic Type Theory [14, 18] and Girard's polymorphic $\lambda$-calculus $F_\omega$ [8]. Terms in CIC are typed and types are also terms. Such a type theory can be treated as a logic through the *Curry-Howard isomorphism* (see [25, 18] for introductions of the Curry-Howard isomorphism) where propositions are expressed as types. For instance, a conjunction $A \wedge B$ is represented by a product type $A \times B$, and an implication $A \Rightarrow B$ is represented by a function type $A \rightarrow B$. Also, a term of type $\tau$ can be seen as a proof of the proposition represented by $\tau$, and thus theorems in the logic are nonempty types. For example, the function

$$curry = \lambda f.\lambda x.\lambda y.f(x, y)$$

which has type $((A \times B) \rightarrow C) \rightarrow A \rightarrow B \rightarrow C$ is a proof of the theorem $((A \wedge B) \Rightarrow C) \Rightarrow (A \Rightarrow B \Rightarrow C)$. Objects which have the same normal form according to $\beta\delta\iota$-conversion are called convertible, and are treated as the same term by the logic. $\delta$-conversion involves the substitution of a constant by its defining term and $\iota$-conversion is automation of inductive definitions. The CIC implemented in Coq differs from that of LEGO [22] by having two sorts of universes, an impredicative universe for sets in which functions are computable, and a predicative universe for types and propositions in which functions (predicates) need not be computable (decidable).

Due to the Curry-Howard isomorphism, theorem proving corresponds to the construction of well typed terms and the core inference engine of Coq is basically a type checking algorithm of CIC terms. Terms whose type is a theorem are usually called proof objects and are stored in Coq theories. The Coq system provides the specification and proof language `Gallina` in which users perform the actual interactive theorem proving. `Gallina` constructs include commands for specifying definitions and for tactic based theorem proving (section 4 discusses this in more detail), and Coq users can extend the `Gallina` language by implementing new contructs in CAML. The files which `Gallina` accepts during theorem proving are usually called scripts (or proof scripts).

## 2.2 HOL

The HOL system implements (in Standard ML of New Jersey for the case of HOL90) a classical higher order logic based on Church's simple theory of types [3] extended with polymorphic types and inference rules for definitions. Thus, HOL terms are typed, where types represent *nonempty sets* and can be either type constants, type variables (which make the type theory polymorphic), function types (which make the logic higher order) or the application of some type operator to a number of types[1]. Terms are either constants, variables, lambda abstractions or applications; sequents consist of a finite set of terms (the assumptions) and one term (the conclusion), and theorems are sequents which are proved by one of a number of primitive inference rules.

Theorems in the HOL system are represented by an abstract datatype (with name `thm`) having as constructors a small number of functions corresponding to the logic's primitive inference rules. The implementation of this datatype is the core inference engine of HOL, and the type checking mechanism of ML ensures that objects of type `thm` are constructed only by using the type's constructors. Theorem proving in HOL involves the implementation of programs in the metalanguage which yield terms of type `thm`. All support for specifying definitions, constructing types and terms (which can be done by *quotation* in which a system function parses expressions written in a readable syntax into HOL representation), and theorem proving is provided through ML functions which are visible to HOL users. Thus, users can extend the system by implementing new ML functions representing higher level inference rules, decision procedures, proof strategies, definition mechanisms, etc..

## 3 Definitions

A definition can be considered as a name given to a term or type by which it can be referred to in a theory. For example the definition

`computable` $n$ $f$ $=_{def}$ $\exists p.$ `computes` $p$ $n$ $f$

introduces the new object `computable` in the current theory and makes the two expressions `computable` $n$ $f$ and $\exists p.$ `computes` $p$ $n$ $f$ for any term $f$, in some sense interchangeable. In a mechanisation (or formalisation) of a theory, giving definitions is a mechanism by which mathematical concepts are formalised

---

[1] A function type $\alpha \rightarrow \beta$ can be considered as the application of the operator $\rightarrow$ on the types $\alpha$ and $\beta$, and type constants as type operators with arity 0.

by specifying them as being equivalent to expressions containing only already defined terms. The above example illustrates how the concept of a computable $n$-ary function can be formalised. A concept can also be formalised through the declaration of axioms and both systems allow users to introduce axioms in theories. However, an axiomatic theory can be inconsistent while the definition mechanisms of Coq and HOL guarantee that purely definitional theories are always consistent.

The definition mechanism in Coq introduces new constant names in an environment and allows these terms to be convertible with their defining terms. This applies to both simple abbreviations ($\delta$-conversion) and inductive definitions ($\iota$-conversion). Since proofs and theorems are first class objects in CIC, the name of a theorem is actually a constant definition given to its proof term. In fact, although the specification language Gallina gives different constructs for defining terms and for theorem proving, one can, for instance, use tactics to define terms and the definition mechanism to prove theorems. The system differentiates between definitions and theorems by labeling the former objects as *transparent* and the latter as *opaque*. Transparent objects are convertible with their defining terms while opaque objects are not. Gallina commands for labeling objects as opaque or transparent are also provided.

The HOL logic treats type and constant definitions differently, and the core system provides one primitive inference rule for type definitions and two for constant definitions. Other inference rules are given for deriving theorems. The function of the HOL primitive rules for definitions is illustrated below, where the differences between the definition mechanism in HOL and in Coq are discussed.

## 3.1 Type Definitions

The HOL system has one primitive rule for type definitions, which introduces a new type expression $\alpha$ as a nonempty subset of an existing type $\sigma$, given a term $P: \sigma \to bool$ which denotes its characteristic predicate. However, in practice, the user introduces new types through the type definition package [15] which specifies ML style polymorphic recursive types as well as automatically deriving a number of theorems specifying certain properties about the type (such as the fact that the type constructors are injective).

Such types are specified in Coq by inductively defined sets and types, and the corresponding theorems derived by HOL's type definition package are either returned as theorems by the definition mechanism of Gallina or follow from the elimination and introduction rules of the set or type.

The obvious advantage of having types as terms in CIC over HOL's simple type theory is a much more expressive type system which allows quantification over types and dependent types. A dependent type is a type which depends on the value of some particular term. The 'classical' examples of dependent types include $Nat(n)$, the type of the natural numbers less than $n$, and $vector(A, n)$, the type of vectors (or lists) having $n$ elements of type $A$. This type is defined inductively in [27]:

```
vector A =def Vnil: (vector A 0)
         | Vcons: (n: nat) → A → (vector A n)
                  → (vector A (S n)).
```

and by defining the type for relations

```
Rel =def λA,B:Set. A → B → Prop.
```

the type of $n$-ary partial functions over the natural numbers can be defined to be single valued relations between `vector nat n` and `nat`:

```
one_valued =def λA,B:Set, R:Rel A B. ∀a:A, b1,b2:B.
                (R a b1) → (R a b2) → (b1 = b2).
```

```
pfunc arity =def mk_pfunc
    { reln     : (Rel (vector nat arity) nat);
      One_valued: (one_valued (vector nat arity) nat reln)}.
```

```
pfuncs =def Pfuncs: (n: nat) → (pfunc n) → pfuncs.
```

The type `pfunc` is a record where the field `reln` is a relation between vectors and natural numbers, and the field `One_valued` is a theorem stating that `reln` is single valued. It can be seen that this is a dependent record as the type of the second field depends on the value of the first field. The type `pfunc` can be seen in some sense as a subtype of `reln`, as objects of type `pfunc` are the objects of type `reln` which are proved to satisfy the property given by `One_valued`.

With this type system one can define the notion that a program computes a function by

```
∀n:nat, p:prog, f:(pfunc n). computes p n f
   =def ∀v:(vector nat n), x:nat. exec p v x ⇔ reln n f v x
```

which is more compact and elegant than an equivalent HOL definition, since the information stored in types has to be specified as terms:

```
∀n:num, p:prog, f:pfunc. computes p n f =def one_valued n f ∧
     ∀v:num list. length v = n ⇒
        ∀x:num. exec p v x ⇔ apply f v x
```

A mechanism which translates objects in a dependent type theory into HOL objects is illustrated in [13] and an extension of the HOL logic to cover quantification over types is proposed in [17].

## 3.2 Constant Definitions

Here we list the different mechanism by which constant definitions can be specified in Coq and in HOL.

**Simple Definitions** In HOL given a closed term $x : \tau$, a new constant $c :$ $\tau$ can be introduced in the current theory by the primitive rule of constant definition which also yields the theorem $\vdash c = x$. Thus, while in the Calculus of Constructions constants are convertible with their defining terms, in HOL the interchangeability of $c$ and $x$ is justified by the above theorem, which needs to be used whenever $c$ and $x$ have to be substituted for each other in other theorems.

**Specifications** The second primitive rule which introduces constants in HOL theories is called the rule of constant specification. It introduces a constant $c : \tau$ obeying some property $P(c)$, if its existence can be shown by a theorem $\vdash \exists x.P(x)$. The theorem $\vdash P(c)$ is returned by the rule. Note that only the existence of some $x$ is required, rather than the existence of a unique $x$, and nothing else can be inferred about $c$, apart from $P(c)$ (and anything which can be inferred from $P(c)$). There is no such rule in the Calculus of Constructions although any constructive proof of $\exists x : \tau.P(x)$ is actually a pair $(w : \tau, p : P(w))$ containing a term of type $\tau$ and a proof stating that this term satisfies $P$. The HOL manual [10] introduces a primitive inference rule for type specification as well but there is no implementation of this rule yet.

**Recursive Definitions** The definition of primitive recursive functions over a recursive type is justified in HOL by a theorem stating the principle of primitive recursion which can be automatically derived by the type definition package. A library for defining well-founded recursive functions, which in general requires user intervention for proving that a relation is well-formed, is also included in the HOL system [24]. In Coq, primitive recursive functions are defined by a fixpoint operator. The syntax of actually defining such functions implicitly in the Coq is very crude. However, a mechanism which allows function definitions in an ML like systax with pattern matching is provided in the Gallina language as a macro for specifying case expressions. This mechanism can also be used on the definition of functions over dependent types.

**Inductive Definitions** The CIC includes rules for inductive definitions and are thus inbuilt in Coq. The Gallina specification language provides constructs for introducing (possibly mutually) inductive definitions as well as tactics for reasoning about them. Inductive definitions can be used for introducing inductive types and sets as recursive datatypes (as seen in section 3) and also for inductively defined relations. Since the implementation of the CIC in Coq includes rules for coinductive types, support for coinductive and corecursive definitions and reasoning by coinduction is also provided.

The HOL system provides a number of packages for defining inductive relations, which include Melham's original package [16, 2], support for mutually inductive definitions [23] and the more recent implementation due to Harrison [12]. Besides providing a mechanism for specifying definitions these packages include ML functions for reasoning about them and for automating them. It is argued (for instance in [11]) that inductive definitions can be introduced earlier in the HOL system and a number of frequently used relations in existing theories (such as the inequalities on natural numbers) can be redefined inductively so that users can for instance apply the principle of rule induction on them, much in the same fashion that it is done by Coq users.

# 4 Theorem Proving

This section illustrates the different proof strategies by which users of the Coq and HOL systems perform the actual theorem proving.

## 4.1 Forward Proving

Forward theorem proving is performed in HOL by applying ML functions which return theorems. This is done in Coq by constructing terms whose type corresponds to theorems. However since HOL users have direct access to the metalanguage, one can implement more elaborate inference rules for forward theorem proving than simple constructions of terms in Coq. In general, theorem proving in Coq is done in a backwards manner by applying tactics.

## 4.2 Backward Proving

Both theorem provers support interactive tactic based goal directed reasoning. Basically the required theorem is stated as a goal and the user applies tactics which break the goal into simpler subgoals until they can be proved directly. Tactics also provide a *justification* for the simplification of a goal into subgoals, which derives the goal as a theorem from derivations of the subgoals. A goal usually consists of the statement which is required to be proved together with a number of assumptions which a proof of the goal can use.

Backward proving is supported in HOL through an implementation of a *goalstack* data structure which provides a number of operations (including specifying goals, applying tactics, moving around subgoals, etc. ) as ML functions. Tactics and tacticals[2] are also ML functions and users can implement new tactics during theory development. On the other hand, Coq tactics and tacticals are provided as constructs of the Gallina language, and so are the operations on the internal goalstack. As a result, implementing a new tactic in Coq involves the non-trivial task of extending the Gallina language and in general Coq users tend to implement less tactics during theory development than HOL users do. Moreover, HOL users can also implement tactics 'on the fly' by combining different tactics, tacticals, and ML functions in general. For instance, the HOL tactic

---

[2] Tacticals are operations on tactics which produce tactics, for example, the tactical then, implemented in both HOL and Coq takes two tactics $t_1$ and $t_2$ and returns a tactic which when applied to a goal, it first applies $t_1$ and then applies $t_2$ on all the resulting subgoals.

```
REPEAT (STRIP_GOAL_THEN
  (fn t => if is_disj (concl t)
            then DISJ_CASES_TAC t
            else RULE_ASSUM_TAC (REWRITE_RULE [GSYM t])));
```

when applied to a goal of the form

$$\forall x_{11}, \ldots, x_{1n_1}.t_1 \Rightarrow \ldots \Rightarrow \forall x_{m1}, \ldots, x_{1n_m}.t_m \Rightarrow c$$

specialises all the quantified variables $x_{ij}$ and strips the terms $t_i$ from the goal; if $t_i$ is a disjunction then the goal is broken down into two, each one having one of the term's disjuncts as an assumption. For each term $t_i$ which is not a disjunction, the tactic rewrites all the assumptions with GSYM $t_i$ which is the result of substituting all the subterms in $t_i$ representing some equality $x = y$ with their symmetry $y = x$. Such a tactic is impossible to construct in Coq within a Gallina theorem proving session.

We also remark that HOL tactics are much more elaborate and numerous than Coq ones. One reason for this arises from the different nature of the Calculus of Inductive Constructions and the HOL logic. Since theorems in Coq are essentially types, tactics correspond to the different ways terms can be constructed and broken down (the introduction and elimination rules of the constructs). On the other hand, tactics in HOL have to be implemented using the much less powerful (and less general) primitive inference rules. Moreover, the powerful notion of convertible terms of CIC makes inference rules such as rewriting with the definitions and beta conversion unnecessary in Coq. However, tactics for unfolding definitions and changing a goal or assumption to a convertible one are also provided, both because it facilitates theorem proving and also because higher order unification is undecidable and user intervention may sometimes be essential.

The considerable difference between the number (and nature) of tactics in HOL and in Coq and the availability of a specification and proof language makes Coq an easier system to learn. New HOL users are faced with hundreds of inference rules and tactics to learn, and possibly a new programming language to master in order to be used effectively as a metalanguage. New Coq users need to learn how to use about fifty language constructs and most theory development can be done without the need of extending Gallina.

Finally we note that assumptions in Coq are named while in HOL they are not. This affects the way user of the systems use assumptions during the construction of a proof. Basically Coq users select the assumptions they need by their name while HOL users apply tactics which try to use all the assumptions. Nevertheless, HOL users can implement tactics which select a subset of, or a particular element from, the list of assumptions through filtering functions and other techniques discussed in [1]. However we stress that selecting an assumption simply by its name is definitely more straightforward than any such techniques. During the implementation of [26] the need of writing several filtering functions was sometimes tedious and overwhelming. Tactics which make use of all the assumptions can however be quite powerful and may save several repetitive proof steps. One can for instance consider the power of ASM_REWRITE_TAC in HOL which repetitively rewrites with all the assumptions, a number of theorems supplied by the user and a list of basic pre-proved theorems (such as $\vdash \forall A.\ \top \vee A = \top$.)

## 4.3 Automation

The HOL system is equipped with more decision procedures and automation tools than Coq. HOL (HOL90 version $9.1\alpha$) includes automation for rewriting (by a simple rewriting engine, an implementation of Knuth-Benedix completion, and a contextual rewriter), a tautology checker, semidecision procedures for first order reasoning (a tableaux prover with equality, and a model elimination based prover), a decision procedure for Presburger arithmetic and for real algebra, as well as an implementation of Nelson and Oppen's technique for combining decision procedures. Since most proofs in [26] are of a highly technical nature, the use of such decision procedures saved a lot of time and thinking about trivial proofs. The Coq system (version 6.1) provides tactics for tautology checking, decision procedures for intuitionistic direct predicate calculus, for Presburger arithmetic, and for a number of problems concerning Abelian rings. The Gallina language contains also a user definable hint list, where tactics can be included into the list and goals can then be automatically solved by the application of one or more of these tactics.

## 4.4 Reasoning with Equality and Equivalence

HOL's notion of equality is extremely powerful and since equivalence of propositions is defined as equality on boolean values, the same properties enjoyed by equality hold also for equivalence. Equality is introduced in HOL by a primitive rule, REFL, which returns the theorem $\vdash t = t$ for any term $t$; and the primitive rule of substitution allows any subterms of a theorem to be substituted by their equals. The rule of extensionality (which can be derived in HOL) yields the equality of any two functions which give the same results when applied to the same values. (More formally, the rule of extensionality is $\forall x.f(x) = g(x) \vdash f = g$.) As a result, equivalent predicates can be substituted for each other and assumptions can be substituted with the truth value $\top$. Hence, theorem proving in HOL can rely a lot on rewriting, for example, statements like $a \wedge b \Rightarrow a \vee c$ can be easily proved by the tactic:

```
REPEAT STRIP_TAC THEN
ASM_REWRITE_TAC []
```

The importance of equality in HOL theorem proving is emphasized by a class of inference rules called *conversions* which are specialised for deriving equalities. Basically, a conversion is an ML function which takes a term, $t_1$, and proves that it is equal to some other term $t_2$ deriving $t_1 = t_2$.[3] Conversions can be used for

---

[3] Note that the term $t_2$ is constructed by the conversion and not given by the user. The use of a particular conversion is actually the transformation of the term $t_1$ into some term $t_2$ justified by the theorem $\vdash t_1 = t_2$.

instance to simplify a term based by rewriting with a particular definition, or to transform a term based on some calculation such as natural number arithmetic or reduction into conjunctive normal form. In general, conversions form the building blocks of more powerful automation tools.

Equality in CIC is introduced by the inductive definition

$$\text{Eq } A =_{def} \text{refl\_equal: } \forall a\!:\!A. \; (\text{eq } A \; x \; x)$$

and results like symmetry, transitivity and congruence can then be derived. However functions are intensional and equivalence of propositions is different from their equality. Basically, two propositions, $a$ and $b$, can be proved to be equivalent in Coq by constructing a term with type $(a \rightarrow b, b \rightarrow a)$ and little support is given for taking advantage of the symmetric nature of bi-implication. The need for a more powerful support of equality is reduced by having the notion of convertible terms. However, here we remark on the inability of constructing a term $t\!:\!T_1$ directly, where $t$ has type $T_2$ which is not convertible with $T_1$ and it can be proved that $T_1$ and $T_2$ are equal. For example, given some term $v$: (vector nat $(n+m)$), then one cannot specify $v$ as having type vector nat $(m+n)$ even though $(n+m)$ and $(m+n)$ are equal. This problem is encountered in [27] and for this particular example it is solved by defining a function Change_arity, such that, given a vector $v$: (vector $A$ $n$) and a proof $t$ of $(n=m)$, then Change_arity $n$ $m$ $t$ $A$ $v$ has type (vector $A$ $m$):

```
Change_arity
   =def λn,m:nat, t:(n = m), A: Set, v: (vector A n).
      eq_rec nat n (vector A) v m t).
```

and it is proved that:

```
∀n:nat, t:(n = n), A:Set, v:(vector A n).
      Change_arity n n t A v = v
```

This theorem is proved using the eq_rec_eq axiom.

Now, if plus_sym represents the theorem $\forall n, m.n+m = m+n$, and the term $v$ has type vector nat $(n+m)$ then

```
Change_arity (n + m) (m + n) (plus_sym n m) nat v
```

has type vector nat $(m+n)$.

# 5   Miscellaneous

This section lists some other considerations of the differences between the approaches of Coq and HOL to the mechanisation of theories.

## 5.1 Classical and Constructive reasoning

HOL's logic is classical, and the axiom of the excluded middle is introduced in the HOL theory which defines boolean values. One can ask however whether any support can be given to users who may want to use HOL and still reason constructively. The CIC is essentially constructive in which the law of the excluded middle cannot be derived and all Coq functions have to be computable. However, one can still reason classically to some extent in Coq by loading a classical theory which specifies the law of the excluded middle as an axiom, although it should be stressed that this does not give Coq the full powers of classical reasoning.

Since all functions in Coq are computable, $n$-ary partial functions in [27] are specified as single valued relations (see section 3.1) rather than as Coq functions, so that functions which are not computable can still be specified in the mechanisation. On the other hand, functions in HOL need not be computable (since the logic is not constructive and because of the rule of constant specification and Hilbert's operator $\epsilon$), and $n$-ary partial functions in [26] are defined as HOL functions mapping lists of natural numbers to possibly undefined natural numbers. The type of possibly undefined numbers is defined as the type of natural numbers together with an undefined value. The advantage of the formalisation of partial functions in HOL is that a function application can be directly substituted by its value.

## 5.2 The Use of Proof Objects

The Coq system stores proof terms in its theory files and uses for these terms include:

1. Program extraction: Given some program specification $S$, a constructive proof that there is some program satisfying it contains an instance of a program for which $S$ holds, hence one can obtain a certified program from a proof of its specification. This facility is supported by the Coq system which provides a package which extracts an ML program from a proof term, as well as providing support for proving the specification of functions written in an ML syntax [20, 19, 21].

2. Extracting proof texts written in a natural language: A proof term of type $\tau$ can be seen as an account of the proof steps involved in deriving the theorem $\tau$, and Coq provides tools for extracting a proof written in a natural language from proof objects [6].

3. Independent proof checking: Proof terms can be checked by an independent proof checker to gain more confidence in their correctness. Moreover, such proof terms can be easier to translate into proof accounts of another theorem prover than an actual proof script or an ML program (as HOL proof scripts actually are). The HOL system is truth based rather than proof based and it does not store proofs in its theories.

## 5.3 The Sectioning Mechanism

The Gallina specification language allows Coq proof scripts to be structured into sections, and one can make definitions and prove theorems which are local to a particular section. The need of local definitions and results is often encountered during theory development, where for instance, the definition of some particular concept can facilitate the proof of a number of results but does not contribute much to the overall formalization of the theory. This point is also discussed in [26] where the following example is given. During the proof of the theorem stating that primitive recursive functions are URM computable, a program $P$, say, which computes some particular function is defined. This program can be broken down into three subroutines: $P_1$, $P_2$ and $P_3$. A number of lemmas concerning these subroutines are derived and used in the proof of the required theorem. However the definitions of $P_1$, $P_2$ and $P_3$ as well as any results concerning them are used only during the proof of one important theorem, and the lack of structure in HOL theories resulted in having to represent them as local variables within the metalangauge.

## 6 Conclusions

The two case studies, and especially more extensive mechanisations of different mathematical theories, show that both HOL and Coq are robust systems and practical in mechanising simple mathematical results. The strongest point of HOL is the flexibility given to the users by means of the metalanguage; while Coq theorem proving relies on the power of the Calculus of Inductive Constructions. Here, we give some concluding remarks on these features.

### 6.1 The Flexibility of the Metalanguage

By allowing a theorem proving session to be given within a general purpose metalanguage, HOL offers a higher degree of flexibility than Coq. As a result, HOL users implement a larger number of new inference rules during theory development than Coq users. For example, the mechanisation of the theory of computation in HOL includes several conversions for animating the definitions, simple and more elaborate tactics which avoid repetitive inferences and most backward proofs include tactics implemented 'on the fly'. The syntax of Gallina can be extended, say with (metalanguage) predicates on terms so that one can filter a sublist of assumptions to be used by some tactic, but then one asks whether a specification language as powerful as the metalanguage is required to implement the required filtering functions during theorem proving. Having a specification language surely has its advantages: the system is easier to learn by new users, and proof scripts are in general easier to follow; also, theorem proving support tools like a debugger or a graphical user interface are probably easier to develop for a specification language with a limited syntax rather than for a general purpose programming language. However, the power of a Turing complete metalanguage is not to be underestimated, for it can be used for instance to derive theorems through the manipulation of proof terms.

## 6.2 The Power of the Calculus of Inductive Constructions

The restrictions due to the specification language are relieved by the power of CIC. The fact that theorems are proved by simply constructing and breaking down terms makes the implementation of tactics specialised for particular logic constructs unnecessary and the powerful notion of convertibility replaces the implementation of conversions for every definition. No new tactics or inference rules are implemented in the mechanisation of the theory of computation in Coq, both because the inference power of the simple constructs of Gallina is enough for most reasoning, and also because the non-trivial task of actually implementing a new elaborate tactic in Coq discourages the development of simple tactics which are used only to substitute a number of inferences. The power of CIC is also emphasised by its highly expressive type system which allows quantification over types and dependent types and thus gives a more natural formalisation of mathematical concepts than a simple type theory. We have seen however, how the stronger notion of equality and equivalence in HOL simplifies most formalisations.

The primitive inference rules of HOL are too simple and are rarely used in practice, most reasoning is performed by higher level inferences. The simplicity of the primitive rules gives a straightforward implementation of the core inference engine, on whose correctness the soundness of the HOL system relies. Although CIC is more complex than the HOL logic, it is sound and due to the Curry-Howard isomorphism theorems in CIC can be checked by a type checking algorithm, on whose correctness the soundness of the Coq system relies. Thus, one can have a very powerful logic whose theorems can still be checked by a simple algorithm.

The feasibility of actually doing so may however be questioned. Proof terms may become very large, and $\beta\delta\iota$-convertibility may become infeasible for large objects. These factors do not yield any significant problems for the mechanisation of the results in [27] but may make Coq unsuitable for large scale 'real-world' theorem proving required by the industry.

## 7 Acknowledgements

I would like to thank my supervisor, Simon Thompson, for his support and encouragement as well as the anonymous referees for their comments and suggestions on an earlier draft of this paper.

## References

1. P. E. Black and P. J. Windley. Automatically synthesized term denotation predicates: A proof aid. In E. T. Schubert, P. J. Windley, and J. Alves-Foss, editors, *Proceedings of the 8th International Workshop on Higher Order Logic Theorem Proving and Its Applications*, volume 971 of *Lecture Notes in Computer Science*, pages 46–57, Aspen Grove, UT, USA, September 1995. Springer-Verlag.

2. Juanito Camilleri and Tom Melham. Reasoning with inductively defined relations in the HOL theorem prover. Technical Report 265, University of Cambridge Computer Laboratory, August 1992.

3. Alonzo Church. A formulation of a simple theory of types. *Journal of Symbolic Logic*, 5:56–68, 1940.

4. Thierry Coquand and Gérard Huet. The calculus of constructions. Rapport de Recherche 530, INRIA, Rocquencourt, France, May 1986.

5. C. Cornes et al. The Coq Proof Assistant Reference Manual, Version 5.10. Rapport technique RT-0177, INRIA, 1995.

6. Yann Coscoy, Gilles Kahn, and Laurent Théry. Extracting text from proofs. Rapport de Recherche 2459, INRIA, Sophia-Antipolis Cedex, France, January 1995.

7. N.J. Cutland. *Computability: An introduction to recursive function theory.* Cambridge University Press, 1980.

8. J.-Y. Girard. *Interprétation fonctionelle et élimination des coupures dans l'arithétique d'ordre supérieur.* PhD thesis, Université Paris VII, 1972.

9. Michael J. Gordon, Arthur J. Milner, and Christopher P. Wadsworth. *Edinburgh LCF: A Mechanised Logic of Computation,* volume 78 of *Lecture Notes in Computer Science.* Springer-Verlag, 1979.

10. M.J.C. Gordon and T.F. Melham. *Introduction to HOL: a theorem proving environment for higher order logic.* Cambridge University Press, 1993.

11. John Harrison. HOL done right. Unpublished Draft, August 1995.

12. John Harrison. Inductive definitions: Automation and application. In E. T. Schubert, P. J. Windley, and J. Alves-Foss, editors, *Proceedings of the 8th International Workshop on Higher Order Logic Theorem Proving and Its Applications,* volume 971 of *Lecture Notes in Computer Science,* pages 200–213, Aspen Grove, UT, USA, September 1995. Springer-Verlag.

13. Bart Jacobs and Tom Melham. Translating dependent type theory into higher order logic. In *TLCA '93 International Conference on Typed Lambda Calculi and Applications, Utrecht, 16–18 March 1993,* volume 664 of *Lecture Notes in Computer Science,* pages 209–229. Springer-Verlag, 1993.

14. Per Martin-Löf. *Intuitionistic Type Theory.* Bibioplois, Napoli, 1984. Notes of Giovanni Sambin on a series of lectues given in Padova.

15. T.F. Melham. Using recursive types to reason about hardware and higher order logic. In G.J. Milne, editor, *International Workshop on Higher Order Logic Theorem Proving and its Applications,* pages 27–50, Glasgow, Scotland, July 1988. IFIP WG 10.2, North-Holland.

16. T.F. Melham. A package for inductive relation definitions in HOL. In M. Archer, J.J. Joyce, K.N. Levitt, and P.J. Windley, editors, *International Workshop on Higher Order Logic Theorem Proving and its Applications,* pages 350–357, Davis, California, August 1991. IEEE Computer Society, ACM SIGDA, IEEE Computer Society Press.

17. T.F. Melham. The HOL logic extended with quantification over type variables. In L.J.M. Claesen and M.J.C. Gordon, editors, *International Workshop on Higher Order Logic Theorem Proving and its Applications,* pages 3–18, Leuven, Belgium, September 1992. IFIP TC10/WG10.2, North-Holland. IFIP Transactions.

18. Bengt Nordström, Kent Petersson, and Jan M. Smith. *Programming in Martin-Löf type theory: an introduction.* Clarendon, 1990.

19. C. Parent. Developing certified programs in the system Coq - the Program tactic. In H. Barendregt and T. Nipkow, editors, *International Workshop on Types for*

*Proofs and Programs*, volume 806 of *Lecture Notes in Computer Science*, pages 291–312. Springer-Verlag, May 1993.

20. C. Paulin-Mohring. Extracting $F_\omega$'s programs from proofs in the Calculus of Constructions. In Association for Computing Machinery, editor, *Sixteenth Annual ACM Symposium on Principles of Programming Languages*, Austin, January 1989.

21. C. Paulin-Mohring and B. Werner. Synthesis of ML programs in the system Coq. *Journal of Symbolic Computation*, 15(5-6):607–640, ?? 1993.

22. Robert Pollack. *The Theory of LEGO: A Proof Checker for the Extended Calculus of Constructions*. PhD thesis, University of Edinburgh, 1994.

23. R. E. O. Roxas. A HOL package for reasoning about relations defined by mutual induction. In J. J. Joyce and C.-J. H. Seger, editors, *Proceedings of the 6th International Workshop on Higher Order Logic Theorem Proving and its Applications (HUG'93)*, volume 780 of *Lecture Notes in Computer Science*, pages 129–140, Vancouver, B.C., Canada, August 1993. Springer-Verlag, 1994.

24. K. Slind. Function definition in higher-order logic. In J. von Wright, J. Grundy, and J. Harrison, editors, *Proceedings of the 9th International Conference on Theorem Proving in Higher Order Logics (TPHOLs'96)*, volume 1125 of *Lecture Notes in Computer Science*, pages 381–397, Turku, Finland, August 1996. Springer.

25. Simon Thompson. *Type Theory and Functional Programming*. Addison-Wesley, 1991.

26. Vincent Zammit. A mechanisation of computability theory in HOL. In *Proceedings of the 9th International Conference on Theorem Proving in Higher Order Logics*, volume 1125 of *Lecture Notes in Computer Science*, pages 431–446, Turku, Finland, August 1996. Springer-Verlag.

27. Vincent Zammit. A proof of the $S_n^m$ theorem in Coq. Technical Report 9-97, The Computing Laboratory, The University of Kent at Canterbury, 1997.

# Author Index

# Springer
# and the
# environment

At Springer we firmly believe that an international science publisher has a special obligation to the environment, and our corporate policies consistently reflect this conviction.

We also expect our business partners – paper mills, printers, packaging manufacturers, etc. – to commit themselves to using materials and production processes that do not harm the environment. The paper in this book is made from low- or no-chlorine pulp and is acid free, in conformance with international standards for paper permanency.

 Springer

# Lecture Notes in Computer Science

For information about Vols. 1–1210

please contact your bookseller or Springer-Verlag

Vol. 1248: P. Azéma, G. Balbo (Eds.), Application and Theory of Petri Nets 1997. Proceedings, 1997. VIII, 467 pages. 1997.

Vol. 1249: W. McCune (Ed.), Automated Deduction – CADE-14. Proceedings, 1997. XIV, 462 pages. 1997. (Subseries LNAI).

Vol. 1250: A. Olivé, J.A. Pastor (Eds.), Advanced Information Systems Engineering. Proceedings, 1997. XI, 451 pages. 1997.

Vol. 1251: K. Hardy, J. Briggs (Eds.), Reliable Software Technologies – Ada-Europe '97. Proceedings, 1997. VIII, 293 pages. 1997.

Vol. 1252: B. ter Haar Romeny, L. Florack, J. Koenderink, M. Viergever (Eds.), Scale-Space Theory in Computer Vision. Proceedings, 1997. IX, 365 pages. 1997.

Vol. 1253: G. Bilardi, A. Ferreira, R. Lüling, J. Rolim (Eds.), Solving Irregularly Structured Problems in Parallel. Proceedings, 1997. X, 287 pages. 1997.

Vol. 1254: O. Grumberg (Ed.), Computer Aided Verification. Proceedings, 1997. XI, 486 pages. 1997.

Vol. 1255: T. Mora, H. Mattson (Eds.), Applied Algebra, Algebraic Algorithms and Error-Correcting Codes. Proceedings, 1997. X, 353 pages. 1997.

Vol. 1256: P. Degano, R. Gorrieri, A. Marchetti-Spaccamela (Eds.), Automata, Languages and Programming. Proceedings, 1997. XVI, 862 pages. 1997.

Vol. 1258: D. van Dalen, M. Bezem (Eds.), Computer Science Logic. Proceedings, 1996. VIII, 473 pages. 1997.

Vol. 1259: T. Higuchi, M. Iwata, W. Liu (Eds.), Evolvable Systems: From Biology to Hardware. Proceedings, 1996. XI, 484 pages. 1997.

Vol. 1260: D. Raymond, D. Wood, S. Yu (Eds.), Automata Implementation. Proceedings, 1996. VIII, 189 pages. 1997.

Vol. 1261: J. Mycielski, G. Rozenberg, A. Salomaa (Eds.), Structures in Logic and Computer Science. X, 371 pages. 1997.

Vol. 1262: M. Scholl, A. Voisard (Eds.), Advances in Spatial Databases. Proceedings, 1997. XI, 379 pages. 1997.

Vol. 1263: J. Komorowski, J. Zytkow (Eds.), Principles of Data Mining and Knowledge Discovery. Proceedings, 1997. IX, 397 pages. 1997. (Subseries LNAI).

Vol. 1264: A. Apostolico, J. Hein (Eds.), Combinatorial Pattern Matching. Proceedings, 1997. VIII, 277 pages. 1997.

Vol. 1265: J. Dix, U. Furbach, A. Nerode (Eds.), Logic Programming and Nonmonotonic Reasoning. Proceedings, 1997. X, 453 pages. 1997. (Subseries LNAI).

Vol. 1266: D.B. Leake, E. Plaza (Eds.), Case-Based Reasoning Research and Development. Proceedings, 1997. XIII, 648 pages. 1997 (Subseries LNAI).

Vol. 1267: E. Biham (Ed.), Fast Software Encryption. Proceedings, 1997. VIII, 289 pages. 1997.

Vol. 1268: W. Kluge (Ed.), Implementation of Functional Languages. Proceedings, 1996. XI, 284 pages. 1997.

Vol. 1269: J. Rolim (Ed.), Randomization and Approximation Techniques in Computer Science. Proceedings, 1997. VIII, 227 pages. 1997.

Vol. 1270: V. Varadharajan, J. Pieprzyk, Y. Mu (Eds.), Information Security and Privacy. Proceedings, 1997. XI, 337 pages. 1997.

Vol. 1271: C. Small, P. Douglas, R. Johnson, P. King, N. Martin (Eds.), Advances in Databases. Proceedings, 1997. XI, 233 pages. 1997.

Vol. 1272: F. Dehne, A. Rau-Chaplin, J.-R. Sack, R. Tamassia (Eds.), Algorithms and Data Structures. Proceedings, 1997. X, 476 pages. 1997.

Vol. 1273: P. Antsaklis, W. Kohn, A. Nerode, S. Sastry (Eds.), Hybrid Systems IV. X, 405 pages. 1997.

Vol. 1274: T. Masuda, Y. Masunaga, M. Tsukamoto (Eds.), Worldwide Computing and Its Applications. Proceedings, 1997. XVI, 443 pages. 1997.

Vol. 1275: E.L. Gunter, A. Felty (Eds.), Theorem Proving in Higher Order Logics. Proceedings, 1997. VIII, 339 pages. 1997.

Vol. 1276: T. Jiang, D.T. Lee (Eds.), Computing and Combinatorics. Proceedings, 1997. XI, 522 pages. 1997.

Vol. 1277: V. Malyshkin (Ed.), Parallel Computing Technologies. Proceedings, 1997. XII, 455 pages. 1997.

Vol. 1278: R. Hofestädt, T. Lengauer, M. Löffler, D. Schomburg (Eds.), Bioinformatics. Proceedings, 1996. XI, 222 pages. 1997.

Vol. 1279: B. S. Chlebus, L. Czaja (Eds.), Fundamentals of Computation Theory. Proceedings, 1997. XI, 475 pages. 1997.

Vol. 1280: X. Liu, P. Cohen, M. Berthold (Eds.), Advances in Intelligent Data Analysis. Proceedings, 1997. XII, 621 pages. 1997.

Vol. 1281: M. Abadi, T. Ito (Eds.), Theoretical Aspects of Computer Software. Proceedings, 1997. XI, 639 pages. 1997.

Vol. 1282: D. Garlan, D. Le Métayer (Eds.), Coordination Languages and Models. Proceedings, 1997. X, 435 pages. 1997.

Vol. 1283: M. Müller-Olm, Modular Compiler Verification. XV, 250 pages. 1997.

Vol. 1284: R. Burkard, G. Woeginger (Eds.), Algorithms — ESA '97. Proceedings, 1997. XI, 515 pages. 1997.

Vol. 1285: X. Jao, J.-H. Kim, T. Furuhashi (Eds.), Simulated Evolution and Learning. Proceedings, 1996. VIII, 231 pages. 1997. (Subseries LNAI).

Vol. 1286: C. Zhang, D. Lukose (Eds.), Multi-Agent Systems. Proceedings, 1996. VII, 195 pages. 1997. (Subseries LNAI).

Vol. 1289: G. Gottlob, A. Leitsch, D. Mundici (Eds.), Computational Logic and Proof Theory. Proceedings, 1997. VIII, 348 pages. 1997.

Vol. 1292: H. Glaser, P. Hartel, H. Kuchen (Eds.), Programming Languages: Implementations, Logigs, and Programs. Proceedings, 1997. XI, 425 pages. 1997.

Vol. 1294: B. Kaliski (Ed.), Advances in Cryptology — CRYPTO '97. Proceedings, 1997. XII, 539 pages. 1997.

Vol. 1299: M.T. Pazienza (Ed.), Information Extraction. Proceedings, 1997. IX, 213 pages. 1997. (Subseries LNAI).

Vol. 1300: C. Lengauer, M. Griebl, S. Gorlatch (Eds.), Euro-Par'97 Parallel Processing. Proceedings, 1997. XXX, 1379 pages. 1997.